TRAVELLERS SURVIVAL KIT

Mauritius,
Seychelles & Réunion

James & Deborah Penrith

Published by Vacation Work, 9 Park End Street, Oxford
www.vacationwork.co.uk

TRAVELLERS SURVIVAL KIT: MAURITIUS, SEYCHELLES & RÉUNION

by James & Deborah Penrith

Editor: Ian Collier

ISBN 1 85458 240 2

Cover Design: Miller Craig & Cocking Design Partnership

Maps by Andrea Pullen

Illustrations by Beccy Blake

Cover photograph courtesy of Mauritius Tourism Promotion Authority

Typesetting by Worldview Publishing Services

Printed by William Clowes Ltd., Beccles, Suffolk, England.

Contents

MAURITIUS AND ITS PEOPLE

MAURITIUS: PRACTICAL INFORMATION

REGIONS OF MAURITIUS

SEYCHELLES

SEYCHELLES: PRACTICAL INFORMATION

EXPLORING SEYCHELLES

SMALLER ISLANDS

RÉUNION

RÉUNION: PRACTICAL INFORMATION

EXPLORING RÉUNION

MAPS

Acknowledgements

The Indian Ocean is the planet's third largest body of water and getting around even a small portion of it calls for planning and organisation that can be achieved only with the help and co-operation of others. We have been fortunate while gathering material for this guidebook in meeting some highly knowledgeable and superbly efficient people. They came from a wide spectrum: from airline and hotel group executives, to tour operators, guides, waiters, and taxi drivers. All shared a common love for their islands and all shared their expertise and knowledge with us in the hope that others will be encouraged to visit and enjoy these Indian Ocean gems.

In particular, we would like to record our thanks and appreciation for the help and support we received from Marie-Claude Janner of Air Mauritius; the indefatigable Suzy Edouard of the Mauritius Tourism Promotion Authority; Sulaiman Patel, communications director of Beachcomber Hotels; Patrick Leal, managing director of the excellent and ubiquitous MauriTours; Willy Auguste, of the Marouk-Ebony Hotel in Rodrigues, his assistant director Thierry Félicité, and PR executive and expert guide Francois Félicité; Greta Jeanne Du Bois and Robert Bourquin, of that impeccable Indian Ocean airline Air Austral; Stéphan Ulliac and Raoul Vincent at the Comité du Tourisme de la Réunion in St Denis; and Alan Mason, of Mason's Travel, in Victoria, Mahé.

Special thanks must go to film-maker, fellow scribe and diving buddy Al J Venter, now resident in the US, for his suggestions and the invaluable help he gave us in compiling the scuba-diving sections of this guidebook.

Sources of Information

In the course of our travels and research for this and other books we noticed in many of the sources consulted a repetition of stories and anecdotes from some largely forgotten original. If there has been any one inspiration and major source of reference for this guidebook then that is the late TV Bulpin's meticulous and monumental *Islands in a Forgotten Sea*, published in Cape Town in 1958 by Howard Timmins. We rarely see this ground-breaking work acknowledged, and the same can be said for the works of the late Lawrence G Green, a contemporary of Bulpin's and an industrious chronicler of southern yarns and legends for the same publisher.

While every effort has been made to ensure that the information contained in this book is as up-to-date as possible, some details are bound to change within the lifetime of this edition, and readers are strongly advised to check facts and credentials themselves.

The *Travellers Survival Kit: Mauritius, Seychelles and Réunion* will be revised regularly. We are keen to hear comments, criticisms and suggestions from both natives and travellers. Please write to the authors at Vacation Work, 9 Park End St, Oxford OX1 1HJ. Those whose contributions are used will be sent a complimentary copy of the next edition.

Preface

The spark of life would have to be extinct in anyone not feeling a thrill at words such as tropics, islands, paradise, palm trees, turquoise seas, pirates and buried treasure. These, usually the stuff of dreams, are everyday reality in the Indian Ocean, where countless idyllic islands evoking them dot the boundless blue between the tropics of Cancer and Capricorn. Mauritius, Rodrigues, Seychelles and Réunion are foremost among these islands, offering tranquil holiday havens to the quirky individualist, the adventurous, the curious, the jaded or simply the stressed-out.

In the centuries since the first European seafarers and explorers unlocked the Indian Ocean gateway to the east, reports of the exotic uninhabited islands they found along the spice route have stirred the imagination of armchair travellers down to the present day. Some of the more famous visitors recorded their impressions for posterity. In April 1836, towards the end of his five-year voyage round the world in *HMS Beagle,* naturalist Charles Darwin visited Mauritius and found 'the whole island...adorned with an air of perfect elegance' and mused, 'How pleasant it would be to pass one's life in such quiet abodes.' Later in the century Mark Twain followed Darwin to Mauritius and penned a thought that has been gold for its publicity wizards ever since. 'You gather,' he wrote, 'that Mauritius was made first, and then heaven, and that heaven was copied after Mauritius.' Joseph Conrad dropped anchor in Mauritius in his youth and, in spite of an unhappy love affair there, called the island 'a pearl distilling sweetness upon the world.' Before going off to die for queen and country at Khartoum, General Charles Gordon visited Seychelles and outdid even Mark Twain's advertising gem. After a visit to Praslin island in 1881 Gordon rhapsodised that not only did he believe he had found the biblical Garden of Eden, but that the fruit with which Eve naughtily tempted Adam had not been an apple, but a 50lb coco-de-mer nut, erotically shaped like her nether regions.

For modern readers whose knowledge of this sublime area of the globe might be restricted to a whiff of cloves and cinnamon at the local curry house we'd add that once you have followed Darwin, Twain, Conrad, and Gordon to any of these magical islands their relapses into advertising slogans will become more understandable. The islands have all the requisite ingredients for the determined latter-day escapist – endless sunshine, equally endless unpopulated beaches of dazzling sand, clear waters, friendly laid-back islanders, unbelievable marine life, birds, animals, plants and trees found nowhere else on earth...

To add a further touch of spice to their attraction is the knowledge that they were used throughout a swashbuckling era as hideouts and bases by some of the most infamous pirates and corsairs roaming the seven seas during the 18th century, and legends abound of the gold, silver and jewels they buried there that still await some lucky treasure hunter. Paradise is an overworked word these days, but if there is any merit in its use it is as a descriptive umbrella for what the late Lawrence G Green poetically called the wondrous 'Isles of the Great Hush.'

On a more practical note it is reassuring to report that the islands we write about are not afflicted by the diseases and infections common in many other tropical islands; there are no dangerous wild animals or poisonous snakes and insects; crime of a serious nature is virtually non-existent; and levels of healthcare, hygiene and sanitation compare favourably with those of the developed world. Creole and French are spoken throughout the islands, but this should not deter unilingual travellers. English is widely understood and spoken, if haltingly, by locals, and in the hotel and hospitality industry staff are usually fluent in English, as well as any number of other European languages. As tourism is a relatively recent import in the life of these islands it's nice to report that they have not suffered from the overkill that in other tourist destinations seems to have turned waiters into deaf statues, taxi drivers into grasping, gibbering maniacs, and everyone else in the service industry into unhelpful or uncomprehending automatons. Let's hope that never happens in paradise.

James and Deborah Penrith
St Denis, Réunion

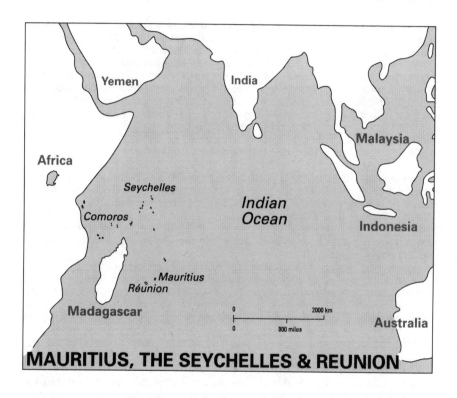

MAURITIUS, THE SEYCHELLES & REUNION

Mauritius

The Dodo

Winging in towards Sir Seewoosagur Ramgoolam International Airport – helpfully better known by its abbreviation SSR – on a clear day you get a bird's-eye view of a reef-ringed tropical island whose dominating features are white sand beaches and turquoise lagoons fringing seemingly limitless swathes of lush green sugarcane fields, punctuated by startlingly spiked and twisted mountain peaks rising abruptly from a well-watered central plateau. Such contrasts set the theme for virtually all other aspects of Mauritius, an island paradise known as the key and star of the Indian Ocean.

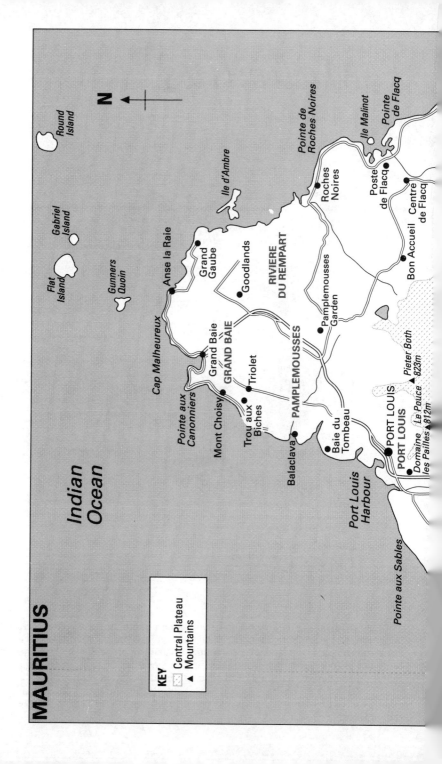

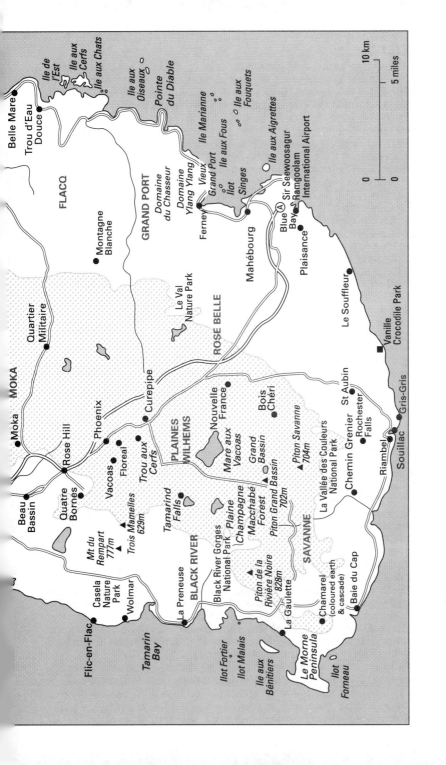

GEOGRAPHY
Mauritius is one of a trio of islands which make up the Mascarene archipelago. It was thrown up and formed along with neighbours Réunion and Rodrigues by a series of undersea volcanic eruptions some 10-million or more years ago. Mauritius is situated just north of the Tropic of Capricorn on the 20th parallel, and lies 1,265 miles (2,036 km) from the nearest point on the east coast of Africa, 2,920 miles (4,700 km) from Bombay, 500 miles (805 km) from eastern Madagascar, and 143 miles (230 km) from Réunion, the French *département* whose volcanic dome is sometimes visible on the horizon to the west.

The island – 38 miles (61 km) from top to bottom and 29 miles (47 km) wide – is poised on what was once a land bridge between Asia and Africa. It has a total area of 787 sq miles (2,040 sq km), slightly less than 10.5 times the size of Washington DC. This is made up of the main island of Mauritius, with an area of 720 sq miles (1,865 sq km); the island of Rodrigues 40 sq miles (104 sq km) to the east; the Agalega Islands to the north and the Cargados Carajos Shoals (the St Brandon Group) to the north-east, which have a combined area of 27 sq miles (71 sq km).

From a lower plain in the north, the terrain rises to a great fertile plateau covering the central part of the island. The southern region is mostly mountainous, with its highest point the **Piton de la Petite Rivière Noire** at 2,710 ft (828 m), in the **Black River Gorges National Park.** There are several lakes on the plateau and numerous perennial streams rise in the highlands and run down to the coast.

The island's interior is dotted with extinct volcanic craters, some water-filled such as the crater lake of **Grand Bassin,** which is a Hindu pilgrimage site in the south of the island, lava boulders, waterfalls, and thick sub-tropical forests, including more than 80 species of palms. Particularly noteworthy geological formations are the striated **Coloured Earth** of volcanic ash at Chamarel, in the south, and the Black River Gorges on the Plaine Champagne, in the south-east. The whole forms a landscape of often stunning beauty. The 205-mile (330 km) coastline is surrounded almost entirely by one of the largest unbroken coral reefs in the world, enclosing a vast limpid shoreline lagoon offering safe bathing, good fishing, and a wide range of aquatic sports. A number of small uninhabited islands dot the ocean around Mauritius, both inside and outside the lagoon.

CLIMATE
Mauritius lies south of the equator, which means that when it is summer on the island it is winter in the northern hemisphere, which makes it an ideal getaway for Europeans and Americans eager to escape their own chilly weather and grey skies. Summer and winter in the tropics are, however, relative terms and while the Mauritian calendar notes a winter season from May to October and a summer lasting from November to April it is much like the West Indies, pleasantly warm throughout the year. Prevailing south-easterly and north-easterly winds fan the island to temper both heat and a year-round humidity which seldom drops below 75%-85%. There are no clearly defined dry and rainy seasons. Although it is wetter during the period December to the end of March, especially on the central plateau, the rain showers don't usually last long and can be a welcome and refreshing change. The hot, rainy, and cyclone seasons all overlap during December to April. Average annual precipitation ranges from about 35 inches (900 mm) of rain on the coast to 59 inches (1,500 mm) in the plateau region.

Mauritius sits in the cyclonic belt of the Indian Ocean and torrential downpours accompany the cyclones that strike the island from time to time, most often between January and March. Cyclonic storms bad enough to cause widespread damage have, however, occurred on only about a dozen days during the past 90 years. Cyclone Carol, the most violent ever to hit Mauritius, occurred at the end of

February 1960 when wind gusts from the south-east exceeded 140 mph (225 km/h). Cyclones passing close to Mauritius give an average of only four days a year of the dismal windy and rainy weather you might be more accustomed to in temperate northern latitudes. Air temperatures range from 80°F (27°C) at the coast to 73°F (23°C) on the central plateau in summer (November to April); and 70°F (21°C) on the coast to 63°F (17°C) on the central plateau in winter (May to October). If you do not enjoy overly warm weather or plan an active holiday July is the coolest month 71°F (22°C). The temperature can drop to 61-65° F (16-18°C) at night on the coast so a light sweater is a good idea. February is the warmest month 83°F (28°C). Sea temperatures range from 72-81°F (22-27°C). Hours of daylight are from 5am to 7pm in summer, and 7am to 5pm in winter. Mauritius is really an all-year-round holiday destination but the **best time to visit** is between April and June and September and November. Whenever you go, don't forget to take a hat, a good pair of sunglasses, and some reputable sun protection products with adequate ultra-violet filtering. For local weather forecasts, tel 302-6071.

HISTORY

Arabs and Portuguese
Mauritius is a breathtaking landfall on the vast air and sea lanes linking Europe, Africa, Asia and Australia. Its inviting azure lagoon and luxuriant green vegetation must equally have been a feast for the eyes of the tired Arab seamen who were the first to record the existence of an island whose main inhabitants were black parrots, gigantic tortoises and an enormous friendly and flightless bird called the dodo. Around 1507, less than a decade after Vasco da Gama first rounded the Cape of Good Hope and entered the Indian Ocean, doughty Portuguese seafarers stumbled on the island in the course of their extensive voyages of discovery and planted it on the European maps of the time. The Arabs had already marked the island they called *Dina Mashriq* ('Eastern Isle') or *Dina Robin* ('Isle of Silver') on their charts at least a century earlier. The recognised Portuguese 'discoverer' was Fernandez Pereira, who gave it the name of his ship *Cerne*, although recent research credits fellow navigator Diego Dias with a sighting in 1500. Although the Portuguese never settled on the island they used it as a victualling stop on their way to Goa and Malacca, and left pigs and goats there as emergency food supplies – the first unwitting assault on the island's delicately balanced eco-system.

First Dutch Settlement
The Dutch were the next on the scene. In 1598, Admiral Wysbrand van Warwyck sailed his Dutch squadron into present-day Ferney Bay, near **Mahébourg**, and claimed the island for his country, naming it Mauritius in honour of Maurice of Nassau, Prince of Orange and Stadtholder of Holland. Although they now regarded Mauritius as their property the Dutch made no attempt to settle or colonise the island and ships of all the major maritime powers – Dutch, English and French – trading in the Indian Ocean and the entrepots of Asia made use of Mauritius to water, replenish supplies, and repair their vessels. Afraid that one of their trading rivals might seize the island in its undefended state the Dutch East India Company sent Cornelius Gooyer to Mauritius in 1638 as its first governor. He was given 25 men to keep both French and English at bay, as well as to found a settlement, grow food and tobacco for visiting Dutch ships, cut and send to Holland the prized ebony trees and any ambergris they could find, and provide a base for convalescent officials from the Dutch East Indies.

In 1658, after 20 years of uphill slog, the Dutch destroyed everything that might be of value to their enemies and pulled out of Mauritius, moving to their more secure bases in Batavia (Java) and the Cape of Good Hope. Behind them they left stands of sugarcane and the herds of deer they had introduced from Java as meat on the hoof, some cattle, and less useful monkeys and rats, which quickly proliferated and further upset the ecological balance. One thing they did not leave behind was the dodo. The once prolific trusting and ungainly bird was ruthlessly slaughtered for its meat and at the end of only 20 years of Dutch occupation was extinct. It lives on only in the saying 'as dead as a dodo' and as a woebegone reconstruction in a glass case at the Natural History Museum in Port Louis.

Second Dutch Settlement

In 1664 the Dutch returned to Mauritius for another attempt at settlement. This time they held out for 46 years, but their colonisation never really flourished and in 1673, after a succession of inept governors, the settlers asked to be allowed to abandon the island again. This appeal was refused and they were told to buckle down under a new governor, Hubert Hugo. During his four-year tenure roads were improved, the fort was rebuilt and a sawmill was erected. Vegetables, bananas, pineapples, and some rice were grown. The sugarcane previously introduced from Java and destined to contribute to the future prosperity of Mauritius was the source of a fiery drink called arrack, which kept most of the Dutch colonists in a state of perpetual inebriation. Cane was not processed to produce sugar until 1696. The climate of Mauritius was a healthy one and Governor Hugo reported to his superiors that the only disease prevailing among his settler community was gluttony.

More governors came and went, their troubles compounded as English pirates, expelled from their lucrative raiding grounds on the Caribbean's Spanish Main, hoisted the skull and crossbones in increasing numbers in the Indian Ocean and used Mauritius as a convenient base for operations. This was the last straw and in 1710 the dispirited Dutch once more destroyed all their buildings, crops and stores and withdrew – this time forever. They had given the island a name that was to endure and the foundation of its sugar industry. Apart from exterminating the dodo, they had also denuded the once-rich forests of some of the world's finest ebony.

French Occupation

In 1715, five years after the Dutch scuttled off, the French took possession of the abandoned island, partly to repress the piracy flourishing among all the Mascarene islands – Mauritius, Rodrigues, and Reunion – and partly for its strategic value on the sea routes to India. The French renamed Mauritius *Ile de France* and late in 1721 they established their first settlement on the site of present-day **Port Louis**, which they named after King Louis XV. During his administration (1735-1746) Governor Bertrand Francois Mahé de Labourdonnais transformed Mauritius from a rundown outpost into a prosperous French colony. He invigorated the town of Port Louis and established the harbour as a naval base and ship-building centre, built roads, a hospital and a fresh-water aqueduct, made sugar the main crop, and established law and order. Some of the numerous public buildings which went up during his governorship still stand, among them the Chateau de Mon Plaisir at Pamplemousses, the Line Barracks in the capital, and part of Government House. Labourdonnais is regarded as the greatest of all the island's governors and his statue is now a prominent landmark on the Port Louis waterfront.

The trade in slaves, begun by the Dutch, was resumed by the French and blacks were shipped in from Madagascar, Mozambique and West Africa to work from dawn to dusk every day except Sundays on the sugarcane plantations. Many escaped to the mountains and forests, and often threw themselves off cliffs rather than be taken by the soldiers sent to recapture them. For much of the 18th century

Britain and France were at war and the Ile de France became a nest of French corsairs who attacked and plundered British merchantmen plying the Indian Ocean. It was a boisterous era, when rich loot poured into bustling Port Louis, which at one stage offered buccaneers a choice of more than 100 taverns.

In 1767, the French East India Company, ruined by the ongoing wars, ceded the island to the French government. An energetic French administrator of the period was Pierre Poivre (1767-1772), a botanist who introduced many spices, exotic trees and plants to the island, and created the famed botanical gardens at Pamplemousses, near Port Louis, which remain a fitting monument to his genius. During the Napoleonic wars the Ile de France remained loyal to France, despite the colonists' strong disapproval of a pledge by their motherland's National Assembly to free all Mauritian slaves, on whose backs the sugar industry of the island rested. Meanwhile pirates and corsairs alike continued preying on British shipping. The most famous Ile de France corsair captain of the time was Robert Surcouf, who was popularly known as 'King of the Corsairs.' Surcouf was so highly esteemed he was cheered by the island's colonists every time he appeared in his box at the theatre in Port Louis. The British were not amused and put a hefty price on his head, but he lived to retire in prosperity to his native Brittany and was rewarded with a title by a grateful Napoleon.

British Rule and Independence

Determined to neutralise the troublesome island which posed a threat to their supremacy in India the British blockaded it and made shore raids to test the strength of the French forts and batteries. In August 1810, a British squadron of four ships sailed into Grand Port Bay to engage a French flotilla of similar strength. Within the beautiful turquoise bay which air travellers now glimpse as they fly in to land at the international airport, a savage battle was fought. It was won by the French, although most of the ships involved were sunk or badly damaged. The Battle of Grand Port Bay was France's only naval victory during the years of the Napoleonic wars and is the only foreign battle commemorated on the Arc de Triomphe in Paris. In 1809, the British had occupied the little island of **Rodrigues**, about 348 nautical miles (560km) to the east of Mauritius, and in December 1810 launched an expeditionary force of 9,000 men, ferried by 50 transports and escorted by 18 warships, and invaded Mauritius at Cape Malheureux, the northernmost point of the island. After four days of skirmishing at Grand Baie, Arsenal Bay and Tombeau Bay the British under General John Abercrombie were in the streets of Port Louis, where they accepted the surrender of French Governor General Charles Decaen, effectively starting 158 years of British rule. The 1814 Treaty of Paris ratified the cession of Mauritius and its dependencies, Rodrigues and the Seychelles, to the British, but Réunion, which was also captured by the British, was returned to France.

The island returned to its old name of Mauritius, English became the official language, and all the colonists were required to take an oath of allegiance to the British crown. The gallows replaced the guillotine. The French were granted generous peace terms by the British, who allowed the colonists to retain their laws, customs, language, civil service posts, property and the Roman Catholic religion. This generosity helped to perpetuate that Frenchification of Mauritius which is obvious to the present day. Mauritius continued to be a strategic island for the British until the opening of the Suez Canal in 1869. The abolition of slavery in 1835 had far-reaching effects on the population and character of the island. Not surprisingly, the freed African and Madagascan slaves rejected work in the canefields, so Indian and Chinese labourers were imported to replace them. Within 30 years Indians formed the majority of the population. They still do, and have played a major role in Mauritian political life since the franchise was broadened in

1948 to give all literate adult men and women the vote. Universal suffrage, which enfranchised more of the Indian majority, was introduced in 1959, speeding up the march to independence. This was attained on 12 March 1968 under Sir Seewoosagur Ramgoolam's Hindu-dominated Labour Party, the *Parti Travailliste*. Ramgoolam steered the island to independence within the British Commonwealth and saw its adoption of the British parliamentary system.

POLITICS

No summary of political developments in Mauritius would be complete without reference to the late Sir Seewoosagur Ramgoolam, who was born in Mauritius of humble Hindu parents and trained as a doctor in London. He returned to the island in 1955 after 14 years in England and entered politics to represent the interests of downtrodden Indian workers and struggling small planters. He became a member of the legislative council, was elected mayor of Port Louis and, at independence in 1968, became the island's first prime minister. He is now revered as 'Father of the Nation' and his name is today blazoned on everything from clinics and shopping centres to airports and public gardens. Like subsequent governments, Ramgoolam's administration faced problems of overpopulation, unemployment and the vulnerability of a monocrop economy depending heavily on sugar, a staple at the mercy of both weather and fluctuating world prices. Social services and assistance programmes were extended, and in 1970 the export-processing zone (EPZ) scheme was launched, which has succeeded in attracting foreign investment, particularly in manufacturing industries such as textiles.

That period also saw the rise of extreme left-wing movements, notably the radical *Mouvement Militant Mauricien* (MMM), led by Paul Bérenger, a Franco-Mauritian from a well-to-do island family who had become a Marxist in his student days in Wales and France. He returned to Mauritius in 1968, a revolutionary dedicated to the redistribution of the wealth of the island among the Indian and Creole peasantry. He sought this principally through a declared policy of nationalisation, especially of the sugar industry. In the mid-seventies the slump in the price of sugar, together with higher fuel prices, plunged the island into an economic crisis. To extricate it, the government in 1979 adopted a structural adjustment programme, supported by the World Bank and the International Monetary Fund, to diversify and stimulate the economy while simultaneously tackling the problems of unemployment, overpopulation and poverty. Before the scheme had a chance to succeed Ramgoolam's administration, weakened by corruption and nepotism, was defeated. In 1982, in an historic sweeping victory, Berenger's MMM captured all 60 seats, leaving only four 'best loser' seats to his humiliated opponents. The landslide victory by the Marxists sent shock waves through Western capitals.

The administrative inexperience of Bérenger and his left-wing regime was such that within nine months the MMM was out of office, rejected by shaken islanders of all ethnic groups, who saw that Marxist policies were wrecking the economy. In the election of 1983 the MMM was replaced by a three-party coalition comprising the *Parti Maricien Social Démocrate* (PMSD), the *Mouvement Socialiste Mauricien* and most of the old Labour Party. The government of Anerood Jugnauth initiated an economic recovery in a spirit of co-operation with the private sector, which has been continued by other administrations, including the present Labour government of Dr Navinchandra Ramgoolam, prime minister and son of the old nationalist stalwart. Mauritius retains the multi-party political system it has supported since independence and opted to become a republic on 12 March 1992, the 24th anniversary of its independence.

Mauritian political life is characterised by coalitions and often uneasy alliances. Legislative power rests with the unicameral 62-seat National Assembly, which is elected by universal suffrage for a five-year term. Eight additional members ('best losers') are also appointed from among defeated candidates to ensure an ethnic balance in the Assembly. Although the government is nominally Labour, Mauritians will tell you that there has been no noticeable left, right or centre in the political spectrum since the Marxists' short and disastrous takeover of government in 1982. Politics is not generally the topic of conversation for Mauritians that it is in Europe and the US – and islanders generally seem happy with the way the government is running their country. There seems little doubt that Labour will continue to hold the reins for some time to come.

Women. Whatever the government in power the legal status and rights of women have never been a primary plank in any political platform. Islanders the world over are notoriously conservative and Mauritius is no exception. Add to this the predominant religions' historical relegation of women to subservient roles and you'll realise why there's been no rush to burn bras on the island. Strangely enough in this age of women's lib there is no strong agitation for radical reform, although an organisation known as the Mauritian Alliance of Women occasionally makes genteel noises about the 'glass ceiling' that keeps women from rising beyond middle management levels in public and private sectors. In the words of the US State Department women continue to face 'legal and societal discrimination'.

THE ECONOMY

Looking at the vast fields of sugarcane seemingly carpeting most of the island's arable land you'd never guess that old King Sugar is finally taking a back seat in the economy of Mauritius. The fields dotted with the monumental mounds of black volcanic rock cleared from the terrain by the black slaves of old still cover 40% of total land area and around 90% of all cultivated land, but sugar's long paramount rule is ending. To understand sugar's pivotal role in the economy of Mauritius and its sweet and sour history we have to look back to its rather sordid beginnings when the Dutch settlers shipped in the first canes from their East Indian possessions and then proceeded to go on a 46-year-long binge on the spirit they produced from the crop. It was left to the administration of the indefatigable French Governor Mahé de Labourdonnais to encourage production of sugar on a significant commercial scale. By 1755, enough sugar was being produced on the island to meet the needs of both the inhabitants of the colony and the sister island of Bourbon (now Réunion), as well as to supply visiting vessels.

By 1801, sugarcane plantations were thriving and some 60 mills were producing 3,000 tons of sugar a year. Towards the end of the 19th century Mauritius, with its rich volcanic soil and abundant sunshine and rain, was the main producer of sugar for the British Empire. **Railways** were built by the British to improve internal communications and where once oxcarts and barges had been used to haul sugar to Port Louis for export to Europe, bridges, viaducts, imposing stations and post offices appeared. By 1904, there were 124 miles (200 km) of British standard-gauge track on the island. The railway was ripped up after World War 2 and the locomotives and wagons were replaced by motor transport, but relics in the form of bridges and embankments transformed into roads and rural post offices in old stations are still to be seen. The most important event for planters and millers during British rule was undoubtedly the abolition in 1825 of the special import duty on Mauritian sugars entering the United Kingdom. This made competition with West Indian sugar possible and was the beginning of the industry's development in Mauritius. Apart from the constant uncertainty of market prices sugar's other setbacks have included natural causes – cyclones, droughts, pests and diseases – as well as labour unrest and, in more recent years, worldwide inflation. In 1973, island factories achieved a record production of 718,464 tons – a figure unlikely ever to be exceeded with the lessening dependency on sugar.

Sugar's contribution to national gross domestic product (GDP) has dropped to around 7.7%, although the trim estates of major producers, whose brands are household names throughout the world, still mechanically reap cane for the dwindling mills during the June to November cutting season. Other small plots, leased from the government, are manually harvested and sent to the co-operative by Creoles in much the same backbreaking way their slave forebears worked until their emancipation by the British. The vulnerability of an economy dependent on a monocrop culture at the mercy of wide global price swings was the reason the government started the process of economic diversification after independence. In the years since then, successive governments have concentrated on building up other economic sectors. While agriculture – sugar, tea, vegetables and cut flowers – is still the main prop, the diversification of the economy is paying off and manufactured products now account for about 23% of GDP. The **tourism** industry is the vibrant third largest hard-currency earner for Mauritius, bringing in 600,000 visitors and holidaymakers in 1999 and growing by an average 10% a year. Well over half of the island's tourists come from Europe, with France, Britain, and Germany – in that order – accounting for most of them. Canadian and US tourists are still relatively few, but numbers are growing and Mauritius is looking to attract even more with tour operator packages that link the island with safaris in East and South Africa.

The national economy has grown at an average rate of 6% over the past decade, and full employment was achieved in the late 1980s. Unemployment (below 2%) is not a problem, thanks to the rapid growth of the **export processing zone** (EPZ), as well as to the government's success in curbing the annual population growth to 1.21% (1997). Skilled labour shortages are, however, now becoming evident in industry. The performance of the manufacturing sector is largely influenced by the evolution of the EPZ, which is predominantly involved in textile and knitted products, electronic and electrical components, as well as food, flowers, leather products and footwear, ship models, watches, jewellery and toys. Some 800 textile companies manufacture for top global brand names, including such famous labels as Christian Dior, Hermes and Diesel, for export to European and American markets. Mauritius has a rapidly growing financial sector with developing offshore and freeport activities. The financial sector comprises 20 commercial banks, 10 of them domestic and 10 others offshore banks. There are also seven non-bank financial institutions that are authorised to transact deposit-taking in Mauritius, three *bureaux de change* and two foreign exchange dealers. The creation of the Stock Exchange of Mauritius in 1989 to finance increased investment needs was a milestone in the development of a modern capital market for the island. Mauritius aims to become not only a regional offshore centre, but an international financial services provider. Activities of the freeport, geared in the main towards entrepot trade and distribution on a regional basis, started at the end of 1993, and have become a fast-developing sector of activity that underscores the new outward orientation of the economy.

Foreign direct investment often depends, among other things, on a country's human rights' record and the US Department of State indicates that trials in Mauritius are considered to be generally fair. Procedural law in both criminal and civil litigation is mainly English, while the substantive law is based mainly on France's Napoleonic Code – tricky, but it seems to work. There are strong ties between Mauritius and the democratic countries of the West due to both its political heritage and a dependence on Western markets. Mauritius has established close links with the European Community, particularly with the United Kingdom and France. India and Mauritius share particularly close relations, based on traditional cultural and ethnic ties.

Environmental Concerns. These have been given increased priority in the government's economic development plans and steps have been taken to provide the legal framework necessary to protect the island environment and its fragile ecosystems. This has cast a shadow over some odd little activities – for instance, sand mining in lagoons. This has been limited by the government to four designated sites which produce an estimated 800,000 tons of sand a year for the construction industry. As sand is only a slowly renewable resource (it builds up again at the rate of about 1.5 tons a year), the government has come under fire from environmentalists and is planning to ban this mining. From 1 January 2001 the island's sand diggers will have to find other work.

THE PEOPLE

The country's 1,150,000 people are the colourful ingredients of an ethnic pot-pourri inhabiting one of the most densely populated countries in the world. The overall population density is about 1,436 per sq mile (about 554 persons per sq km). In Mauritius, the Constitution classifies everyone by ethnic origin and religion for electoral purposes. The Constitution recognises four main groups: **Hindus** (Indians), representing about 52% of the population, a loose category officially called the **general population**, which covers **Creoles, Franco-Mauritians** (white descendants of the original settler families and landed gentry), **Europeans,** and anyone not fitting into any other classification and constituting about 29%, **Muslims** accounting for more than 16% and Sino-Mauritians (**Chinese**) about 3%.

Port Louis, the island's capital city, has a population of 160,000. The lively Creoles are of mixed African and European descent. Most of them are Roman Catholics. The one thing all communities have in common is that they are all descended from immigrant communities, as less than four centuries ago the island was uninhabited. Despite ethnic and cultural differences the people form a cosmopolitan blend with a reputation for being among the friendliest and most hospitable people in the world. If you despair of people ever overcoming national boundaries, religious bigotries and racial prejudices, Mauritius is a wonderful example of diverse races living together in peace and harmony. The only time tolerance has been strained in recent years has been during communal soccer matches and, in 1999, when popular seggae Rastaman musician Kaya died in jail under mysterious circumstances after being arrested for smoking a mind-altering substance at a public meeting.

From the time the French took possession of the island in 1715, after two unsuccessful Dutch attempts to settle, the populating of Mauritius took the form of a series of overlapping waves of immigration, each wave bringing with it different customs, languages and religions. The French imported slaves from Africa, particularly from Senegal, Guinea, Mozambique and Madagascar, to work in the sugarcane fields. The British became interested in the island in the early 18th century because it provided a good staging post for their ships en route to India, and took the island from the French in 1810. British rule was essentially administrative and the French colonists were allowed to stay and retain their language, culture and lifestyles. Things did not change for the slaves until, yielding to the pressure of abolitionists, the island colonists freed them in the mid-1830s. To make up for the subsequent labour shortage the British shipped in indentured labourers from India – mainly from Bihar, Uttar Pradesh, Tamil Nadu, Andhra Pradesh, Maharashtra, and Gujarat – and within a few decades people of Indian origin were in the majority. The latter part of the 19th century saw the arrival of Hakka and Cantonese Chinese settlers who set up shop in the retail trade, which they now virtually dominate. The result of all this is that many towns and villages have a Catholic church, a Muslim mosque, and a Hindu temple sited virtually cheek by jowl. Buddhist temples and Chinese pagodas add to the religious medley and one little-known cemetery at Bambous has a Muslim burial ground with a Jewish section.

The story is that Jewish refugees from eastern Europe tried to reach Palestine in the early 1940s to escape Nazi persecution. They sailed down the west coast of Africa, rounded the Cape of Good Hope and travelled on into the Indian Ocean. At this point they were brought to Mauritius by the British authorities and stayed on the island until the end of the war. Some of them died during their sojourn and were buried in a special section of the Muslim cemetery.

Western traditions generally prevail in social situations and a handshake is the customary formal greeting. Visitors should respect the traditions of their hosts, particularly when visiting a private home, where the type of hospitality depends on the religion and social customs of the host. It is considered appropriate to offer a small gift as a token of appreciation if you are invited to share a meal with a Mauritian family.

LANGUAGES

You should have no communication problems in Mauritius as the average Mauritian is a polyglot, and an oddity on the island is someone who speaks only one language. **English** is the country's official language and, with **French**, is used for administrative and international communications. Virtually all hotel and travel agency staff speak English and French, and to a lesser degree German, Italian, and Spanish. Most tourist brochures and pamphlets are printed in English and French. **Creole** has established itself as a national *lingua franca* and it is understood and spoken by all Mauritians irrespective of ethnic or cultural origins. Bhojpuri, a Hindi patois, is spoken in the more rural areas, but is steadily losing ground to Creole. Schoolchildren are taught in English and French, and most Mauritians also speak their native community's language, such as Hindi, Chinese, Urdu, Tamil, Telegu, or Bhojpuri, and there are 13 recognised languages in all. A census carried out in 1983 listed no fewer than 63 ancestral languages, although most of them are used principally on socio-cultural and religious occasions. Variants of Creole are spoken throughout the islands of the southern Indian Ocean but are not similar enough to be generally understood by Creole speakers. The Mauritian government rates its national literacy level at between 90% and 94%.

Useful Words and Phrases

If you want to be really friendly or raise a smile try some of these in Mauritius:

English	French	Creole
Good morning	Bonjour	Bonzour
Please	S'il vous plaît	Si ou plai
Goodbye	Au revoir	O révoir
How are you?	Comment ça va?	Qui maniére?
What's your name?	Quel est votre nom?	Comman ou apéle?
Where is...?	Où se trouve...?	Cotte?
What time is it?	Quelle heure est-il?	Qui lère là?
Do you understand?	Avez-vous compris?	Oune compran?
How much is it?	Combien?	Combien?
Where do you live?	Où habitez-vous?	Cotte ou resté?
Is it near?	Est-ce près?	Li près?
Is it far?	Est-ce loin?	Li loin?

Where are we now?	Où sommes-nous maintenant	Cotte nous été là?
Where are we going?	Où allez-vous?	Cotte ou pé allé?
Do you like cakes?	Aimez-vous les gâteaux?	Ou content gato?
Do you want to eat?	Voulez-vous manger?	Oullé manzé?
A lot/a little	Beaucoup/peu	Boucou/ti guitte
It's good	C'est bon	Li bon
I like mangoes	J'aime les mangues	Mo content mangue
Give me more	Domnez-m'en plus	Donne moi plis
I'm leaving	Je m'en vais	Mo pé allé
My room	Ma chambre	Mo la çambre
My luggage	Mes bagages	Mo bagaze
Today	Aujourd'hui	Zordi
Tomorrow	Demain	Dimin
Time	Le temps	Lé temps
Eat	Manger	Manzé
To drink water	Boire de l'eau	Boire di lo
Meat	La viande	La vianne
Salt	Le sel	Di sel
Sugar	Le sucre	Di sic
Bread	Le pain	Di pin
Tea	Le thé	Di thé
Coral reef	Les récifs	Brisants
A shell	Un coquillage	Ene coqui
A basket	Un panier	Ene panié
Market	Le marché	Bazar
I'm hungry	J'ai faim	Mo faim
I'm thirsty	J'ai soif	Mo soif
It's too expensive	C'est trop cher	Li trop çèr
I need a doctor	J'ai besoin d'un médecin	Mo bisin ène doctère

The patois, which developed from the pidgin French of the old plantation slaves, is rich in expressive and often ribald words and phrases, most of which don't make it into the Creole dictionaries on sale in Mauritius. One interesting curiosity is the use of numbers as a form of shorthand for certain words. If a man refers to his 35 it means his girlfriend; 17 is a boyfriend; 2 is a monkey; 6 is a homosexual; 15 means a woman's breasts; 32 is a Chinese person; 27 is a policeman; and 40 refers to your bum. Even Creoles can't explain how this numbering came about.

Everywhere you go you'll hear two English words which sum up the laid-back philosophy of all islanders. They are: 'No problem.'

RELIGION

All the great religions of the world have adherents in Mauritius and in half a day in capital Port Louis you can visit Christian churches, Hindu shivalas and Tamil kovils (temples), Muslim mosques, Buddhist temples, Chinese pagodas, and the places of worship of other sects. The voice of the muezzin calling the faithful Muslim to daily prayer may have its counterpoint in the sound of the gong. Please remember when visiting Hindu temples and Muslim mosques that the wearing of shoes or sandals is regarded as a grave affront and can create unpleasant scenes.

Christianity

In the form of Roman Catholicism, this was originally brought to Mauritius by the first French settlers, who arrived in 1715. Today out of a population of more than a million some 30% are Christians, of whom about 95% are Catholics, the remainder comprising Anglicans, Presbyterians, Baptists, Seventh Day Adventists,

Methodists, Jehovah's Witnesses and others.

Hinduism
The Indian immigrants who came to Mauritius were a heterogeneous lot. Most came in great waves from the north of India; a good many came from the south of India, with a few coming from Bombay, in the west. Hinduism incorporates a wide range of practices and traditions, which are followed by about 52% of the Mauritian population.

Islam
The indentured Indian workers brought in to replace the freed slaves also comprised many Muslims, who came in the main from the north and south of India. The Muslim population also included a group of enterprising traders who came mostly from Gujarati-speaking areas in the west of India. These were followed soon afterwards by traders from Surat. The Muslims now make up more than 16% of the population, some 95% of them are Sunni Muslims, the rest are Shiites and Ahmadists.

Chinese
Mauritius has become the homeland to two distinct Chinese groups: the Cantonese and the Hakkas, the latter being the much larger group. Early Chinese immigrants practised Confucianism, Taoism and Buddhism, ways of life rather than religions. Today, however, about four-fifths of Mauritian Chinese have become Christians, predominantly Roman Catholics. Notwithstanding such conversions, many Chinese are still attached to their ancestral cultures, customs and traditions.

NATIONAL ANTHEM AND FLAG
The Mauritian flag has, from top to bottom, four equal bands of red, blue, yellow, and green. The words of the national anthem are:

Glory to thee, Motherland,   *As one people,*
O Motherland of mine.   *As one nation,*
Sweet is thy beauty,   *For peace, justice and liberty.*
Sweet is thy fragrance,   *Beloved country, may God bless thee*
Around thee we gather   *Ever and ever.*

FURTHER READING
Islands in a Forgotten Sea by TV Bulpin (Howard Timmins, Cape Town);
Randonnée au Coeur des Localities Mauriciennes by Bhurdwaz Mungur and Breejan Burrun (Editions Le Printemps, Mauritius 1993);
A New History of Mauritius by J Addison and K Hazareesingh (Editions de l'Océan Indien, Mauritius 1999);
Underwater Mauritius by Al J Venter (Ashanti, Gibraltar 1989);
Where to Dive in Southern Africa and off the Islands by Al J Venter (Ashanti, Rivonia 1991);
Rodrigues by Katerina and Eric Roberts (Editions Le Printemps, Mauritius); and
The Island of Rodrigues by Alfred North-Coombes (privately printed, Mauritius 1971).
Culture Shock! Mauritius by Roseline NgCheong-Lum (Times Books International, Singapore 1997).
Eight Bells at Salamander by Lawrence G Green (Howard Timmins, Cape Town 1960).
Harbours of Memory by Lawrence G Green (Howard Timmins, Cape Town 1960).

MAURITIUS: PRACTICAL INFORMATION

Getting There

BY AIR

Mauritius has become the aerial crossroads of the Indian Ocean, linking not only the neighbouring islands of Madagascar, Réunion and Rodrigues, but also Europe, India, South-East Asia, the Far East, Australia and East and South Africa, and this status now matches its former importance as a port of call for world shipping. An Indian Ocean success story has been the rapid growth of **Air Mauritius** the national flag carrier of the island republic in which the state has the majority shareholding in a joint venture with the private sector. Since it was founded in 1967, Air Mauritius has grown its fleet from a single, leased six-seater Piper Navajo into a leading international airline, with a fleet of five Airbus A340-300s, two Boeing 767-200 ERs, and three ATR 42s. The airline today flies to 29 destinations across four continents, with more than 80 departures a week from Mauritius.

Among other destinations around the globe Air Mauritius has regular flights to and from London (Heathrow and Gatwick), Manchester, Paris, Brussels, Frankfurt, Vienna, Geneva, Zurich, Milan, Rome, Munich, Mumbai, Melbourne, Perth, Hong Kong, Nairobi, Harare, Johannesburg, Cape Town, and Durban. The airline has a schedule of regular inter-island services between Mauritius and Rodrigues,

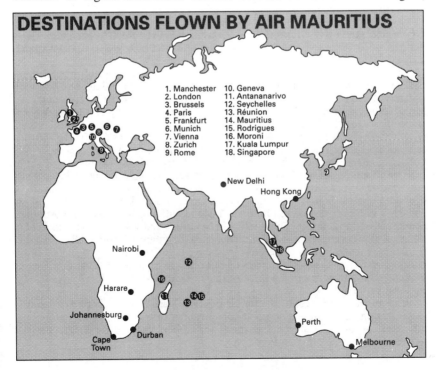

DESTINATIONS FLOWN BY AIR MAURITIUS

1. Manchester
2. London
3. Brussels
4. Paris
5. Frankfurt
6. Munich
7. Vienna
8. Zurich
9. Rome
10. Geneva
11. Antananarivo
12. Seychelles
13. Réunion
14. Mauritius
15. Rodrigues
16. Moroni
17. Kuala Lumpur
18. Singapore

New Delhi
Hong Kong
Nairobi
Harare
Johannesburg
Durban
Cape Town
Perth
Melbourne

Réunion, Mahé (Seychelles), and Madagascar. The airline is also general sales agent for Air India, SAS, Swissair, and Thai Airways. Other major airlines serving Mauritius include Air Europe, Air France, Air Austral, Air India, Air Madagascar, Air Seychelles, British Airways, Cathay Pacific, Singapore Airlines, Condor, South African Airways, Air Zimbabwe, and Kenya Airways.

Flights from London airports cost from around £450-£700 (US$675-US$1,050) per person; British Airways operate flights from New York out of JFK and Newark via Gatwick for around US$4,200, before airport taxes. These prices will vary according to carrier and class of ticket.

Distance in miles (km) from Mauritius

London	6,076 (9,779)	Nairobi	1,810 (2,913)
Paris	5,876 (9,456)	Singapore	3,472 (5,588)
Munich	5,872 (9,450)	Johannesburg	1,917 (3,086)
Frankfurt	5,712 (9,193)	Durban	1,789 (2,879)
Geneva	5,615 (9,037)	Antananarivo	690 (1,110)
Zurich	5,622 (9,048)	Rodrigues	376 (605)
Rome	5,184 (8,343)	Réunion	143 (230)
Mumbai	2,916 (4,693)	Hong Kong	4,824 (7,764)
Melbourne	5,292 (8,517)		

Non-stop flight time London-Mauritius is 11 hours 30 minutes.

Mauritius is served by the Sir Seewoosagur Ramgoolam International Airport (named after a former prime minister and better known simply as SSR) which is situated on the south-east coast of the island, about 30 miles (48 km), an hour's drive, from Port Louis, the capital.

OFFICES AND INFORMATION DESKS AT THE AIRPORT

Air Mauritius, information, reservations, enquiries (tel 603-3060); Civil Aviation, information concerning the airport terminal (tel 603-3390).

Tour operators await you in the arrivals hall and if you are on one of their package tours will be ready to take you to your hotel. If travelling solo, you will find lots of taxis outside. Make sure you've agreed on the fare before choosing one. Most big hotels have a helipad and Air Mauritius runs a helicopter transfer service from the airport. To the north of the island will cost you 8,400 rupees (£210/US$317); to anywhere else on the island is 6,900 rupees (£173). To use this service you should preferably arrange a booking through an airline agency before you leave home. Their telephone number at SSR airport is 603-3754/5.

The airport has been extensively renovated and extended and facilities include duty-free shops, a bank, *bureaux de change*, a tourist office, snack bar, tour operator and car hire (Avis, Europcar, Hertz) desks. Duty-free shops allow passengers to buy goods when both leaving and entering, so unlike in most other countries you can stock up as you arrive in Mauritius and save yourself a packet on things such as wines, spirits, film, chocolate and gourmet foods. All prices are marked in French Francs (FF), but they take Mauritian rupees at a pinch. Until recently, an airport tax of 300 rupees (about £8) was payable on departure. This is now thankfully included in the price of the air ticket, which saves you scratching for local currency.

It is important to reconfirm your air ticket at least 72 hours before departure. Don't imagine that you've got a seat home just because you booked it before you left. You can do this on your arrival at the airport, at your hotel, or you can telephone the airline office in Port Louis.

AIRLINE OFFICES:

In Mauritius
Air Mauritius: Air Mauritius Centre, Rogers House, President John F. Kennedy
Street, Port Louis (tel 207-7070, fax 208-8331, e-mail: resa@
airmauritius.com); SSR International Airport (tel 603-3030, fax 637-3266).
Other airlines in Rogers House are *Air Austral* (tel 212-2666, fax 211-1411); *Air
France* (tel 212-2666, fax 211-1411); *Air Madagascar* (tel 208-6801, fax 212-
0218); and *South African Airways* (tel 208-6801, fax 208-8792).

Airlines elsewhere in Port Louis:
Air Zimbabwe: IKS Building, corner Farquhar and La Paix streets (tel 242-4032,
fax 240-5305).
British Airways: Duke of Edinburgh Avenue (tel 208-1039).
Cathay Pacific: 10 Dr Ferriere Street (tel 212-4044).
Condor: 18 Edith Cavell Street (tel 208-4802).
Malaysian Airlines: 3rd Floor Blendax House, Dumat Street (tel 208-4935, fax
208-2417).
Singapore Airlines: 5 Duke of Edinburgh Avenue (tel 208-0791, fax 208-1535).

Air Mauritius Offices Around the World:
Australia: Mezzanine Level, 261 George Street, Sydney NSW 2000 (tel 2-9247
1444, fax 2-9247 1110); LVL 3, 250 Collins Street, Melbourne, Victoria 3000
(tel 3-654 1788, fax 3-654 3366); and Level 3, 178 George Street, Perth WA
6000 (tel 8-9442 6044, fax 8-9481 0590).

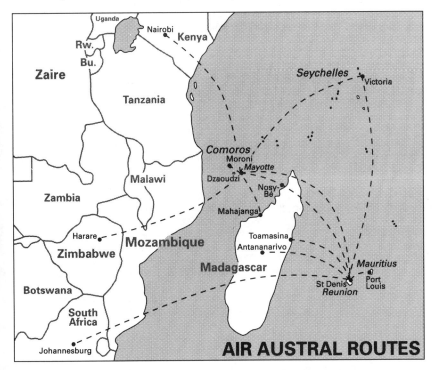

AIR AUSTRAL ROUTES

Austria: Hilton Center Top 1742-44, A-1030 Vienna (tel 1-713 9060, fax 1-713 9052, e-mail: info.air.mauritius@vienna.at).

Benelux: Boulevard Emile Jacqmain 6, B.P. 15, B-1000 Brussels, Belgium (tel 2-218 5705, fax 2-218 5104, e-mail: air-mauritius@unicall.be).

Britain: 49 Conduit Street, London W1R 9FB (tel 020-7434 4375, fax 020-7439 4101); and Room 3067, Terminal 2, Manchester International Airport, Manchester M90 4QX (tel 0161-498 9909, fax 0161-437 6069).

Canada: Airways Center Business Park, 5925 Airport Road, Suite No 752, Missisauga, Ontario L4V 1W1 (tel 905-405 0188, fax 905-405 0191, e-mail: airmauritius_ca@compuserve.com).

France: 11 bis Rue Scribe, F-75009, Paris (tel 1-44 51 15 64, fax 1-44 51 15 55, e-mail air.mauritius.paris@wanadoo.fr).

Germany: Herzog Rudolf Strasse 3, D-80539 Munich (tel 89-2900 3930, fax 89-2900 3944, e-mail: info@airmauritius.de); and Frankfurt Airport Center, Hugo Eckener Ring, D-60549 Frankfurt (tel 69-690 72700, fax 69-690 59206, e-mail: atash-fra@t-online.de).

India: Air India Building, Ground Floor, Nariman Point, Mumbai 400021 (tel 22-202 8474, fax 22-202 5340); and 206-207 Arunachal Building, 19 Barakhamba Road, New Delhi 110001 (tel 11-373 1534, fax 11-373 1545).

Italy: Via Barberini 68, I-00187 Rome (tel 06-474 2051, fax 06-482 5252); and Via P. Dea Cannobio 10, 20122 Milan (tel 02-80 4661, fax 02-890 10600).

Madagascar: Ario, 77 Lalana Solombav Ambahoaka Frantsay, BP 3673 Antsahavola, Antananarivo 101 (tel 23-5990, fax 23-5773).

Réunion: Corner Charles Gounod and Alexis de Villeneuve Street, 97400 St Denis (tel 94-8383, fax 41-2326, e-mail: airmauritius@wanadoo.fr).

Rodrigues: ADS Building, Port Mathurin (tel 831-1558, fax 831-1959); and Plaine Corail Airport (tel 831-1301, fax 831-1321).

Singapore: 135 Cecil Street, #04-02 LKN Building, Singapore 069536 (tel 222-3172, fax 224-9726).

South Africa: Grayston Ridge Office Park, Ground Floor, South Wing, Block A, Sandown 2196 (tel 11-444 4600, fax 11-444 4413, e-mail: jnbmk@airmauritius.co.za); Suite 2708, 27th Floor, 320 West Street, Durban 4000 (tel 31-304 6681, fax 31-306 2709); and Strand Towers, 11 Floor, 66 Strand Street, PO Box 1832, Cape Town 8001 (tel 21-421 6294, fax 21-421 7371).

Switzerland: 1-3 Chantepoulet, CH-1202 Geneva (tel 22-732 0560, fax 22-731 1690, e-mail: gdastur@airmauritius.int.ch); Loewenstrasse 19, CH-8001 Zurich (tel 8-212 2316, e-mail: resazrh@airmauritius.int.ch).

USA: 560 Sylvan Avenue, Englewood Cliffs, New Jersey 07632 (tel 201-871 8382, fax 201-871 6983, e-mail: airmkusa@concentric.net).

TOUR OPERATORS

A number of tour operators specialise in Mauritius, among them:

In Britain

Abercrombie & Kent: Sloane Square House, Holbein Place, London SW1 8NS (tel 020-7730 9600, fax 020-7730 9376).

Beachcomber Tours: 1 Portsmouth Road, Guildford, Surrey GU2 5BL (tel 01483-533088, fax 01483-532820).

British Airways Holidays: Worldwide Department, Astral Towers, Betts Way, London Road, Crawley, West Sussex RH10 2XA (tel 01293-723202, fax 01293-722640).

Cosmos Distant Dreams: Tourama House, 17 Homesdeale Road, Bromley, Kent BR2 9XL (tel 020-8464 3444, fax 020-8466 0699).

Elegant Resorts: The Old Place, Little Street, John St. Chester CH1 1RB (tel 01244-350408, fax 01244-897780).

Elite Vacations Ltd: Elite House, 98-100 Bessborough Road, Harrow, Middlesex HA1 3DT (tel 020-8864 9818, fax 020-8426 9178).

Island Holidays: Drummond Street, Comrie, Perthshire PH6 2DS (tel 01764-670107, fax 0176-670958).

Kuoni Travel: Kuoni House, Deepdene Avenue, Dorking, Surrey RH5 4AZ (tel 01306-740500, fax 01306-744222).

Mauritian Connections: 424 Barton Road, Stretford, Manchester M32 9RW (tel 0161-865 7275, fax 0161-865 2501).

Sunset Travel: 4 Abbeville Mews, 88 Clapham Park Road, London SW4 7BX (tel 020-7498 9922, fax 020-7978 1337).

Thomas Cook Faraway: 12 Coningsby Road, Peterborough, Cambridgeshire PE3 8XP (tel 01733-418450, fax 01733-417784).

Tradewinds: Concorde House, 3 Forest Street, Chester, Cheshire CH1 1QR (tel 01244-329551).

Thomson Worldwide: Greater London House, Hampstead Road, London NW1 7SD (tel 0870-550 2555).

In France

Accor Tour: 31, rue du Colonel Avia, Paris Cedex 15, F-75904 (tel 1-41 33 69 19, fax 1-41 33 69 51).

Beachcomber Tours: 1-3, rue Caumartin, Paris F-75009 (tel 1-44 94 72 70, fax 1-44 94 04 34).

Club Aventure: 18, rue Séguler, Paris F-75006 (tel 1-44 32 09 30, fax 1-44 32 09 59).

Eden: 12, rue Godot de Mauroy, Paris F-75009 (tel 1-40 06 88 00, fax 1-42 65 64 05).

Iles du Monde: 7, rue Cochin, Paris F-75005 (tel 1-4326 6888, fax 1-43 29 10 00).

Jet Tours: 23, rue Raspail, Ivry s/ Seine Cedex, F-94858 (tel 1-45 15 70 00, fax 1-45 15 74 06).

Kuoni: 95 rue d'Amsterdam, Paris F-75008 (tel 1-40 16 04 06, fax 1-40 23 06 26).

Nouvelles Frontieres: 87,bd de Grenelle, Paris Cedex 15, F-75738 (tel 1-45 68 71 22, fax 1-45 68 74 50).

Voyageurs Dans Les Iles: 55 rue Sainte-Anne, Paris F-75002 (tel 1-42 86 16 80, fax 1-42 86 17 89).

Ylang Tours: 131 bis, rue de Vaugirard, Paris F-75015 (tel 1-40 61 03 03, fax 1-40 61 07 08).

In Germany

VIP Tours: Munchener Street 35, D-60329 Frankfurt (tel 69-236336, fax 69-232674).

AKL Travel Gmbh: Clemensstrasse 12, D-80803, Munich (tel 89-3401 9615, fax 89-3401 9619).

Club Mediterranean Germany: Königsallee 98a, D-40215 Düsseldorf (tel 211-380500, fax 211-377122).

Fischer Reisen Gmbh: Ballindamm 11, D-20095 Hamburg (tel 40-309070, fax 40-309072).

Ikarus Tours Gmbh: Fasanenweg 1, D-61462 Königstein (tel 016174-29016, fax 016174-22952).

LTU Touristik Gruppe: Parsevalstr 7b, D-40468 Düsseldorf (tel 211-907 8208, fax 211-907 8340).

SR & Partners: Hapsburgerring 18-20, D-50674 Köln (tel 221-257 5820, fax 221-257 5817).

Take Off Reisen Gmbh: Eppendorfer Weg 158, D-20253 Hamburg (tel 40-422 2288, fax 40-422 2209).

World Travel Club: N 6, 3 Holiday Inn Passage, D-68161 Mannheim (tel 621-260900, fax 621-260940).

In South Africa

Beachcomber Tours: PO Box 745, Somerset West 7129, Cape Town tel toll-free 0800 500 800, fax 21-852 6377/8, e-mail: beachcomber@galileosa.co.za).

Club Med: 37 Ashford Road, Parkwood 2193 (tel 011-442 5252, fax 011-442 5035, e-mail: sales@clubmed.co.za).

Sun and Sandals: (budget hotels and self-catering), PO Box 2513, Edenvale 1610, Johannsburg (tel 11-616 7705, fax 11-616 7716).

Unusual Destinations: 13 Gustav Preller Street, Vorna Valley 0686, Johannesburg (tel 11-706 1991, fax 11-463 1469, e-mail: unusdest@global.co.za).

Wild Wet Tours (budget hotels and self-catering), 134 Rabie Street, Fontainbleu, Randburg (tel 011-791 0335, fax 011-791 0337, e-mail: wildwet@iafrica.co.za).

BY SEA

Forget it – unless you are already a yachtie drifting around the Indian Ocean or sitting on the beach in Mombasa with all the time in the world, waiting for a serendipitous cargo boat to give you a berth. A more congenial possibility is to stop off from a cruise ship, but this is an expensive option and tends to limit your time on the island. Check with your travel agent if you're interested. In Mauritius, Port Louis is the main deep-sea port, and although it's primarily commercial there is a limited passenger service to the French island of Réunion and to Rodrigues, that other Eden that is part of Mauritius.

Ferry Services

Mascarene Ferries operates *L'Ahinora*, a catamaran taking 260 passengers, and offering a rapid daily service between Mauritius and Réunion, departing Port Louis at 8am, and arriving at Pointe des Galets at noon. Contact Concord Travel & Tours, La Chausée, Port Louis, tel 208-5041. The *MV Mauritius Pride* cargo and passenger ship operates a service two or three times a month from Port Louis to Rodrigues. This is the popular way Rodriguans get to and from their island to Mauritius, so you should book early to get a cabin. Travel first-class if comfort is a criterion; economy class is much cheaper, but gives you a seat in a communal saloon and you eat in a self-service cafeteria instead of being served by smiling stewards. For more information about sailings and prices contact Mauritius Shipping Co Ltd., Nova Building, 1, Route Militaire, Port Louis (tel 242-5255 or 242-2912, fax 242-5245).

TRAVEL SAFELY

Both the UK Foreign Office and the US State Department have travel information offices which provide regularly updated free advice on countries around the world (see also *Health and Hygiene* page 38 for information on the health situation).

Travel Advice Unit: Consular Division, Foreign & Commonwealth Office, 1 Palace Street, London, SW1E 5HE (tel 020-7238 4503/4504 Website www.fco.gov.uk/travel).

US State Department: 2201 C Street, Washington DC 20520, USA (tel 202-647 4000 Website http://travel.state.gov).

Red Tape

ENTRY REQUIREMENTS

PASSPORTS AND VISAS

Your passport must be valid for a minimum of six months, you should have a return ticket to your point of departure or an onward destination, and you must have adequate funds to cover the length of your expected stay. For more information contact diplomatic representatives of Mauritius or the Passport and Immigration Office, Police Headquarters, Line Barracks, Port Louis, tel 208-1212/1271, fax 212-2398. A visitor's visa is granted normally for one month, but can be renewed on request. Visas can be obtained from Mauritian consulates and embassies. Citizens of most European and Commonwealth countries, as well as some of other countries, including the USA, Canada, and Australia, do not require visas, although you should always double-check this before travelling. Passports issued by the government of Taiwan (Republic of China) are not recognised, although holders can apply to a passport and immigration officer for an entry permit. If you do need a visa you must specify the type – tourist, business or social – and each is available for single or multiple entry. Visas are not necessary if you are in transit, so long as you continue your journey to a third country within 72 hours. Tourist visas are valid for up to six months in any one year; business visas up to three months; and social visas, two months. They are usually issued free of charge from a Mauritian consulate or the consular section of an embassy. Depending on your nationality, an application can take up to 40 working days.

If you are not part of a package tour you should make hotel arrangements before you go, as immigration officials at the airport in Mauritius expect you to specify where you intend to stay and you have to fill in a form to this effect on arrival. If you are in Mauritius only during the stay of a vessel you are travelling on, such as a cruise ship or yacht, you do not need a visa. Further rules and regulations tend to get somewhat complicated, so it's always best to check with a travel agent or a Mauritian diplomatic mission or tourist office.

HEALTH DOCUMENTS

Mauritius is fairly unusual for a country in the Indian Ocean region in that it is free of diseases such as malaria, yellow fever and cholera. This is because of the effective eradication programmes followed by the government. You should, however, double-check with your doctor or a travel clinic well before leaving for Mauritius. It is also advisable to ask a Mauritian consulate or embassy about any restrictions on prescription medicines and the amounts you're allowed to take in. International yellow fever vaccination certificates are required for anyone over one year of age arriving from an infected area, such as some countries in Africa. The Mauritius government considers countries and areas where yellow fever is classified as endemic to be infected, and its missions abroad can provide you with a list of these. Cholera vaccination is no longer required and according to Mauritian health authorities there is no risk of malaria, although mosquitoes can still be an irritant. There are no endemic tropical diseases on the island.

CUSTOMS REGULATIONS

If you are over 16 years of age you are allowed to take into Mauritius, duty-free, 250g of tobacco (including cigars and cigarettes), two litres of wine, ale or beer, one litre spirits, and about 8.8 fluid oz (250 ml) of *eau-de-toilette*, as well as a small quantity of perfume not exceeding 3.5 fluid oz (100 ml). Any more than this and you face paying duty, although in practice customs officials rarely check obvious tourists. Any plants, seeds, fresh fruit or flowers must be declared immediately on arrival, and you must have an import permit from the Minister of Agriculture to bring them in. Firearms and ammunition must also be declared on arrival. There are no restrictions on personal cameras, photographic equipment and film. If your religion or diet calls for specific requirements such as kosher, halaal or vegetarian foodstuffs these are allowed, with the exception of meat and fresh produce. Import of plants and other agricultural products is prohibited. Dogs, cats and other pet animals are subject to a quarantine period of up to six months, but we've not yet seen holidaymakers taking their pets with them. For further information contact the Customs & Excise Department, Port Louis (tel 240-9702, fax 240-0434) or Agricultural Services, Head Office, Réduit (tel 454-1091).

MAURITIAN EMBASSIES, CONSULATES AND HIGH COMMISSIONS ABROAD

Australia: Mauritius High Commission, 43 Hampton Circuit, Yarralumla ACT 2600, Canberra (tel 2-281 1203/282 4436, fax 2-282 3235).

Britain: Mauritius High Commission, 32-33 Elvaston Place, London SW7 5NW (tel 020-7581 0294, fax 020-7823 8437, e-mail: londonmhc@binternet.com). Open 9.30am to 1pm and 2pm to 5pm Monday to Thursday 9.30am to 1pm and 2pm to 4.30pm Friday. Consular section: 9.30am to 1pm Monday to Friday.

Canada: Honorary Consulate of Mauritius, Suite 200, 606 Cathcart Street, Montréal, Québec H3B 1K9 (tel 514-393 9500, fax 514-393 9324, e-mail: gga-mti@sympatico.ca).

South Africa: Mauritius High Commission, 1163 Pretorius Street, Hatfield 0083, Pretoria (tel 12-342 1283, fax 12-342 1286).

USA: Embassy of Mauritius (also deals with enquiries from Canada), Suite 441, Van Ness Centre, 4301 Connecticut Avenue NW, Washington DC 20008 (tel 202-244 1491/2, fax 202-966 0983, e-mail: mauritius.embassy@mcione.com).

Business Hours. Generally from 8.30am to 4.30pm from Monday to Friday, and half-day on Saturday, 9am to noon, although government offices work only from 9am to 4pm during the week.

And now for something completely different...

GETTING MARRIED

Mauritius is the Nevada of the Indian Ocean – not for gambling but for (fairly) quick marriages. The Civil Status Act of Mauritius provides that the marriage of non-citizens and non-residents may be celebrated any time from the day immediately following the day of publication of intention. You should, however, produce to the Civil Status Officer at the time of publication a certificate issued under the authority of the Prime Minister to the effect that you and your wife-to-be are not citizens or residents of Mauritius. You can obtain this certificate on application to the registrar of Civil Status, 7th level, Emmanuel Anquetil Building, Port Louis (tel 201-1727, fax 211-2420). With your application you should include two photocopies of each birth certificate and two photocopies of each passport (the first three pages only) and any other document in case of divorcees or widow/widower. The application for a certificate of non-citizen/non-resident should reach the Civil Status Office not less than 10 days before the date of your proposed wedding.

The wedding may be celebrated at the Civil Status Office, or in any hotel, by the Civil Status Officer of the locality where you and your intended are holidaying. If you are Catholic and wish to celebrate your religious wedding in a Catholic church, your tour operator or the Episcopate in Port Louis (tel 208-3068, fax 208-6607) can provide you with information on what to do. Now that should make it a holiday to remember...

What Money to Take

The import of foreign currency is unlimited, subject to declaration; export is limited to the amount declared on arrival. There are no restrictions on the import or export of local currency. Take Mauritian rupee, French franc, sterling or US dollar travellers cheques. These can be exchanged on arrival at the airport, at banks, hotels and authorised dealers.

MONEY IN MAURITIUS

This is the Mauritian Rupee (MRs), which divides up into 100 cents. Notes come in denominations of 2,000, 1,000, 500, 200, 100, 50, and 25, while rupee coins are 10, 5 and 1. Cents come in 50, 20, and 5 cent coins. You can't buy anything for less than 50 cents and this will get you only a gooey sweet or two.

Exchange Rates

These are subject to fluctuation, but are usually around 40 rupees to the pound sterling, 4 or so to the French franc, around 25 to the US dollar, and about four to the South African rand. If you have access to the internet www.oanda.com/converter/classic is an easy to use and highly regarded currency conversion website which can provide exchange rate information daily. Mauritian rupees are not in much use outside Mauritius, so take only enough to have cash ready for taxis and tips on arrival. The exchange rate for travellers cheques is weirdly much better than for hard cash.

Banks and Banking

Many international banks are represented on the island. The two biggest local banks are the Mauritius Commercial Bank and the State Bank of Mauritius. Mauritius Commercial Bank has a 24-hour service at tel 208-5250.

Hours. Monday to Thursday 9.15am to 3.15pm, Friday 9.15am to 5pm, and on Saturday 9.15am to 11.15am.

Credit Cards and ATMS

MasterCard, Visa, Diners Club and American Express are widely accepted. Credit cards are accepted in hotels, restaurants and also in some shops and supermarkets – but don't buy anything or incur any bills without first checking that your plastic is acceptable. You can also use credit cards to obtain cash in the banks or use them with your PIN number to get money from cash dispensers (ATMs). You can contact American Express, Diners Club, MasterCard, and Visa through the Mauritius Commercial Bank in Port Louis (tel 202-5010, or on the emergency number 208-8720) and Barclay Card at Barclay's Bank, in the city suburb of Bell-Village (tel 208-9700).

Tipping

Mauritius is that unusual holiday destination – a place where most waving palms are of the coconut variety. The island is not, in general, a tipping society, although many open-handed tourists are helping to change this.

A 12% Government Tax is added to all hotel and restaurant bills, so tipping is not compulsory and still remains an old-fashioned gesture of appreciation. Don't tip more than 10% of the bill, even if you are really impressed with the service. The average salary on the island is less than 4,000 rupees (£100/$160) a month. Locals advise you not to tip taxi drivers, even if they whine. Their fares are inflated enough as it is, especially for visitors.

 **Health**

BEFORE YOU LEAVE

Remember that when you go on an island holiday it might be difficult to get hold of many of the things you take for granted. If you are on any sort of medication, take it along with you. It's also a good idea to take along a broad spectrum of antibiotics, medicine for stomach upsets and pills or suppositories for nausea. Suppositories are a good idea because usually, when you get a stomach bug on holiday, whatever you swallow comes straight up again. Suntan lotion or cream with a protection factor of 15 is recommended, and so is sunblock. Take the stuff that doesn't wash off in the pool or the sea. A medical and dental check is a good idea before you leave. Take copies of any accident insurance documents, and important medical records. Make sure you take an adequate supply of all prescription and any other medications you use. Take a letter from your doctor on his/her letterhead stationery (signed and dated) certifying your need for any medications you might be carrying. Keep all medications in their original wrapping and pack them in your cabin bag so they don't get lost en route. Check that your health insurance covers you for any treatment you may need in Mauritius before you leave. However, it's a good idea to check out all health requirements two weeks before you leave in case there have been changes. See *Travel Safely* (page 34) and *Useful Addresses* (page 41).

When You Return

A disease or ailment picked up on holiday sometimes takes weeks or even months to become evident after returning home and the connection between the problem and your holiday can easily be missed. You should keep this in mind, especially if you suffer an intestinal illness; if it does not clear up within three or four days, see your doctor and tell him/her where you were, what you did, how long you were there, what you ate and drank, and whether you can remember being bitten by any insects.

MEDICAL SERVICES

Medical and dental standards in Mauritius are advanced and basic treatment in state clinics and hospitals is free, to visitors as well as to locals. There are also private clinics on the island, generally offering a more attractive environment, as well as having more modern medical equipment. These, however, are not free.

Doctors and Dentists

You'll find them in the telephone directory under *Docteurs* and *Dentistes*. There are well-stocked pharmacies throughout the country, but medications do not always carry their international name on the island and it is advisable to take extra supplies of prescription medications, contact lenses, and contraceptives.

Two of the main **hospitals** in Mauritius are: Doctor Abdool Gafoor Jeetoo Hospital, Volcy-Pougnet Street, Port Louis (tel 212-3201, fax 212-8958); and the Sir Seewoosagur Ramgoolam National Hospital at Pamplemousses (tel 243-3661, fax 243-3740). There are also more than a dozen fee-charging private clinics around the island. The main ones are: City Clinic, Sir Edgar Laurent Street, Port Louis (tel 241-2951, fax 240-7042); Clinique de Lorette, Higginson Street, Curepipe (tel 675-2911, fax 676-2695); and Med Point Clinic, Sayed Hassen Avenue, Quatre-Bornes (tel 426-7777, fax 426-5050). The Ministry of Health is in Port Louis (tel 212-3223). The **emergency number** for the ambulance service is **999**.

EVERYDAY HEALTH

Sensible Precautions

Mauritius has no major health hazards, but with the change of water and the generally spicy food some simple precautions are worthwhile. The local tap water is relatively clean and Mauritians drink it. Use it to clean your teeth, but it's safer to drink the bottled water which you can buy in shops everywhere. Best known and most widely available bottled waters are Vital and Crystal, which come in small easy-to-carry plastic bottles and in litre and 1.5 litre sizes. When buying bottled water, always check to make sure the cap seal has not been broken. Some vendors fill up used bottles from the tap and sell them as the real thing. If you are in a self-catering establishment or you are camping it is wise to boil any tap water before drinking it. The same thing goes for local milk, which is unpasteurised. You can use powdered or tinned milk, but make sure its reconstituted with pure water. Avoid dairy products which are likely to have been made from unboiled milk, cook all vegetables, and peel all fruit. It's also wise to avoid ice cubes – a difficult thing to do after a steamy day at the beach or an evening at the disco. If all this sounds pernickety, remember that contaminated food and water is the main reason for most travellers' sickness. All this, of course, is academic if you are on a package tour and staying in a super-duper hygienic hotel.

AIDS

Acquired Immune Deficiency Syndrome (AIDS) is an infectious disease in which is transmitted primarily through blood or semen. Major risk factors include the sharing of contaminated needles and syringes, the use of infected blood or blood products in transfusions, and sexual contact with an infected person. If you have a medical condition which requires injections, such as diabetes, you should carry your own supply of needles and syringes. A letter from your doctor covering these should prevent problems with suspicious customs officers. Abstinence from any homosexual or heterosexual activity is a prime safety measure. If this doesn't appeal you should at least use a condom. AIDS is officially not a major problem in Mauritius and Seychelles, but the threat of infection is always there.

HEALTH HAZARDS

Malaria. Although the health authorities say there is no risk of malaria in Mauritius some travel clinics and doctors probably err on the side of caution when they recommend the usual precautions against this mosquito-borne infection. Use a mosquito repellent cream or spray to keep mozzies at bay. Rooms in the better hotels are equipped with electrical repellent devices which you switch on at night after inserting a small chemically impregnated tablet. This produces a protective vapour which is effective for about eight hours.

Rabies. Rabies is present in some rural areas of the island, and so is typhus. Vaccinations against these should be considered, but be guided by the medical experts.

NATURAL HAZARDS

Sun

Avoid over-exposure to the sun for the first few days of your holiday. The Mauritius sun can be scorching, so wear a hat and sunglasses when out during the day. You should stay out of the sun between 11am and 3pm and regularly apply sunscreen while tanning or swimming. Protect your eyes from ultra-violet radiation by wearing quality sunglasses which block more than 90% of visible light and have protective side-shields. Cream to protect your lips from exposure is also recommended.

Prevention protect your skin by using a sunscreen that filters out damaging UV rays. SPF stands for Sun Protection Factor, and the number indicates the degree of protection a product offers. The higher the number, the better the protection. Children and those with sensitive skins or pale complexions need higher protection than adults with darker or less sensitive skins. Apply the stuff regularly, especially after you have been swimming or exercising. The back of your neck, upper arms and upper legs need special attention. Protection is necessary even on cloudy or hazy days, and especially at altitude. Apart from burning, you can also get **sunstroke (heatstroke)** or suffer from heat exhaustion from over-exposure to the sun.

Symptoms of sunstroke are chills, fever, nausea and delirium. Itching and peeling may follow any degree of sunburn and normally begin four to seven days after exposure. Severe sunburn or sunstroke should always be treated by a doctor.

Heatstroke and **heat exhaustion** are different conditions and are treated differently. The first is a medical emergency. If in doubt, treat for heatstroke, which occurs when high temperatures overwhelm the body's heat-control system. Immediate medical help is necessary. Heat exhaustion is caused by loss of salts and fluid during heavy sweating and can be rectified by drinking fresh fruit juice, which contains the right combination of water and electrolytes to fix you up. Avoid strenuous activity during the hottest hours and make sure you drink plenty of non-alcoholic, caffeine-free liquids to make up for the loss of body fluid through sweating.

Humidity

Constant high humidity may affect you if you have an arthritic condition. If you suffer from sinusitis or hay fever you could be affected during July and August when the sugarcane-cutting season gets under way.

SEASHORE HAZARDS

Coral

Mercurochrome solution – that staining red stuff – is particularly useful, especially where there is a risk of cutting or grazing yourself on coral. Mauritius is virtually surrounded by a coral reef. Dab on mercurochrome as soon as possible after contact with sharp coral. Wounds otherwise tend to fester.

Sharks

The chance of encountering a shark outside the dusty marine displays at the natural History Museum in Port Louis is remote in the extreme. Any self-respecting shark wouldn't be seen dead in the shallow waters of a lagoon. If it were, it would be – which means that all the ones which conjure up the movie *Jaws* are safely swimming in the deep blue yonder beyond the protective reef. So, as far as we can ascertain no one has ever been attacked or bitten by a shark in Mauritius.

Stonefish

This is an ugly, squat spiny fish that lies camouflaged on the sea-bottom waiting for a meal to pass by. At least it used to. Continuing coastal erosion and the washing down to the lagoon of topsoil from the interior by rivers and streams have upset it and it has generally moved away from the beaches. Tread on one and venom-filled hollow spines down its back bring agonising pain and sometimes, without rapid treatment, death. With no punning intended locals call this nasty piece of work a *laff*.

FIRST-AID HINTS

A basic first-aid kit is a good thing to carry. You can buy one from any outdoor equipment store or make up your own. See that it contains at least a disinfectant or anti-bacterial agent, anti-histamine cream, bandages, gauze and adhesive tape, a small pair of scissors, tweezers, a thermometer, aspirins, an anti-diarrhoea preparation, a bottle of medicinal alcohol, and a small bottle (30ml) of 2% mercurochrome solution.

Useful addresses and websites

MASTA (Medical Advisory Service for Travellers Abroad): London School of Hygiene and Tropical Medicine, Keppel Street, London, WC1E 7HT; tel 020-7631 4408; fax 020-7323 4547 Website www.masta.org. For a health brief tailored specifically to your journey you have to call the Travellers' Health Line on 09068 224 100 (this is a premium line available from the UK with calls charged at £0.60 per min).
World Health Organisation (WHO): Website www.travelhealth.com/index.htm (up-to-date vaccination and health advice for travellers, country by country.)

CLOTHING

Keynote for dress in Mauritius is cool and casual – swimsuits and *pareos* (the local colourful cotton sarong) for the day and smart-casual for the evenings. During cooler months from June-September, a jacket or light sweater is recommended for evening wear. Pack light cotton casual wear, beach-wear, sunglasses, a hat or two, comfortable walking shoes and sandals. Rubber-soled shoes you can wear in the sea for protection against coral, stonefish, and sea-urchins are also worth their space in your bag. Light rainwear is advisable all year round. Take lots of T-shirts and shorts, although you can buy from a wide range locally. If you are travelling with a baby remember that disposable nappies cost three times the price they do in Europe or the USA. Either take enough nappies with you or pack some washable ones. As more than half the population is Hindu, you should show respect when visiting religious shrines by dressing appropriately (no shorts, mini-skirts or skimpy dresses). Some up-market hotels require smart-casual dress for their restaurants and more formal wear for the casinos. Mauritian men are quite formal when at work. No matter what the temperature is jackets and ties are normally worn in the office and long trousers are usual for dinner in hotel restaurants.

Although the younger generation of Mauritians, especially working women, show a preference for everyday western dress, the traditional sari still remains the last word for the Hindu woman and the *salwar-kameez* (a knee-length tunic and a pair of slacks) worn with an *horni* (long, light scarf) and the *ghagra-choli* (long embroidered skirt and blouse) are finding favour among the younger generation with a taste for fashions from India. Men also opt for western clothes for daily wear, although on formal and ceremonial occasions Hindus will wear the *dhoti-kurta* (long-sleeved loose shirt and a draped lower garment), the Muslim will favour the *kurta-pajama* and *topi* (loose shirt, drawers and a *haaji* cap), and the Tamil will wrap himself in a *lunghi* (a length of cloth wound around the waist) and a shirt.

Communications

TELEPHONES

The telephone system might not be extensive but it provides a good service. There are many public telephones all over the island which take telephone cards. You can buy a Mauritius Telecom telephone card from post offices, at supermarkets, curio shops, and some hotels. In an emergency you can always use a hotel telephone and most also have a fax facility. Fax facilities are available at the Mauritius Telecom Offices in Port Louis, at Rogers House, President John F. Kennedy Street (tel 208-1036); at the Telecom Tower in Edith Cavell Street (tel 208-7000); and in Cassis (tel 208-0221).

International direct dialling is available throughout the island. To call an overseas number dial the international code 00, then the country code and finally the telephone number. Some country codes are: France (+33), Great Britain (+44), South Africa (+27), Réunion (+262), Germany (+49), Italy (+39), India (+91) and the USA (+1). The country code for Mauritius is +230 (no area codes are required).

Mobile phones

Mauritius has a mobile telephone network which conforms to the international GSM standard. Roaming contracts exist with most developed countries and Mauritius Telecom is busy extending these to other countries. Mauritius has its own cellular network (Cellplus). Discuss details with your own service provider before you leave home. You can rent a GSM cellphone from Cellplus Mobile Communications during your stay in Mauritius. You will find them at Telecom Tower, Edith Cavell Street, Port Louis (tel 203-7500, fax 211-6996).

Telegrams

Telegrams can be sent from Mauritius Telecommunications Service offices in Port Louis and Cassis. There are also facilities at Overseas Telecoms Services (OTS) in Rogers House, President John F. Kennedy Street, Port Louis.

MAIL

Rarities

In 1847, Mauritius became the first British colony to issue postage stamps, and thereby hangs a fascinating tale. The stamps were engraved by a watchmaker at the request of the wife of the governor, Sir William Gomm, who was giving a ball and wanted to send out stamped invitations. At the time the postage stamp was still something of a novelty, even in Britain. The watchmaker engraved a one penny and a twopenny stamp. Five hundred of each were printed, the penny stamp orange-red and the twopenny a deep blue. Similar to the first British stamps, they carried Queen Victoria's head, with the addition of the word 'Mauritius' on them. They should have also carried the words 'Post Paid,' but 'Post Office' was engraved in error. When the ball was over the error was noticed and the remaining stamps were withdrawn. About 27 of the stamps survived to become among the rarest in the world. If you are offered one of these rarities on the street, wet the corner of your handkerchief and test the colour. If it comes off, it is a forgery, if it doesn't it's your lucky day. The result of a lady's whim is today worth a fortune.

Post Offices

Port Louis has several post offices. The main GPO is in Quay Street, near the harbour, down Sir William Newton street and across the motorway dividing the central business district from the port (tel 208-2851, fax 212-9640). There are post offices in all the major towns and villages and at a pinch any hotel reception will post mail for you, provided its already adequately stamped. Airmail to Europe usually takes about five days; surface mail takes 4-6 weeks. Post Office hours are generally 8.15am to 11.15am and noon to 4pm Monday to Friday, and 8am to 11.45am on Saturday.

E-mail. E-mail is still a novelty, but it's growing rapidly on the island.

MEDIA

Television

The government controls all communications media, most notably the Mauritius Broadcasting Corporation. Television programmes are broadcast by MBC on the TV1, TV2 and TV5 channels. MBC also broadcasts the Canal+ programmes from Réunion island on channel 3 and an English programme on channel 4. Mauritian television is an educational experience. Radio and TV broadcasts feature mainly French and Hindi programmes, but also some in Creole, English and other oriental languages. Satellite Television is available, but is still limited. You can watch Sky TV from Britain early in the morning. Television and radio programmes are broadcast in a dozen languages.

Radio

You can listen to five different public stations: RM1, RM2, Sugar FM, Planet FM, and Sansar FM. You can also tune in to the BBC and Voice of America radio in Mauritius. BBC World Service and Voice of America frequencies are MHz 19.55 15.31 9.510 5.975 and MHz 17.89 15.60 9.575 6.035 respectively. From time to time these frequencies change.

Newspapers and Magazines

There are more than 30 newspapers and magazines for a population of just over a million, which claims one of the highest literacy rates in the world. Of the six daily newspapers, two are printed in Chinese and most of the others are in French, with occasional English articles. Of these, *L'Express* and *Le Mauricien* have the highest circulations. You can buy overseas English language newspapers in bookshops such as well-stocked Bookcourt, at the Caudan Waterfront in Port Louis (tel 211-9262, fax 211-9263) or read them free of charge in some of the better hotels. They are also sometimes available at the airport, where a 35p British newspaper will cost you the equivalent of £2.50.

Getting Around

Maps

We find *Globetrotter's* 1:80,000 scale travel maps, published by New Holland, the best all-round maps to the islands of the Indian Ocean. They've got useful inset layouts of the larger towns and places of interest to visitors, as well as several colour illustrations and various snippets of information. For more detailed coverage look for IGN *(Institut Géographique Nationale)* maps, published in France.

In Britain there are several options: *Blackwell's* (53 Broad St, Oxford OX1 3BQ; tel 01865-792792 Website www.bookshop.blackwell.co.uk); *Daunt Books* (83 Marylebone High Street, London W1M 4DE; tel 020-7224 2295); *Newcastle Map Centre* (55 Grey St, Newcastle upon Tyne NE1 6EF; tel 0191-261 5622 Website www.newtraveller.com); *The Map Shop:* (30a Belvoir St, Leicester LE1 6QH tel

0116-247 1400) and *The Travel Bookshop* (13 Blenheim Crescent, London W11 2EE; tel 020-7229 5260 Website www.thetravelbookshop.co.uk). In London, map-seekers usually make a bee-line for the bookshop *Stanford's*, 12/14 Long Acre, Covent Garden, London WC2 9LP (tel 020-7836-1321 Website www.stanfords.co.uk); there are also branches at 156 Regent St, London W1R 5TA (as part of the British Airways Travel Shop); 52 Grosvenor Gardens, London SW1W 0AG (adjacent to Victoria railway station and part of the Usit Campus store); and 29 Corn St, Bristol BS1 1HT (tel 0117-929 9966). Stanford's also has a mailing service.

Once you are in Mauritius the best place to get free maps of the island is the *Mauritius Tourism Promotion Authority* (MTPA), which you'll find on the 11th Floor of the Air Mauritius Centre, President John F. Kennedy Street, Port Louis (tel 208-6397, fax 212-5142). MTPA and tour brochures containing simple maps are also available in the reception area of all hotels. *Bookcourt* on the Caudan Waterfront in Port Louis (tel 211-9262, fax 211-9263), offers a range of more detailed maps. Maps of Mauritius, including Rodrigues, have been compiled by the government and are available from the *Ministry of Housing and Lands*, 6th Floor, Moorgate House, 29 Sir William Newton Street, Port Louis (tel 212-7403).

Guides

Wherever you go on the island you'll find free copies of the English/French *What's On in Mauritius,* published by B&T Directories, and MPTA's *Information Guide to Mauritius and Rodrigues*. Both are handy and complementary pocket-sized 50-60 pagers. There's also a useful *Yellow Directory Tourist Handbook,* produced and published by the Mauritius Advertising Bureau (tel 212-2734, e-mail: mab@bow.intnet.mu).

BY AIR

Apart from the thrill of a helicopter jaunt around Mauritius, the island is too small for flights. Within the island Air Mauritius has three Bell-Jet Ranger Helicopters available for airport/hotel transfers and for sight-seeing tours. Different trips are available depending on the length of the flight. Going around the whole island along the coast takes about an hour. An hour in the air costs about 14 000 rupees (£350/US$528). For more information and tariffs contact Air Mauritius Helicopter Services (tel 637-3552, fax 637-41040; Reservations tel 403-3754/5), or contact your hotel PRO.

Island-hopping

Air Mauritius links most of the main islands in this part of the Indian Ocean with weekly flights to Seychelles (3), Madagascar (3), Grand Comore (1) and Réunion (daily). Air Austral also has a daily Réunion-Mauritius service. Air Mauritius operates daily flights from SSR International Airport to the island of Rodrigues (flight time about an hour and 20 minutes). These flights are well patronised by islanders and it is sometimes difficult to get a seat. Book well in advance, and preferably before leaving home. **Note:** As the airline operates small (48-seat) aircraft on this route it restricts your baggage allowance to 33 lbs (15 kg).

Air Mauritius: Port Louis (tel 207-7070, fax 208-8331). SSR Airport (tel 603-3030, fax 637-3266).

Air Austral Port Louis (tel 212-2666).

BY SEA

Ferries and Cruises

Limited passenger ferry services run from Port Louis to Réunion and Rodrigues (see *Regions of Mauritius*). Port Louis is usually a principal port of call for most

Indian Ocean cruise ships. A variety of craft can be chartered by the day, week or month to take you exploring, fishing, or diving. Contact Yacht Charters Ltd, Royal Road, Grand Baie (tel 263-8395); Cybele Charters (tel 674-3596); Cruising Experience (tel 453-8888). There is also a choice of day cruises with *Croisieres Turquoises* (tel 631-8347); and *Croisieres Australes* offers cruises aboard magnificent 12 m sailing catamarans, either in the south-east or in the north of the island, to Ile aux Cerfs or Gabriel islands respectively, where you can relax on some of the most beautiful beaches in Mauritius (tel 674-3695, fax 674-3720). Other cruise and boat rental companies offer similar outings on everything from yachts and catamarans to 19th century schooners. For more information contact *Mauritours*, who seem to be able to arrange just about anything (tel 465-7454/454-1666, fax 454-1682/83, e-mail: mauritours@mauritours.intnet.mu), or the *Mauritius Travel and Tourist Bureau* (tel 208-2041, fax 208-8607).

BY ROAD

Taxis
There seem to be taxis everywhere – until you need one. Taxis can be identified by their number plates, which sport black letters on a white background where private cars have black plates with white letters. They don't cruise, so you have to telephone for one or locate a taxi rank. Hotels seem to be able to whistle them up at any time. Though taxis have meters you should negotiate the fare with the taxi driver before getting into the vehicle. The longer you hire a taxi, the cheaper in ratio it becomes. Most hotels prominently display scheduled taxi fares in their reception area and you should read this to get a ball park figure for your intended journey. A taxi to take you around the island for a day will cost about 1,500 to 1,800 rupees (£38-£45). Without stopping, it takes about four hours to drive around the entire island; with stops about 6-8 hours. The speed limit is 50 mph (80 km/h) but taxis must legally travel at not more than 37 mph (60 km/h) but no one seems to adhere to this limit. Average time by taxi from Port Louis to Curepipe is 20 minutes, Grand Baie 30 minutes, and about an hour to Plaisance, St Geran, Touessrok, and Souillac.

Buses
Island bus services are regular and reasonably inexpensive. Travel by bus is a colourful and novel experience. The services run on tight schedules and the buses are usually prompt and quite reliable. Fares are low and start at 5 rupees (13p). The destination appears on the front of the bus, but it's sensible to double-check with the conductor before boarding. Bus stops are often far apart, so ask the conductor to tell you when your stop is coming up so that you can get off at the right place. Buses run from about 5am to 10.30pm in the towns and from 6.30am to 6.30pm in more remote areas. The MTPA's free *Information Guide* has a useful section detailing bus numbers, departure and destination points, routes, and operators.

Five main bus companies operate on the island, carrying daily and seasonal commuters. They run on standard routes within specified regions and usually start off from the centre of their area's main town. For more information contact *National Transport Corporation* (NTC) (tel 426-2938, fax 426-5489); *United Bus Service* (UBS), *Les Cassis* (tel 212-2028, fax 212-1361); *Rose-Hill Transport* (RHT), 14 Hugnin Street, Rose-Hill (tel 464-1221, fax 464-6023); *Triolet Bus Service* (tel 261-6516, fax 261-5186); or *Mauritius Bus Transport*, Royal Road, Montagne Longue (tel 245-2539).

An easy way to see the sights of Port Louis is to use the hop-on, hop-off bus service operated by *Citirama* to do a 2½ hour tour of exploration (tel 212-2484, fax 212-1222, e-mail: citirama@intnet.mu).

BY RAIL
At the time of writing there is no railway system. However, Mauritius is looking at proposals to introduce a rail-based mode of public transport between Port Louis and Curepipe which would provide the public with a long-delayed alternative to cars, taxis, and uneven bus services.

DRIVING

Licences
An international driving licence is recommended, although not compulsory, and a foreign licence is acceptable. A temporary driving licence is available from local authorities on presentation of a valid British or Northern Ireland licence.

ROADS
Mauritius has a good network of tarred roads which are generally in good condition, but are sometimes narrow and uneven with poor lighting at night. Signposting is fairly poor and a good road map is essential if you are driving. There are 1,156 miles (1,860 km) of highways, of which 1,076 miles (1,732 km) are paved. The island is a **left-hand drive** country, with right-of-way given to traffic from the right. Mauritians are generally reckless and fast drivers and generally treat traffic rules with good-natured contempt. If you are involved in an accident go straight to the nearest police station and report the details before you attract a crowd.

Parking in the larger towns is often difficult to find. You can buy coupons at petrol stations for use in demarcated parking zones.

Fuel
Only super-grade leaded petrol – suppliers Caltex, Esso, Shell, and Total – is available in Mauritius. Petrol costs 12.80 rupees (32p) and diesel 6.80 rupees (17p) a litre.

VEHICLE RENTAL
There is no shortage of vehicle rental companies. You pay the full rental amount when you hire and the necessary adjustment is made when you return your vehicle, unless you pay with a credit card. Fuel is your responsibility. Each vehicle comes with a full tank. Prices naturally vary, but the average for a small car for a day is 1,400 rupees (£35). This gives you unlimited mileage. You must have a valid driving licence and be 21 or over.

Among the better known hire companies are:

Europcar: Airport terminal (tel 637-3240, fax 208-4705); and Grand Baie (tel 263-7948, fax 208-4705); central reservations in Les Pailles (tel 207-2125, fax 208-4705).

Hertz: Airport (tel 637-3219); Curepipe (tel 674-3695, fax 674-3720); Grand Baie (tel 263-8353); Le Morne Brabant (tel 683-6775); and Trou Aux Biches (tel 261-6562).

Budget Rent A Car: Good for 4x4s and mini-mokes. Port Louis (tel 242-0341, fax 465-3700).

Avis: Port Louis (tel 208-1624/208-6031, fax 211-1420; Website www.avis.com).

Beach Car: Airport (tel 637-3186); Rose-Hill (tel 454-1666, fax 454-1682); Port Louis (tel 208-52410).

Dodo: Quatre Bornes (tel 425-6810, fax 424-4309).

Goorye Car Rental: At the service station, next to the Banana Bar in Grand Baie (tel 263-8961/263-6685).

Car hire booked in advance from your own country usually works out cheaper than booking direct on the island.

Motorbikes and Bicycles are available for hire from Centre Sports Nautiques, Royal Road, Grand Baie (tel 263-8017); and Jawa Rental Centre, Route Royale, Pointe-aux-Canonniers (tel 263-7529).

HAZARDS

Human and animal. Watch out when driving for dogs, chickens and other stray animals crossing the road, as well as pedestrians, cyclists and moped riders who all seem to think the road belongs to them alone. Avoiding these hazards is often white-knuckle stuff, on top of which you'll find yourself involuntarily breathing in to enable your car to squeeze past other vehicles on unusually narrow roads. Common road sense seems generally lacking, although courtesy is common.

For such a small island Mauritius is well endowed with hotels. There are more than 90 recognised by the Mauritius Ministry of Tourism and Leisure, providing more than 8,000 rooms and nearly 17,000 beds – and more are opening, including a 205-bed Hilton. There's a wide choice, from luxurious five-star beach resorts to budget self-catering and family hotels. The occupancy averages a high 72% and the repeat rate for visitors returning for a second and third holiday on the island is approaching 30%, which says a lot for its popularity. Hotels usually cater for specific market segments – families, singles, honeymooners – and the primary job of your travel agent should be to establish your customer profile and correctly match it to the accommodation.

The island is famous for some of its world-class hotels and if you want to be spoiled by excellent service and spend your time on the beach, then an all-in package including accommodation is perfect for you. More than 90% of people holidaying in Mauritius are on package tours. While this might seem to make a look at some of the accommodation open to you superfluous, it's as well to know what's in store before you sign up for a travel package.

We have given these in some detail as your choice of hotel and what it offers can colour your entire stay. Food, air-conditioning, sports facilities and entertainment can and do assume major proportions in your life. Hotels are not just places to stay in Mauritius – they are your holiday. Dominant hotel groups on the island are *Beachcomber* with eight hotels and resorts and *Sun International* with five.

The Beachcomber group operates top-quality resorts, going up in price from *Le Mauricia* to the *Royal Palm*, a super-luxury hotel, which is the jewel in the crown of the group, and has soared beyond the usual star ratings awarded by tour operators. Beachcomber hotels give you a card on arrival which entitles you to free entry to their casinos, discounts on car hire and at selected shops in Port Louis and Curepipe, free water sports such as water-skiing, sailing boats, windsurfing, sailing, pedaloes, canoes, snorkelling and cruises on glass-bottom boats, as well as free land sports, such as tennis, volleyball, squash, table tennis and snooker. Activities such as scuba-diving, deep-sea fishing, trimaran/catamaran cruises, bicycle and moped hire come at an extra charge.

Sun International has hotels on both east and west coasts – from the 333-room *Le Coco Beach* to neighbouring 5-star hotel *Le Saint Géran*. A similar variety of free land and water sports to those at Beachcomber venues are available.

SELF-CATERING

If grand hotels and resorts are not for you you can enjoy an affordable, relaxing holiday in a more private self-catering apartment or villa. Some even start you off with a stock of milk, sugar, tea, coffee, bread, butter, condiments, jam, mineral water, soft drinks and eggs, so you don't need to go shopping immediately you arrive. Popular Trou aux Biches on the west coast north of Port Louis and near Grand Baie has a number of these do-it-yourself establishments, among them:

Beachvillas, self-catering bungalows on a small beach just 4 miles (6 km) from Grand Baie. There's a choice of six two-bedroomed bungalows and eight one-bedroomed studios in a garden overlooking a swimming pool. Bungalows sleep up to five people and comprise two air-conditioned bedrooms, fully equipped kitchenette, living/dining-room and terrace and a private bathroom with shower. Studios sleep up to three people in an open-plan bedroom, living and dining area with a fully-equipped kitchenette and private bathroom with shower. There's also a cleaner.

Right on the beach at Trou aux Biches, *Rhapsodie* offers four separate apartments, each sleeping four people, with air-conditioning, fully equipped kitchenette, living/dining-room, private bathroom with shower, two bedrooms and a terrace. Parking bays are available for hired cars or bicycles, and you can stock up at a grocery shop across the road. A good option for a family holiday (tel 263-8771).

Villas Mont Choisy has 10 apartments sleeping up to six people, and five air-conditioned studios with double bedrooms. All accommodation is furnished, with fully equipped kitchenette and private bathroom with shower. Apartments offer two air-conditioned bedrooms, a kitchenette, living/dining-room, terrace and bathroom. Studios are air-conditioned with open-plan living and sleeping area, kitchenette, verandah and private bathroom with shower (tel 265-6070).

The Oasis, just outside Grand Baie, is across the road from the beach. It has 12 two-bedroomed apartments and eight studios, all air-conditioned, furnished, and fully equipped with kitchenettes. The apartments sleep up to five and have two bedrooms, a kitchenette, living/dining room and terrace with a private bathroom. Studios are open-plan, sleeping up to three people, with a dining, sleeping and living area, separate kitchenette and bathroom with shower. The resort has two swimming pools and a wide variety of facilities are available nearby. This resort is across the road from the beach (tel 263-8717).

Also in the Grand Baie area are: *Pereybère Beach Apartments* (tel 263-86790); *Veranda Bungalow Village* (tel 263-8015); *Hibiscus Village Vacances* (tel 263-8554); *Casa Florida* (tel 263-7371); *Villas Le Filao* (tel 263-6149); and *Fred's Apartments* (tel 263-8830). For information on other self-catering options contact a tour operator (see *Getting There*).

| Eating and Drinking | CUISINE |

CUISINE

Some of the great cuisines of the world meet on the Mauritian table, and a holiday on the island can easily become a gastronomic trip round the globe. Mauritians take their food seriously – especially those dishes based on traditional Creole recipes. Three centuries of interracial mixing have given rise to a cuisine which draws on, but never represses, its origins – French, Indian and Chinese – which have absorbed African influences to produce the cuisine known as Creole.

Creole

Fish (fresh and saltwater) and seafood are the foundation stones of Creole dishes, along with wide variety of spices to liven them up. Chillies, tomatoes (*pommes d'amour*), coriander and ginger are prominent in many of the dishes, along with cinnamon, cloves and turmeric. Although often spicy, Creole food is not usually hot on the palate. Mango and coconut are used extensively with lemongrass and anisette, making Creole food flavoursome rather than mouth-searing. You can eat freshly harvested oysters, shrimps, crayfish, crabs, or the giant local prawns usually served with *sauce rouge* and accompanied by the *coeur de palmiste*, the heart of a seven-year-old palm, which is justly known as millionaire's salad as the tree has to be cut down to make it. Delicious local smoked marlin replaces northern salmon on the local buffet. An interesting freshwater fish is the *gourami*, a broad, dark grey fish bred in the lake at Pamplemousses. Local families serve it with a creamy *béchamel* sauce. For the carnivorous there is venison curried Creole-style or casseroled, hare and wild boar. The often fiery side-dish that accompanies every main course is *rougaille,* which is a mix of tomatoes, onion and garlic, with varying amounts of chilli. With the addition of meat or octopus it becomes a substantial stew. Sample both with care.

Vegetables range from boiled watercress (*bouillon de cresson*) and chouchou (a tender small marrow) to king-size aubergines and exotic lady's fingers (okra). The fertile volcanic soil also produces an abundance of some of the sweetest pineapples in the world, papayas, mangoes, litchis, guavas, jackfruit, watermelons, avocados, pears, custard apples, and bananas as well as some fruits you might never have seen before. In the island markets you'll find a great variety of bananas, from the tiny, tasty *gingelis* to giant, woody red plantains. Stalls are covered with breadfruit, pawpaws, limes, mangoes and fresh red litchis. There's also a rare fruit called the *mabolo,* that some call the 'celestial fruit.' It smells like blocked drains, but has a delicious flavour. Rice is eaten with every main meal and the fusion of Creole, African and Indian cuisines has given rise to a dish that is distinguished and delicious enough to have been included by Singapore Airlines on its in-flight menu. This is *Riz à la Creole* (Creole Rice), an enticing mix of basmati rice, vegetables and spices.

Indian

Make it a point to try the *briani,* a masterpiece of Muslim cuisine that is a fragrant preparation of rice and meats or vegetables in saffron-flavoured yoghurt. An authentic Mauritian meal is not complete without an *achard,* which is a medley of vegetables prepared with oil, vinegar and spices, or *chatini,* chutney made with tomatoes or coconuts seasoned with garlic, ginger and vinegar.

Fast-Food

Life in the fast-food lane is almost as interesting. Indian fast food snacks are popular with locals in Mauritius and hawkers sell such savouries as samoosas, rotis, curried rolls, the deep-fried pastry balls of mashed yellow peas with chilli called *gateaux piments* and the Muslim pancake, *puri.* If you get tired of all this exotica a nice plate of grilled marlin or dorado with french fries can give hake and chips a run for its money, and on an island which calls a poor chef a *rosbif* (English) cook, you can always order eggs and bacon or look for a steakhouse, a Pizza Hut, or a Kentucky Fried Chicken outlet.

As can be seen from the lists of restaurants in the different regions (see *Eating Out* in each regional section) Chinese food is extremely popular with Mauritians, although they are more likely to buy it as takeaways at lunchtime or to eat at home in the evening.

DRINKING
When they're not drinking bottled water, vanilla tea, or coffee Mauritians like to relax with the products of the local brewery and competing distilleries.

Beer and Rum
All over the islands you'll see corner shops and bars painted a bright yellow and sporting a large black Phoenix logo and a slogan promising 'friendly moments.' These are well patronised. Phoenix is the name of both brewery and its beer. It's a refreshing drink on a warm day – and it's always warm in Mauritius. The beer is fairly strong – 5% alcohol by volume, although the brewery also makes Blue Marlin beer at 6%. A large bottle of Phoenix costs around 25 rupees (about 60p) from a *boutique* (Creole for grocery store). Hotel bars usually mark up more than double the retail price of any drink and an oddity is that a soft drink or a bottle or water costs exactly the same as a beer. This lesson is quickly learnt by beer-drinking visitors. Don't forget to pack your handy Swiss Army knife or a bottle-opener.

Serious local drinkers – and there are plenty – prefer the rum made on the island, not the up-market Green Island Rum of the hotels and restaurants, but the downmarket one named Goodwill, which is appropriately made in Tombeau ('Tomb') Bay. You can buy a 26 fl oz (750 ml) bottle (40% alcohol) in the store for 40 rupees (about £1) or you can go to a local bar and ask for *ene ferraille* ('an iron'), Creole slang for a shot of Goodwill. Creoles will tell you that you'll never get drunk on rum if you use coconut water as a mixer. Coconuts cost 10 rupees (25p) in the country, double this in the street in Port Louis.

If you ask your hotel to arrange a visit to a distillery you'll probably end up at Domaine Ylang-Ylang, where it is not rum that trickles from the copper stills, but the fragrant oil of the yellow ylang-ylang flowers used to make perfume.

Wine
Wine of sorts is made in Mauritius but buffs prefer to drink the imported French and South African labels, for which you'll pay through the nose. If you ask Mauritians about the local wine they'll usually recount the story of the founder of the island's first winery who called his family together as he lay dying to tell them the secrets of wine-making, ending his recital with: 'You can even make it with grapes!'

Soft Drinks
You'll find a wide range of non-alcoholic fresh fruit and fizzy sweet drinks available on the island. Buy whatever takes your fancy, but we insist you try the almond drink called *alouda,* and the refreshing thirst-quencher Orangina. Oh yes, and try coconut water fresh from the nut – without the rum.

Tea and Coffee
Tea is grown on the island and is plentiful in the shops in a wide variety of flavours. Vanilla is added to the most unlikely food and drinks, often with surprisingly pleasant results. It's so popular in tea that doctors are worried about the heart problems some of its properties can cause. Locals rarely drink ground coffee, although an excellent bean called Cafe Chamarel is grown on the island. They seem to prefer instant coffee. Coffee in restaurants and hotels can be a subtle and delicious drink, and it often comes spiced with vanilla, *à la Créole.*

Entertainment

DANCE AND MUSIC

Sega

The traditional dance in Mauritius is the *sega* and you can't truly say you've seen the island until you've watched the sensual and at times frankly obscene gyrations of this dance, a legacy of the old black slaves interwoven with themes from other cultures. The *sega* is a colourful and vibrant dance and most resort hotels have a toned-down version at least once a week. All around the island the traditional instruments are still used – the *ravane*, a drum made from a wooden hoop covered with taut goatskin; the *coco* (maracas), and the metal triangle. Another traditional instrument, the bowed single-string attached to a dried gourd, has been replaced by the more sophisticated electric guitar. The beat is definitely African, with hip movements reminiscent of the South Seas, hand movements resembling those of South-East Asia, and a shuffle that could come from almost anywhere. Onlookers are invariably invited to take part in the dance. A few hints – the man usually stands hands on hips, waiting while the girl shuffles towards him, wiggling and waving an inviting colourful handkerchief. Partners then face each other holding waist and shoulder. When you hear *En Bas! En Bas!* ('Down, Down') bend your knees and bend backwards while swaying your hips to the rhythm. Women are advised not to wear mini-skirts; formal wear for men can be a handicap. **Riviere Noire** is a Creole fishermen's district where *sega* dancing is especially lively on Saturday nights. The dance is common throughout all the Mascarene islands, although in Rodrigues the rhythm beats faster, in Réunion the *sega* has developed into the sultry, slow *maloya*, while in Agalega, small seashells are clapped together as an accompaniment.

Among other music and dance forms in Mauritius are the *jhumar* (Bhojpuri dance songs), the *jhaakri* (Marathi religious dance songs), the *kolattum* (Tamil folk dance), and the *raas* (Gujarati folk dance).

Dancing

If the dance floor calls, nightclubs open from 10.30pm or 11pm and swing till dawn. Most of the hotels have in-house nightclubs. An entrance fee is payable if you are not a resident. Discothèques abound for late-nighters, particularly in the Grand Baie area, a magnet for the young and the young-at-heart and the island's answer to the Côte d' Azure. Look for names such as *Club Climax* (tel 263-8701), *Le Rocking Boat Pub* (tel 212-2403), *Number One* (tel 263-8434), *Saxophone* (tel 465-3021), *Speedy* (tel 263-7829), and *Zanzibar* (tel 263-8540).

Music

For a relaxed musical evening, spend some time in one of the many piano bars. *Phil's Pub* (tel 263-8589), *La Plantation* (tel 686-5370), *Le Privé* (tel 263-8766), *Alchemy* (tel 263-5314), *Banana Café* and *Tom Cat Jazz Club* (both at tel 263-8540) are some of the better known.

FESTIVALS

Nothing is more representative of the multi-cultural and religious nature of Mauritian life than the succession of Hindu, Muslim, Chinese and Christian festivals throughout the year, occasions that can be either impressive and spectacular, solemn and austere, or simply colourful and a time for fun and frolics. With origins rooted in three continents, Europe, Asia, and Africa, the number and variety of religious festivals celebrated is not all that surprising. Along with Christian festivals such as Christmas and Easter, each month seems to bring yet another celebration.

The Mauritian calendar includes such religious events as:

Thaïpoosam Cavadee (mid-January) – A Tamil event dedicated to Muruga where adepts, after 10 days of fasting, pierce their bodies with dozens of tiny needles and parade in colourful, animated processions. These are followed by fire-walking in temple grounds.

Chinese New Year and **Spring Festival** (January/February) – Traditional Dragon Dances can be seen in various parts of the island.

Eid-ul-Fitr (March) – Represents the end of the Muslim month-long fast of Ramadan and many colourful celebrations mark the event.

Maha Shivaratree (February/March) – This is the annual pilgrimage to Grand Bassin, in the Plaine Champagne area, when Hindus offer homage to Shiva. To the Hindus Grand Bassin is known as Ganga Talab ('Lake of the Ganges').

Pére Laval Pilgrimage (September) – Catholics go in procession to gather at the tomb in Sainte-Croix of the saint-like French priest and missionary, Father Désiré Laval, who died in 1864 after converting thousands of Mauritians to Christianity. He ministered to the liberated slaves during the 23 years he lived on the island.

Ougadi (March/April) – A religious event for the Telegus, when they pay homage to the Telegu New Year, which coincides with the beginning of the Indian harvest. Get-togethers, prayers and cakes mark this event.

Ganesh Chaturthi (August/September) – A religious event for the Marathis celebrating the anniversary of the god Ganesh, the ceremonial deity, who is half-man, half-elephant, the son of Shiva. Followers pray and make flour or clay statues of Ganesh, which they throw into a sacred river or at holy water points.

Divali (October/November) – A religious event for Hindus celebrating the victory of good over evil, light over darkness. During this occasion, the whole island sparkles with thousands of small lights and lanterns. **Bonne Terre**, near Vacoas, and the village of **Triolet** are places to visit at this time.

Wherever you go in Mauritius you'll see boxes mounted on pedestals or rocks, lining the roads and dotted throughout the towns, and containing small statues and icons. Some are Catholic, some Hindu, some Tamil, others Islamic, and some are mysterious perfumed and garlanded figures, which Mauritians are not keen to discuss. These often involve the voodoo rites of the old plantation slaves, which some old Creole women still keep alive. In every town and village you'll also see innumerable Indian houses with two red or yellow flags fluttering on long bamboo poles in the front garden. These are planted behind the small shrine of whatever deity in the pantheon has been chosen to protect the house. Halumana, the god of victory, seems to be the most popular choice for this task.

GALLERIES AND MUSEUMS

Although the **Port Louis Art Gallery** (tel 212-0639) in the capital has been around for years, art galleries do not flourish the way they do on other islands in the region. Art is kept alive by exhibitions at alternative venues, such as the **Colonial Coconut Hotel** (tel 263-8720) in Grand Baie and the **Eureka Creole House** (tel 212-1539) at Moka, whose top floor is given over to local painting.

Museums are more varied. The **Natural History Museum and Mauritius Institute** (tel 212-0639) in Port Louis is the best known, housing most of the nation's important historical records and relics, as well as a comprehensive research facility and library. The **Musée de la Photographie** (tel 454-5242) in the heart of Port Louis, exhibits some of the oldest photographs in the world. The first was taken less than five years after the invention of photography. The museum contains a priceless collection of 19th century cameras. The **Naval Museum** (tel

631-9329) in Mahébourg is the second most popular museum on the island. It contains relics such as the ship's bell from the wreck of the **St Géran**, which sank off the coast of Mauritius in 1744, inspiring the country's best-loved national novel *Paul et Virginie*. The museum was used in 1810 as a hospital for officers wounded in the French and English naval battle at Grand Port. The **Robert-Edward Hart Museum** (tel 625-6101), near Souillac, is dedicated to the Mauritian poet of that name, whose restored cottage **La Nef** has a comprehensive collection of his original manuscripts. At Tamarin, the **Shellorama Museum** houses what is regarded as the largest collection of Indian Ocean shells in the world.

CINEMAS AND THEATRE
Cinemas. There are cinemas in all the major centres, but unless you are at least fluent in French or an oriental language stick to the more sophisticated three-screen entertainment complex at the Caudan Waterfront in Port Louis if you want to go to the movies. Tel 211-9500 to find out what's on.

Theatre
Television, and particularly home video, has dealt a blow to live theatre in Mauritius. During the past few years, however, there have been moves to revive both theatre and the performing arts in general. The Ministry of Arts, Culture and Leisure promotes an annual festival of the dramatic arts. Fresh attention is being paid to venues and, with help of the French Embassy's cultural co-operation mission, the southern hemisphere's oldest theatre (1822) has been renovated in Port Louis. Tourist offices distribute a regular news sheet detailing shows and plays at island theatres, as well as dances and *sega* nights at hotels and discos.

GAMBLING

Horse-Racing
If you like a flutter there are lots of casinos on the island and a major racecourse, *Champ de Mars*, in Port Louis where locals have been watching horse-racing since it was founded in 1812 during the Napoleonic wars. The Mauritius Turf Club is the second oldest race club in the world after the English Jockey Club. When it opened it was the first racecourse in the southern hemisphere. The track is a magnet for gambling islanders and visitors alike, and on Derby Day, the Maiden Cup in late August, it seems that most of the population of Port Louis is crammed into the amphitheatre on the outskirts of the capital. The racing season runs from May until December.

Casinos
Many of the larger up-market hotels have their own casinos on or adjacent to their premises. Games include American roulette, blackjack, slot and poker machines. Some popular venues are:
Le Caudan Waterfront Casino, tel 210-3518
Le Coco Beach Hotel & Casino, Belle Mare Beach, tel 415-1089.
Casino de Maurice, Curepipe, tel 675-5012.
La Pirogue Sun Hotel & Casino, Wolmar, Flic-en-Flac Beach, tel 453-8441.
Berjaya Le Morne Beach Resort & Casino, Le Morne Plage, tel 622-6450.
Grand Casino du Domaine, Port Louis, tel 212-0400.
L'Amicale Casino Chinois, Port Louis, tel 242-3335.
Belle Mare Plage Hotel & Casino, Poste de Flacq, tel 415-1515.
Le Saint Geran Hotel & Casino, Poste de Flacq, tel 415-1825.
Trou aux Biches Village Hotel & Casino, Triolet, tel 265-6619.
For the cash-strapped, dominoes is a popular game.

FLORA AND FAUNA

For an island only the size of the British county of Surrey and slightly smaller than America's District of Columbia, Mauritius abounds with fascinating flora and fauna. Virgin forests and fertile plains provide ideal ecological niches for myriad species of wildlife, many of them found only on the island. Active nature conservation is a vital aspect of government policy in Mauritius and the establishment of nature reserves has enabled many threatened species to thrive in a protected environment, while allowing visitors to enjoy nature without upsetting delicate eco-systems.

Flora

A month seldom passes in Mauritius without a variety of trees, shrubs and plants bursting into magnificent blossom. More than 1,000 plants are indigenous to Mauritius, of which about 300 justify the abused word 'unique.' Among the most beautiful blossoms in Mauritius are those of *Trochetias*, from the *Sterculiacea* family. *Trochetia boutoniana*, particularly, has huge carmine-red flowers and is found in the mountains of the south-west. It is the national flower of Mauritius. Several locations on Mauritius are also blazoned with snow-white clustered blossoms of *Trochetia triflora*; although by far the commonest among the island's species is *Trochetia blackburniana*. Hibiscus flourishes in several localities, usually in more acid terrain. *Hibiscus columnaris* is a tree of great beauty, with a blossom rich reddish-yellow on the outside and sulphur yellow on the inside. *Hibiscus boryanus* has vermilion-red flowers. The **rainforests** of Mauritius are fascinating for anyone with the slightest interest in botany. In the forests you can see giant endemic trees such as the **black ebony** (*Diospyros tesselaria*), and various other ebony species. Growing in the rain forests of Pouce Mountain is *Roussea simplex*, or *Liana rousseau* (dedicated to the memory of Jean-Jacques Rousseau), an escalioniaceae with thick fleshy yellow petals. Among the many tree species are beautiful **palms**, spectacular **pandanus**, known locally as *vacoas*, downy-leafed **veloutiers**, and the **oil tree** *Hornea mauritiana*, a huge tree growing on the drier side of the island. The **Curepipe Botanical Gardens** are well worth a visit; there you will find a unique palm, the world's only surviving *Hyophorbe amaricaulis*.

Fauna

Plant life of Mauritius is matched in its diversity by the island's fauna, among the richest in the Indian Ocean, from the lowliest insects to some of the world's most exotic birds. Pretty little **fairy terns**, brilliantly hued **cardinals**, **weaver birds**, and the **pic-pic** should delight twitchers, as well as species such as the **bespectacled white-eye**, **Mauritius fody**, **paradise flycatcher**, the white-tailed tick-bird – the *paille-en-queue* ('straw-in-the-tail') which is the emblem of Air Mauritius – and the recently endangered falcon called the **Mauritius kestrel**. This has been pulled back from the brink of extinction by a captive breeding programme supported by the Mauritius Wildlife Foundation. Several hundred of these little raptors have been released into the wild. The **pink pigeon**, a long-necked bird with a back and tail suffused by subtle shades of pink, is another success story. In collaboration with the Mauritius Wildlife Foundation the government is also working on the captive breeding of local parakeets, which have declined to a dangerous level. There are about 15 species of reptiles in Mauritius and on its outlying islands. Round Island alone harbours eight endemic species. There are also more than 2,000 insect species in Mauritius and its butterflies are among the most beautiful in the Indian Ocean. One of the larger spiders spins a useful silk which Mauritian society ladies once collected to weave a pair of gloves for the empress Eugénie, wife of Napoleon III. Mauritius has no indigenous species of mammals except for the **Mauritius fruit bat**, or flying fox. **Java deer** were introduced by the Dutch in the 17th century, and the **mongoose** came with the earlier Portuguese. Monkeys and wild boar, feral descendants of domestic pigs, roam the forests. The latter, with the deer, are hunted for their meat.

CONSERVATION

The **dodo** is probably the first thing that springs to mind when Mauritius is mentioned. When Portuguese seafarers first landed on the island they found a previously unknown species of bird, which they called *dodo,* the equivalent of a simpleton – because they mistook its lack of fear for stupidity. The dodo weighed 44-55 lb (20-25 kg) but had small, weak wings and was flightless. It was easy prey for the Portuguese who would club it to death as it waddled trustfully up to them. Those that survived had to contend with animals such as dogs and pigs, left behind on the island by seamen. Dutch colonists joined the onslaught on the dodo, and by 1681 there were none left in Mauritius. The eco-vandalism not only wiped out the dodo, but had other unexpected effects. Soon after the dodo became extinct the seeds of a local tree stopped sprouting, because they needed to first soften by passing through the dodo's digestive system to enable them to germinate (turkeys were eventually used as substitute dodos and the tree was saved). The dodo (*Raphus cucullatus*) survives only in museum reconstructions and as a supporter in the Mauritian national coat-of-arms. The only known dodo egg in the world is an exhibit at the East London Museum in South Africa. Though the dodo is long gone it still attracts scientific attention and there's been a fresh interpretation of its shape by a scientist of the National Museum of Scotland who has constructed a new, slimmer model than that found in the museum in Port Louis.

In close collaboration with the government the Mauritian Wildlife Foundation works to ensure that the sad story of the dodo is never repeated. Alerted by Sir Peter Scott, international organisations started getting involved in conservation projects in Mauritius back in 1973. The first major project was the rescue and conservation of the Mauritius kestrel at a time when only four kestrels – the only bird of prey in Mauritius – were known to exist, making it the rarest bird in the world. An intensive programme of captive breeding and release has saved the kestrel from extinction. The bird is still on the endangered species list and the management of its population will have to continue for many years to ensure its survival.

In 1976, international naturalist and conservationist Gerald Durrell visited Mauritius and Rodrigues and sparked the involvement of the Jersey Wildlife Preservation Trust in local conservation projects. The JWPT got involved in efforts to save the pink pigeon, the Mauritius echo parakeet, and the Rodrigues fruit bat. The wild population of pink pigeons now numbers more than 250 birds, from a low of 15-20 in 1985. The echo parakeet is the world's rarest parrot and its catastrophic decline in its native habitat has been halted but the population will have to reach 500 before the threat of extinction is averted. The bats which Durrell thought looked like pomeranians hanging in the trees have also made a comeback.

DIVING AND WATERSPORTS

Sun, sand and sea is what Mauritius is all about for holidaymakers, and for those who take their aquatic sports seriously the waters around this cross-roads of the Indian Ocean are the ideal playground – especially for scuba-diving and snorkelling, big-game fishing, and sailing.

DIVING

International diving film-maker and author Al J Venter rates some diving spots in Mauritius and sibling island Rodrigues as among the best in the world. The Mauritian diving season continues throughout the year, but the summer months are particularly popular. Visibility near the reef which virtually girdles the island is particularly good during winter. Sea and surface temperature outside the reef ranges from 72°F (22°C) in August and September to 81°F (27°C) in March. Lagoon waters within the reef have higher temperatures in summer.

Mauritius has nearly 30 diving centres – many of them based at leading hotels and resorts – which hire equipment, offer tuition and certification, and take you on boat excursions to the best dive sites for whatever your level of underwater competence might be. For beginners, lessons start in the swimming pool and, if you show aptitude, quickly progress to shallow diving within the lagoon. Beginners should be able to progress to supervised scuba-diving in the sea during the course of a two-week holiday. You can get on-the-spot advice or information before you go from Mauritius Scuba Diving Association (MSDA), 36 bis Meldrum Street, Beau Bassin (tel/fax 454-0011, e-mail: MSDA@intnet.mu) or from the Mauritius Underwater Group (MUG), Railway Road, Vacoas (tel 696-5368), which also hosts the Mauritius Marine Conservation Society, which has sunk a number of old hulks off some resorts to create artificial reefs. All the best diving centres on the island are affiliated to the MSDA and can be found at most of the large hotels and resorts along the north, east, and west coats. All of them are fully equipped with wetsuits, life jackets, compressors, regulators, and other underwater paraphernalia. The Special Mobile Force at Vacoas has a decompression chamber (tel 686-1011, fax 696-4956). You can hire equipment from MUG by the day, which can be considerably cheaper than outfitting at one of the resort hotels' dive centres.

Mauritius has outlawed the use of spearguns and the collection of shells and corals, which means that snorkelling and scuba-dives among the island's coral gardens in pleasantly warm waters is memorable both for the beauty of the surroundings, and the diversity of the marine life. There's a great variety of angelfish, colourful *demoiselles*, targetfish and a large variety of eels, including smaller moray eels and the harmless, but often alarming, banded snake-eel, which often makes straight for you if you disturb it in its lair. Parrot fish, thick-lipped groupers, boxfish, wrasse, trumpetfish, sweetlips, angel, clown, squirrel and the beautiful but poisonous lionfish can also grab your attention against a backdrop of sponges, corals, and anemones. The island is also noted for its shells; conches, cowries, cones; some common and a few rare. Beyond the reef, where temperatures and depths drop sharply, you should be a certificated open-water diver. An introductory dive at **Trou aux Biches** is a good idea for anyone unused to local conditions. Wear some form of body protection, either a thin wetsuit or even a long-sleeved vest to protect against coral cuts and grazes. The depth there is about 66 ft (20 m), there is good visibility, and little current. Boats usually anchor about 230 ft (70 m) beyond the reef in sheltered water when the weather is fine.

The **Ambulante Passe** which lies just off the Le Morne area is one of the deeper natural channels in the encircling reef through which the marlin boats set out in season in search of marlin and other game-fish. The Passe offers excellent snorkelling, with maximum depth in the area at about 33 ft (10 m) and visibility ranging from 33-98 ft (10-30 m), depending on the tide. Fish here are mainly streaker, a species of kingfish, parrotfish and dog-toothed tunny. Sharks are rarely seen.

Islets to the north-west offer great sport, although diving in this area is not for novices. The islands lie exposed to the ocean swell, and tidal streams can cause the occasional dangerous race. Deeper and more spectacular dives are to be found near Flic en Flac. This lies in the area of the west coast which Al J Venter recommends as the best coast for diving, particularly around Flic en Flac and the Albion coastal area of Black River, where visibility on a good day rarely falls below 98 ft (30 m). The best places to dive are in the south-west at Le Morne, along the west coast and northward towards Trou aux Biches and Grand Baie. There is also good diving in the east in the area around Pointe de Flacq and in the southerly region in the vicinity of Grande Port. The northern offshore islands have some wonderful spots on their leeward shores.

BEST DIVES AND DIVE CENTRES
Here's a choice of some of the best dives, selected by island experts:

NORTH-WEST
Trou aux Biches: The lagoon here is protected by a fairly extensive coral barrier reef about 984 ft (300 m) and is a paradise for snorkel divers as it rarely gets any surf. Moray eels here have become accustomed to being hand-fed by divers. Instructors warn against this, saying hungry eels will follow you throughout your dive and can become aggressive.

Aquarium: This site in Grande Baie has an average depth of 49 ft (15 m), but in deep gullies it falls to 59 ft (18 m). The humpbacked scorpionfish, *Scorpaenopsis gibbosa,* is commonly found here, so wear gloves. If you are diving in the north you shouldn't miss this site.

Tortoise: A 43 ft (13 m) site at Grand Baie which comprises a cluster of four flat reefs, with resident morays. Octopus and lionfish are frequently seen and on the sand you'll stir up sole and sand eels. The site is usually dived in the late afternoon when the current slackens.

Coral Gardens: This Grande Baie site begins at 59 ft (18 m) and can be explored to about 79 ft (24 m). Sand gullies between bank after bank of coral attracts many species of bivalves, and there are many fish, including squirrelfish, trumpetfish and goldies. Crayfish can be found in some of the crevices.

Dive Centres in the North:
Atlantis Diving Centre: Trou aux Biches (tel 265-7172, fax 263-7859).
Blue Water Diving: Le Corsaire, Trou aux Biches (tel 265-7186, fax 265-6267).
Cap Divers: Paradise Cove Hotel, Anse La Raie (tel 262-6511, fax 262-7736).
Canonnier Diving Centre: Le Canonnier Hotel, Pointe aux Canonniers (tel 263-7995, fax 263-7864).
Diving World: Le Mauricia Hotel, Grand Baie (tel 263-7800, fax 263-7888).
Dolphin Diving Centre: Grand Baie (tel 263-9428, fax 263-7888).
Islandive: Veranda Bungalow Village, Grand Baie (tel 263-6260, fax 263-7369).
Turtle Bay Nautics: Maritim Hotel, Balaclava (tel 261-5600, fax 261-5670).
Merville Diving Centre: Merville Hotel, Grand Baie (tel 263-8621, fax 263-8146).
Paradise Diving: Coastal Road, Grand Baie (tel 263-7220, fax 263-8534).
Pereybère Diving Centre: Casa Florida, Pereybère (tel/fax 263-6225).
Nautilus: Trou aux Biches Hotel, Trou aux Biches (tel 204-6565, fax 265-6661).
Sinbad: Kuxville, Cap Malheureux (tel 262-8836, fax 262-7407).

WEST COAST
The waters between Wolmar and Flic en Flac have some of the best sites on the island, with dives of 49-197 ft (15-60 m) only minutes from the beach. There are corals, rock caverns and abundant marine life, as well as shipwrecks and the fabulous 39 ft (12 m) high, 33 ft (10 m) long Cathedral Cave to explore.

Aquarium: A shallow dive descending from 26 ft (8 m) down a rocky terrace to 49 ft (15 m). You start by following the anchor cable down; after that your skipper will haul it up and follow divers from the surface, an easy job in such excellent visibility. This area is well-known for its huge anemones and their resident clownfish. Many of these fish are tame and can be fed by hand. This is an outstanding spot for beginners.

Cathedral: A wall dive on an interesting rock formation. The dive begins from the top of one rock at 59 ft (18 m), and you slowly descend down the side of two sheer cliff-faces to 125 ft (38 m). Once inside this enormous cave, with light filtering through a crack in the roof 33 ft (10 m) up, there is a churchlike sense of peace and tranquillity.

Couline Bambou: A 59-112 ft (18-34 m) dive through chimney tunnels, bridges and rock caves. Expect to see large game-fish such as wahoo, tunny and kingfish. Besides the many schools of large fish there are plenty of colourful small reef fish, turtles and various types of large rays. Good spot for photography.

Manioc: A deep dive of 131-197 ft (40-60 m) on a series of rock-faces that is recommended **only for experienced divers**. White-tip reef sharks are sometimes seen but pose no danger to divers. There are always a few shoals of game-fish – kingfish and barracuda – and there are large emperor angelfish.

Rempart L'Herbe: Known as Shark Place, this is a 138-164 ft (42-50 m) dive on a rock pinnacle that almost always provides close-ups of rays, sharks and barracuda. Plenty of small tropical reef fish among the coral and large rays are seen, but the main denizens of interest are the white-tip reef sharks that congregate. Approach quietly and they will stay around.

L'Eveille: A medium-depth dive that starts at 98 ft (30m) and ends at 59 ft (18 m). There's a series of drop-offs where there are several patches of anemones with attendant clownfish. Coral and lots of oyster-clams grow here.

Rempart-Pat: A dive of 66-92 ft (20-28 m) on a rock formation that ends on a small drop-off. Beware of the camouflaged stonefish that are sometimes seen on this dive. Watch where you place your hands.

Rempart-Suisse: This is one of the longest reefs in Mauritius, with an average depth of 82 ft (25 m). It's full of small caverns where lobsters hide. There's plenty of marine life and a good variety of fish, especially balloonfish. There are more than 30 diving spots here, with depths ranging from 39-262 ft (12-80 m).

Canon: At 72 ft (22 m), a 19th century wreck lies almost completely buried in the sand. You can grub around an old cannon; copper nails are occasionally found in the sand.

Pointe Koenig: This dive is off Black River, on the side of a 66-82 ft (20-25 m) channel in the reef, where there are some excellent coral formations.

Shark Reef: This dive is normally a drift-dive, almost always in crystal-clear water with a vis up to 131 ft (40 m). There is a drop-off at 131 ft (40 m) down to 164 ft (50 m). The area has many fish, and large shoals of hundreds of kingfish are often seen. Throughout the year you are likely to encounter black-tip reef sharks, and as many as 40 have been spotted on a single dive.

Dive Centres in the West

Exploration Sous-Marine: Villas Caroline, Flic en Flac (tel 453-8450, fax 453-8807).

Klondike Diving Centre: Klondike Hotel, Flic en Flac (tel 453-8335, fax 453-8337).

Abyss: Flic en Flac (tel/fax 453-8109).

Sofitel Diving Centre: Sofitel Imperial Hotel, Wolmar (tel 453-8700, fax 453-8320).

Sun Divers: La Pirogue Hotel, Wolmar (tel 453-8441, fax 453-8449).

Punto Blue: Pearle Beach Hotel (tel 453-8453/253-3348, fax 683-6230).

SOUTH-WEST COAST

The hotel resort at the foot of towering Le Morne mountain on the south-western corner of the island has diving spots that are within 30 minutes' boat trip. The more popular dive sites are all on the seaward side of the barrier reef, and have been named by local fishermen and divers.

Needle Hall

A shallow dive of 46 ft (14 m) in an area of coral pillars that look like needles protruding from the sea-bed. This area teems with fish, there is hardly every any current, and visibility is excellent, making it a perfect spot for underwater photography.

Anthony

A 53 ft (16 m) dive round a rock and coral pinnacle surrounded by coral and white sand in deep gullies. You begin your dive at the main pinnacle, referred to as Anthony, which rises steeply from the sand with a sheer cliff face round it. Shells are common where the reef and sand meet in the gullies, and a variety of cone and cowrie shells, and large open clams are all around.

Michel's Place

A 125 ft (38 m) dive in an area of flat corals where lots of clownfish, triggerfish, and the picasso triggerfish can be seen. The area is well-known for its hawksbill and green turtles, which you might occasionally catch napping under a coral overhang.

Cliff

A large coral drop-off, this 79 ft (24 m) site is on the other side of the barrier reef – magnificent vistas, coral and reef fish. An underwater camera is imperative on this dive.

Japanese Gardens

Begins at 82 ft (25 m) and ends at 49 ft (15 m). It gets its name because of its obvious resemblance to a garden, with many different coral types and small tropical reef fish.

Casiers

A 92-115 ft (28-35 m) site. Tuna, wahoo and hammerhead sharks are occasionally seen over the reef, which is flat and full of small corals. The area is well-known for its abundant shells. Snorkelling in the channel of the Ambulante Passe can be very interesting on the incoming tide. This Passe is only a few metres deep, with small coral cliffs patrolled by shoals of kingfish, barracuda and colourful surgeonfish.

Dive Centres in the South-West
Black River Diving Centre: Centre de Pêche, Rivière Noire (tel 683-6503, fax 683-6318).

Easy Dive: Berjaya Hotel, Le Morne (tel 683-6800, fax 683-6070).

Diveplan: Le Morne (tel 401-5050, fax 450-5140).

SOUTH COAST
There's not a great deal here to attract the scuba-diver, although the snorkelling in Grande Port is excellent and there are a number of old wrecks in the bay worth a scuba-diver's attention. The most interesting is that of *HMS Sirius* which, with the *Magicienne* was lost on 24 August 1810 during the Grand Port naval battle between the British and the French, although you are not officially allowed free access to this underwater museum piece.

Blue Bay in the south-east doesn't have many reefs, but you'll see quite a few crabs, lobsters, squid and sharks if you dive here.

EAST COAST
Most vacationers, particularly divers, wind up in Grand Baie or Black River/Flic-en-Flac region. Hotel group Sun International, which operates upmarket hotels and resorts along this coast, says that Eden, on its first morning, must have looked like this area. Apart from the hype, dive sites in the area are well worth sampling. A drift-dive through the Passe in the barrier reef is regarded as one of the finest dives in Mauritius. Carried by the current through the Passe, you float past coral walls and through clouds of brilliantly-coloured tropical fishes, including some of the biggest parrotfish around.

Dive Centres in the South-East and East
Coral Dive: La Croix du Sud, Pointe Jérôme (tel 631-9041/9601, fax 631-9603).

Shandrani Diving Centre: Shandrani Hotel, Plaine Magnien (tel 637-3511, fax 637-4313).

East Coast Diving: Saint Géran Hotel, Belle Mare (tel 415-1825, fax 415-1983).

Sea Fan Diving Centre: Hotel Ambre, Palmar (tel 415-1545, fax 415-1594).

Neptune Diving Centre: Belle Mare Plage Hotel, Belle Mare (tel 415-1501, fax 415-1082).

Pierre Sport Diving: Tousserok Hotel, Trou d'Eau Douce (tel 419-2451, fax 419-2025).

WRECK-DIVING
There are more than 50 wrecks strewn offshore around the island, many of them accessible to reasonably fit and experienced scuba-divers. One of the more interesting lying within easy reach of the shore is off Mahébourg in the south-east. This is the *Sirius,* sunk in the naval battle that pitted the British against the French at Grande Port in 1810. To this day her cannon can be seen lying in neat rows on the bottom at about 98 ft (30 m). Other relics of this engagement can be seen in the local museum. The French novel *Paul et Virginie*, by Bernardin de St Pierre, is set in Mauritius and was inspired by the wreck of the *St Géran*, which lies in less than 33 ft (10 m) of water off the north-east coast. Old silver coins are occasionally found among the coral and conglomerate at this site and her anchor and cannon are still visible. A dive on the wreck entails a long boat trip, which must be made in fine weather as the wreck lies off an exposed coast. More modern vessels have been scuttled around the island by local marine conservation society divers to form artificial reefs. In the west are the *St Gabriel,* lying on a flat rocky bottom at a depth

of 121 ft (37 m); the *Kai Sei 113* at 118 ft (36 m) on a flat rock reef; and the *Tug II* on sand at 66 ft (20 m). All attract lots of fish life, especially the colourful but dangerous stonefish and lionfish.

HELMET DIVING

This is an experience not to be missed – forget about the copper helmets and heavy lead boots. No special training is needed – you don't even have to be able to swim – and you can wear glasses or contact lenses during a guided sea-bed stroll. You'll don lightweight see-through headgear, supplied with air from the surface to enable you to go for an unforgettable undersea tramp. If this doesn't appeal you can go for a trip on a semi-submersible, which opens up magnificent views of coral reefs and marine life previously limited to divers and snorkellers. A one-hour trip in guaranteed safety and air-conditioned comfort provides spectacular views of the silent world.

Contact:

Undersea Walk: Grand Baie (tel 423-8822/263-7820).

Alpha II: Grand Baie (tel 263-7664).

Coral Garden Water Sports: Blue Bay (tel 631-1651).

Blue Safari Submarine: Grand Baie (tel 263-3333).

Captain Nemo's Undersea Walk: Pointe aux Canonnieres (tel 263-7819).

Aquaventure: Belle Mare Plage Hotel (tel 415-1515, fax 415-1993).

Embadilo Open Helmet Diving: Grand Baie (tel 263-7290/423-7082, fax 263-7290).

There is also the semi-submersible *Le Nessee* at Grand Baie (tel 674-3695, fax 674-3720). All of these places will also organise or point you in the right direction for glass-bottom boat excursions in various spots around the island.

BIG-GAME FISHING

Mauritian waters offer exciting hunting grounds for deep-sea anglers in search of marlin, sailfish, tuna, dorado, bonito, wahoo and other ocean-roving pelagic fish. So rich are these waters in these game-fish that the island regularly hosts many top international fishing competitions, which have chalked up many world records for fighting fish. The **best deep-sea fishing season** stretches from September to March, and this is the time serious anglers from all over the world congregate on the island, and when Mauritius hosts the annual World Marlin Cup. During the season it's not unusual to hear of up to 600 marlin being boated and weighed. March and April draw fishing enthusiasts to Mauritius for its yellowfin tuna season when shoals of 140-200 pounders move inshore, although big-game fishing is an all-year-round sport. Launches for big-game fishing are available for half-day or full-day hire from most beach hotels and a number of private fishing centres. These launches are rented fully equipped and include the services of an experienced skipper whose knowledge of the sea can be relied upon to see you casting and trolling in the right spots. As well as hiring sophisticated fishing boats you can buy fishing equipment and tackle locally free of tax, and you can obtain temporary membership of yacht or angling clubs and take part in their activities. Deep-sea fishing boats are well-equipped with ship-to-shore radio and trolling equipment for both live-bait and artificial lures as standard equipment. Six hours' fishing – 7am to 1pm – is the minimum hire time, but charter boats can be shared by a group of three to six anglers. Boats can be booked through most of the hotels, although the largest fleets are based at the Corsaire Club at Trou aux Biches, at the Hotel Club Centre de Pêche and Le Morne Anglers Club, both at Black River. Mauritius is one of the few places on earth where you can catch big fish well within sight of the shore. The big predators feed about a mile from the shoreline, where the bottom falls away to more than 2,000 ft (610 m), and fast-running wahoo, yellowfin tuna, barracuda, bonito, sea bass, blue, black and striped marlin, along with sailfish, dorado and sharks such as blue, hammerhead, tiger, mako, black fin and white fin, provide some of the best big-game fishing in the world. Blue marlin tipping the scales at weights of 1,000 lb (454 kg) or more are not uncommon and scores of these whoppers have been boated in recent years, with the biggest weighing in at 1,430 lb (649 kg).

There is probably no other place in the world where giant marlin can be hooked within 15 minutes of boarding the boat and the all-tackle world record for a 1,100 lb (499 kg) boated Pacific blue marlin taken here in 1966 was not beaten until 1982. Mauritius still hangs on to the world records for mako shark (1,114 lb/505 kg), as well as a 41.5 lb (19 kg) bonito. Local Mauritian records include: blue marlin 1,430 lb (649 kg), black marlin 794 lb (360 kg), dorado 65 lb (30 kg), yellowfin tuna 212 lb (96 kg), and wahoo 125 lb (57 kg).

MAIN FISHING ORGANISATIONS

Beachcomber Fishing Club: Le Morne (tel 450-5050, fax 450-5140).

La Pirogue Big Game Fishing: Flic en Flac (tel 453-8441/683-6579, fax 453-8449/683-6162).

Morne Anglers' Club: Rivière Noire (tel 683-6528, fax 683-5801).

Killer Sportfishing: Trou aux Biches (tel 423-6091/265-6595, fax 265-7449).

Sofitel Imperial Big Game Fishing: Wolmar (tel 453-8700/683-6579, fax 453-8320/683-6162).

Organisation de Pêche du Nord (Corsaire Club), Royal Road, Trou aux Biches (tel 265-5209, fax 265-6267).

Domaine du Pêcheur: Vieux Grand Port (tel 634-5097, fax 634-5261).

Centre de Pêche: Black River (tel 683-6522/682-6503, fax 683-6318).

Professional Big Game Fishing Charter Association: La Preneuse, Black River (tel 683-6579, fax 683-6162).

Black River Sport Fishing: Black River (tel 683-6547).

Surcouf: Trou d'Eau Douce (tel 419-3198, fax 419-3197).

Sportfisher: Coastal Road, Grand Baie (tel 263-8358, fax 263-6309).

Sportfisher on the water's edge in Grand Baie, is a good example of a professional island deep-sea fishing charter company. They fish mainly from the northern coastline, near the outlying islets where there are superb ocean drop-offs, and concentrate on blue and black marlin, sailfish, dorado, yellowfin and skipjack tuna, wahoo and sharks, which include hammerhead, mako, black and white fin, and they've even had a thresher shark on their scales. Boats are hired out on a full-day or half-day basis and the prices are for the boat, not per person. They generally do not recommend more than six anglers on board any one charter boat. Most boats for hire on the island have three fighting chairs in the stern and outriggers to troll five baits at a time. For a full day: 7am (departure from jetty) to 4pm (arrival on jetty) Sportfisher charges US$400, and for a half-day: 7am (departure from jetty) to 1pm (arrival on jetty) or 1.15pm (depart from jetty) to 6.30pm (arrival on jetty) US$340.

The Centre de Pêche also specialises in big-game fishing and has an excellent restaurant, swimming pool, disco, snooker, TV room and bar. After a good day's sport you can relax with a local beer among the mounted heads and pictures of giant marlin and talk about the one that got away.

For deep-sea fishing equipment browse at *Quay Stores*, 3 President John F. Kennedy Street, Port Louis (tel 212-1043); and *Rods & Reels*, La Preneuse (tel 683-6579, fax 683-6162).

SAILING

Most hotels and resorts in Mauritius offer their guests a variety of water and land sports free of charge, such as boats for sailing inside the lagoon, windsurfing, water-skiing, golf and horse-riding. If you want to strike out on your own or you're staying in a budget hotel or self-catering villa without access to these sports the island offers you a good choice of facilities, especially anything to do with aquatic recreation. If you'd rather sail over the waves than swim through them and want to venture beyond the placid water of the lagoon you can charter boats, yachts and catamarans suitable for open-sea sailing or simply join an organised cruise. For a different view of Port Louis join a harbour cruise (tel 211-65600).

Yacht Charter Contacts

Yacht Charters: (Schooner) Coastal Road, Grand Baie (tel 263-8395, fax 263-7814).
Cybele Charters: (Catamaran) Blue Bay (tel 674-3596/631-9630/499-7800, fax 674-3596).
Kaparine Pleasure Yacht: Grand Baie (tel 254-1360).
Croisières Turquoises: (Catamaran) Riche en Eau-St Hubert (tel 633-5835, fax 633-5379).
Croisière Océane: Trou d'Eau Douce (tel/fax 419-2767).
Croisières Australes: (Catamaran) Rue Gustave Colin, Forest Side (tel 674-3695, fax 674-3720) and at Grand Baie (tel 263-6426, fax 263-8440).
Cruising Experience: 10 Nenuphar Complex, Coastal Road, Flic en Flac (tel 453-8888, fax 453-9688).
Ocean Pearl: Grand Baie (fax 263-8055).
Effendi: (sailing yacht) tel 422-9037, fax 263-6102.
Yacht Charters: Grand Baie (tel 263-8395, fax 263-7814).
The Grand Yacht Club: tel 263-8568.
Aquarelle: tel 419-2767/421-0197.

SURFING

Mauritius is definitely not a destination of choice for surfers. The huge encircling reef and protected lagoon means that there's not much prospect of hanging ten in any serious way, although you can catch some good swells at Tamarin, in the south-west. Sea breezes and the water do, however, make board-sailing a less demanding option. Watch out though for people scooting around on pedaloes and in canoes.

OTHER ACTIVITIES

GOLF

Golf is probably the most hectic exercise you'll find during a holiday in Mauritius. Until a few years ago this was regarded by most islanders as a highly exclusive pastime, but that has changed and there are now many enthusiasts. Tournaments are organised throughout the year and attract many willing sponsors. You can sign up as a temporary member of a local club, so long as you bring your own equipment. A few hotels have nine-hole courses while others offer some golfing to their guests.

The 18-hole (par 72) championship course at *Le Paradis*, designed by South African golfing maestro **Gary Player**, is situated on a secluded private peninsula on the south-west coast, the course has been designed to offer some unique golfing challenges to players of varying handicaps. Six miles (9 km) of fine sandy beaches, a mountain backdrop and spectacular landscape give to the course a special attraction. The Mauritian-style clubhouse, as well as the impressive opening par-4 hole, are only 66 ft (20 m) from the beach. This 6,500 yard (5,943 m) championship course is accessible to all Beachcomber guests and only one hour from the other hotels in the group. The golf club has a clubhouse with a store-room for guest's golf equipment; a bar and toilets on the course; group lessons twice a week, free of charge for hotel guests; two full-time pros, and a pro-shop; practice balls, clubs and trolleys can be hired at the clubhouse. Beachcomber also has a nine-hole (par 32) golf course at Trou aux Biches; and a nine-hole (par 27) mashie course at Shandrani Hotel at Blue Bay in the south-east.

Although attached to Le Saint Géran hotel, the course is open for casual visitors at a cost of around 640 rupees (£16) for nine holes. The par-68 golf course at the Gymkhana Club, near Curepipe, is a sight to behold for visitors more used to ample facilities. Tees are shared, fairways operate in two directions at once, or intersect, and it's not unusual to be required to drive directly over the heads of oncoming players. Some club members wisely take the precaution of wearing polo helmets.

Renowned as one of the finest and most inclusive sporting complexes, *Belle Mare Plage* on the east coast offers challenges for both amateur and professional golfers. The centrepiece is the Championship Golf Course, the first of its kind in Mauritius, which was opened in January 1994. Designed by South African champion **Hugh Baiocchi** it features 18 holes, with the expected manicured greens, fairways and winding waterways. The outstanding hole is the par 3, 160-yard (2,890 m) 17th with its spectacular views from the tee across the turquoise waters of Sandy Bay. This is the home of the Johnnie Walker Classic and the Mauritius Open, and the course also hosts the PGA of Mauritius, affiliated to the PGA of Africa. The course record belongs to UK golfer Mike MacLean, with 62 (10 under par) notched up in December 1995.

Tennis

Courts are often part of the complex of facilities available in hotels, irrespective of size, with a choice of hard, synthetic and lawn courts, including flood-lit ones for those who like to exercise at night. Tennis coaches are also available. A few hotels have squash courts, although the temperatures are not really conducive to this form of strenuous exercise.

Horse-Riding

Most hotels and a few clubs offer to lovers of equestrian sports the opportunity to indulge their favourite form of exercise. Some leisure complexes organise riding excursions for youngsters and experienced riders will find riding on open beaches and rural inland lanes and valleys a delight. There are equestrian centres in Floreal (tel 696-4387); Le Morne (tel 683-6775); Palmar (tel 415-1625); Domaine les Pailles (tel 208-1998); and also at a number of beach hotels.

RAMBLES AND SCRAMBLES

Three main mountain ranges with some amazingly shaped peaks dominate the island. Around Port Louis the Moka range stretches for about 12 miles (20 km), beginning at Mount Ory and finishing at Nouvelle Decouverte. In the south, the Grand Port range covers some 15 miles (24 km), starting at Mount Lagrave and stretching to the mouth of the Grand River. The third range, the Black River chain, reaches from Rempart Mountain to the south of Bambous village and stretches down to Le Morne in the south-west. There is also a series of small peaks, the Savanne Mountains, in the extreme south above Souillac. All the rugged peaks have been sculpted over the aeons by volcanic action and subsequent erosion and call to all who love the heights. If they call to you you'll be pleasantly surprised to find that the tops and ridges are yours alone on your outing; Mauritians generally would rather spend their leisure time picnicking at the seaside than rambling and scrambling in the hills. There are no really high climbs, and no really difficult ones, with the possible exception of **Pieter Both**, the peak named from its supposed resemblance to the profile of a Dutch admiral drowned in Tomb Bay in 1615.

Towering over Port Louis from the encircling Moka range is the peak descriptively known as **Le Pouce** ('The Thumb'). It is an easy climb, which can be done from St Georges Street in upper Port Louis or from Moka, near the turn-off to Eureka. **Pieter Both** forms part of the Port Louis/Moka range and at 2,685 ft (818 m) rears its singular profile on the skyline along with **Le Pouce**. It has steep sides and is topped by an enormous boulder, which looks – but isn't – precariously balanced. The climb is possible for the athletic, weather permitting, but you should venture this only if accompanied by someone familiar with its peculiarities. There have been several fatal falls on this climb over the years since Frenchman Claude Penthé planted the *Tricolore* on top of the pear-shaped boulder in 1790. Islanders used to believe that the British would leave Mauritius if the boulder ever fell. The Brits left with independence in 1968, the boulder still stands.

Near Quatre Bornes and Rose Hill on the Central Plateau is **Corps de Garde.** Start from Rose Hill – it's a pleasant walk and an easy climb to the 2,362 ft (720 m) summit. The view from the top is well worth the effort. The striking, crouching shape of **Lion Mountain** is on the south-east coast and its 1,575 ft (480 m) summit offers a good view of Mahébourg and the bay of Vieux Grand Port. The climb is quite easy but can sometimes be dangerous as the steep slopes can get tricky when wet. The mountain of **Le Morne** on the south-west coast close to the magnificent lagoon is imposing but only 797 ft (243 m) and easily climbed. It is recorded that during French rule in the early 19th century escaped slaves hid on its summit. On one tragic occasion they jumped to their deaths from the top on seeing soldiers coming up the slopes – not realising that slavery had been abolished.

On the west coast behind the Casela Bird Park, but best viewed from the Curepipe area, is **Montagne du Rempart** at 1,788 ft (545 m). The climb starts off from the beginning of the road to Magenta, and it's a difficult one. The final stretch to the top can be reached only by a stiff rock climb. Best access for this climb is at Bassin, between La Louis and Pierrefonds. In the foothills are the appropriately named trio of peaks **Les Trois Mamelles** ('The Three Breasts'). **Piton de la Petite Rivière Noire** is the highest peak on the island. It is in the south-west and the route leading to its 2,716 ft (828 m) peak is a beautiful one through Plaine Champagne and the Macchabee Forest in the Black River Gorges National Park. It's an easy climb and along the meandering path some rare endemic birds can sometimes be seen.

You'll find an interesting out-of-print book in the library of the Mauritius Institute in Port Louis which is a useful reference source if you plan to tackle any of these mountains. This is *Climbing and Mountain Walking in Mauritius*, by Alexander Ward. In the bookshops you might be lucky enough to find a copy of Robert VT Marsh's *Mountains of Mauritius*.

It might not be shop-till-you-drop territory but Mauritius has a lot of stores, many of them duty-free, with a wide variety of products. Clothing and knitwear, jewellery, Chinese goods, textiles, leather items, quilts, shells and crafts such as ceramics, basketry, embroidery, wood carvings, and model ships are among the choices you face. Port Louis and Curepipe are the most popular shopping areas, and they are probably the best places to buy souvenirs. Good buys include model ships, knitwear, and sportswear, Indian fabrics, cotton and silk, Chinese and Indian jade, diamonds, basketry, pottery, and spices to bring back memories of the island when you are in your kitchen at home.

OPENING HOURS
Port Louis Monday to Friday 9.30am to 5pm, Saturday 9.30am to noon. Central Market Monday to Saturday 9am to 6pm, Sunday 9am to noon. Shops in Curepipe, Rose Hill, Quatre Bornes, Beau Bassin, Phoenix and Vacoas open Monday to Wednesday 10am to 6pm, Friday and Saturday 10am to 6pm. On Thursday and Sunday they open at 10am and close for the day at noon.

GIFTS AND SOUVENIRS
The most popular gifts and souvenirs are the beautiful hand-made wooden models of famous ships, which are usually of an amazingly high standard. Choose, for instance, from scale replicas of such historical vessels as Captain Cook's *Endeavour*, Nelson's *Victory*, Captain Bligh's *Bounty*, the *Cutty Sark*, and a host of others from the old days of sail. Most manufacturers can provide a packaging and dispatching service and can handle the relevant export and customs paperwork for you. Without doubt, the mecca for model and boat lovers is **Historic Marine**, in Goodlands (tel 283-9304, fax 283-9204) where 150 craftsmen and women build and rig 1,000 models a year. A copy of the *Amerigo Vespucci*, for instance, takes a thousand hours' painstaking work. Models cost from 5,000 to 100,000 rupees (£125-£2,500). There are dozens of other smaller model shipmakers scattered around the island. On Route Royale, Floreal, Curepipe, tour the tiny model workshop of **Thalassa**, tel 697-5929.

Glass
Another good place for unusual gifts is the *Mauritius Glass Gallery*, where glass blowers and other craftsmen produce a wonderful variety of glass and stained-glass products from recycled bottles and other glass. Beautiful glass paper-weights featuring endangered birds as well as little statues of the extinct dodo make ideal gifts. The gallery is near the roundabout which links the highways to Port Louis, the airport and Curepipe, but there's also a gallery shop in Port Louis, in the Craft Market on the Caudan Waterfront.

Music
Take home some Mauritian music to bring back memories of the exotic *sega*. The group *Casinga* has a CD called *Marsan Coco* which is just the thing for long, cold, northern hemisphere nights. Try Philanne Music Centre, in the Happy World Shopping Centre on 37 Sir William Newton Street, Port Louis (tel 211-8091, fax 234-5976).

T-shirts
Exotic T-shirts of the 'been there, done that' variety are on sale just about everywhere, but nowhere will you find such a wide range of export quality T-shirts at reasonable prices as in the markets of Port Louis and Quatre Bornes.

Sugar and Spice
Easy to carry take-home gifts are packets of Mauritian vanilla, sugar and spices; miniatures of island rum, miniature dodo replicas in wood, copper, brass or glass; cotton or silk *pareos* (sarongs); local music cassettes; vacuum packs of smoked marlin; and the boxed fresh-cut anthurium flowers grown on the island for export.

Coral
Don't buy any coral products – you'll be contributing to the destruction of the reef eco-system.

DUTY-FREE SHOPS
Duty-free jewellery shops are worth checking for competitively priced precious stones and locally crafted jewellery, which can also be found in shops selling Chinese ornaments, silks and porcelain.

Mauritius Shopping Paradise: at SSR International Airport (tel 637-3794); and at Air Mauritius Centre, Port Louis (tel 211-6835).

Poncini Duty-Free Boutique: for jewels, diamonds and watches, in Port Louis (tel 212-4723); St Géran Hotel (tel 413-2825); and Sunset Boulevard, Grand Baie (tel 263-5061).

Adamas: duty-free diamonds, Mangalkhan, Floreal (tel 686-5783/4).

Parure: Le Maurica Shopping Centre (tel 263-3030.

Sashena: Floreal (tel 698-1556).

Payment can be made only in foreign currencies and you must show your passport and air ticket. Your purchases will be ready at the airport for collection as you leave. For more folksy souvenirs try the National Handicraft Centre, 3rd Floor, Ken Lee Building, Edith Cavell Street, Port Louis (tel 208-1847, fax 208-9813).

Crime and Safety

POLICE
The national police force includes the paramilitary Special Mobile Force (SMF), Special Support Units (SSU), and the National Coast Guard. Policemen are usually conspicuous by their absence, and considering the amount of contraventions, you don't see many involved in booking traffic offenders, although they are supposed to be on the look-out for everything from unclipped seat belts to drunken drivers. If you have to call the cops telephone 208-7013/20, or the emergency 999 number and ask for the service needed.

Theft
Petty crime is common, especially pickpocketing, and the central market in Port Louis is a prime place for this. Pickpockets are as likely to be small children as adults, one begging for money, while another lifts your wallet. Mauritians are generally laid-back and friendly people, although there are sporadic disturbances. Visitors are unlikely to be the target of these but you should at all times avoid crowds and street demonstrations. Do not leave anything of value in your hotel room to tempt the cleaners.

DRINK, DRUGS AND THE LAW
Booze is a problem in the city areas – they can't get enough. There's a perception among more affluent Mauritians that the poorer members of the population (read Creoles) drink too much. Maybe that's why they are so laid-back and jolly. The Hindu-dominated government's response has been to increase taxes on alcohol, but this doesn't seen to have had the desired affect, although we never saw any of the rolling drunks of Europe, Australia, and the USA in our travels.

Drugs
The anti-drug enforcement agencies do, however, seem to take their jobs seriously. While we were visiting the Black Gorges National Park, police helicopters were quartering the area, looking for the patches of *ganja* (marijuana) being grown there by enterprising merchants. Mauritius is an illicit producer of cannabis both for local consumption and for the international drug trade. Hard drugs are not, yet, a major problem. Sentences for illegally importing drugs into

Mauritius can get offenders from 20 years to life imprisonment. As they don't import it, local users seem to ignore these prohibitions, although they are quick to tell you they don't actually inhale. Users can expect a fine or 3-6 months in jail for exhibitionist smoking.

Help and Information *i*	**TOURIST INFORMATION CENTRES** *Mauritius Tourism Promotion Authority (MTPA):* 11th Floor, Air Mauritius Centre, President John F. Kennedy Street, Port Louis (tel 208-6397 or 210-1545, fax 212-5142, e-mail: mpta@intnet.mu).

TOURIST OFFICES AND REPRESENTATIVES ABROAD

Britain: MTPA, 32-33 Elvaston Place, London SW7 5NW (tel 020-7584 3666, fax 020-7225 1135, e-mail: mtpa@binternet.com Website www.mauritius.net). Open 9am to 5pm Monday to Friday.

France: Office du Tourisme de l'Île Maurice, 24 rue Eugène Flachat, F-75017 Paris (tel 1-44 01 46 11, fax 1-47 63 49 56, e-mail: mrouet@edelman.com).

Germany: Mauritius Informationsbüro, Postfach 101846, Frankfurt am Main D-60018 (tel 69-980354, fax 69-980652, e-mail: wbcom@t-online.de).

India: Mauritius Tourism Information Bureau, Trikaya Grey, 28 Rampart Row, Opposite Max Mueller Bhavan, Fort Bombay 400023 (tel 22-285 6746, fax 22-287 2270).

Italy: Ufficio del Turismo dell Isole Mauritius, Foro Buonaparte, 46, I-20121 Milan (tel 02-865984, fax 02-864605).

Japan: Mauritius Tourism Information Services, Ginza Stork Building 5F, 1-22-1 Ginza, Chuo-Ku Tokyo 104 (tel 3-5250 0175, fax 3-5250 0176).

South Africa: Mauritius Tourist Information Service, 41 Brand Road, Glenwood, Durban, PO Box 118, Durban 4000 (tel 31-562 1320, fax 31-562 1383, e-mail: mtis@iafrica.com).

Switzerland: Mauritius Tourism Information Service, Kirchenweg 5, CH-8032 Zurich (tel 1-383 8788, fax 1-383 5124).

USA: Mauritius Tourist Information Service, Port Executive Building, 8 Haven Avenue, Port Washington, New York 11050 (tel 212-944 3763/4, fax 212-944 8453).

EMBASSIES AND CONSULATES

British High Commission: Les Cascades Building, Edith Cavell Street, Port Louis (tel 211-1361, fax 211-1369, e-mail: bhc@intnet.mu).

Embassy of the United States of America: Fourth Floor, Rogers House, President John F. Kennedy Street, Port Louis (tel 208-2347, fax 208-9534, e-mail: usembass@intnet.mu Website htp://usis.intnet.mu/embassy.htm). US citizens visiting Mauritius are advised to register with the embassy's consular section where they can get information on travel and security.

Australia: (tel 208-1700).
Austria: (tel 208-6801).
Belgium: (tel 208-1241).
Canada: (tel 208-0821).
France: (tel 208-7062).
Germany: (tel 240-7425).
India: (tel 208-3775).
Italy: (tel 208-7700).
Japan: (tel 208-2811).
Madagascar: (tel 686-5015).
Netherlands: (tel 208-2811).
New Zealand: (tel 208-8042).
Seychelles: (tel 208-1241).
Spain: (tel 208-2811).
Switzerland: (tel 208-8763).

GAY TRAVELLERS

Homosexuality has been decriminalised in Mauritius, but a largely religious and conservative population still frowns on overt displays of same-gender relationships. There are no especially gay-friendly restaurants, clubs or other gathering places, although the Grand Baie area would seem to be the best place to look for them.

Nudists. Nudism is illegal in Mauritius, although the influence of sun-worshipping tourists over the years has led the authorities to ignore topless sunbathing on resort beaches. There are, however, no legal beaches for tanning or frolics in the altogether.

DISABLED TRAVELLERS

Before travelling to Mauritius disabled UK and US vacationers are advised to make enquiries about facilities on the island at the Royal Association for Disability & Rehabilitation, 25 Mortimer Street, London W1N 8AB (tel 020-7242 6061), or the Society for the Advancement of Travel for the Handicapped, 26 Court Street, Brooklyn, New York NY 11242 (tel 212-858 5483).

Grand Gaube Hotel, on the north-east coast, is one of the few in Mauritius which has made an obvious effort to be wheelchair-friendly. All public areas, bedrooms, and even the beach, can be reached by ramps and close to the central hotel buildings are three ground-floor disabled-friendly rooms.

USEFUL INFORMATION

Time Zone

Mauritius time is four hours ahead of GMT in winter and three hours in summer. It is three hours ahead of mid-European time, nine hours ahead of US Eastern Standard Time, and two hours ahead of South African time.

Electrical Appliances

The power supply throughout the island is 220 volts AC, 50 cycles Hertz. Three-pin British type and two-pin French and American type plugs are usual. Take a travel plug and continental adaptor to be on the safe side, especially if you take electrical appliances with you.

Weights and Measures. The metric system is in force, although you'll find street vendors and market traders still talk in old Imperial pounds and ounces.

USEFUL ADDRESSES AND TELEPHONE NUMBERS

Emergency Calls:

Dial 999 for Police, and for Ambulance services (also 114).
Fire Service dial 995.
Police headquarters are at Line Barracks, Lord Kitchener Road, Port Louis (tel 208-7013/20).
Hospitals:
        Dr Jeetoo Hospital: Port Louis (tel 212-3201).
        SSR National Hospital: Pamplemousses (tel 243-3661).
        Hospital Candos: Quatre Bornes (tel 425-3031).
Tourism Information: tel 208-6397, fax 212-5142.
Mauritius Wildlife Foundation (MWF): 4th Floor, Ken Lee Building, Edith Cavell

Street, Port Louis (tel 211-1749, fax 211-1789).
Central Post Office, Place du Quai, Port Louis (tel 208-2851, fax 212-9640).
Overseas Telecommunications Services (OTS), Cassis (24-hour service) (tel 208-0221); Port Louis (tel 208-1036). Enquiries and help with overseas phone, fax or telex.
National Transport Authority, tel 212-1448, fax 212-9399/86.
Mauritius Shipping Company, Nova Building, 1 Military Road, Port Louis (tel 241-2550, fax 242-5245).
Customs & Excise Department, IKS Building, Farquhar Street, Port Louis (tel 240-9702, fax 240-0434).
Passport and Immigration Office, Sterling House, 11-12 Lislet Geoffrey Street, Port Louis (tel 210-9312/17, fax 210-9322).
Weather forecast, tel 302-6071.
Camping Gaz, Port Louis (tel 208-2011).
Mauritius Breweries, Phoenix (tel 601-2000).

Public Holidays

Until the Marxist MMM party enjoyed a brief spell of power islanders enthusiastically celebrated 26 public holidays a year, probably more than any other country in the world. Intent on boosting worker productivity the party cut the number down to 13 in 1982, and there it remains.

Fixed Dates

New Year's Day	1-2 January
Independence Day (Republic Day)	12 March
Labour Day	1 May
Assumption	15 August
All Saints' Day	1 November
Christmas Day	25 December

The remaining seven public holidays on the Mauritian calendar are religious festivals. Hindu and Muslim festivals are timed according to sightings of various phases of the moon, and Chinese festivals according to local astronomical observations (see *Festivals* p.51). This makes it difficult to forecast the exact dates of their occurrence each year.

REGIONS OF MAURITIUS

TOURIST ATTRACTIONS

Pamplemousses Garden, created by Pierre Poivre in the 18th century, and 7 miles (11km) north-east of Port Louis ranks with the finest in the world. Its lakes and ponds are a riot of Amazon and Indian water lilies and among the myriad tropical plants and trees the talipot palm is a curiosity, blooming only once before dying.

Grand Bassin, in the highlands of Savanne at 1,800ft (549 m), is a secluded lake holy to hundreds of thousands of Mauritian Hindus. Every year they go on pilgrimage to wash themselves in its waters and celebrate the festival of Maha Shivarati in February/March.

Chamarel Coloured Earth, in the Savanne area, is a natural curiosity of volcanic origin, with exposed layers of coloured volcanic ash. Striations of its seven different colours, including ochre, violet and red, are best seen from a viewing tower late in the afternoon.

Black River Gorges National Park encloses 16,245 acres (6,574 ha) and is in the south-west at the heart of the Plaine Champagne. The area contains the only indigenous forest areas of the island and is home to many endangered plants and birds, including the Mauritius kestrel and the pink pigeon.

La Vanille Crocodile Park lies in the unspoilt south near Souillac. The crocodile farm has a zoological garden housing animals and reptiles of the Mascarene islands. There's an open-sided tree-top restaurant, as well as a boutique selling various crocodile products and Mauritian memorabilia.

The picturesque **Rochester Falls** in the south of the island are reached by following the signposts through the sugarcane fields near Souillac. There's a tempting swimming pool below the falls.

Named after Governor Mahé de Labourdonnais, attractive **Mahébourg** has a rich historical past, located as it is around the Grand Port bay where the Dutch (the first settlers) disembarked. Mahébourg was the scene of a famous naval battle in which, for the first and only time, a Napoleonic fleet defeated the British.

Casela Bird Park is situated in the west of the island, where more than 2,500 birds of 180 different species flutter in a hundred aviaries in 62 acres (25 ha) of beautiful tropical gardens. You can see the Mauritian pink pigeon here, one of the rarest birds in the world.

Domaine de Ylang-Ylang lies in a magnificent sub-tropical valley at the foot of Anse Jonchée Mountain, at Vieux Grand Port. From its plantation come the fragrant yellow ylang-ylang flowers which are distilled on the estate to produce the oils used in Europe as a base for expensive perfumes. You can watch this process, and enjoy short walks on trails up the mountain.

Le Saint Aubin and **Bois Chéri**. The colonial house at Saint Aubin, dating from 1819, is magnificent. You can see an anthurium and vanilla garden and lunch in exquisite surroundings before visiting the nearby Bois Chéri tea plantations. A guided tour of the factory traces the leaf from growth to cuppa.

The **Caudan Waterfront** in Port Louis, with its shops and food centres – including top-class restaurants as well as inexpensive snack bars – makes for an interesting half-day wander. Caudan lies on a tongue of land protruding into the harbour basin and once housed an assortment of disused storage and general purpose warehouses.

Creole Houses. There are a number of public and private old colonial houses and chateaux whose preservation recalls a more gracious, if often turbulent, age. You can see **Château de Mon Plasir** built in 1735 by the governor of the island, Mahé de Labourdonnais, and situated inside the Pamplemousses Garden; **Château du Réduit**, built in 1778, residence of the President, is in the Rose-Hill Moka area. It is open to the public only once a year; and **Eureka**, an old colonial house which is now a museum. It's off the motorway from Port Louis to Curepipe, through Montagne Ory.

PORT LOUIS AND THE NORTH COAST

PORT LOUIS

Historic Port Louis, the capital of Mauritius, was founded by French governor Mahé de Labourdonnais in 1736. It lies in a broad amphitheatre of the Moka mountain range and when the sun rises over the volcanic peaks the new high-rise buildings of the city take on an attractive golden hue. Despite being the business centre of the country, Port Louis has preserved many of its green open spaces, its old colonial buildings, and picturesque if threadbare neighbourhoods. The city has a population of some 160,000 – 15 per cent of the island's population – and covers only 17 sq miles (45 sq km), but as the centre of business activities it draws in more than 100,000 extra people every morning. Towards the outskirts of the city, at the foot of the Moka chain, is the **Champ de Mars**, now a race-track and once a military parade ground during the French administration. In the 19th century it provided a popular weekend promenade venue for locals. High above Port Louis stands a sturdy old fortress known as La Citadelle, or **Fort Adelaide,** the name of the wife of William IV, reigning English monarch when it was built by the British in 1834. Its grey stone walls rise in true British fashion two barracks-like storeys and from the knoll it stands on at an altitude of 272 ft (83 m) you get a bird's-eye view of the city and its port. Fort Adelaide was built after slavery was abolished and resistance from French sugar plantation owners was feared. Today concerts, exhibitions and cultural events are held at the fort and it houses a souvenir gift shop selling handicrafts from the Mascarene islands, as well as the Comoros and Seychelles. In the heart of the city is the **Company Gardens,** the original site of the headquarters of the French East India Company. Towering banyan trees festooned with creepers and lichen dominate the shady square, which is full of statues, busts and memorials to the men and women who helped to shape the character and history of the island. The city's main market was in these gardens before moving to its present site between Queen and Farquhar streets, where the gates are fine examples of Victorian wrought ironwork. The **central market** is a must-see for any visitor and souvenirs can be bought here at bargain prices. Stallholders compete with pavement vendors in displays of colourful wares and consumables. The fruit and veg stalls alone are a photographer's delight. The **Natural History Museum** alongside the Company Gardens, has a dowdy collection of casts and shells of giant turtles and tortoises, sea creatures, land animals and fish, as well as displays of mounted birds, butterflies and insects in glass cabinets. Its prize attraction is a sad-looking reconstruction of a dodo and the replica of an egg and fossilised femur of another extinct bird *Aepvornis maximus,* whose egg was three to four times the size of a modern ostrich egg. The museum is in need of a general sprucing up and its staff need coaching in public relations, but the museum is nonetheless worth a visit.

Throughout the city are elegant homes of the colonial era. Some, even though built of wood, are survivors of countless cyclones. The city's Anglican **Cathedral**

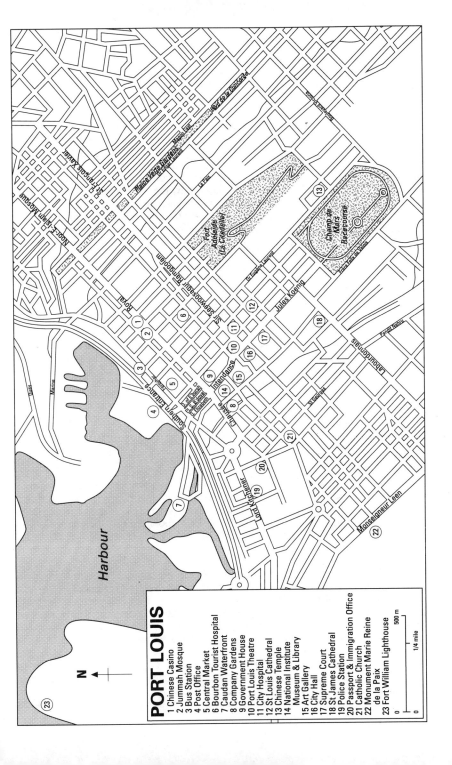

PORT LOUIS

1 Chinese Casino
2 Jummah Mosque
3 Bus Station
4 Post Office
5 Central Market
6 Bourbon Tourist Hospital
7 Caudan Waterfront
8 Company Gardens
9 Government House
10 Port Louis Theatre
11 City Hospital
12 St Louis Cathedral
13 Chinese Temple
14 National Institute
   Museum & Library
15 Art Gallery
16 City Hall
17 Supreme Court
18 St James Cathedral
19 Police Station
20 Passport & Immigration Office
21 Catholic Church
22 Monument Marie Reine
   de la Paix
23 Fort William Lighthouse

0   1/4 mile

0   500 m

N

Harbour

of Saint James was converted from a building once used as a gun-powder magazine. With walls 10 ft (3 m) thick and window ledges wide enough to sleep on, it was often used as a cyclone shelter in the past. At the end of the palm-lined Place d'Armes is **Government House (1738),** still fronted by a statue of Queen Victoria. It is not open to the public. **Chinatown** is near the island's principal place of worship for Muslims, the **Jummah Mosque,** and is a great place for tasty inexpensive meals or snacks. For gamblers there's a Chinese-style casino called L'Amicale in the Chinese quarter, and for the superstitious there are Chinese astrology parlours ready to tell you what's going to win at the next race meeting. A notable city landmark is the *Old Post Office,* which was completed in 1868. The **Philately Museum** at the Post Office is definitely worth a visit if you are interested in stamps. The **Caudan Waterfront** became a new landmark in Port Louis in 1996, offering sophisticated shopping and up-market entertainment. An interesting mix of 50 retail outlets and a craft market has made Caudan one of the most popular shopping and leisure areas for locals, as well as for tourists. A three-screen cinema entertainment complex, five restaurants and a wide range of fast-food outlets offering typical Mauritian, Eastern and Western cuisine share the waterfront with a themed casino. It's right next to the central business district of Port Louis, and there's parking for 600 vehicles – as well as a marina to moor your boat.

Port Louis grew to be the economic and administrative capital of Mauritius after it superseded early capital Mahébourg in the 18th century because it had a better harbour. Until the Suez Canal was built, Port Louis was the usual port of call for ships on their way to India, and it was largely because of this, that Mauritius earned itself the title 'Star and Key of the Indian Ocean.' The skyline of the city has changed dramatically in the years since independence, with new high-rise towers competing with buildings from more gracious colonial times. Port Louis is unrecognisably quiet after business hours and at weekends, except when the Champs-de-Mars track hosts the popular horse races.

Guided Tour. You can take a three-hour guided tour of Port Louis, conducted by Citirama. The itinerary includes the Central Post Office and Museum; the 'Coolie Ghat;' Robert Edward Hart Garden; St Sacrement Church; Cassis; Marie Reine de la Paix Memorial; Thien Thane Pagoda; St. James Cathedral; the Company Gardens; Natural History Museum and Mauritius Institute; Line Barracks; Government House; Port Louis Theatre; City Hall; Supreme Court; St Louis Cathedral; Central Market; Jummah Mosque; Chinatown; Sir Seewoosagur Ramgoolam Memorial Centre; St Francois Xavier Church; Nicolay Road Tamil Temple; Père Laval Church; Ste Croix; and La Citadelle (Fort Adelaide). Contact Citirama, Yiptong House, Royal Road, Cassis (tel 212-2482, fax 212-1222).

THE NORTH COAST

There is no real north coast as the island of Mauritius comes to a point at Pointe l' Hortal, near Cap Malheureux, and you are then left heading for either north-west or north-east coastal areas. The north-west coast runs from Pereybère in the north to Port Louis in the south, a stretch noted for its miles of wonderful sandy beaches. This is said to be the warmest part of the coast, because it is the area most protected from trade wind snorters, especially in winter. **Cap Malheureux** is a small fishing village on the northernmost tip of the island, with a magnificent view of the offshore islands and **Coin de Mire,** a distinctively shaped rocky islet 2 miles (4 km) offshore. This is of some historical importance as it was from here in September 1810 that the British embarked to invade and wrench the island from the occupying French. It is also a popular subject for photographers and local postcards.

Whatever name it has been known by – and there have been many – the botanical garden at **Pamplemousses,** 7 miles (11 km) north-east of Port Louis, is one of the glories of Mauritius and has been aptly, if somewhat fulsomely, described as one of the marvels of the world. Back in 1916 W Edward Hart rhapsodised: *Its groves of century-old trees, its clumps of rare, precious and interesting plants...its hundreds of raffias, palm trees of all sorts mingling the gleaming blades of their metallic foliage with the sombre boughs of forest species; its lake, strewn with small islands rimmed by lush belts of aquatic plants, with their rustic pavilions fringed with bamboo, wallflowers or latanier trees – enchanting settings reflecting the transparent mirror of the limpid waters into infinity.* Well, yes, it is all that. More prosaically the garden boasts no fewer than 600 different species of plants and trees, including 80 distinct types of palm. Since the garden was established in 1735 by famous French Governor Mahé de Labourdonnais next to his residence, the original Mon Plaisir, as a vegetable plot to supply the needs of his household and the growing capital, with the surplus going to passing ships, it has successively been known as Jardin de Mon Plaisir, Jardin de Mont Plaisir, Jardin des Plantes, Le Jardin National de l'Isle de France, Jardin Royal, Jardin Botanique des Pamplemousses, The Royal Botanical Gardens, Pamplemousses, and since 17 September 1988 it has officially been the Sir Seewoosagur Ramgoolam Botanic Garden – although Pamplemousses Garden is enough for locals and taxi drivers.

It was not until the French appointed Pierre Poivre *Intendant* (administrative officer, or quartermaster) of the island in 1767 that its fame took root. In that year Poivre took control of the veggie plot and started to turn it into a botanical showpiece. For the next five years he tirelessly worked to develop it into what is still one of the wonders of Mauritius. In 1770 he took the opportunity to buy the estate for himself so that he could be close to his passion. In addition to establishing a nursery for the acclimatisation of his precious nutmeg and clove trees from the Moluccas, he also collected numerous trees and plants from other parts of the world, together with as many indigenous plant species as he could lay his hands on. Thanks to Poivre and his successor, Nicolas Céré, Pamplemousses became known to leading naturalists and eventually acquired worldwide fame. When the malaria epidemic struck Mauritius in 1866, much of the gardens was used as a nursery to grow thousands of the eucalyptus trees introduced in an early attempt to control the spread of the infection by drying out the marshes in the country, the prime breeding places for malarial mosquitoes.

There are two ways to enjoy Pamplemousses, one is a whirlwind quick visit taking less than an hour, and another one taking at least two hours or longer, or you can while away at least a morning, or an afternoon. To get the most out of your walk through the gardens you should have a guide – not necessarily one of the many official and unofficial touting for business at the gates, but a handy booklet such as the concise guide *Sir Seewoosagur Ramgoolam Botanic Garden* written in 1976 by then Conservator of Forests AW Owadally, B.Sc (Hons). This costs the equivalent of £3 at a bookstore, or you can get one from the office at the gate. If you do opt for a human guide you'll fork out 50 rupees (£1.25) per person for one to four people, or 40 rupees (£1) per visitor for five to 10 people.

The garden covers 62 acres (25 ha) of landscaped gardens, with pools, streams, palm avenue and some truly amazing species of tropical plants. You should not miss the prize jewels among the many attractions, especially the Talipot and bottle palms and the water lily and lotus ponds. The **Talipot** palm blooms only once in its 40-60 years' lifetime. After a floral display of its more than 50-million tiny blossoms the palm tree dies. Islanders believe that whoever sees this palm in flower will have lots of luck, so cross your fingers. The aptly named **bottle palms** come from Round Island, off the north coast, where only six are still growing. When young the bulging palm trunk looks, at least to wine lovers, like a full-bodied and narrow-necked chianti bottle. Another Round Island fugitive at Pamplemousses is the endangered hurricane palm. Altogether there are some 80 species of palms in the garden, including the royal raffia, sugar, toddy, thief, cabbage, fish-tail, fan, oil, areca, and lady palms, as well as the famed coco-de-mer. Trees more than match the palms in their variety, with such evocative names as marmalade box, sausage, rubber, lucky bean, nutmeg, African tulip, camphor, litchi, mango, fish poison, and chewing gum tree.

The **water-lily pond** is a natural magnet for visitors, with its remarkable Amazonian lilies and their gigantic floating leaves like huge green circular tea trays. These can reach 5 ft (1.5 m) in diameter and are said to be sturdy enough to bear the weight of a child. The flowers open on two successive days late in the afternoon and remain open until the middle of the following morning. On the evening of the first day the fragrant flowers are creamy-white and on the second day they turn pink. Further along the path is the **lotus pond,** in season, full of lovely pink and white flowers, of which the *Nelumbo* is the lotus sacred to the Hindus. To see these in full bloom the **best time** to visit the garden is between December and April. The lake of **Grand Bassin** is surrounded by shady spots which are ideal for a rest on a hot day's tour. This islet-dotted stretch of water is full of tilapia, or bream, long-whiskered *gourami*, eels and swarms of small fish known simply as 'millions.' The lake is also home to Madagascan moorhens and herons, as well as a variety of frogs and harmless reptiles. There's also a fernery (ferns, orchids, begonias and anthuriums), a tiny stag park, a couple of fish ponds, and some pens housing tortoises large and small. Their ancestors, and maybe a couple of the larger present inhabitants, were brought from Aldabra in 1875 at the prompting of Britain's Royal Society of Arts and Sciences, which was worried that the remote atoll tortoises were on their way to join the dodo. Near the tortoise pens is an early **sugar mill** and the imposing residence called the **Chateau de Mon Plaisir,** which is a proclaimed Ancient Monument, although it was built by the British towards the middle of the 19th century. It is used for occasional official receptions and is not open to visitors.

Scattered around the garden are monuments, statues and other interesting historical relics. The first you'll see on entering Pamplemousses through the elaborate wrought iron gates – they won first prize at the Crystal Palace International Exhibition in England in 1862 – is the **Liénard Obelisk.** This graceful white marble column, incised with the names of notables who contributed to the agricultural and botanical development of the island, is a useful landmark for visitors without a guide. There are busts of the garden's creator **Pierre Poivre** and of naturalist and novelist **Bernardin de Saint Pierre,** and a monument commemorating the planting of trees by the Duchess of Cornwall and York, later Queen Mary, in 1901, and by the Duchess of York, afterwards Queen Elizabeth, the Queen Mother, in 1927. More difficult to find is the **Concession Stone.** It's at one of the corners of the concession originally granted to settler P Barmond by the French government in 1729. The stone bears an impression of the royal emblem of France, the fleur-de-lis.

Outside of Port Louis, the main focus of the northern region of Mauritius is the largely Hindu city of **Grand Baie,** which is noted for its many temples. Excellent Indian cuisine and some first-rate beaches add to its tourist allure. Grand Baie Bay beach and the Royal Palm Hotel beach are both prime stretches of sand, with a wide range of facilities. Grand Baie owes its popularity to its clean turquoise waters and to its liveliness by day or by night. It offers safe swimming, sailing, windsurfing, and water-skiing, as well as a variety of fashion and craft shops, hotels, and nightclubs. It is the departure point for helicopter flights, and for deep-sea angling and boat excursions. This is the Saint-Tropez of the island with its Indian, Chinese, Creole and French restaurants, elegant shops and kiosks, and pubs and bars that are open all day and don't close until late at night. At **Pointe aux Canonniers** is Club Med, one of the best known and most popular resorts on the island with younger generation holidaymakers. Day visitors are allowed into the resort. A prime dive site in the area is the deep chasm at Whale Rock. Glass-bottom boat excursions, yachting and sailing are all excellent from here, and you can also take an undersea walk inside the reef and hand-feed the fish. **Mont Choisy,** south of Grand Baie on the north-west coastline, has a great beach, but you'll probably have to share it with hordes of locals and other tourists, although if locals enjoy spending weekends in a place it must be worth a visit. At the approach to the beach is a monument commemorating the first flight by a Mauritian aviator in November 1933 between Réunion and Mauritius. This historic flight was completed by Mauritian pilot Jean Hily, who lost his life on a second attempt to fly between the islands in October 1934. **Trou aux Biches** is a premier vacation area. The beach is spectacular and the Trou aux Biches Hotel has an excellent watersports centre, as well as a nine-hole golf course and a casino. Facing the lagoon between Trou aux Biches and Pointe aux Piments further south is the **Aquarium,** where 220,000 gallons (1m litres) of seawater pour every day through the 36 glass tanks showcasing 200 species of fish, invertebrates, live coral and sponges, all from the waters around the island (tel 261-6187).

ISLANDS

If you want to see what Mauritius looks like from the sea you have a wide choice of excursions by boat along the coast and among the islets scattered offshore to the north and you can book a cruise from Trou aux Biches, Grand Baie, and Pereybère. Few places in the world can boast as many rare and endangered plants, reptiles and birds for their size as these islands and islets. Lying 12 miles (20 km) north among the surrounding islets of **Flat Island, Ilôt Gabriel** and **Gunners Quoin** is **Round Island.** Nearby is **Snake Island,** where are no snakes, although they exist on Round Island. Contrarily, Snake Island is the one with the rounded shape. Round Island is a 380-acre (154 ha) nature reserve, with strictly controlled access. The absence of beaches makes landing by boat difficult but well worth the effort. The summit of the island rises 984 ft (300 m) above the sea. Only 150 years ago Round Island was clothed in dense vegetation and covered by a large variety of trees. Rabbits and hares were introduced by the British to supply the mainland population with meat, a decision which proved to be a recipe for ecological disaster. Today, the trees have almost completely disappeared from the whole northern part of the island and the soil has been severely affected by erosion. The Ministry of Agriculture, in collaboration with the Mauritius Wildlife Foundation, has set up a rehabilitation programme and regular expeditions are organised to the island to make an inventory of rare plants and establish new trees to contain erosion and rid the island of alien life. Rabbits and goats were successfully eradicated by 1986. Round Island's northern side is dry and arid, while the southern slopes are covered with vegetation. The endangered Talipot palm and the bottle palm still cling to life here, but only just. There are two species of harmless snakes on the island, the Burrowing Boa and the Keel Scale Boa. The first was last seen in 1975 and might have become extinct. The latter is faring better and an estimated 300 still live on the island, along with six species of lizards, including Gunther's gecko, which is unique to the island, and the Telfair skink. Hundreds of thousands of sea-birds congregate on Round Island, among them the white-tailed tropic bird and a petrel found only here and on the island of Trinidad in the Caribbean.

ACCOMMODATION

Port Louis
The capital city is for visiting and not for staying, unless you are on a business trip. The *Labourdonnais Waterfront Hotel* (tel 202-4000, fax 202-4040, e-mail: lwh@intnet.mu) is the business person's hotel. It is situated on the Caudan Waterfront within walking distance of the city's central business district. All rooms and suites are air-conditioned, with harbour and marine views, TV and video, telephone, safe, and mini-bar. There is an executive health centre with swimming pool, steam room and massage area. Informal restaurant *L'Escale* serves international cuisine, the gourmet *La Rose des Vents* is an elegant restaurant offering seafood specialities. A casino, theatre, cinema and other restaurants are nearby on the waterfront. There's a complimentary boat shuttle to the beach four times a week and a sundowner harbour cruise. Watersports available include scuba-diving, windsurfing, and water-skiing. The Labourdonnais Sport Fishing Club will take you fishing for a fee and yacht and boat charters for deep-sea fishing are also available.

The North Coast
There's a mix of luxury and budget hotels mainly in the lively Grand Baie area on the north-west coast, and in the north-east between Cap Malheureux and Grand Gaube.

Le Mauricia (tel 209-1100, fax 263-7888, e-mail: mauhot@intnet.mu) is in the heart of Grand Baie, 16 miles (25km) from Port Louis and 47 miles (75km) from the airport. All rooms air-conditioned, sea-facing with their own balcony, en-suite bathrooms, TV, mini-bar and room safe. It has two restaurants, the *Grand Bay* serves breakfast and buffet meals, while *Le Palmier* dishing up grills, salads, pizzas, and Mauritian cuisine, for lunch and dinner.

Le Canonnier (tel 209-7000, fax 263-7864, e-mail: hotcan@intnet.mu) is at Pointe aux Canonniers, 3 miles (5km) from Grand Baie, 16 miles (25km) from Port Louis, and 43 miles (70km) from the airport. All rooms are air-conditioned, with shower and toilet, TV, mini-bar. Disco and resident band, nightly theme shows. *Le Frangipanier* is the main restaurant for breakfast and dinner. *Le Navigator* is on the beach and serves a la carte lunch and dinners. There are two bars to choose from.

Sharing the peninsula is the *Club Med* village (tel 209-1000, fax 263-8617), one of this chain's 120 resorts in nearly 40 countries. The village has 281 air-conditioned rooms, equipped with en-suite shower room/wc, mini-fridge and personal safe. There are two restaurants serving a variety of buffets, and three bars. Other facilities include a boutique, conference room, washing machines, and car hire. Also available are leisure island excursions, deep-sea angling and trips (two-days) to Réunion. All aquasports are on offer, with tuition where necessary.

Beachcombers's up-market *Trou aux Biches* (tel 204-6565, fax 265-6611, e-mail: tabhotel@intnet.mu) is at Triolet, 12 miles (20 km) from Port Louis, and 43 miles (70 km) from the airport. All air-conditioned rooms in the chalets face the sea, and one of the most beautiful beaches on the island. *La Caravelle* restaurant serves breakfast and buffet dinner, while the *L'Oasis* is a romantic restaurant adjacent to the swimming pool serving breakfast, lunch and a la carte dinners. All the usual sports are included free, except for the catamaran/trimaran cruises, scuba-diving and lessons, deep-sea fishing, nine-hole golf, parasailing and undersea walks.

Beachcomber flagship *Royal Palm Hotel* (tel 209-8300, fax 263-8455, e-mail: rpalm@intnet.mu) at Grand Baie is 14 miles (22 km) from Port Louis, and 47 miles (75 km) from the airport. It is the last word in luxury, with 57 rooms, 22 suites, a penthouse, three Presidential suites and a Royal suite. *La Goelette* serves gourmet dishes in a terrace restaurant overlooking the sea. *Le Surcouf* serves speciality dishes in a candlelit, romantic atmosphere, and *Captain's Table* is a small exclusive restaurant suitable for private dinner parties.

The exclusive, elegant *La Maison* is 5 miles (8 km) north of the Royal Palm at Cape Malheureux. Its seven luxury suites must be booked in their entirety through the Royal Palm Hotel (tel 209-8300).

Casuarina Hotel (tel 265-6552, fax 265-6111, e-mail: casuarina@intnet.mu), at Trou aux Biches, is within five minutes of Grand Baie, 11 miles (18 km) from Port Louis, and 32 miles (52 km) from the airport. Comfortable air-conditioned accommodation in whitewashed stone walls under thatch with private balconies, TV, mini-bar, bathroom. Swimming pool, bar, restaurant. Public beach nearby.

Le Grand Gaube Hotel and Resort (tel 283-9350, fax 283-9420, e-mail: reservationgg@illovo.intnet.mu) is a 15-minute drive from Grand Baie. Air-conditioned rooms, all with terrace/balcony, private bathroom with shower, TV, mini-bar and safe. *La Caze* restaurant overlooks the pool and serves buffet breakfast, a la carte or theme dinners. *Le Rocher* is a seafood restaurant. Light meals at the poolside *Sundeck Pool Bar*, or try a lunchtime barbecue.

Le Maritime Hotel (tel 261-5600, fax 261-5670), overlooking Turtle Bay and its national marine park on the north-west coast, is set in the private 18th century estate Balaclava. The bay provides good conditions for a variety of watersports. The hotel has its own yacht for sunset cruises and excursions to Port Louis, Grand Baie, and Coin de Mire island. There is also a nine-hole golf course, gym and three tennis courts. All rooms are sea-facing, air-conditioned, with terrace/balcony, private bathroom, TV, safe and mini-bar. *Belle Vue*, the main terrace restaurant, offers breakfast and dinner, *Mon Desir* is a gourmet a la carte restaurant, *La Maree* a beach restaurant for seafood and grill dinners, and the *Quarter Deck* offers happy-hour relaxation.

Merville Beach Hotel (tel 263-8621, fax 263-8146), within walking distance of Grand Baie, has sea-facing rooms with balconies, or luxury thatched cottages, air-conditioned, en suite bathroom, TV, mini-bar, safe. The hotel is home to the Mauritius Yacht Club. Watersports are available and fully inclusive in the rate. During dinner guests are entertained by folk singers. Brazilian carnival evenings, *sega* and Mexican cabaret and Chinese floor shows are also staged.

Le Beach Club (tel 423-9698, fax 208-1035) is 1.2 miles (2km) from the centre of Grand Baie. Bus stops, taxi stand, restaurants and shops are all within a short walk. Studios with double room, shower and toilet, kitchenette, and living room.

L'Archipel (tel 283-9518, fax 283-7910, e-mail: archipel@maurinet.com), on north-east coast, is 1.9 miles (3 km) from the fishing village of Grand Gaube. It has eight bungalows and four studios, restaurants, swimming pool, pedaloes, and canoes. You can swim in the ocean at high tide and at low tide you can cross to a nearby island and swim there.

EATING OUT

Le Domaine les Pailles (tel 212-4225, fax 212-4226, e-mail: domaine@intnet.mu), a short drive from Port Louis, claims it has four of the best restaurants in Mauritius to sample Indian, Creole, Chinese, and Italian dishes. You can also visit an 18th century sugar mill and rum distillery on its 3,700 acre (1,500 ha) estate.

Le Carri Poule (tel 212-1295/4883), interesting authentic Indian/Creole food, buffet served Wednesdays to Fridays.

La Bonne Marmite (tel 212-2403), mainly Creole.

Café du Vieux Conseil (tel 211-0393), local and English cuisine.

La Flore Mauricienne (tel 212-2200), local and English cuisine.
Le Chinois (tel 242-8655), Chinese.
Le Boulevard (tel 208-8325), local, Chinese and English cuisine, good salads for
   vegetarians.
Stax Steak Ranch tel 211-1977.
L'Escale Restaurant (tel 202-4000), is an all-day restaurant in the Labourdonnais
   Waterfront Hotel overlooking Place du Caudan and the harbour, with a terrace
   from which you can watch the capital go by.

Grand Baie

Le Grillon (tel 263-8540), Creole and European seafood restaurant and snack bar.
Le Jonque (tel 263-8729), mainly Chinese food, restaurant near the beach.
Palais de Chine (tel 263-7120), overlooking the bay, serves mainly Cantonese and
   Szechwan food.
Phil's Pub (tel 263-8589), breathtaking view of the bay, specialises in Creole-style
   seafood. Pricey, but worth it. Stocks good South African wines.
La Pagode (tel 263-8733), excellent Chinese food, good value for money.
La Capitaine (tel 263-8108), local and Indian dishes, with spicy seafood served on
   a banana leaf.
La Casa Creole (tel 263-8432), local, English cuisine, steaks and grills.

Grand Gaube

The Nomad (tel 263-8199), Mediterranean and Creole cuisine.
Le Dauphin (tel 263-8199), Creole, Chinese, Mediterranean cuisine.

Pereybère

Hibiscus (tel 263-8554), Creole restaurant in an open bamboo building on the
   beach.
Café Pereybère (tel 263-8700), Chinese restaurant excellent value for money,
   exceptional food.
Epicure (tel 262-6711), local and English cuisine.
Chez Roland Auberge des Songes (tel 262-8326), Creole cuisine.

Pointe aux Cannoniers

Le Bateau Ivre (tel 263-8766), specialising in French and Creole.
Le Carnivore (tel 263-7020), African theme restaurant serving all kinds of meat.
Le Navigator (tel 263-7999), excellent seaview restaurant in an old colonial house.

Trou aux Biches

Le Pescatore (tel 265-6337), an up-market seafood restaurant on the beach with an
   excellent sea view.

THE WEST COAST

EXPLORING

The island's western coastal area south of Port Louis is probably the driest, hottest
region of the island and is known, rather obviously, as the Sunset Coast. Its premier
attraction is the peerless blue-water fishing grounds beyond the reef. The Black
River area is one of the main centres for big-game fishing and most of the hotels
can organise charter boats. Le Morne mountain dominates the landscape in the
south-west of the Black River district. The coastal area at **Tamarin** is known for
some good surfing in winter (June-September), when sea and winds combine at

their most violent, and in summer Tamarin is a draw for watersports fanatics and a hopping off point for the charming **Tamarin Falls**, inland. The **Shellorama Museum** is situated here, displaying one of the biggest private collection of shells in the Indian Ocean. You can buy shells at the museum but make sure you can take them out of the country legally. The salt marshes, salt-pans and the charming fishing villages of La Gaulette, Case Noyale and La Preneuse, all add to the charm of this region. Perched on a mountain slope in the Riviere Noire district not far from the small coastal village of Flic en Flac is **Casela Bird Park**, a zoological garden and bird sanctuary with a magnificent view of the entire west coast. It is 10 miles (16 km) south of Port Louis. Casela is home to about 2,500 birds of 140 different species. There are also tortoises, monkeys, leopards, lemurs, and tigers, all in a restful atmosphere enhanced by trees, streams and small cascades. In the flowering season the orchids are superb. Casela covers more than 20 acres (8 ha) of land and contains specimens from five continents, but the main attraction is the Mauritian pink pigeon, one of the rarest birds in the world and still fighting to avoid the fate of the less fortunate dodo. Look out also for the white peacock. Among the giant tortoises at Casela is one said to be more than 150 years old (tel 452-0693/4).

Chamarel is perched atop the thickly wooded Black River mountain range and the steep route winding and twisting its way to the village offers a panoramic view of the entire west coast. Near the village is one of the best known curiosities of the island: the **Coloured Earth** of Chamarel, in a privately owned estate. In an open glade are waves of multi-coloured layers of earth, each wave glowing with its own distinct colours. This oddity of nature is said to have been caused by the erosion of ancient volcanic ashes, the remains of a lava flow which over time has weathered into ripples of wrinkled earth with colours ranging from burnt oranges and reds to deep purple. There are raised vantage points which give you a bird's-eye view of these strange rainbow soils. Late afternoon if the sun is out is a good time to visit, because the softer light enhances the colours of the earth, particularly from the western side. As a memento you can buy a small bottle filled with different layers of coloured sands from a small kiosk at the site. This is near a sign which warns against the disturbance or removal of coloured earth. It costs 25 rupees (63p) per person to enter the area, but for that you can also visit and admire the nearby **Chamarel Cascade** plunging down a sheer drop into an inviting pool.

With its towering Le Morne Mountain the imposing Le Morne peninsula is one of the most beautiful sites for a hotel in Mauritius and there are a couple here, next to each other. A horseshoe of white beach stretches for 4 miles (7km) and the reef-protected waters lend themselves to every kind of watersport. The lagoon in the south-west between Le Morne and to Grande Riviere Noire Bay is 4 miles (7km) wide, with well-developed reef flats and sand banks which provide good and safe swimming for all ages, although you've got to watch out for *fond blancs* – deep circular basins rimmed by coral. In the lagoon off La Gaulette is the crescent-shaped plantation islet of **Ile aux Bénitiers**. Only 1.2 miles (2 km) long it's a lovely spot for a picnic, surrounded as it is by casuarinas and coconut palms. **Wolmar** and **Flic en Flac** offer one of the longest ribbons (7 miles/12 km) of soft white coral sand on the island, ideal for sunbathing and swimming. Cliffs overlook the sea in parts at heights of 26-66 ft (8-20 m) and at **Montagne Jacquot** you can watch local divers attempt breathtaking dives in imitation of those at Acapulco.

ACCOMMODATION

Le Victoria (tel 261-8219, fax 261-8224, e-mail: victoria@intnet.mu), renowned for its long stretch of white sand beach, is at Pointe aux Piments, halfway between Port Louis and Grand Baie, 9 miles (15km) from the capital, and 37 miles (60km) from the airport. Rooms are sea-facing with air-conditioning, safe, TV, mini-bar, and bathrooms with separate shower and toilet. Resident band, sega shows and cabarets. Restaurants include the poolside *Le Superbe* where breakfast and themed dinners are served, *La Casa* specialises in Italian food, and *La Case Creole* serves Mauritian delicacies. *L'Horizon Bar* is open for lunch, as is *Le Recif* which offers light snacks, salads and sandwiches.

The *Paradis* (tel 401-5050, fax 450-5140, e-mail: parahot@intnet.mu for villas and hotel) is on the Le Morne peninsula in the south-west. Port Louis is 28 miles (45 km) away and the airport 43 miles (70 km). The calm reef-protected waters are ideal for watersports and beyond is one of the most prolific marlin breeding grounds in the world. Sports include an 18-hole par 72 international golf course, accredited and recognised by the European PGA. Rooms are air-conditioned, and have a mini-bar, TV and safe. The *Paradis* restaurant serves breakfast, lunch and dinner. The *Blue Marlin* on the edge of the sea serves a la carte and grilled seafood. *La Palma* specialises in Italian cuisine and *La Ravanne*, on the beach, serves seafood, grills and Mauritian specialities. The *Le Paradis Villas* are three-bedroom luxury villas, with a main en-suite bedroom, while the other two bedrooms share a bathroom. There are four restaurants to choose from, or you make meals in your own fully equipped kitchen or grill seafood and steaks on the private barbecue on the beach. Each villa has a valet who prepares breakfast, washes up and cleans the place.

At Wolmar, on the leeward coast about 12 miles (20 km) from Port Louis, 16 miles (25 km) from Curepipe, and 25 miles (40 km) from the airport, is *La Pirogue Hotel and Casino* (tel 453-8441, fax 453-8449, e-mail: infolap@sunresort.com) set in a huge landscaped garden of coconut palms, frangipani and hibiscus, with secluded bougainvillea-clad bungalows. Each room is on the ground floor, has a private bathroom with separate shower, telephone, satellite television, radio, mini-bar, individually controlled air-conditioning and a private terrace. On one of the longest beaches on the island, well-protected by a coral reef, there is a superb boathouse and watersports facilities including a scuba-diving centre. La Pirogue big-game fishing centre at Black River is internationally renowned. There are four restaurants and three bars, as well as beach service and a mobile beach bar. The children's club is for children from 4-12.

Next door, with free access between the two, is the five-star *Sugar Beach Resort* (tel 453-9090, fax 453-9100, e-mail: infosbr@sunresort.com), a 238-room ensemble of buildings in traditional Franco-Mauritian estate style, set in a tropical garden with sugar-white beaches dotted with thatched umbrella-shaped *paillots*. Accommodation is divided into rooms in the main Manor House, and in the surrounding garden villas. Each room has either twin or king-size beds, bathroom en-suite with shower, satellite TV, multi-lingual video channels, international direct-dial (IDD) telephone, air-conditioning, electronic safe, and mini-bar. All rooms open on to a private balcony or patio. There are four restaurants, two bars and a beach bar trolley.

The 276-room *La Plantation* (tel 261-5821, fax 261-5709, e-mail: balaclava@intnet.mu) is on the west coast at Turtle Bay, about 15 minutes drive from Port Louis and Grand Baie. On 20 acres (8 ha) of tropical gardens, it has spacious air-conditioned rooms overlooking either lagoon or gardens, with TV, mini-bar, and safe. There is a choice of three restaurants: *Le Domaine des Epices*, *La Cocoteraie*, and *L'Amiral*. Bars, boutiques, swimming pool, beach, tennis. All watersports, including scuba-diving and deep-sea fishing, as well as a fitness centre. In the evening, you can try your luck in the casino or dance the night away in the nightclub.

EATING OUT

Belle Mare
Symon's (tel 415-1135), Creole and Chinese cuisine. Seafood a speciality, beautiful tranquil setting.

Flic en Flac
Sea Breeze (tel 453-8413), extremely popular Chinese restaurant, specialising in Chinese fondue.
Mer de Chine (tel 453-8236), local and Chinese cuisine.
Ocean Restaurant (tel 453-8627), Chinese, seafood and duck.

Riviere Noire
Pavillon de Jade (tel 683-6151), praised for its Chinese cuisine.
Le Bonne Chute (tel 683-6552), specialising in European and Creole seafood.

THE SOUTH COAST

EXPLORING
The extreme south of the island is quite picturesque, with a wild coast below some striking heights. Sandy beaches are scarce and a rugged coastline creates seas too turbulent for all but the strongest – or craziest – swimmers, so you are advised to look rather at the popular attractions along the stretch from Mahébourg and Blue Bay to the Le Morne peninsula. From Mahébourg to Le Morne, the south offers vistas of ever-changing scenery. A majestic chain of mountains, the Creole range, dominates the bay of Vieux Grand Port, which once saw a naval battle between the French and English fleets. Offshore are the islands of Ile aux Aigrettes, Ile de la Passe, and Ile aux Fouquets. South of Mahébourg small sandy beaches appear along a coast that is largely bare rocks and boulders. **Riambel** is one of the more attractive with a wide beach that is 2 miles (3.2km) long, it is the most protected lagoon along this coastal stretch and the casuarina-fringed beach takes its name from a Madagascan word meaning 'sunny beach.' During low tide here you can stroll across the lagoon as far as the outlying reef itself. *Souillac*, the main southern village, is perched on high cliffs. It was named after the Viscomte de Souillac, who was the French governor of Mauritius from 1779 to 1787. A pleasant feature of Souillac is a garden overlooking the sea, named after Dr Charles Telfair, a local 19th century landowner, botanist, and sugar industry innovator – who was also a champion of slavery. Near the village is the **Robert Edward Hart Museum**, a restoration of this popular Mauritian poet's coral beach cottage *La Nef*. It contains some of his manuscripts and personal effects. Nearby **Gris-Gris** has a popular tanning beach and the summer season brings hordes of local surfers to the area as the absence of reef at this end of the island can bring in some violent waves. No one is sure how Gris-Gris came to be named, although one popular explanation is that an astronomer and early cartographer of Mauritius, Abbé de la Caille, named it in memory of his pet dog. Another is that it refers to Creole black magic practices, with one of the rocks said to be an enchantress of old. Gris-Gris is a regular stopover for travellers along the coast. The short (328 ft/100 m) beach is a real find, set in a small cove between two headlands. A narrow path provides a panoramic trail along the cliff above.

They say they have discovered the perfect equilibrium between flora and fauna at **La Vanille Crocodile Park** and its nature reserve at Senneville. It is, therefore, perhaps unfortunate that they advertise among the specialities of their restaurant,

The Hungry Crocodile, a variety of croc meat dishes – or maybe this is one of the ways they preserve the balance of nature. Having said that, the croc park can still claim to be one of the island's most-visited tourist attractions. The park breeds Nile crocodiles from stock imported from Madagascar, and has more than 1,000 of these saurians to attract the interested – or tempt the taste-buds of the hungry. There are also animals and reptiles from all the Mascarene islands, among them fruit bats, monkeys, deer, mongooses, and tenrecs (a larger Madagascan relative of the common English hedgehog), as well as iguanas, lizards, chameleons and tortoises. The park, near Riviere des Anguilles, is open every day of the week from 9.30am to 5pm (tel 626-2503, fax 626-2844). Not far away, to the north of Souillac, are the **Rochester Falls**, where water cascades over some spectacular volcanic rock formations. The falls are wider than they are high (26 ft/8 m). They are reached by a road crossing a sugar plantation that is open to visitors. Towards the south-west corner of the coast is one of the island's biggest waterfalls. This is the 295 ft (90 m) **Riviere du Cap** cascade. There's a path down, leading to a basin where you can take a refreshing dip. Halfway along the coast between Souillac and Blue Bay, in an area of lava boulders and jagged cliffs, is the **Le Souffleur** blowhole. Stand above the blowhole and you'll feel the knee-shaking power of the sea rumbling through the cavities below. Circled by casuarina trees lies another fine bathing spot at **Blue Bay**. Situated on the south-east coast, not far from Mahébourg, Blue Bay offers a fine stretch of white sandy beach and deep, clear, light-blue waters for safe bathing. There is also lots of yachting and windsurfing activity. One great advantage of the south coast is that it has not yet been subjected to the waves of tourist development prevalent elsewhere on the island, although it can offer some fine, if small and intermittent, beaches.

ACCOMMODATION

There are few hotels along the south coast, which features long stretches of tidal flats rather than alluring beaches.

The sophisticated five-star *Shandrani* (tel 603-4343, fax 637-4313, e-mail: shandrani@intnet.mu) on Blue Bay is a 10-minute drive from the airport. It has wide open spaces under thatch housing the main public areas and leading out to the pool and the bay beyond. The hotel places a strong emphasis on family holidays, with family apartments and interleading rooms. There is a choice of three separate beaches, one in front of the hotel which is the centre of the sports facilities, another for more quiet relaxation, and a wilder third beach where the waves pound through a gap in the reef to break on the shore. Rooms are luxurious, with separate shower, bath, toilet and dressing room, air-conditioning, TV, mini-bar, and safe. Breakfast and theme dinners are served at *Le Grande-Port* restaurant, which is set on a wide terrace with views over the swimming pool and sea. *Le Sirius* is set under the trees at the edge of the sea and serves grills, Mauritian specialities and seafood for lunch. Resident band, cabarets and astronomy – yes, star-watching from the pool.

The five-star *Berjaya Le Morne Beach Hotel and Casino* (tel 683-6800, fax 683-6070) is on the south-west coast's Le Morne peninsula, an hour's drive from the airport. Malaysian-style villas in tropical gardens, with air-conditioned, en-suite bathroom, TV, mini-bar and room safe. Snorkelling, windsurfing, water-skiing, glass-bottomed boat, sail boats, kayaks and pedaloes are all free, as are billiards, games room, fitness centre, squash and tennis. The main restaurant is *La Cascade* with buffet breakfasts and dinners. There's Chinese cuisine in the *Oriental Pearl*, *Bel Ombre* is a beach grill for snacks, lunch and pool bar, and the *La Caze* is a fun pub and disco.

La Croix du Sud (tel 631-9505, fax 631-9603), a holiday village hotel near Mahébourg, has 169 sea-facing rooms, each with its own balcony; 38 rooms are in luxury thatched cottages. You can admire the magnificent bay from a viewing balcony and enjoy cocktails beside the freshwater pool at *The Badamier*, a thatched bar which also incorporates the terraced dining-room offering English and Chinese cuisine and barbecues and buffets and a covered dancing area. Windsurfing, pedaloes, kayaks, snorkelling, and glass-bottomed boats are all free. There is a charge for water-skiing, deep-sea fishing, scuba-diving and catamaran cruises.

Blue Lagoon Beach Hotel (tel 631-9529, fax 631-9045, e-mail: blbhotel@bow.intnet.mu), is on the south-east coast, 10 minutes from the airport and close to the historical village of Mahébourg, 50 minutes from Port Louis. It has air-conditioned rooms, TV, mini-bar, live entertainment, bar, and a pool.

EATING OUT

Mahébourg
Restaurant La Phare (tel 631-9728), seafood restaurant.

Pointe aux Roches
Green Palm Restaurant (tel 625-5016), the only one in the area, Indian, Creole and Chinese food.

THE EAST COAST

EXPLORING
The east coast – the 'Sunrise Coast' – has some of the longest and whitest beaches on the island. Inland it meets mountainous areas thick with ebony and other indigenous trees which are the haunt of deer, wild boar and a variety of birds, including the rare Mauritian kestrel. The eastern coastal district of *Flacq* takes its name from the flat terrain here – in Dutch *vlakt*. Coral was burned locally in kilns to produce lime, which was used in sugar processing and for agricultural purposes. **Centre de Flacq** is the only town in the district. The district courthouse is a copy of Sir Arthur Hamilton Gordon's ducal house in Aberdeen, Scotland. Further along the coast in the north-east is **Grand Gaube** a small fishing village whose fishermen have earned a well-deserved reputation for their skill in making sailing boats and for their deep-sea fishing lore. Cycling excursions are popular from here. Off the coast near here are the **Ile d'Ambre** and the adjoining **Ilôt Bernache** with a couple of secluded beaches tucked away here and there among a jumble of rocks and boulders. There are numerous hotels and good beaches here, especially at **Belle Mare**, which has a beautiful white sandy beach with fine bathing. The coast, with its white sweeps of sand, stretches down to Grand Port where the beach narrows and the road closely follows the coastline to Mahébourg in the south-east. **Roches Noires** and **Poste Lafayette** are both favoured seaside resorts, especially in the hotter months, because of the prevailing fresh sea winds that blow inshore almost all year-round. All in all this is a rock-strewn coastline punctuated by some attractive sandy stretches. **Trou d'Eau Douce** is a typical fishing village which is said to retain its natural charm and leisurely pace of life year after year. South of the village there is 8 miles (12 km) of continuous beach along the straightest length of coastline on the littoral and with some excellent holiday resorts. The beaches are wide and, because the coast runs almost parallel to the path of the south-east trade winds, it is the most protected area along the east coast. The **Ile aux Cerfs** ('Stag Island') is a gem of an island off the coast south of Trou d'Eau Douce and belongs to the Sun International group of hotels. The island is an idyllic place to spend the day. Easiest access is by a boat ride of 20 minutes across the lagoon from Sun's

Touessrok Hotel, or by taking a small local pirogue from Pointe Maurice. The promontory **Pointe du Diable** was, according to local legend, named by French sailors whose navigational instruments went haywire as they sailed around this point. They thought this was the work of the devil. French battery cannon still point out to sea, placed here to guard the offshore pass in more turbulent times. The battery is a popular viewpoint. **Mahébourg** was once the capital of Mauritius and is the nearest town of any size (population 20,000) to the Sir Seewoosagur Ramgoolam international airport. The town lies in the bay of **Grand Port**, the only natural harbour in Mauritius. It still retains its old-world charm, with many of its quaint little buildings painted in cheerful red and white. It is regarded as the most Mauritian of all the island's villages, although it was laid out like a town in metropolitan France. This appellation will most likely change if plans to develop a waterfront area with an esplanade, pier, restaurants, shopping centre, a discothèque, a nautical centre and much more, come to fruition. The town was named after French governor Mahé de Labourdonnais and was once a busy little sea port. It is still one of the island's main fishing centres. The islet at the entrance of Mahébourg harbour is the **Ile de la Passe**, which guarded the pass through the reef into the lagoon and was the launch pad in 1810 for a disastrous attempt by the British to invade Mauritius from the south.

After securing the vital entrance, a British squadron comprising the frigates *HMS Sirius*, Iphigenia, Magicienne and *Nereide*, and the brig *Staunch* entered the harbour and engaged the French vessels *Bellone, Minerve, Ceylan* and *Victor*. Cannon balls and grapeshot whistled for four days. During the battle the *Magicienne* and the *Sirius* ran aground and were set on fire by their own officers. The *Nereide* was captured and the *Iphigenia* surrendered to French reinforcements from Port Louis. This, the sole French victory over the British, led Napoleon to order the name of Grand Port carved on the Arc de Triomphe in Paris. A plinth in the bay also commemorates the battle. Many of the guns of the *Magicienne*, a former French frigate earlier taken as a prize by the British, were salvaged in 1933-34. The **Naval Museum** has some interesting relics from this battle and from some old shipwrecks. The museum is housed in the French colonial plantation mansion where in 1810 wounded English and French naval officers were ferried in to receive medical attention. Captain Sir Nesbitt Josiah Willoughby, commander of the British fleet, who had lost an eye, and French commander Duperré, who was badly wounded at the beginning of the engagement, recovered under its roof and became good friends. You can also see the ship's bell (recovered by divers in 1966) of the *St Géran*, which sank further up the east coast in 1744 and gave rise to the romantic but historically inaccurate story of *Paul et Virginie*, the name of Bernardin de St Pierre's famous novel. The vessel drifted on to the rocks at Ile d'Ambre, off the north-east coast, in August 1744. Among the passengers were the mesdemoisselles de Mallet and Caillou, who were engaged to officers de Payramon and de Longchamp. As the masts crashed down and the ship splintered on the rocks the two young women were urged to take off their voluminous clothes, jump into the sea and swim for it. They refused because they thought the idea indelicate and died for their prudery, clasped in the arms of their lovers. In St Pierre's fictionalised account the heroine Virginie is returning to Mauritius. Paul waits on the shore, only to see the ship bearing his beloved wrecked within sight of the shore. Virginie is drowned and washed up at his feet. He then dies of a broken heart. Prints of Paul and Virginie, furniture and articles belonging to Mahé de Labourdonnais and relics recovered from British battleships sunk in the bay are among the museum's exhibits. There's a handicraft section of the museum which is built in typical island architectural style (tel 631-9329). An interesting sidelight for lovers of biscuits is **La Biscuiterie de Manioc**, a factory on the outskirts of Mahébourg, where the same local family has been making biscuits based on manioc (cassava) for the past hundred years. These biscuits are said to go well with cheese.

Present day **Ferney** is the site of the first Dutch landing in the bay, which they named Warwyck Bay, in honour of the admiral who sailed his squadron in here in September 1598 to step ashore among the mangroves. Visible from the road and visitable by a narrow path is a monument at the water's edge commemorating this momentous event in island history. Slap-happily this pillar erected in 1948 anglicises the good admiral's surname. Ferney was also where the French established one of their first sugarcane plantations in 1740 and there's still a sugar mill there, but it's no longer used. Out in the bay, just off the coast at Pointe d'Esny, is the pretty **Ile Aigrettes**, a reserve for native plants. This small island is home to about 40 different species of endemic plants characteristic of the flora that once existed on the coastal mainland. Among the rare indigenous trees here is an endemic ebony known as *Bois Fer*. The island covers a bare 25 acres (10 ha) and was established as a nature reserve in 1985. It serves as a quarantined breeding station for the country's rare pink pigeon and its national kestrel. There are two restaurants on the island, and a few curio sellers. All kinds of aquatic sports are on offer from the island's watersports centre. A leisurely half-hour walk will take you right around the island. Walk across a narrow strip of sand and you can explore the tiny, untouched **Ilôt Mangénie**, also known as **Ile de l'Est**. Along with other islands, it is undergoing rehabilitation and regeneration in terms of a United Nations Development Programme (UNDP). The Mauritius Wildlife Appeal Fund has been busy on the island for some years trying to save endemic flora from extinction.

Tucked in the hills above Anse Jonchée, not far from Mahébourg, is the magnificent 2,000-acre (809 ha) park of **Domaine du Chasseur**. The forest-clad slopes shelter more than 1,000 **deer**, as well as **wild boars** and monkeys, among luxuriant vegetation containing wild orchids and stands of ebony, eucalyptus, palm trees, and **ravenals**, the local name for the famed **Travellers Tree**, whose fan-like stems can be pierced in an emergency to produce a copious flow of stored fresh water. Some **rare birds**, such as the Mauritian kestrel, can be seen by the sharp-eyed in these woods. There are a few hikes of 3-9 miles (5-15 km) and 4x4 trails on the estate. The estate has thatch-roofed, rustic chalets for accommodation and an open restaurant (tel 634-5097, fax 634-5261), overlooking the hills. A wide choice of specialities, including venison and wild boar, as well as seafood, is available. As well as being a nature reserve the estate is also a hunting ground for locals eager to pot the descendants of the deer brought in by the Dutch from Java in the 17th century.

Also near Anse Jonchée, 9 miles (15 km) from the international airport at Pleasance, is the **Domaine de Ylang-Ylang**, a 200-acre (81 ha) plantation of more than 15,000 ylang ylang (*cananga odorata*) trees whose fragrant yellow flowers feed the only distillation plant in Mauritius producing ylang-ylang (pronounced ee-lang) and other pure essential oils from camphor, citronella, vetiver, eucalyptus, and pink pepper trees and plants. The tree with the odd-sounding name was introduced to the island from the Philippines in 1750. Trees of four or five years old yield 22-27 lb (10-12 kg) of flowers during the picking season from October to May. Flowers must be distilled the day they are picked. To make a couple of pints of essential oil takes 110 lb (50 kg) of flowers. Second distillation oils are used for aromatherapy treatments, and the third distillation is used for soap and toiletries. Trees flower for 25 years and then they must be pulled up and replaced. There are nature trails through the scenic woodlands of the estate, which is open seven days a week from 9am to 5pm. A variety of perfumed products and essential oils are on sale at the gift shop. A small (10 ml) vial of ylang-ylang oil costs 203 rupees (about £5) – or more than £500 a litre. There's a 100-seater restaurant on the estate which has such mouth-watering dishes as pancake with crab meat (£3.75/US$5.60), roast venison with royal sauce (£5.60/US$8.45), wild boar with chasseur sauce (£5.75/US$), and there's even stag steak with french fries (£7.25/US$10.94). Bookings are advisable for both restaurant and distillery tours (tel 634-5668, fax 634-5230). **Le Val Nature Park** is also in the south-east, at Cluny, and derives its name from the valley it sits in surrounded by mountains. The park has anthurium and andreanum greenhouses, prawn, fish and watercress ponds, deer enclosures, and monkeys and a variety of bird species also call the park home. You can catch your own freshwater fish and *camarons* (giant *Rosenberghis* prawns) for lunch (tel 633-5051).

ACCOMMODATION

Le Coco Beach (tel 415-1010, fax 415-1888, e-mail: infococo@sunresort.com), on Belle Mare peninsula, 27 miles (43 km) from Port Louis and 25 miles (40 km) from Curepipe, is set in 80 acres (32 ha) of indigenous gardens with palm trees and casuarinas, on nearly a mile of white sand beaches. It is the largest resort on the island. It is a good value-for-money hotel for children and families. All rooms have twin or double beds, private bath, shower and toilet, satellite TV, mini-safe, air-conditioning and a private balcony or patio. There are two restaurants, seating 600 in five separate sections, serving breakfast and nightly themed buffet dinners. There's a multi-entertainment area, comprising a central 100-seater bar with electronic games, karaoke, snooker tables, daily disco, live band and themed shows on selected evenings and a dance floor. There is also a mobile beach bar; a children's club for ages 6-12 years and a créche for ages 2-6 years. The hotel has retail shops selling clothing, beach articles, international press, and gifts and services include a launderette, baby-sitting, car hire, excursions, secretarial services, gym and massage, beauty therapy, helicopter service, fully-equipped fitness centre, vending machines for soft drinks and snacks, games room with pool tables, video games and chess, and a kiddies jungle-gym.

The five-star *Le Touessrok Hotel* (tel 419-2451, fax 419-2025, e-mail: infotsk@sunresort.com), 29 miles (46 km) from the airport, is recognised as one of the most romantic resorts in the world and rated 'best hotel in the world' by British magazine *The Spectator*, an opinion shared by Conde Nast's *Traveller*. Sited on its own cluster of tiny islands, it is built in the local vernacular style, with wooden bridges connecting some of the rooms to the main hotel. Rooms at Le Touessrok follow a circular pattern around the beach and all have electronic safe, mini-bar, satellite TV featuring Canal Plus and Sky News, video channel, radio and taped music, air-conditioning and en-suite private bathroom with tub and shower. Non-smoking rooms are available. The private Ile-aux-Cerfs is a short ride away on the courtesy shuttle boat. The exclusive Îlot Mangenie is a private, uninhabited Robinson Crusoe-style island in the middle of the lagoon, open only to hotel guests. The *Captain Sharky Bar* on the beach serves a daily barbecue lunch. There is a free shuttle bus between the hotel and *Le Saint Géran* for guests who want to use the facilities or visit the casino there. There are eight restaurants and four bars with beach service from a mobile beach bar at both Ile-aux-Cerfs and Îlot Mangenie.

The first resort to be built in Mauritius, *Le Saint Géran Hotel, Golf Club and Casino* (tel 415,1825, fax 415-1983, e-mail: infostg@sunresort.com) is a 60-minute drive from the airport, and about 15 minutes by shuttle bus from *Le Touessrok*. It has 12 suites overlooking the sea and all 163 rooms open on to a sea or lagoon-facing terrace. Each room features a mini-bar, CD music channels, internal video system, direct-dial telephone, radios, satellite TV featuring Canal Plus and Sky News, teletext information system, bathroom telephone, electronic room safe, air-conditioning, ceiling fan, and luxury en-suite bathroom with shower and bidet, and courtesy bathrobes. Gary Player designed the par-33 nine-hole golf course. There are four restaurants and four bars, as well as a mobile beach bar. A shopping arcade offers jewellery, clothing, books, international press, and beach articles as well as branded goods from the hotel's special gift collection.

The *Hotels Apavou* group has three hotels in Mauritius. The 246-room four-star *Hotel Ambre* (tel 415-1544, fax 415-1594, e-mail: hotel.ambre@intnet.mu) at Belle Mare is 45 minutes from Port Louis by car. It has elegant Creole-style rooms, large bathrooms equipped with bath, bidet, double-basin and separate toilet. All rooms are air-conditioned, with a sea view, TV, radio, mini-bar, and safe. The hotel is on a long white sandy beach bordering a protected lagoon. Restaurants include spacious *Les Filaos*, open to the bay. *Les Alizées*, right on the beach, and *L'Etoile des Indes*, a chic restaurant for evening buffets featuring Indian, Creole, Chinese and French cuisine. Bars are open all day long, and there's entertainment every evening. The *Hibiscus* is a piano bar. The *Nautilus* night-club opens at 11.30pm. Four flood-lit tennis courts, volleyball, French bowls, water-skiing, sailboards, sailing dinghies, canoes, pedaloes, snorkelling, glass-bottom boat. Fitness studio, swimming pool, two jacuzzis, balneotherapy centre, boutiques, and disco. Supplementary charges for parasailing, horse-riding, catamaran cruising, deep-sea fishing, hunting and golf. Excursions can be arranged through the PR at the hotel.

Belle Mare Plage (tel 415-1083/4/5/6, fax 415-1082, e-mail: resachsl@intnet.mu) has 213 rooms, suites, and villas and is set in tropical gardens near Poste de Flacq. Rooms are air-conditioned with shower or bath, and toilet. Two swimming pools, complimentary watersports, as well as beach volleyball, French bowls, tennis, squash, two open-air jacuzzis, sauna and massage, complete fitness centre, 18-hole golf course (home of the Mauritius Open and the PGA of Mauritius), scuba-diving and deep-sea fishing. Main restaurant *La Citronnelle* serves breakfast and dinner. *Le Veloutier* offers a la carte dining in the evening, and *Le Beach Rendezvous* and the coffeeshop have light lunches and snacks.

Also at Belle Mare is Apavou's *Emeraude Hotel* (tel 415-1107, fax 415-1109, e-mail: emeraude@intnet.mu), with 60 air-conditioned rooms grouped in bungalows, a tropical garden, restaurant, bar, swimming pool, jacuzzi, watersports.

Le Tropical (tel 419-2300, fax 419-2302, e-mail: letropical@intnet.mu), near Trou d'Eau Douce, is a small, intimate colonial-style hotel facing Ile aux Cerfs and is ideal for anyone looking for a quiet, romantic get-away. All rooms are air-conditioned and sea-facing, with balconies or terraces. Two free daily speed-boat shuttles to Ile Aux Cerfs, where watersports are available, including trips in a glass-bottomed boat, deep-sea fishing, scuba diving, mountain biking and horse-riding.

EATING OUT

Ile aux Cerfs
Paul et Virginie (tel 419-2541), seafood served on the beach.
Le Chaumiere (tel 419-2541), Creole, Chinese, and Mediterranean.

Trou d'Eau Douce
Chez Tino (tel 419-2769), seafood served on the beach.

Vieux Grand Port
Le Barachois (tel 634-5643), gourmet restaurant.

THE CENTRAL PLATEAU

EXPLORING

Most of the residential towns are situated in the central plateau where the climate is cooler and in the old colonial days was a much healthier place to live than the coast. The central region does, however, have to put up with more frequent downpours than any other area, and is the source of six of the island's main rivers. The road takes you through the highest part (2,430 ft/740 m) of the central plateau where craters, waterfalls, reservoirs, and natural lakes are all part of the landscape and leads to magnificent panoramic viewpoints of mountains, forests and gorges.

Only a 10-minute drive out of Port Louis on the Curepipe road is **Domaine Les Pailles**, which provides a good opportunity to see how some of the islanders lived centuries ago; this is virtually a reconstruction of colonial Mauritius in a magnificent natural setting. You can visit an old oxen-driven sugarcane-crushing mill and a traditional still used to produce the estate's own potent white rum, and explore the 3,000-acre (1,214 ha) estate on foot, on horseback, by horse and carriage, and train. Other attractions include a spice garden and a two-hour guided 4x4 safari through indigenous forest to the foot of La Pouce mountain, overlooking the capital. There are four acclaimed restaurants on the estate serving gourmet dishes of Mauritian, Indian, Chinese and Italian food (tel 212-4225/6003, fax 212-4226). South of Port Louis are the major residential towns of Beau Bassin, Rose Hill, Quatre Bornes, and Vacoas, all on the main road to the island's second largest town, Curepipe. Of these Quatre Bornes is the more interesting, with a market held on Thursdays and Sundays that is a real treasure trove for bargains, especially handicrafts. The other towns seem to be largely places to live and work. Near Rose Hill is the French colonial pile of **Le Chateau du Réduit** residence of the former Governor-General of Mauritius, set in 325 acres (132 ha) of magnificently landscaped gardens, and now the official residence of the president of the Mauritius Republic. The gardens were designed more than 200 years ago by the Frenchman responsible for laying out the grounds at Versailles. Few official residences in the world can compare with the Le Réduit site. The double-storey chateau stands on a promontory between two ravines. Paved verandas run the full length of the building, which has 240 doors and windows. Le Réduit ('The Redoubt') was first built to serve as a stronghold and place of refuge against invasion. Not far from Le Réduit at Moka is the **Eureka Creole House** (1830), a magnificently restored colonial estate house with more than 100 doors and windows, which contains furnishings used by early European settlers. Eureka stands in a five-acre (2 ha) estate surrounded by streams and waterfalls from the Moka River. It has an andreanum garden and a restaurant serving Creole and local dishes. Afternoon tea is a speciality (tel 433-4951).

CUREPIPE

In the old coach-and-horses days drivers used to rest their sweating teams at an inn in the upland forests. They took this opportunity to light up their pipes, first cleaning them (*curer la pipe*). This spot eventually became known as **Curepipe** – at least, that's the fanciful story you'll hear for the origin of in this town. Curepipe became a popular residential town in the 19th century when islanders left the west coast for the healthier if wetter highlands. The town today has a population of nearly 80,000 and is a good central starting point for forays into the surrounding countryside. Before setting out pay a visit to the town's superb botanical gardens, a peaceful 5-acre (2 ha) oasis, its colourful vegetable market, and the shops and model ship makers for which the town is renowned. In the evening gamblers throng the local Casino de Maurice.

Between Curepipe and neighbouring Floreal is the spectacular extinct crater known as **Trou aux Cerfs**. This is 280 ft (85 m) deep and nearly 656 ft (200 m) wide and its interior is clothed in bush and tropical plants. From the crater rim you get an extensive view of the island, with its sugarcane fields stretching away to the horizon and the mountain ranges of the Plaines Wilhems and Black River districts. If it's really clear you can even get a glimpse of the highest mountains on Réunion island. Not far to the south-west, through the Plaines Wilhems, lies an area that contains many of the island's main natural attractions, including **Mare Aux Vacoas**, the largest lake and reservoir on the island, the Mare Longue and the **Tamarin Falls**. On through the Plaine Champagne lies Grand Bassin, and the **Black River Gorges National Park**. This area is at its best between September and January. The Black River Gorges were proclaimed the island's first national park in 1994. A number of nature trails leading to cascades and rivers meander through the 16,245 acre (6,574 ha) park, and traverse some of the most beautiful forests on the island. At Le Pétrin a tourist information centre has been developed where you can see a map showing all the trails and walks in the area. There is also a picnic area. There's a boardwalk into the dwarf forest that's typical of the region and a fenced conservation management area from which alien plants have been removed. This protects a stretch of the island's remaining heathland. From here you can stroll through the **Macchabée Forest**, a circular 4 mile (7 km) walk. The forest is full of gnarled trees and vegetation not found anywhere else on the island. The vegetation grows heath-like close to the ground, among stands of Travellers Trees full of chattering monkeys. Other trails take you down through the gorges to Black River, a hike of 9 miles (15 km). Longer walking trails include one to the highest point in Mauritius, **Piton de la Petite Rivière Noire**, which is 2,716 ft (828 m) high. From the road across Plaine Champagne towards Chamarel you'll find easy access to a number of viewpoints. The one near the central parking ground affords a splendid view of an immense canyon over which white straw-tailed tropic birds float in the warm upward eddies. As well as Macchabé, all major areas of native forest are now nature reserves, among them Perrier, Bel Ombre, Corps de Garde, Pouce, Cabinet, Combo, Les Mares, Bois Sec, Ile Ronde, Ilôt Gabriel, Ile Plate, Coin de Mire, Ilôt Marianne, Ile aux Aigrettes, Ile aux Serpents, and both the Ile aux Cocos and the Ile aux Sables off the island of Rodrigues.

Bordering the national park are the small nature reserves of Les Mares, Bois Sec, and Gouly Père, surrounding **Grand Bassin**. This lake is revered by Hindus as a religious pilgrimage site and known to them as *Ganga Talab*, ('Lake Ganges'). The lake fills an extinct volcanic crater at 2,303 ft (702 m). The annual pilgrimage to Grand Bassin and its shrines is one of the most important dates on the Hindu religious calendar and is celebrated as a national holiday. The festival of Shiva on this day is an occasion for pilgrims to strew the lake's surface with flowers and offerings before they dip in pots to fill with its sacred water for their local temples. To the east of Grand Bassin are the tea plantations, factory and museum of **Bois Chéri**, a privately owned estate where you will be invited to a tea tasting after a guided tour of the factory. The museum on the estate gives you a quick look at the history of the beverage. Not far away are the estate's anthurium and vanilla gardens at **Le Saint Aubin**, where you can learn all the things you've always been afraid to ask about these two flowers (vanilla in the seedpod of an orchid). The early 19th century restored colonial house at Le Saint Aubin stands in lovely gardens, inviting a stroll after a Mauritian lunch in the mansion (for both these places tel 626-1513, fax 626-1535). The **Tamarin Falls**, to the north of the national park near the reservoir of the same name, are pretty rather than spectacular. Their attraction has been enhanced now that the falls have become a site for the increasingly popular sport of canyoning. Under the watchful eye of trained instructors you can abseil (rappel) down the falls from heights of 82-180 ft (25-55 m).

EXCURSIONS

Visits to all attractions detailed in this section of the book are available through MauriTours, the slickest and most knowledgeable of all the operators in Mauritius, with a reputation built up in the local tourism industry over nearly 30 years. This family owned business has a trained staff of 350, as well as guides and representatives on hand in all the hotels and resorts on the island. Collectively, they are fluent in English, French, German, Spanish, Italian, Swedish, Japanese, Hindi, and Russian. MauriTours has the island's largest fleet of air-conditioned mini-buses, coaches, and chauffeur-driven cars to take you around the sights, or can provide rental self-drive vehicles. They can even fix you up with a self-catering apartment in Residence Le Tamaris, a complex they own in the heart of Grand Baie. **MauriTours** has offices in all the main centres, including Port Louis (Centre), Port Louis (Caudan), Rose Hill, Quatre Bornes (St Jean), Quatre Bornes (Orchard), Curepipe, Phoenix, and Grand Baie. Contact MauriTours at PO Box 125, Rose Hill, Mauritius (tel 465-7454/7331, fax 454-1682/83, e-mail: mauritours@mauritours.intnet.mu). They also have agencies in Rodrigues, Comoros, and Madagascar.

EATING OUT

Plaine Champagne
Le Chamarel (tel 683-6421), European and Creole cuisine.

Quatre Bornes
Green Dragon (tel 424-4564), Chinese cuisine.
Rolly's Steak and Seafood House (tel 464-8267), local and English cuisine.
Happy Valley (tel 454-9208), Cantonese seafood.
Golden Spur Steak House, tel 424-9440.

Rose Hill
Le Pékinois (tel 454-7229), Chinese specialities.

BEACHES

Mauritius has some of the loveliest beaches in the Indian Ocean. In the extreme north, offering magnificent views of the volcanic coastal islands of Flat Island, Round Island and Gunners Quoin, are the beaches of the little fishing villages of **Cap Malheureux** and **Grand Gaube**. The north-west coastline has some equally delightful beaches; among them **Pointe aux Piments**, famous for its underwater vistas, **Trou aux Biches**, with its splendid Hindu temple, then further up the coast **Mont Choisy**, one of the most popular beaches on the island, offering safe bathing, sailing, windsurfing and water-skiing; **Grand Baie**, main centre for yachting, fishing and water-skiing; and **Pereybère**, a delightful little cove mid-way along the coastal road between Grand Baie and Cap Malheureux, which is arguably one of the island's best, but usually crowded, bathing beaches.

On the west coast are the public beaches of **Tamarin**, **Flic en Flac**, with its casuarina trees and fine lagoon, **Albion**, **Pointe aux Sables** and **Baie du Tombeau**, among others. Along the east coast are long, white, sandy beaches such as **Roches Noires**, which extends to Poste Lafayette and is noted for its good fishing. A few miles away, **Belle Mare** has fine bathing and a beautiful white sandy beach. **Palmar** and **Trou d'Eau Douce** are the names of fine crescents of sugary sand and gin-clear water which are the sites of some leading resorts.

Blue Bay in the south-east offers a deep, clear, bathing area and a fine stretch of white sandy beach. In the south, the coast is largely a barricade of high cliffs dropping abruptly into the sea. Le Bouchon, Gris-Gris, Souillac and Baie du Cap are beautiful viewpoints along this wild stretch, but are certainly not recommended for bathing. The odd pleasant beach does exist here, however, and **Riambel** and **Pomponette** are two that deserve closer inspection.

The beaches tagged by locals the **best and most popular** are to be found at Le Morne, Mon Choisy, Belle Mare, Pereybère, Trou aux Biches and Grand Baie (Grand Bay). Northern beaches are generally where the action is.

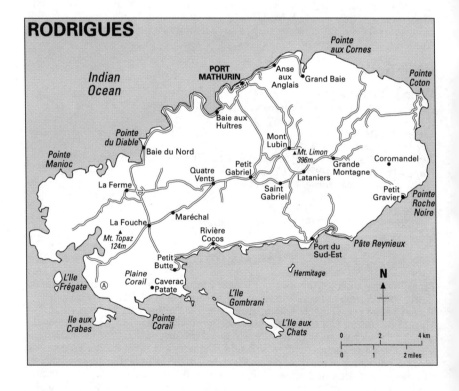

RODRIGUES ISLAND

Whenever we asked local people in Mauritius where they would like to go for a holiday most of them said Rodrigues, their little sister island 348 miles (560 km) away to the north-east. Most of them had never been there, but Rodrigues seemed to represent for them another Mauritius of days long gone. So ignoring the sophisticates who usually chose the nearby French island of Réunion, or England – always to watch Manchester United play – we hopped aboard an Air Mauritius ATR 42 turbo-prop and made the 1½-hr flight to the pinprick Indian Ocean island where time, almost, stands still. It's a short flight to the past that we can unreservedly recommend to anyone yearning for an untramelled spot as yet unsullied by the more garish trappings of civilisation. Tourism authorities and operators will tell you Rodrigues is the perfect antidote for modern stress, and for once the hyperbole is valid. It's a small place. You can travel the full length of the island by car in an unhurried half an hour. Bends in the road on the way take the name of the nearest house or shop, as in Corner Benny outside his café. Villages tend to be named after fruit and vegetables – mangoes, papaws, oranges and bananas, peppers, cabbages, and potatoes. They still call tomatoes by their 16th century name *pomme d'amour* ('love apple'). Everybody knows everyone else on the island and all are laid-back and friendly. Education is highly regarded and children think nothing of walking for two hours to get to school. Mothers do the same trek carrying small baskets of food for their children's lunch. There's no industrial pollution or unseemly litter on beaches and the sea is as clean and blue as it must of been on the first day. All in all this is an island for lovers of islands – or simply for lovers.

GEOGRAPHY

Rodrigues is 340 nautical miles (560 km) to the north-east of Mauritius and lies at the heart of the south-east trade winds. Its greatest length, from Pointe Coton in the east to Pointe Mapou in the west, is a little over 11 miles (18 km). Its greatest breadth, from Jantac in the north to Pointe Poursuite in the south, is 5.25 miles (8 km). As the crow flies, the distance from Port Mathurin to Port South-East – the only harbour on the opposite shore – is about 4.6 miles (7 km), but as there are no crows – and because they don't fly uphill and down dale – and because of the broken, hilly nature of the land, distances on the ground and total actual surface area are considerably greater than the figures would suggest. The area, not including 18 surrounding islets and atolls of various sizes, is 42 sq miles (108 sq km), smaller than Jersey in the Channel Islands or one tenth the size of Rhode Island. A central mountainous ridge runs along most of the island's length, the sides of which are deeply cut by ravines stretching down towards the sea. These are deeper, shorter and more abrupt on the southern than on the northern side. This means that there is very little flat land. Principal peaks along the ridge go from Diamond Peak's 330 ft (101 m) to Mont Limon, at 1 300 ft (396 m) the highest point on the island. Rodrigues is surrounded by a shallow lagoon of brilliant turquoise which is nearly twice the size of the island itself. The virtually unbroken coral reef creating this placid expanse surrounds Rodrigues, varying in distance offshore from its narrowest point, a bare 20 yards (18 m) away at the eastern end of the island, to 5 miles (8 km) out in the south. A couple of tricky openings in the reef are used by fishermen as gateways to their deep-water fishing spots.

The coastline is so indented that the perimeter is 50 miles (81 km) long and is full of capes and bays, even the most insignificant of which has a name. Heading south from Port Mathurin the capes, or *pointes* as they are known locally, are Monnier, Diamant, Malgache, Diable, Nicolas, Pistache, Manioc, Mangue, La Fourche, Afine, Mapou, Matourin, Palmiste, de l'Herbe, Corail, Caverne, Raffin, Roche Noire, Tasman, Coton, Sel, Grenade and aux Cornes. Chief bays heading counter-clockwise along the coast from Grand Baie in the north are Anse aux Anglais, Mathurin Bay, Oyster Bay, Baie Diamant, Baie Malgache, Baie du Nord, Baie Pistache, Baie Lascars, Baie Topaze, Anse Quitor, Anse Grand Var, Anse Tamarin, Anse Raffin, Anse Baleine, Anse Mourouk, Baie de l'Est, Anse Ally, and Anse aux Caves. *Anse* is the word generally used to describe an inlet or cove.

Many small islands, some volcanic, others of limestone or sand lie scattered on the reef platform around the island. Off the northern coast there are only two, Diamant and Ile aux Fous (Booby); off the western shore lie Ile aux Sables and Ile aux Cocos. Five islets called Marianne, Catherine, Frégate, Destinée, and Crab lie off the south-west coast. Inside the lagoon off the south are the islands of Pintades, Paille en Queue, Gombrani, Cats, Plate, Misel, and Hermitage. A large limestone plain, the Plaine Corail, forms the extreme south-western part of Rodrigues and covers about 2,000 acres (809 ha). This plain is honeycombed with caves. The island's little airport is on this plain, and plans to extend its short runway to take bigger jets are hampered by the existence of these underground caverns. Environmentalists are also against the idea, arguing that the fragile eco-systems in the area have yet to be fully explored and described.

CLIMATE

Rodrigues can be visited all year round, but if there are going to be any, January and February are the months to watch out for cyclones. These bring rain, and without them water supplies for the island would be seriously curtailed. The main tourist season is from November to May. From November to April you can expect the mercury to hover between 84°-90°F (29°-32°C) and from May to October the island chills out to between 59°-84°F (15°-29°C). The driest time of the year is from September to November. The south-east trade winds are more constant here than in Mauritius or Réunion, but when they stop blowing, a pleasant sea breeze takes over and sweeps the island as the land warms up throughout the day. The breeze usually drops just before sundown. The winds and breezes fanning the island effectively serve to divide the island year into summer and winter seasons. The most settled weather occurs in winter from June to October, when it is delightfully cool and dry, the sky is clear, and the nights are superb. Summer extends from November to May, with the hottest months being January, February and March. Life at the coast can then be somewhat uncomfortable, although the temperature is less trying and the nights are cooler in the hilly interior. The sea surface temperature in summer averages 81°F (27.5°C) and in winter it's 74°F (23°C).

HISTORY

As with most of the other islands in the Indian Ocean the true discoverers of Rodrigues will never be known. It is probable that the island was first seen by Arab merchants in an ocean-going dhow blown off-course from its usual trading routes; there's even a case to be made for according the honour to early Indonesian navigators who, after all, made it as far as Madagascar. Certainly the island appeared on mediaeval Arab maps as *Dina arabi*. Portuguese sources credit the discovery of Rodrigues to Diego Rodriguez some time in February 1528 and in the late 16th century Portuguese navigators found the island a useful landmark on their way to India and the east. On the 25 June 1638 the French vessel *Saint-Alexis*, called at Rodrigues on its way to Mauritius and formally claimed the island for France, even though a Dutch squadron had landed men on the island in mid-1601, and these shore parties had spent five or so days exploring the vicinity of what is now Port Mathurin. Three years later some Dutch sailors were marooned on Rodrigues for three months before sailing to Mauritius in a long boat. They arrived safely having made the first recorded crossing between the two islands in an open boat. During the 17th century, when there was a free-for-all over the lucrative Indian Ocean trade routes to the east, there were reports of many well-known navigators landing at Rodrigues. In 1642, the French annexed the still uninhabited islands of Réunion and 'Diego Ruis' for monarch Louis XIII.

First Colonists

By a quirk of history the first colonists of an island that is today overwhelmingly Catholic were Huguenot Protestants. They arrived in May 1691 following Louis XIV's earlier revocation of the Edict of Nantes, a Protestant charter which had allowed French Huguenots the freedom to practise their religion. Among those who had been accepted to form the new colony at an undisclosed destination known only – and appropriately – as 'Eden' was Francois Leguat. The new colony's first inhabitants numbered eight men, who got their first sight of their future home from the deck of the frigate *Hirondelle*. Some crewmen went ashore and brought back a bag of 'great and good birds,' providing Leguat and his companions with their first meal of the soon to be extinct *solitaire*. On the 1 May 1691 Leguat and his party landed on Rodrigues and settled at the mouth of Grand Rivière, not far from present day Port Mathurin. The cereal they planted died so they had no bread, but there were birds and their eggs, all kinds of fish, eels, crabs, lobsters and oysters, tortoises and turtles, palm cabbage, and plenty of fruit and indigenous vegetables. In spite of delectable meals such as 'even kings might envy' they grew bored by the monotony – there were no women among the settlers – and made toddy and arrack from palm tree sap. Waiting for the promised other colonists, who never came, they built a boat, showing real ingenuity. They used fibrous stalks from the latanier palm for cordage, a large rock was the anchor, the sail was made from cloth they had brought with them, and a cheap toy pocket compass was their sole navigational instrument. On 19 April 1693 they set sail, but foundered not far from the beach. A month after this attempt they finally left Rodrigues and the settlement where they had lived for two years. They reached Mauritius nine days later. This landfall was not the end of their troubles. Soon after landing the Dutch authorities in Mauritius discovered that one of Leguat's party had a piece of ambergris, to which the Dutch had long claimed exclusive right. Assuming that this had been found in Mauritius, Leguat and his companions were banished to the *Isle aux Fouquets,* at the entrance to Grand Port Bay. Leguat and three others were sent to Batavia in 1696, still prisoners. Leguat didn't get back to Europe until 1698, where he joined French Protestants seeking refuge in Britain. He settled in London, became a British subject, and died in September 1735 at the age of 96. Leguat's trials and tribulations are given here in some detail, as not only is he today firmly established in island folklore, but the account he wrote, *Voyages and Adventures*, became famous over the next 250 years in the literature of travel and natural history and sparked an interest in this remote little island that still continues.

Second Colonisation

Neither the British nor the French governments showed any immediate interest in the newly uninhabited island, although the Admiralty conducted a survey of the coastline and its anchorages. A subsequent French plan to establish another colony on Rodrigues was considered, relying on strong, hardworking peasants. Such worthies, however, were not among the next settlers to arrive. Instead, a motley band of 38 women of ill-repute and men who had lived by theft rather than by work were shipped from Bourbon (Réunion) on 6 September 1725 in *La Ressource*. For guidance, the captain was given a copy of Leguat's book and a chart on which the anchorage was marked. Six weeks later *La Ressource* was back after an unsuccessful attempt to land the settlers. Five men did make it ashore, however, and one of them, second mate Tafforet, passed his time until they were taken off again in 1726 writing a *Relation de l'Isle Rodrigues*. This fascinating account was mislaid, only to turn up in Paris nearly 150 years later. The Seven Years' War in Europe did not begin, at least formally, until 1756 and once again Britain decided to invade and capture Mauritius to prevent its continued use as a base for French maritime nastiness. In 1761 Rodrigues was chosen as the assembly point for British forces. British ships gathered there waited in vain for reinforcements. Meanwhile, as the plan fizzled out, the British lost men, not to enemy action, but to venomous fish and to a diet that included the shoots of a poisonous type of palm. The first permanent settlers arrived in Rodrigues after news of the French Revolution had percolated to Bourbon. Among them was Philibert Marragon, who had visited Rodrigues in 1791, and liked it so much he applied for and secured the post of French civil agent there. Marragon and his wife both died on the island, after living there for 32 years, and their tomb can still be seen at L'Union. Marragon, incidentally, took the first population census of Rodrigues in 1804, and reported that there were 22 settlers and 82 slaves.

British Occupation

Following the armed truce in March 1802 that was the Peace of Amiens it was obvious to the British that only by taking Mauritius and Bourbon could they neutralise the French threat. With Rodrigues once again as their assembly point and supply base the British attacked. Bourbon surrendered in July 1810 and by Christmas of that year Mauritius had also capitulated. The British kept a token force on Rodrigues, before withdrawing to India in 1812. Today, the only traces in Rodrigues of that brief occupation are the ruins of a circular gun emplacement on the top of Mount Venus. Under the Treaty of Paris of 30 May 1814, Bourbon was handed back to France. Seychelles, Mauritius and Rodrigues came under direct British rule. Once the islands became British slave trading became, at least officially, illegal. In fact, slavery was abolished by Act of Parliament in August 1833 and a period of seven years for the gradual emancipation of slaves was declared. Slaves in Mauritius were finally freed in March 1839 and three months later all slaves in Rodrigues were also ostensibly free.

Integration

From the time the British took over the administration of Mauritius in 1810 until 1968, when Mauritius attained independence within the British Commonwealth, Rodrigues was governed as its dependency. This is a polite way of saying Rodrigues was a largely forgotten and neglected island. Independent Mauritius itself even seemed to forget its other island. When the Post Office issued a series of stamps to commemorate the 25th anniversary of the international airport in 1971 Rodrigues did not appear on them, even though it had at that stage been constitutionally integrated with Mauritius for three years. Rodrigues continued to feel neglected until the Mauritian government appointed one of their own community as Minister of Rodrigues and gave him a resident Island Secretary.

THE ECONOMY

Fishing is the most important economic and survival activity. There are around 2,000 registered fishermen – 40% of them can't swim – but this does not include the many other men and women who fish by wading or sailing their pirogues in the 81 sq mile (210 sq km) lagoon virtually every day for food, or as a source of income. Look out on the wide lagoon and invariably you'll see groups of women, and often entire families, up to their knees in the placid water hooking out octopuses from the coral crevices. Drive along the shoreline and you'll see dozens of these cephalopods hanging out on racks to dry like lines of tattered washing. The octopus is a prized ingredient in many of the island Creole dishes. It's also exported to Mauritius dried or frozen. Prawns and crabs, on the other hand, do not have the same cachet with fishing families, who usually sell these catches to hotels and restaurants. Most families also keep a few cows and pigs and raise their own vegetables. Everyone seems to have a garden, and in the fertile island soil almost anything will grow. Maize, plantains, and manioc are major staples; rice is imported from India and China. Tourism didn't really take off in a big way here until 1994 with the opening of two quality hotels and the formation of the Association of Rodrigues Tourism Operators (ARTO), but islanders have been quick to realise that increased tourism means more job opportunities and a ready market for many of their traditional handicrafts, such as wickerwork and basketry, and their famed bottled diabolical chillies. It's all a far cry from only a decade ago when there were no souvenir shops and visitors had to search hard to find even a faded old postcard of Rodrigues.

THE PEOPLE

The island has a population of 37,000, 97% of them Catholic Creoles, whose relaxed lifestyle and general friendliness and hospitality to visitors is one of the most pleasing features of the island. Rodriguans pride themselves on their warmth and inbred courtesy. The relatively recent advent of tourism has barely affected them in this respect and they still exhibit the characteristics of a more leisurely age. They certainly haven't changed in the 30 or more years that have passed since Alfred North-Coombes noted that 'the Rodriguan is well-behaved, law-abiding to a great extent, and respectful. You would be surprised how many would greet you in the streets and all over the country in the most friendly way. This is a really delightful experience. This sense of respect is not reserved for strangers. It is ingrained in the people.' The island's Creoles are descendants of slaves who came from Africa during the days of French rule. In explanation of the *café au lait* complexion of many, locals will tell you that over the past 200 years sufficient Europeans posted to Rodrigues had liaisons with island women to, in the words of a Creole saying, 'leave one or two portraits behind.'

As the population census of 1804 revealed, there were 22 settlers and 82 slaves living on Rodrigues. A century later there were barely 3,300, but by the mid-1930s at treble this figure it had grown enough to worry the British authorities that island resources might soon be insufficient to support many more people. This led many islanders to seek new lives, across the water to nearby Mauritius and Réunion, and as far away as Australia. Even today it's estimated that as many again Rodriguans as are on the island are living and working in other countries. Rodriguans adore children – even if they belong to someone else – and being strict adherents to their religion frown on contraception and family planning, a mixture of elements that could eventually see this little corner of paradise bursting at the seams. One bright light is that when TV arrived on the island the birth rate suddenly dropped, and has yet to recover.

LANGUAGES

As in Mauritius, the official language is English, although school children are taught in French as well. At home they speak Creole, like everyone else. If you are reading this you should have no problem communicating, although there are plenty of older Creoles who cannot understand any language except their own island patois. Some of these have perplexingly been given jobs as guardians at popular tourist attractions.

RELIGION

As mentioned earlier, virtually all islanders are **Catholic,** and the tenets of their church coupled with a natural conservatism have reinforced an almost Victorian approach to mores and morality in the scattered small communities. Church is a popular meeting place for young Rodriguans as both sexes can be together for the two of three hours it takes to walk there. Girls are not otherwise allowed to be with young men without a chaperone. Grown men don't even smoke in front of their father – they will either stub out or swallow a cigarette they are smoking if they see him coming. Men build houses for their future wives near their parents to ensure an extended family.

There are a few **Muslims** on Rodrigues, whose religious needs are catered for by the mosque in Jenner Street, Port Mathurin, the only one on the island, and there is one **Hindu** temple, at Pointe Canon.

RODRIGUES ISLAND: PRACTICAL INFORMATION

Getting There

BY AIR

Not so long ago the only way you could get to Rodrigues was by sea, an often miserable two to three days' voyage if the sea was rough, and there was a boat only once a month. Now you can fly into Plaine Corail Airport at Point l'Herbe in comfort in just under 90 minutes. Entry regulations are the same as for Mauritius. Try to get off the aircraft quickly when you land, otherwise you'll wind up in a long, tedious queue while airport officials tick off your name on the airline passenger list. You might even be asked for your passport. Once inside the tiny terminal it's advisable to reconfirm your departure flight at the Air Mauritius desk. Air Mauritius operates two flights a day between SSR Airport and Rodrigues with 48-seater ATR42 turbo-jet aircraft. Remember that the luggage allowance on these flights drops to 15 kg per person.

Air Mauritius Offices

Port Mathurin (tel 831-1632, fax 831-2128).
Plaine Corail Airport (tel 831-1301, fax 831-6301).
Port Louis Head Office, Mauritius (tel 207-7070, fax 208-8331).
If you are calling from Mauritius dial 095 followed by the number in Rodrigues.

There are no car hire facilities at the airport and no waiting taxis, so arrange with your hotel beforehand to be picked up. If you've neglected to take this precaution look for the Supercopter bus that is there for every arriving and departing flight in the hope of picking up people like you. This 25-seater will take you to Port Mathurin, 11 miles (18 km) away, in half an hour for 100 rupees (£2.50), or to anywhere else on the island. At night the fare increases by 25%.

BY SEA

The *MV Mauritius Pride* sails to Port Mathurin, Rodrigues, from Port Louis two or three times a month. The vessel can carry 250 tourist-class passengers, but has only a dozen first-class cabins. The sea route takes a minimum of 27 hours, but at least white-jacketed waiters serve mouthwatering Creole dishes, which helps to pass the time so long as you don't suffer from sea-sickness. A first-class single costs the equivalent of about £40, about the same as a ticket on the plane. For a little extra you can arrange to have the use of your cabin while the ship is berthed in Port Mathurin – and save on hotel bills. For bookings contact Mauritius Shipping Corporation (tel 241-2550 or 242-5255, fax 242-5245) in Mauritius; in Rodrigues (tel 831-1555, fax 831-2089).

There's no problem with money changing, as you'll obviously be arriving from Mauritius and carrying Mauritian rupees and whatever other currency or travellers' cheques you brought from home.

Banks

Barclays Bank is in Jenner Street, the main thoroughfare in Port Mathurin (tel 831-1553). There is an ATM outside where you can use Visa or MasterCard to withdraw funds. Also in Port Mathurin are the *State Commercial Bank* (tel 831-1642); *Mauritius Commercial Bank* (tel 831-1831); and the *Indian Ocean International Bank* (tel 831-1591). Banks are usually open Monday to Thursday from 9am to 3.30pm, and on Friday from 9am to 4pm.

There is no malaria on the island, nor any other of the common diseases of the tropics. The tap water is safe to drink, but it's not advisable if you want to avoid intestinal upsets. As in Mauritius, buy the bottled water, still or carbonated. Rodriguans naturally drink the local water, although doctors have noticed an increase in hypertension among men which they believe is due to the water's high saline content. Water, or lack of it, has always been a big problem on the island. There are no reservoirs, so when it rains the water runs wastefully off into the lagoon. It also often comes out of domestic taps looking rather evil. Most islanders filter and boil their water. Not too long ago drinking water at Port Mathurin was so full of odd matter that some locals could not see the bottom of their wash-basins through water only two or three inches deep. As you travel around you'll notice that every village has a large communal water tank, provided by the United Nations' agency Unicef, from which residents can draw water for two hours, three times a week. Until these tanks arrived water was even more strictly rationed. Remember this, and use water sparingly while you are on the island.

NATURAL HAZARDS

The advice given for Mauritius about **sun-bathing** applies to Rodrigues. The same goes for **sharks** – there aren't any inside the lagoon, although there are plenty of sizeable but shy **octopuses**. If paddling or swimming rather watch out for spiny **sea-urchins**, **scorpionfish** and **stonefish** (both *laff* in Creole). The first is a sluggish but beautiful fish with poisonous dorsal fins that is found in the lagoon all round the island; the ugly stonefish is the more dangerous one as it lies on the bottom, perfectly camouflaged. It isn't aggressive, but it's easy to stand on one. Wear something on your feet when paddling. This will also protect you against the **pen shells** (*hatches d'armes*), whose razor-sharp edges can give you a nasty cut.

TELEPHONE

To call Rodrigues dial the international direct dialling (IDD) access code, followed by 230 and the number you want. When calling from Mauritius, dial the IDD access code, plus 095, followed by the number. To call Mauritius from the island dial the subscriber number as it appears in the telephone directory. Calls are cheapest if made from the Overseas Telephone Service (OTS), in Jenner Street, Port Mathurin. You'll find a public telephone in almost every village on Rodrigues. As yet there are no cellular (mobile) phones on the island.

MAIL

You'll find the main Post Office next to the Anglican church of St Barnabas on Jenner Street, in Port Mathurin, along with Mauritius Telecomm. The status of Lubin and La Femme villages is enhanced by the fact that they each have a post office, a bank, and a health clinic. Just how close-knit the communities are is illustrated by the fact that there are no house numbers and no street addresses on local mail, just the name of the addressee and the village. Postmen deliver mail on foot. If they have post for someone far away on their rounds they simply hand it to the nearest villager and it goes from hand to hand to the recipient, who usually gets it the same day.

TELEVISION

There is only one TV channel. From Monday to Friday transmission starts at noon and goes on until 11pm, and at weekends from 9am to 11pm. Programmes screened are usually canned Mauritius Broadcasting Corporation productions, although news bulletins are transmitted live via satellite between 7.30pm and 8pm. Satellite TV arrived recently and some 50 homes sport the distinctive dishes. Rodriguans say they never go to the beach for relaxation – they watch TV instead.

Radio. A small local radio station broadcasts news and views-type snippets for a couple of hours early every day.

If you have the time and the energy there is no better way to see this island than on foot. If you need a break on the road bus services connect Port Mathurin with most of the island villages and are reliable if slow. The **bus terminus** is at the end of Port Mathurin, near the harbour. Probably the best option if you are on holiday for a limited time is to make use of one of the island's tour operators (see *Useful Addresses and Telephone Numbers*), who in the end will probably save you time and money by taking you to all the right places and some you probably didn't even know about. The next best, if you're heavily loaded, is to hire a car (see *Vehicle Rental*), or one of the island's three **taxis**. Two are usually at Cotton Bay Hotel, the other somewhere in Port Mathurin. At a push a motor-cycle should be considered, but don't go for a hire bicycle unless you are super-fit and can tackle virtually continuous hill climbs.

DRIVING

Vehicle Rental

Cars, 4x4s and motor-cycles can be hired through Ecotourisme (tel 831-2801, fax 831-2800). Ecotourisme, in Douglas Street, Port Mathurin, also arranges excursions and airport collections. For other vehicle rentals try:
Rod Tours: Port Mathurin (tel 831-2249, fax 831-2267).
Ebony Car Rental: Port Mathurin (tel 831-1640, fax 831-2048).

Comfort Cars: Port Mathurin (tel 831-1603, fax 831-1609).
Spring Lovers: Petit Gabriel (tel 831-4431).

Fuel, keep an eye on the fuel gauge if you are driving yourself. There is only one garage where you can top up the tank, and that's in Port Mathurin. It's open every day, but only between 6am and 2pm.

Roads
These are generally narrow, twisting, unlit at night, and in a poor state of repair. Locals will tell you that when they see a road gang filling in pot-holes they know an official from Mauritius will soon be visiting. The only major road works that were in progress when we visited were on the road between the airport and Port Mathurin. The job of widening and upgrading this road is expected to be finished by about 2005.

Hazards are the same as in Mauritius. Humans and animals seem to have equal rights on the road.

HOTELS
On the rugged south side of the island at Paté Reynieux, is the *Mourouk Ebony Hotel* (tel 831-3350, fax 831-3355), which can accommodate up to 70 people in 30 cosy bungalows, equipped with bathroom, toilet, and ceiling fans. It is a Creole-style complex set in an exotic garden. All the bungalows have terraces looking out over the lagoon. It also has a dive centre, and windsurfing is a speciality. Mountain-biking is also catered for, as well as water sports and fishing expeditions. A freshwater swimming pool fronts the hotel and overlooks a fine sandy beach. The stretch of lagoon in front is a famous spot for fun-boarding and diving (see *Sport and Recreation*). There's wonderful food, too, especially the Rodriguan specialities, and a friendly bar.

Further along, on the north-east coast at Pointe Coton, is the up-market *Cotton Bay Hotel* (tel 831-6001, fax 831-6003, e-mail: cottonb@intnet.mu) which offers accommodation in 40 air-conditioned rooms, six luxury rooms and two suites, all facing the lagoon. Service and local and international cuisine are first-class. The hotel is managed by Air Mauritius. Activities include watersports, fishing, mountain-biking, horse-riding, and tennis courts. It is on a blinding white sand beach, and only 30 minutes from Port Mathurin. Sports and leisure equipment is free, except for scuba-diving gear. You can expect some interesting evening entertainment.

Within walking distance of the capital Port Mathurin, in the hills at Fond la Digue, is *Escale Vacances* (tel 831-2555, fax 831-2075, e-mail: escal.vac@intnet.mu), a pleasant 23-bedroomed Creole-style guest-house with air-conditioned bedrooms, showers, bathrooms, and a swimming pool. At night you might even see golden fruit bats circling overhead in the valley of Cascade Pigeon River. The hotel can arrange car and bicycle rental and excursions around the island, as well as boat and fishing trips. It has good Chinese and Creole cuisine.

MauriTours owns *Les Cocotiers* (tel 831-1058, fax 831-1800, e-mail: lescocotiers@intnet.mu) at Anse aux Anglais. It has 14 comfortable sea-facing rooms with TV, restaurant, swimming pool, and a fine view of the bay.

Medium and Budget Price Hotels
Le Tamaris: (tel 831-2715, fax 831-2720, e-mail: letamaris@intnet.mu), also MauriTours owned, which has 15 self-catering flats of one, two or three bedrooms, all with a living room and equipped kitchenette. The terrace restaurant serves

breakfast, lunch and dinners. This is ideal for families and is within walking distance of central Port Mathurin.

Beau Soleil Guest House: (tel 831-1916, fax 831-2004), has 30 rooms, a restaurant and bar .

Guest House Ciel d'Eté: (tel 831-1507, fax 831-2004), with 15 rooms, in central Port Mathurin.

Guest-Houses

There is a concentration of guest-houses at Anse aux Anglais, just minutes from Port Mathurin:

Auberge Anse aux Anglais: (tel 831-2179, fax 831-1973) has 22 rooms, a bar and restaurant.

Beau Séjour Guest House: with five rooms (tel 831-1753).

Auberge Les Filaos: (tel 831-1644, fax 831-2026) with 12 rooms.

Self-Catering

Domaine de Décidé: (tel 262-6788, fax 262-6708) situated in a forest off the road to Graviers, in the south-east. It has six comfortable rooms with cook/maid services.

Auberge de la Montagne: (tel 831-46070) in Grand Montagne, inland near Mt Limon, has three rooms.

For modest but comfortable **backpacker accommodation** try the simple *Sunshine Boarding House:* (tel 831-1674) in Port Mathurin, although there are only four rooms.

Eating and Drinking

RESTAURANTS

Restaurants don't flourish in a place where residents can, with little effort, pull tasty fish and other seafood out of the lagoon at their door and fill a basket in their garden with fresh fruit and vegetables bursting with goodness and flavours long gone from the supermarkets of less fortunate countries. What few restaurants there are on the island serve mainly the dishes of Mauritius, with a few hearty island specials such as a baked redfish called *vieille rouge*, red bean curry – served for fast-food junkies on a take-away banana leaf – and reef octopus, either dried and chopped into a salad, or simmered in a succulent stew with fiery local chillies.

Meals are usually built around something that comes out of the sea, although Rodriguan pork with the small local onions is quite a popular culinary departure. As with their fellow citizens in Mauritius, the islanders don't usually eat out in the evening, unless it's a special occasion. They do patronise street corner cafés and shops for lunchtime snacks and take-aways. The result is that most restaurants open during the day and are closed by late afternoon or early evening. Visitors can eat in any of the hotels, even if they are not staying there. Particularly good are *Escale Vacances* (tel 831-2075) in Port Mathurin, *Les Cocotiers* (tel 831-1058), at Anse aux Anglais, *Mourouk Ebony* (tel 831-3350) at Paté Reynieux, and the more expensive *Cotton Bay* (tel 831-6001) at Pointe Coton.

You can always find a change of pace at one of Port Mathurin's handful of restaurants. These include: *Le Capitaine* (tel 831-1581), in Johnston Street, serving mainly seafood and chicken, including a spicy chicken-burger that's a filling and inexpensive feed; *Le Gourmet* (tel 831-1571) is a Chinese restaurant in Duncan Street which also sells take-aways; *Paille en Queue* (tel 831-2315), is also in Duncan Street; and, for the budget conscious, there's *Lagon Bleu* (tel 831-1823), in

Morrison Street. In Mont Lubin you'll find the *Phoenix d'Or* (tel 831-1417), and in Mangue there's *John's Resto* pub and restaurant, which is worth a visit to try some Rodriguan specialities, and this usually means something spiced up and chilli hot.

Chillies

Even in the most unlikely places you'll see old half-jack rum bottles filled with mixtures of yellow, orange and green island chillies. Even if you are a lover of these little capsicums you should treat them with respect here. This is a sauce that Rodriguans regard as only mildly hot: Pound 100 chillies in five tablespoons of oil, then add 30 roughly chopped boiled and drained lemons and pound into a smooth paste, let it amalgamate in the bottle for several days before using.

DRINKING

Phoenix, the pride of Mauritius, is the beer drunk locally. For teetotallers the island's bountiful fresh fruits provide some tantalising ingredients for refreshing long drinks. Some of these amazing fruits also find their way into more potent beverages. A popular drink is called *rhum arrangé*, which can loosely be translated as 'arranged rum.' This is local rum in which various fruits and spices are arranged and left to macerate until they have imparted their exotic scents and flavours to the alcohol. Every family, every bar, seems to have its own special recipe.

Rhum Arrangé

Anthony Edouard is a barman at the Mourouk Ebony Hotel; this is how he arranges his special brew: Take a bottle of 40% Goodwill Mauritian rum, the cheap one with the red and white label, pour it over three sliced oranges in a wide-mouthed jar, add a couple of chopped lemons or limes if you feel like it, throw in a dozen coffee beans, two large sticks of cinnamon and two pods of whole vanilla. Seal and leave to mature as long as possible. Serve large tots in a glass and stir in a generous spoonful of honey. Good for keeping colds and 'flu at bay.

The **sega-tambour** of Rodrigues is regarded as being closer to its African and Madagascan origins than the *sega* known in Mauritius and Réunion, and this is probably explained by the greater isolation of the island. In Rodrigues the *sega* rhythm is faster and the women do most of the actual dancing. Their male partners switch at short intervals, a rapid succession explained by the fact that in the early days of colonisation there were many more men than women on the island. The Ebony Club in Port Mathurin is a good place to watch an unhibited display of this dance on Fridays and Saturdays from 9pm. You can see a more stately version every Wednesday and Saturday evening at the Mourouk Ebony Hotel, Paté Reynieux (tel 831-3350, fax 831-3355). As well as the seductive *sega*, islanders still dance the highly charged polkas, cotillions and waltzes brought to the Mascarene islands from Europe in the 17th and 18th centuries.

Nightlife

If you're into nightlife you might suffer withdrawal symptoms in Rodrigues. There are only two night-clubs on the island, both of them in Port Mathurin. *Club Ebony* is one (tel 831-1540, fax 831-2030). This is a discothèque in a corrugated iron structure where parents and middle-aged singles dance to American pop songs and reggae and share the dance floor with their teenage children. When *sega-tambour* dance music is played – and it is at least once every half-hour – the dance floor is packed tight. The bamboo bar then does a thriving trade in soft drinks, beer and rum.

The other focus of nightlife in the capital is the restaurant-bar *Le Capitane* in Johnston Street (tel 831-1581). This has a weekend disco which is locally regarded as more sophisticated than the Rodriguan-style Ebony. Both discos open for business only at the weekend.

Cinema there's one cinema on the island, the *ABC* in Port Mathurin, where a ticket costs the equivalent of £1.

FLORA AND FAUNA

More than any other ecological disaster the sad story of the solitaire (*Pezophaps solitarius*) has been a cautionary tale for island conservationists. This ungainly flightless bird was apparently not even as tasty as the similarly ill-fated dodo of Mauritius, but it joined it in extinction all the same, and not too long after its first brush with human beings. The solitaire, an overweight pigeon resembling a turkey with a swan-like neck, excited the interest of naturalists ever since it was drawn and described by early French colonist Francois Leguat, whose account tells us that the bird was given its name because although still abundant when he arrived on the island in 1691, it was seldom seen with other birds of the same species. As their wings were too small to support their weight, solitaires never flew, but in the woods and on stony ground they could move faster than a running man. On open ground they were easily overtaken and clubbed. They were usually killed for the pot between March and September, when they were extremely fat. Fledgelings were said to be tastier than adult birds. Solitaires could not be domesticated and when caught and caged, said Leguat, 'they shed tears without crying and refuse all manner of sustenance till they die.' They had been hunted and otherwise driven to extinction by the late 18th century. In 1875, an entire skeleton was reconstructed from bones found in the Caverne Patate to provide science with perhaps the most perfect existing specimen of the extinct solitaire's anatomy. Since then many naturalists who have studied the solitaire have tried to arrive at an explanation for its final disappearance. Many theories have been expounded, but so far none has found general acceptance.

The innumerable giant tortoises of Rodrigues were also seen as a valuable take-away food. Again, when Leguat lived on the island there were so many that 'sometimes you see 200 or 300 of them in a flock; so that you may go above 100 paces on their backs...without setting foot to ground.' The biggest tortoise Leguat saw weighed about 100 lb (45 kg). Soon after Leguat published his book recounting all his observations passing ships began calling at the island to load all the tortoises they could find. In 1725, the Governor of Bourbon seems to have had conservationist ideas. He instructed that tortoises were to be consumed only according to permits issued by him to each settler, but by 1735 many hundreds of thousands of tortoises had already been plundered and at least 10,000 a year were being caught. In 1759, one ship alone loaded 5,000. As a result of this indiscriminate slaughter Rodrigues lost virtually the whole of its tortoises, whose population at its peak is estimated to have numbered between 150,000 and 200,000. The last two tortoises were seen alive in an inaccessible ravine in 1795.

Down the years other species endemic to Rodrigues have come under pressure. The dugongs that once lived and grazed in the shallow waters of the lagoon and gave rise to sailors' stories of mermaids have vanished, but there is hope for other rare and endangered flora and fauna on the island. When British naturalist Gerald Durrell visited Rodrigues in the 1970s in search of the island's remaining **fruit bats** he found there were only 120 left. There are now several thousand of them on the island and they can still be seen around the Cascade Pigeons River forest area outside Port Mathurin where Durrell found the last surviving colony. The Wildlife Preservation Trust International (WPTI) is involved with a breeding project in Mauritius and there are also programmes on Rodrigues designed to educate locals on the importance of protecting the island's bats. Only two species of endemic birds survive, the **Rodrigues fody** and the **Rodrigues warbler**. The Mauritian Wildlife Foundation (MWF) is active in conservation work on the island and this has resulted in a significant increase in the numbers of these birds. MWF is also involved in habitat and vegetation restoration on Rodrigues and some offshore islets. Out of 45 surviving endemic island plant species, the majority are said to be critically threatened, and seven species are down to less than 10 specimens in the wild.

The MWF is a registered charity organisation and depends on donations from people who care about wildlife. If you would like to contribute to MWF projects for the long-term survival of a unique heritage, you can get more information from the Director of Development, MWF, 4th Floor, Ken Lee Building, Edith Cavell Street, Port Louis, Mauritius (tel 211-1749, fax 211-1789). The Association of Rodrigues Tourism Operators is also promoting eco-tourism and is keen to ensure that the island won't go the tourist high density route that can only put already fragile eco-systems under more of a threat.

SPORT AND RECREATION

DIVING AND WATERSPORTS
Instructors at the island's two diving centres say that the lagoon and its coral reefs, the most unspoilt on earth, justify Rodrigues' claim to have some of the best diving sites in the world, and having dived other sites around the world that make the same claim we are inclined to agree. The banning of spearfishing, lagoon water-skiing, and the use of fishing nets during the six-month spawning season have all helped immeasurably to preserve the island's prolific and exotic marine life.

DIVE SITES
Just a few of the many worthwhile are:

Coral Gardens – Grand Pâté
Just beyond the channel into Port Mathurin, are corals of every conceivable colour – branching corals, terraces of layered plate corals, coral towers rising to within a few feet of the surface, and colonies of fan-shaped stinging corals. The experts say there are 170 species of coral in this part of the Indian Ocean. Among the most magnificent are the **blue corals**, huge coral heads of vibrant cobalt. Some of these seemingly dead corals under overhangs and in deep gullies glow with a weird iridescent blue light.

Grand Bassin
You may find **sharks** swimming at the base of the many coral pinnacles in this area. These are white-tip reef sharks, but grey sharks and even hammerheads have been seen. There have been no recorded attacks on divers.

Ile aux Sables and Ile aux Cocos
These are two of the many islands lying within the extensive fringing reef. Shoals

of black kingfish patrol the outer edges of the reef, and large parrotfish feed among the corals. Look out for huge **plate corals** in this area.

Pointe Coton

At depths of 12-15 ft (4-5 m) you will see huge parrotfish and more of a spectacular coral reef that is unspoilt and vibrant with marine life of all kinds.

Port South-East

This is an area best dived on an incoming tide; and you should not miss the 60 ft (18 m) dive in the passage near the entrance to the barrier reef. Shoals of quicksilver garfish, kingfish and black chub patrol the passage. The best diving is on the northern wall at a depth of only 13-23 ft (4-7 m). The **undersea cliff** walls are crowded with soft corals of lavender and yellow sea-fans and are full of caves and tunnels where gigantic trumpetfish hang almost motionless; wary squirrelfish vanish and reappear among swirling clouds of multi-hued and see-through tiny fish, and enormous tiger cowries feed among the corals. Stunning stuff.

WRECK DIVING

Most of the ships lost on the reefs here were inter-island traders, as Rodrigues lies far from the main shipping routes. A few, however, have come to grief elsewhere and been brought to their final resting place by wind and ocean currents. One strange example of this occurred in 1997 when a Russian yacht abandoned by her crew three years earlier in Australian waters thousands of miles to the east grounded at Rodrigues, to the mystification of the islanders. A number of old wrecks have been located which make for interesting dives.

Some of the better known include the following baker's dozen: the *Swift*, wrecked in August 1827, the *Victoria*, lost in 1843, the *Oxford*, bound for Liverpool from Calcutta with a cargo of silk shawls, and wrecked on the south-west reefs in September 1843. The 388-ton barque *Trio* went down in March 1846, the *Samuel Smith*, bound from Penang for London was wrecked in November 1847 and lies in 20 ft (6 m) of water. The bones of the *Nussur Sultan* also lie in the south at the same depth. The *Masaniello* was wrecked in March 1862, and in May 1863 the 15-ton *Jemima* was abandoned after striking.

On the south-western barrier reef you can see the remains of the 1,250-ton *Clytemnestra*. She went down in September 1870 on a voyage from Rangoon with a cargo of rice and now lies in 20 ft (6 m) of water. The wreck of the 1,194-ton *City of Venice*, lost in 1871, lies nearby in 16 ft (5 m) of water.

In the north-west, at Booby Island, you can dive on the wreck of the *White Jacket*, also lost in 1871, and now lying in pieces in 10 ft (3 m) of water. In 1872, the 292-ton *Clare Sayers* was lost off southern Rodrigues on her way from New South Wales to Mauritius with a cargo of coal. A year later the *Bella Maria* also foundered off the island.

Old anchors can still be seen in the shallow coral forests off Port Mathurin, and divers can visit the remains of other vessels at the edge of the channel to the harbour, although visibility in this area can be poor.

DIVE CENTRES

To find the above and other wreck sites you need someone with local knowledge. Best places to look for the experts are the Bouba Diving Centre, based at the Mourouk Ebony Hotel (tel 831-3350, fax 831-3355, e-mail: ebony@intnet.mu) in the south-east, and further north at the Cotton Dive Centre, Cotton Bay Hotel, at Pointe Coton (tel 831-6001, fax 831-6003, e-mail: cottonb@bow.intnet.mu). These are the only two fully equipped diving centres on the island and both are affiliated to the Mauritius Scuba Diving Association (MSDA), which recognises BSAC, CMAS, NAUI, PADI, and MUG diving qualifications. There is no decompression chamber on Rodrigues, although with most scuba-dives taking place at relatively shallow depths this should not pose a problem. The deepest place inside the lagoon is a 105 ft (32 m) *passe*, or channel.

SURFING

The Club Nathalie Simon, based at the Mourouk Ebony Hotel and owned by former French windsurfing champion Nathalie Simon (tel 831-3355) can provide boards for windsurfing, sailboarding in addition to mini-Malibu boards and bodyboards for surfing. The reef on the western part of the island has some impressive waves with tubular sections and at **Jimmy's Pass**, on the way to Ile aux Cocos, you might even catch an unforgettable ride. The centre can also fix you up with a pirogue and fishermen to take you sailing. You can accompany them as they collect lobsters, crabs, and octopus from the traps they sink overnight in the lagoon.

BIG-GAME FISHING

The deeps beyond the lagoon offer great blue-water angling for black, blue and striped marlin, sailfish, tuna and sharks, as well as smaller fish such as barracuda, bonita, and wahoo. The sport fishing season starts at the beginning of October and runs through to the end of May. There are five big-game fishing boats available for hire for the equivalent of about £200 for a 6-hour outing for six passengers. This gives you a 37 ft (11 m) cabin cruiser, with skipper and crew, and fighting chairs for three anglers at a time. As well as sport fishing you have a choice of trawling and night fishing. Contact Mourouk Ebony Hotel (tel 831-3550, fax 831-3355), or Sail Fish, in Port Mathurin (tel 831-7228, fax 831-7241).

OTHER ACTIVITIES

Hiking and Trekking

Even though the island is small it offers some interesting trails. Walks can be arranged through the three reserves that protect remaining endemic flora and fauna. A good place to contact if you want to hike or trek in the hills is Becara Tours, at Baie aux Huîtres (Oyster Bay) (tel 831-2198). Two to three-hour guided hill treks can also be arranged through the Club Nathalie Simon, based at the Mourouk Ebony Hotel (tel 831-3355), which can also provide **mountain bikes**.

Football

Football is a passion on Rodrigues and inter-village matches take place at Port Mathurin and throughout the island every Saturday. There's even an all-girl team. An oddity for visiting football fans is to watch villagers kicking a ball around pitches on dried-out mangrove flats which are playable only when the tide is out. It's an odd sight to see the goal posts on these pitches sticking above the waves when it's high water.

Basketry and wickerwork are crafts at which islanders excel, and you'll find examples in even the smallest village. If you've neglected to buy **souvenirs** there's a well-stocked little store at the airport with hats, briefcases, baskets, bottle-holders and other knick-knacks. It's open only as planes arrive and depart.

CRAFT-AID

You'll find the best selection of gifts and crafts at an enterprising centre called **Craft-Aid**, which is in Trevor Huddleston House at Camp du Roi, Port Mathurin (tel 831-1766, fax 831-2276). The Craft-Aid gift shop here is the outlet for a wide range of handicrafts and other products from the workshop adjoining the Special Learning Centre for handicapped children, headed by Paul Draper, a British former freelance broadcaster who received an MBE for his work. Nearly all the **coconut jewellery** and other handicrafts made are exported all over the world to raise money for the centre.

HONEY

Don't leave without buying a jar of Craft-Aid's island honey. The centre opened a special department for the production of this superb honey at the end of 1997 after its entry in Britain's National Honey Show, in Kensington, won the second prize silver medal. Since then Rodrigues honey has gained an award every year. The centre's workshop makes the beehives which are supplied to families of the severely disabled so that they can learn bee-keeping. Surplus honey produced – 7 tons a year – is bought and marketed by Craft-Aid. Production took a dive a few years ago when chameleons were introduced by accident in container shipments and proceeded to eat the honey bees. The editor of craft-aid's newsletter, Katy Roberts, has co-authored a local guidebook with her husband Eric which is on sale at the centre's gift shop. The centre also has a shop in Jenner Street, Port Mathurin, which is open every day from 8am to 4pm. The work done by Craft-Aid definitely deserves support. Visit them, or buy their products in the UK from Oxfam.

An interesting little **market** is held every Saturday morning in Port Mathurin, in Fisherman Lane, but you've got to get there early. It opens between 5am and 6am and is gone by 9am. People come from miles around – and even from Mauritius – just to buy the redoubtable fresh and bottled chillies. These are modestly claimed to be the hottest in the world.

Shopping Hours

There seem to be no hard and fixed opening and closing times on the island. Shops generally open between 6.30am and 8am and close around 4pm during the week, Saturday 8am to noon. Most shops are closed on Sunday although a few open for half the day, depending on how the owner feels. Whatever the closing time, if you need anything from a small store you simply knock on the door and the shopkeeper opens for you. That's da island style...

 Police stations have little to do, as crime is virtually non-existent on the island and common offences such as pilfering of state timber, poaching, and evading animals taxes are not regarded as crimes, although everyone knows that they're unlawful. Rodriguans believe that while it is a disgrace to be jailed for theft, illegal fishing or tax evasion carries no such stigma. Men who have been in prison for anything remotely serious usually have difficulty in finding a wife in this prim society. A Mauritian magistrate dispenses justice once a month, and there's a prison on the island, but it's not much used. While we were there it housed a couple of men inside for brawling while drunk. The prison is sited on the headland at Pointe la Guele, Oyster Bay, and has a nice view of the sea. Police officers usually go fishing at the end of a hard day looking after inmates. Prisoners are allowed out every day to buy cigarettes or snacks and to see that their animals have sufficient grazing. It is safe to walk alone anywhere on the island, day or night. The main police station is in Port Mathurin (tel 831-1536, fax 831-2302).

Help and Information *i*

Time Zone, Rodrigues is in the same time zone as Mauritius, in other words GMT +4 hours in winter and 3 hours ahead in summer.
Electricity at 220V this is also the same as Mauritius, and all the other details likewise apply.

USEFUL ADDRESSES AND TELEPHONE NUMBERS

Rodrigues Administration Office: Port Mathurin (tel 831-1515, fax 831-2128).
Ministry of Tourism: Jenner Street, Port Mathurin (tel 831-1504, fax 831-1815).
Ministry for Rodrigues: Fon Sing Building, 5th Floor, Edith Cavell Street, Port Louis, Mauritius (tel 208-8472, fax 212-6329).
Association of Rodrigues Tourism Operators (ARTO): c/o Escale Vacances, Fond la Digue (tel 831-2555, fax 831-2075).
Air Mauritius: Port Mathurin (tel 831-1558/1632, fax 831-2128); at Plaine Corail Airport (tel 831-1301, fax 831-6301).
MV Mauritius Pride: Port Mathurin (tel 831-1555).
General Post Office: Port Mathurin (tel 831-2098).
Port Mathurin Pharmacy: tel 831-2279.
Police Station: Port Mathurin (tel 831-1999/1536, fax 831-2302).
Queen Elizabeth Hospital: Crève Coeur (tel 831-1521).
Rod Tours: (a branch of MauriTours) Port Mathurin (tel 831-2715/2249, fax 831-2267/1125).
Henri Tours: Port Mathurin (tel 831-1823/1635, fax 831-1125).
Rodrigues 2000 Tours: Port Mathurin (tel 831-2099, fax 831-1894).
Ecotourisme: Port Mathurin (tel 831-2801, fax 831-2800).

EXPLORING RODRIGUES ISLAND

PORT MATHURIN

This has got to be one of the smallest capitals in the world, but it has a charm and atmosphere that bigger places lack. In effect it's still a village, criss-crossed by a few streets lined with a jumble of shops and stores selling just about everything. Don't miss the **general store** of Maxime Wong in the middle of town, it's the oldest one around and should appeal to photographers. Everything is a five-minute stroll from central Jenner Street, including the **official residence** of the Island Secretary in an old colonial house (1873) behind a high wall concealing lush gardens and guarded at the entrance by two cannons of more recent vintage. Two notable events for locals are the **weekly market** and the arrival two of three times a month of the *MV Mauritius Pride* with passengers and provisions. The first settlement on Rodrigues was made on the sand-spit on which Port Mathurin now stands. The exact origin of the capital's name is uncertain, although one of the original settlers was known to be a Mathurin Morlaix. Jenner Street, the principal thoroughfare, is named after resident magistrate George Jenner, who administered the island between 1862 and 1871.

Near the central village of Mont Lubin, the highest village on the island, is the highest point on Rodrigues. This is **Mt Limon** at 1,289 ft (398 m). It's an easy walk to the top up one of the paths from the road and your reward is a magnificent view across the island from coast to coast.

Islands

Idyllic reef-fringed **Ile aux Cocos** and its smaller neighbour **Ile aux Sables** are both proclaimed nature reserves and two of the 18 islands dotting the ocean around

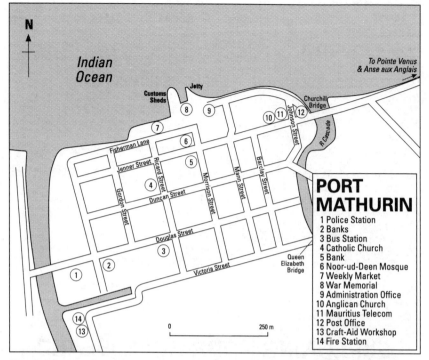

N

Indian Ocean

To Pointe Venus & Anse aux Anglais

Jetty

Customs Sheds

Churchill Bridge

Fisherman Lane

Jenner Street

Ricard Street

Gordon Street

Duncan Street

Douglas Street

Morrison Street

Mann Street

Barclay Street

Johnson Street

R. Cascade

Victoria Street

Queen Elizabeth Bridge

0   250 m

PORT MATHURIN

1 Police Station
2 Banks
3 Bus Station
4 Catholic Church
5 Bank
6 Noor-ud-Deen Mosque
7 Weekly Market
8 War Memorial
9 Administration Office
10 Anglican Church
11 Mauritius Telecom
12 Post Office
13 Craft-Aid Workshop
14 Fire Station

Rodrigues. Thousands of **noddies, fairy terns** and other seabirds breed on these island reserves, 7 miles (11 km) from Port Mathurin, making them, in particular, a magnet for bird-watchers. Sail there by pirogue from Oyster Bay or take the one-hour boat ride from Baie du Nord, which is closer to the islands. The Ebony Mourouk hotel can organise the full-day trip and the permits necessary to visit (tel 831-3350).

Caves

Caverne Patate is the most intriguing of the island's 25 known caves. It's in the south-west coral plain at Butte l' Herbe and has some weird and wonderful natural formations along its 1,094 yard (1 km) length, with such fanciful names as the Great Wall of China, Winston Churchill's Head, King Kong, the Dragon, Lion, and the Buddha. It's advisable to hire the services of a guide. If it has rained for 24 hours it's not possible to visit until the water inside subsides. This can take a week. Over the past two centuries the cave has yielded calcined bones of the extinct solitaire, the dodo of Rodrigues.

Coral Cutting

Near the cavern is the **Carrière de Corail** where you can watch men laboriously sawing coral building bricks by hand in an open quarry. They pay the state one rupee for each brick they cut and sell them for 10 rupees (25p) each. One man can cut 10 bricks a day. You can also buy crudely carved coral figurines, ashtrays and other mementoes here.

BEACHES

Without doubt the main attraction is the vast **lagoon** around the island, 81 sq miles (210 sq km) of beautiful, warm, limpid water of colours that would make an old Hollywood movie-maker salivate. To protect the surrounding coral water-skiing is not allowed in the lagoon, but every other kind of water sport and activity is possible. One picture postcard place that shouldn't be missed along the lagoon is **Trou d'Argent**, a cove bounded by high rocks sheltering a small white beach lapped by water of an unbelievable aquamarine. You can walk down to this beach or go by boat with a fisherman. Further north is **Pointe Coton** which locals say is the best beach in Rodrigues. Residents of the hotel managed by Air Mauritius there have easy access to this heavenly stretch, but it's open to all, as is every other beach on the island. Each of the many inlets and coves around the island has its own particular appeal, but **Anse aux Anglais** ('Bay of the English') is a pretty spot not far from the capital that also has interesting historical associations. This is where, in 1761, a squadron of British men o' war anchored and took the island from the French. They waited here some months for the troop reinforcements required to attack Mauritius. They sailed away when these failed to arrive.

Treasure

One of the island's best known legends about buried pirate's treasure pinpoints **Anse aux Anglais** inlet as the spot where gold pieces and precious gems still lie awaiting discovery. Treasure hunting was an obsession with a local magistrate, who studied plans and documents at the British Museum to discover what special signs were used by pirates. He decided Anse aux Anglais was just the place pirates would have chosen to bury treasure and started to look for such signs. He found some marks carved on a rock, which led to other clues. In 1913 the magistrate made a mistake he was to regret all his days. He told his assistants to keep digging while he was away on business. They found a large stone with an arrow carved on it and removed it for safety. Unfortunately when the magistrate returned no one could remember exactly where the stone came from. He spent the rest of his tour of duty digging all over the sandy flat – without success.

Tour operators will take you on an excursion to islets **Hermitage** and **Ile aux Chats**, on one of which infamous buccaneer Laurent Lemoine is believed to have buried his booty while escaping from pursuing British. He was never able to return to Rodrigues, and when he was dying reportedly gave someone a plan of the place where his treasure was hidden. This, however, was so complicated it was virtually indecipherable and locals are still wondering whether the treasure still lies there on one of these lovely islands.

Seychelles

La Digue

GEOGRAPHY

The main Seychelles islands are granitic fragments of the ancient mega-mass now referred to as Pangaea, which stretched from Pole to Pole, and embraced all of today's continents. Geologists believe that this land mass was torn apart to form a northern land mass, Laurasia, and the southern super-continent of Gondwanaland. Aeons ago there was a seminal re-shaping of the planet when Gondwanaland burst apart to form Africa, Madagascar, South America, India and Antarctica. The Indian Ocean was another result of this upheaval and the islands were thrust up from its depths by grinding plates and fissures in the earth's crust. Why is this important? Well, it explains the strange existence of granitic islands in the middle of an ocean where most others have grown on coral. Seychelles is unique in being the only mid-ocean group in the world formed from this ancient rock. On Praslin, the second largest island, the granite is often reddish-grey or pink in colour because of coloured alkali feldspars in its composition.

The 115 islands that make up the Republic of Seychelles are tucked away in the ocean, 684 miles (1,100 km) from the northern tip of Madagascar, 994 miles (1,600 km) from the east African mainland and 2,051 miles (3,300 km) south-west of the toe of India, hence Seychelles' favourite advertising slogan: 'A thousand miles from anywhere.' The Seychelles islands are scattered like granite and coralline stepping stones across 517,374 sq miles (1,340,000 sq km) of ocean, but with a total land mass of only 176 sq miles (455 sq km), three-quarters the size of the Isle of Man, or just over 2½ times the area of Washington DC. The islands have a total coastline of 305 miles (491 km). Little more than 17 miles (27 km) long and 3-5 miles (5-8 km) wide, main island Mahé is a paradise of sandy beaches and palm-fringed coves, with rugged granite peaks rising nearly 3,000 ft (900 m) and luxuriant forests.

The inner islands of the Mahé group are all steeply granitic, reaching their highest point on Mahé at Morne Seychellois at 2,970 ft (905 m), and rise from an anchoring base on an ancient submerged land mass. This underwater bank is 13,000 sq miles (33,670 sq km) in extent and holds in its shallow depths a realm astonishingly rich in marine life. The outlying islands are groups of low-lying coral islands. The atolls and island groups of Aldabra – the biggest atoll in the world – Farquhar, and Desroches, stretch away into the south-western expanse of the Indian Ocean. After principal island Mahé, the most popular with tourists are Praslin, La Digue, Bird, Frégate, Silhouette, and Desroches. All the granite islands are less than 40 miles (65 km) from Mahé.

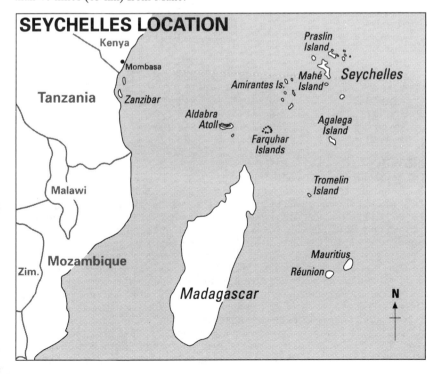

SEYCHELLES LOCATION

CLIMATE

Being fairly close to the equator the islands are blessed with a warm, tropical climate and most of the time the seasons are indistinguishable. Temperatures vary between 79°F (26°C) to 84°F (29°C) throughout the year. There is a mean maximum temperature of 86°F (30° C) and a mean minimum temperature of 76°F (24.5° C). The dry season is from May to September when the south-east monsoon blows and it is fairly hot. Although often promoted in the northern hemisphere as a winter destination Seychelles are at their wettest between December and February, during the north-west monsoon. Average rainfall on main island Mahé is about 93 inches (236 cm) a year and at times this has reached as much as 140 inches (356 cm). The rain can pour down even in the so-called drier months, but these downpours don't usually last long. The north-west monsoon blows between October and April and high humidity is the norm, but at least the sea is calm. The islands lie outside the Indian Ocean cyclone belt, so you don't have to worry about battening down the hatches.

Even though Seychelles is generally a good all year round destination, there are naturally times which are better for certain activities. Scuba divers, for instance, will find April, May, October and November offer the best visibility and calmest seas. For birdwatchers, April heralds the start of the breeding season and seabirds flock to the islands from May to September, before migrating between September and December. Hiking and walking are best from May to September because of the drier conditions, lower temperatures and lower humidity.

Temperatures	Minimum	Maximum
January	75°F (24°C)	86°F (30°C)
February	77°F (25°C)	86°F (30°C)
March	77°F (25°C)	88°F (31°C)
April	77°F (25°C)	88°F (31°C)
May	77°F (25°C)	86°F (30°C)
June	77°F (25°C)	85°F (29°C)
July	75°F (24°C)	82°F (28°C)
August	75°F (24°C)	82°F (28°C)
September	75°F (24°C)	84°F (29°C)
October	75°F (24°C	84°F (29°C
November	75°F (24°C)	86°F (30°C)
December	75°F (24°C)	75°F (24°C)

HISTORY

The Seychelles archipelago lies in that part of the ocean between the equator and the Tropic of Capricorn known to old Arab seamen as *Bahr-el-Zanj*, or the Sea of the Blacks, and to the ancient Greek chroniclers as the *Erythraean*, or Negro Sea. It's likely, therefore, that Arab *nahodas* or dhow masters, first spotted or landed on the then uninhabited islands, but as they obviously preferred trade to cartographic immortality we can't be sure. It is also possible that Arab merchants knew that some of the islands were the source of the rare and valuable coco-de-mer ('nut of the sea') and came here to collect them, keeping the location secret so that they could sell them at inflated prices to potentates who thought they were the last word in aphrodisiacs. We must look to European explorers, with their urge to map and name everything, for the first recorded arrivals. What is regarded as the first representation of Seychelles on a chart appears on the Cantino Planisphere of 1502, but as navigators in those days couldn't determine longitude, places tended to be given a succession of different names. A famous sailing instruction of the time advised mariners to 'sail south till the butter melts.' Portuguese admiral Vasco da

Gama sailed through a scattered group of islands in 1503 and they were named the Almirantes ('Islands of the Admiral') in his honour. In 1506, another Portuguese navigator sighted the islands, and they appeared regularly on maritime charts after this date as the Seven Brothers, or Sisters.

In January 1609, factor John Jourdain, a passenger on the British East India Company vessel *Ascension*, was the first Englishman to set foot on the islands now called North and Silhouette. He wrote in his journal that crew members who went ashore to scavenge provisions 'brought so many tortells as they could carrie. The tortells were good meate, as good as fresh beefe, but after twoe or three meals our men would not eate them, because they did not looke so uglie before they were boyled.' Jordain said he noted 'no signe of any people that ever had bene there.' The ship's bosun was first to describe the islands as 'an earthly Paradise.' Shore parties from his ship saw 'many coker nutts, both ripe and greene, of all sorts, and much fishe and fowle and tortells and manye scates with other fishe.' The isolation of the islands made them perfect places for the buccaneers and corsairs scouring the Indian Ocean during the 17th and 18th centuries in search of ships to plunder. They used the islands to careen and provision their vessels and today many Seychellois will tell you that untold treasure from those days still lies hidden in the archipelago, particularly on Mahé, somewhere in the vicinity of Bel Ombre. British and French warships finally hunted the pirates down in the 18th century and put an end to their reign of terror in the area.

French Colonisation

In 1742, Frenchman Lazare Picault landed on Mahé at Anse Boileau (not Baie Lazare, which now bears his name) and was so impressed with the island that he named it Ile d'Abondance ('Island of Plenty'). He left four days later after stocking his ship with 600 coconuts and some giant tortoises. Picault was sent back two years later to make a more detailed survey and changed the island's name to Mahé, presumably to flatter Mauritian governor Mahé de Labourdonnais, who sent him there. By then the French realised that their war with Britain would probably spread to the Indian Ocean, and that the islands would then be of great strategic important, but it was left to Irish sea captain Corneille Morphey to officially claim Mahé and its seven easterly islands for Louis XV of France by laying a 'Stone of Possession' on 9 November 1756. The stone, which was set above the entrance to the port, is now in the National Museum in Victoria. The group then underwent another name change, this time to honour Vicomte Jean Moreau de Séchelles, the monarch's minister of finance at the time. In 1768, the French also claimed Praslin and named it after the Duke of Praslin; La Digue and Curieuse which were named after ships exploring the islands at the time under Captain Dufresne. Praslin was so beautiful that in later years it moved visiting Charles ('Chinese') Gordon, then a colonel in charge of troops on Mauritius, to opine that it had to be a relic of a long-lost continent on which the biblical Garden of Eden was once to be found. Gordon decided it was the famed garden and that the forbidden fruit was the strange coco-de-mer. He wrote in 1881: 'I think any requirement is fulfilled for deciding that the site of the district of Eden is near Seychelles.' Gordon, so the apocryphal story goes, was wandering through the luxuriant Vallée de Mai on Praslin when he met a member of the island's Adam family. Gordon asked him his name. 'Adam' replied the fisherman. That clinched it for Gordon. Years later one of Adams' descendants, noted for his fish curry, entertained Ronald Reagan at his seaside shack. The future US president signed a book for Adam, writing 'Name: Ronald Reagan. Profession: Politician. Point of Embarkation: Oblivion. Destination: Unknown.'

Colonists started arriving from Mauritius in 1770 and, after trying out various islands, settled on Mahé. By 1774, there were nearly 1,000 slaves at work collecting coconuts, turtles, tortoises and bird guano for fertiliser. When the French Revolution began there were 69 French colonists, 32 freed slaves, and 487 slaves living in the Seychelles. In 1790, they declared independence from Ile de France (Mauritius) and laid claim to the entire island group. Their independence did not last long. In 1794, the French sent in Captain Queau de Quinssy to put an end to dissension, which he did. As governor he became something of a joke, in turn striking the French standard and running up the British flag on at least eight occasions between 1794 and 1811 as he capitulated each time to attacking ships of the Royal Navy.

British Rule and Independence

When the Treaty of Paris was signed in 1814, British sovereignty over the Seychelles was confirmed and De Quinssy was invited to stay on in service of the British monarch. This he did until he died 1827. He is buried in the grounds of the present State House. The British Government abolished slavery in 1835 and more than 6,500 slaves were freed. In 1903, Seychelles became a Crown Colony in its own right and the British governor celebrated the event by erecting the quaint Victoria clock tower, modelled on the one standing outside Victoria railway station in London, which still proudly dominates the town centre. Electricity lit up Victoria for the first time in 1923, and 11 years later the currency was officially changed to the Seychelles rupee (SR). The airport opened on Mahé in 1971, breaking the age-old dependency on sea links, and within five years Seychelles had become an independent republic within the British Commonwealth.

POLITICS

The Seychelles is an independent republic and a relative latecomer to democracy. The seat of government is in the capital Victoria, on Mahé. The president holds executive power, and legislation is in the hands of the 35-member National Assembly. France Albert René is the current president and governs with a Cabinet, or Council of Ministers. Political parties emerge, merge, or disappear like shifting sands, but the ones that are established in the political scene are the ruling Seychelles People's Progressive Front (SPPF), Democratic Party (DP), and the United Opposition (UO) which is a coalition of the Parti Seselwa (PS), Seychelles Democratic Movement (MSPD), and the Seychelles Liberal Party (SLP). There's also a new New Democratic Party (NDP), a 1995 breakaway from the original NDP of 1992.

Political History

The two world wars of the 20th century had little impact on Seychelles except in economic terms, but as in other parts of Britain's colonial empire they heralded political change. As early as the 1940s the Association of Seychelles Taxpayers had protested against Britain's control and management of the islands and following World War Two Britain began to feel the first wind of change and, realising that self-rule in the Seychelles was inevitable, began the process of political change. Seychellois involvement in their own political affairs began to gather momentum in 1948 when Britain granted the vote to some 2,000 adult male property owners, who then elected four members of the governor's advisory Legislative Council. They represented local landed gentry – known colloquially as the *grands blancs* ('great whites') – and spent their time defending their interest in crop marketing and other agricultural issues. They were the principal political force until the early 1960s, when representatives of the small but vocal new urban professional and middle class began to challenge their political monopoly.

In 1964, the Seychelles Democratic Party (SDP), led by James Mancham, and the Seychelles People's United Party (SPUP), led by France Albert René, were founded. Mancham's SDP favoured continued close ties with Britain, whereas René's left-wing SPUP campaigned for total autonomy. Both men were London-educated lawyers who had returned to the islands pledging to improve conditions for Seychellois and to develop popular based local politics. Pressure for independence intensified in 1965 after Britain separated Desroches, the Aldabra and Farquhar island groups from Seychelles and made them part of the British Indian Ocean Territory. In 1967, Britain extended universal suffrage to the colony and established a governing council to run it, the majority of whose members were for the first time elected. That year nearly 18,000 Seychellois voted, and the SDP emerged in control of the council. In 1970, the council became a 15-member Legislative Assembly and Seychellois were given the responsibility of administering all but external affairs, internal security, the civil service, and the government's broadcasting service and newspaper. In the elections for the Assembly the SDP won 10 seats, and the SPUP won five. James Mancham became Chief Minister and Albert René the leader of the official Opposition. The next elections in 1974 were won by the SDP, which took 13 of the 15 seats with only 52.4% of the vote, lending credibility to SPUP charges that results had been rigged. Relations between the two parties, already personalised and bitter, worsened steadily after this. Seychelles achieved internal self-government the following year and the National Assembly then voted for independence. Despite their differences, Mancham and René formed a coalition to lead Seychelles to independence, and a year later, Britain granted the colony complete independence. On June 29 1976, the Republic of Seychelles became a sovereign nation, with Mancham as president and René as prime minister.

As a gesture of its goodwill Britain returned Desroches, the Aldabra and Farquhar islands to Seychelles and made a series of hefty grants to smooth the transition to an independent economy. Both political parties agreed to support the coalition government until elections were held in 1979, but in a shock move on 5 June 1977, René's party, renamed the Seychelles People's Progressive Front (SPPF), staged an armed coup – now celebrated as Liberation Day – that ousted Mancham while he was attending a Commonwealth conference. Soon after this René declared a Marxist one-party state and added the defence and tourism portfolios to his presidential responsibilities. He launched a programme of extensive nationalisation of enterprise including hotels and industries, and established a 1,000-strong paramilitary National Guard allegedly to strengthen the country's defence. The decision to turn the nation into a one-party state based on socialist ideology, as well as nationalisation initiatives, created bitterness, especially among the upper and middle classes. Censorship of the media and control over public expression were also unpopular, and there were a number of attempts to oust René's increasingly authoritarian government between 1978 and 1987. The most serious of these attempts was in 1981, when a group of 50 mercenaries recruited in South Africa and led by Congo veteran Colonel 'Mad Mike' Hoare landed in Mahé. Their weapons were discovered at the airport and they escaped by hijacking an Air India airliner, leaving five of their fellow conspirators behind. Other plots were subsequently uncovered, but in 1984 René was returned unopposed for a second five-year term as president. As a result of political problems and the lack of adequate attention to the islands' infrastructure the tourism industry had started to experience difficulties.

These problems really began with the opening of an international airport on the east coast of Mahé in 1971. The end of the island's relative isolation triggered tourism and concomitant booms in foreign capital investment and the domestic construction industry. The economy then changed over a few years from its traditional fishing and agricultural base to an economy where services accounted for the major portion of employment and gross domestic product. The two parties of the day had differed on the ways to manage the growing tourism industry. The SPUP favoured controlling its growth, whereas the SDP wanted to stimulate rapid tourism growth and to establish the islands as an international offshore financial centre. In view of this it is somewhat ironic today that a government under René has embraced the principles he formerly opposed, especially the capitalist oriented drive to promote Seychelles as a serious financial and business hub. Offshore banking and business has taken off since enabling legislation was enacted during 1994.

René's third term as president began in 1989 but did not reach full term. The crunch for Marxist Seychelles came with the collapse of communism in Eastern Europe. This resulted in the loss of powerful support and in November 1991, at a Commonwealth conference in Zimbabwe, Third World members made it clear to René that his island nation was becoming even more isolated. The Gulf War then brought an alarming drop in the number of foreign tourists, causing the fragile economy to stutter. Faced with political change in the Soviet Union and the eastern bloc countries and an evident swing in Africa to multi-party democracy René had to do some fancy footwork. Other factors which forced his political tap-dance away from one-party rule included indications by Britain and France that they would tie all future aid to democratic progress on the political front. In December 1991, René stunned his party by announcing that Seychelles would return to multi-party democracy. René told the party faithful that from January 1992, political groupings of at least 100 members would be permitted to register and that multi-party elections for a commission to participate in drafting a new constitution would be held within six months.

In April 1992, former president Sir James Mancham, returned from Britain to lead the New Democratic Party (NDP), now more commonly called the DP, and six additional parties were also registered. In September 1992 the government ended the 11-year state of emergency it had declared after the 1981 mercenary-led attempted coup. A draft Constitution was submitted for popular referendum in November 1992 but failed to get the necessary support for adoption. The Catholic Church strongly objected to the proposed legalisation of abortion. A period of unsavoury wrangling ended with an unprecedented alliance between Mancham and René and negotiations resumed on a new draft. Proceedings were conducted more openly this time, and live debate was allowed by the government. A new Constitution was finally accepted by referendum in June, 1993. They emphasised human rights and the separation of executive, legislative, and judicial powers. The presidency was again limited to three terms of five years each. The Constitution provided for a leader of the opposition to be elected by the National Assembly. The assembly consisted of 33 members, 22 of them elected and 11 designated by proportional representation. Probably helped by his political and economic volte-face René was again elected Seychelles president with 60% of the votes cast in the election. Mancham received 37% of the votes and a coalition of the smaller parties took the rest. Of the elective seats for the national Assembly the SPPF won 21 and the NDP one. Of the total 33 seats in the Assembly, 27 went to the SPPF, five to the NDP, and one to the coalition of parties. Liberalisation of the political system and the heavily state-controlled economy continued throughout the 1990s. René won another five-year term as president in the March 1998 elections, when his SPPF won 30 out of 35 seats in the enlarged National Assembly with 66.7% of all votes cast. When the United Opposition (UO) party drew more support (27%) than Mancham's DP (12%) the veteran politician withdrew from active political life. René has seemed at times uncomfortable with the democracy he unleashed, especially the increase in public criticism of various government policies and a perception that in spite of their being in the majority the Kreols lack a significant voice in the white-dominated political life of the islands.

THE ECONOMY

The Seychelles has a mixed economy with tourism, agriculture, and industrial fishing as its mainstays. The tourism industry is the most important economic sector, contributing an estimated 20% of gross domestic product (GDP) and a whopping 70% of the island's total foreign exchange earnings.

Tourism

In spite of being the golden goose, the government curbs the number of visitors to around 140 000 a year to minimise environmental damage and prevent overcrowding of the islands. Most visitors to Seychelles come from Europe – France, Britain, Germany, Italy and Ireland – and about 85% of these are holidaymakers who stay an average of 9.7 nights. There are about 4,500 beds in the country, with an overall room occupancy rate of around 65%. Most sectors of the local economy are tourism related, especially agriculture. Strong growth in the tourism industry since independence in 1976 has helped to push per capita GNP in the archipelago to well above its old near-subsistence level, and in recent years the government has encouraged foreign investment in order to upgrade and increase hotels and the availability of other tourism services. It has done this while endeavouring to reduce its heavy dependence on tourism by promoting the development of farming, fishing and small-scale manufacturing. This seemingly schizoid approach is the result of the tourist sector's vulnerability, which was devastatingly illustrated by a shock drop in arrivals during the Gulf War. The industry took more than five years to recover from this setback. The country's financial situation subsequently deteriorated again through fiscal deficits financed in the main by domestic borrowings and a drawing on reserves which put a severe crimp in its foreign exchange holdings. The government is still committed to the upgrading of tourism facilities to meet the growing challenges of international competition, but the final decade of the last century was characterised by a gradual withdrawal of the government from the tourism sector and increased incentives for private sector initiatives and investments in all areas of its development.

Agriculture

Farmers have a tough time as there is not much fresh water and a mere thousand acres of arable land for crops, and half of this has poor or low-nutrient soil. Weather patterns also restrict the type of crops that can be raised. The sector remains strategic because it not only provides food for the local population, but is a key link in supplying tourist hotels, restaurants, and other services with food. Products and produce to support the tourism industry include tea, tropical fruits, coconuts, cinnamon, vanilla, sweet potatoes, tapioca, bananas, vegetables, beef, poultry and pork. Other foodstuffs, including rice, are imported. The government is trying to reduce the food imports used mainly by the tourism industry and trying to ginger local production. To do this it has exempted farmers from income tax, as well as reducing import taxes and duties on their agricultural equipment and fertilisers.

Fishing

As a result of its vast territorial waters Seychelles has an exceptionally large Exclusive Economic Zone, which has helped to make it a world leader in the trans-shipment of tuna and fish products. Significant income is generated through the licensing of foreign fishing vessels and by supplies and services to these fleets. Indian Ocean Tuna (a majority share of which belongs to Heinz International) processes more than 110 tons a day, giving Seychelles its largest single export. Almost all commercial fishing activity is centred on the harbour at Victoria.

Manufacturing

This is the largest industrial sector, producing mainly soft goods, foodstuffs, tea, coffee, UHT milk, fruit juices, coconut cream, animal feed, tobacco, beer, paints, detergents, plastics and handicrafts for sale to tourists. These are also joint foreign investment ventures in television set assembly. Despite government efforts to promote manufacturing, the sector remains small. Lack of human and natural resources, relatively high wages, remoteness from major import and export markets, and stringent environmental regulations are among the curbs to the further development of manufacturing. Seychelles has a hefty trade imbalance with principal trading partners Britain, France and South Africa. Exports include fresh, frozen and canned fish, tea, vanilla, cinnamon, copra, and guano. The main imports are manufactured goods, food, petroleum products, tobacco, beverages, machinery and transportation equipment.

Investment

Privatisation has been promoted with a view to increasing foreign and domestic investment in the country. The private sector employs 48.2 per cent of the labour force. Privatisation has notably taken place in tourism, fish processing, and agriculture. In tandem with this privatisation, the government has also moved to create a business environment favourable for domestic and foreign investment. Privatisation has changed the sectoral face of employment. In the parastatal sector employment has decreased by more than 20%, while employment in the private sector has increased in recent years to nearly half the total work force. As recently as 1996, 6.5 per cent of the Seychellois labour force worked in agriculture, 16.9 per cent in manufacturing and construction, 14.1 per cent in hotels and restaurants, 11.8 per cent in transport, distribution and communications, and 50.7 in other services. The country has an unemployment rate of 10%, with 1,400 more job seekers swelling the figure every year. Only 400 people retire each year. The UN Human Development Index, an indicator of progress in human development which combines as indicators longevity, educational attainment, and standard of living, has ranked Seychelles, along with Mauritius, ahead of all other sub-Saharan countries in Africa. The 1997 index listed Seychelles 54th among 174 developed and developing nations.

Until the move to privatisation the government's economic policy was driven by socialist-oriented policies, with most enterprises state-controlled and about two-thirds of the labour force working for the government. In the early 1990s, in parallel with the move from a one-party state to a multi-party democracy, the government announced more market-oriented policies and a withdrawal of the government from direct economic activities. The government has shed its holdings in some of the largest manufacturing enterprises, although it still maintains significant interests in manufacturing and food industries, in the service sector, and retains a monopoly on the import of basic foodstuffs, largely through the Seychelles Marketing Board (SMB), which was established in 1985 to ensure a steady flow to consumers of essential commodities at stable prices. Seychelles has made progress in reducing poverty, but the World Bank still regards poverty levels as high for a country with the Seychelles' per capita income.

THE PEOPLE

French enough to have a natural *joie de vivre*, English enough to have an islander's reserve, Asian enough to possess a discreet charm, and African enough to have an exotic beauty and rhythm in their veins, the Seychellois people have blended the influences of their various origins into one potent Kreol concoction – that's how the people see themselves, according to their own tourist spin doctors. It certainly sums up an island race which has sprung up in only 200 years from an intermingling of settlers, slaves and traders. Originally a Creole was a white person born in one of France's overseas possessions in the Carribean or the Indian Ocean. Later the term came to mean, as it does in Seychelles, anyone born in the islands, as distinct from someone arriving from another country. There are today around 77,000 Seychellois, descendants in the main of British and French seamen, freed African slaves and Indian, Arab, and Chinese merchants. The first to settle in the latter part of the 18th century were the French, who brought with them or imported slaves from Madagascar and the African mainland. This trade in slaves continued into the 19th century, and some were still being smuggled into the islands even after 1835, when the British officially abolished slavery. Their numbers swelled in the 1860s when British naval anti-slaving patrols brought ashore liberated Africans, seized from Arab dhows. During the 19th century Indian and Chinese merchants began to settle and still dominate local business and trade. The main European influence is French, recognisable not only in the Kreol patois, but also in island culture and religion. The Asian contribution is its obvious impact on the island's cuisine and on its commerce. This mixture has produced an almost unparalled multicultural community, yet one that is harmoniously integrated and free from stress. Skin can be fair or dark, hair blonde or black, and eyes blue or brown, but all islanders have in common a general cheerfulness, and a refreshingly welcoming and helpful attitude to visitors, a hospitable streak that is matched only in the remote island community of Rodrigues, far to the south-east. Seychellois always have a welcome for you, and friends old and new are never turned away if they visit for a drink or chat. Verandas are the recognised centres of family and communal life and homes are always spick and span in readiness for any visitors that might drop by. Many live in old well-preserved colonial houses, although the original thatching of palm has in most cases given way to a more practical corrugated iron roof. House fronts usually overflow with flowers, often in brightly painted recycled tins. While their wives are busy cooking, or keeping the home clean and keeping up with the local gossip, the men are most likely out at sea fishing for the larder or to make some extra money.

For an agglomeration of peoples forged into a nation in a bare two centuries, the Seychellois have developed a lifestyle and culture which, unlike many others, is based not so much on the accumulation of material things, but on a laid-back approach to life. Most Seychellois believe life is to be enjoyed and to have a good time. Some visitors might regard this approach as indolence, but it is certainly something which, like the islands themselves, is unique. The islander's traditionally broad-minded approach to love and romance is legendary. US consul Thomas Prentice wrote complaining to Washington in 1878 about the large number of American sailors who jumped ship there, although he confessed that they could hardly be blamed. The Americans, who at that time had the biggest whaling fleet in the world, came to Seychelles to hunt the sperm whale, and their most popular port of call was Mahé, where they would often disappear with obliging island girls. The area of Victoria where the ruling regime has established a party museum once also boasted a well-known house of ill fame. It closed when customers realised that Seychellois gave freely what they were paying for.

In spite of their Catholicism, Seychellois family ties are, or were, rather loose, with not infrequent changes of partner. Couples usually married fairly late in life and this is said to have its roots in the time when slaves were not allowed to marry and any children born to them belonged to the slaves owner. These days, as in many parts of the world, a more practical reason why couples do not get married is the expense which, given the large and lavish receptions which are part of Seychellois tradition, can be ruinous. As not all that many couples actually tie the knot the woman is, in many cases, the head of the family. Often she is the one who alone raises and supports her children, with maybe a helping hand from the extended family. The number of births where no father acknowledges paternity of the child is recorded at a high 45%. Maybe they rely on the fact that health care and education are free and social benefits generous.

The islands have a youthful population, with more than 67% of the people under 30 years of age. Most of the people (88%) live on the main island of Mahé. Another 7% live on Praslin, and 4% on La Digue. All the other islands together have an area of less than 740 acres (300 ha) and support few or no inhabitants. The overall population density is about 1.5 people to the acre, or 165 to the sq km. There are slightly more women than men, and the average life expectancy is over 70 years.

Women

Political rights have been established, but violence against women is a recurring evil at all levels of society and is linked to social, religious, cultural and economic patterns and structures which have shaped island society. It stems essentially from a lack of mutual respect and tolerance and on island notions of male superiority. Gender-based violence against women and children is predominantly domestic. Although available statistics indicate a decrease in cases of violence, the full extent of the problem remains submerged and these statistics are, therefore, guesswork. The establishment of various governmental and non-governmental social agencies assist both parties involved in this degrading cycle, but the government realises that the most effective counter is education at school level, through the churches, and the mass media. Women themselves are being counselled that they can learn not to provoke domestic violence by behaving with modesty, dignity and confidence – an admonition that itself smacks of male condescension.

LANGUAGES

There are three official languages in the Seychelles: English, French and Kreol. Most Seychellois are fluent in all three, although their French is generally better than their English. What is commonly called Creole everywhere else in the Indian Ocean is now officially Kreol in Seychelles, and this is how it is spelt and taught to schoolchildren. Children are initially taught in Kreol, followed in later grades by English and French. A recently published Kreol dictionary replaces the French C and S with K and Z. In effect, Kreol is phonetic, with the odd linguistic twist. French words are given a harder pronunciation and syllables which are not pronounced are ignored altogether. You'll get the idea if you look at the following examples. You'll also note the differences between the Seychellois patois and, say, Mauritian Creole (see *Languages* page 26).

USEFUL WORDS AND PHRASES

English	Kreol
Good day, hello	Bonzour
Good evening	Bonswa
What is your name?	Ki mannyer ou apele?

My name is...	Mon apel...
Goodbye	Orevwar
How are you?	Comman sava/komman ou sava?
Very well, thank you	Byen mersi
I am well	Mon byen
Please	Sivouple
Thank you	Mersi
Today	Ozordi
Tomorrow	Demen
Come here	Vini
Over there	Laba
I	Mon
You	Ou
He, she	Li
They	Zot
What?	Kwa?/Ki?
Who?	Ki?/Lekel?
Where	Kote?
Where is...?	Ol i/cote ou...?
What does it cost?	Konbyen sa/konbyeni I vann?
Seychellois	Seselwa

The repetition of a word takes the place of 'very,' as in *dousman dousman* which means 'very slowly,' and *tiggin tiggin*, which means 'very little.' The Kreol equivalent of the English saying 'the older the fiddle, the sweeter the tune' is *Vye marmite i/fer bon/kari* ('an old pot makes good curry'). Interestingly, the word 'stress' does not exist in the Kreol vocabulary.

RELIGION

Although there is no state religion, most Seychellois are Christians, and more than 90% of the population is Catholic, with a small number of Anglicans (8%) and the remainder made up of Seventh Day Adventists, Pentecostal, Jehovah's Witnesses, Bahai, Muslims, Hindus and other minorities. Although sorcery was outlawed in 1958, belief in the supernatural and in *gris-gris*, the old spirits of Africa, co-exists with Christian belief. In this respect the religious life of the islanders reaches back far from the relatively recent influence of the dominant Catholic faith to a centuries-old voodoo-type magic. Its practitioners and adherents seem quite comfortable with both and often people will consult a *bonnom dibwa*, a local adept in the art, for love, luck, or revenge spells and potions, or to keep away evil spirits and *dandotia* ('zombies'). Seychellois, particularly the women, are avid churchgoers and consider going to a church service a social as well as a spiritual occasion.

NATIONAL ANTHEM AND FLAG

There have been three national flags since independence in 1976. The latest Seychelles flag with its five oblique bands of colour radiating from the hoist side was introduced on 18 June 1996 (National Day). The blue represents the sky and sea around Seychelles; yellow is for the sun; red symbolises the people, unity and love; the white band stands for social justice and harmony; and the green is the land and the natural environment. The new flag was adopted as a symbol of Seychelles' new era of democratisation and a return to a multi-party political system. The new flag is non-partisan and includes the colours of all the principal political parties in the country.

The new national anthem is entitled *Koste Seselwa* (Kreol for 'Come Together all Seychellois') and the words are:

With courage and discipline we have broken all barriers.
With the tiller in our hands, we will always remain brothers.
Never, never shall we cease struggling.
Death rather than to live in slavery!
Never, never shall we cease struggling.
Equality for all of us! Freedom for ever!

Chorus

Rise, free men!
Proud Seychellois, our doors are open.
Our path is traced,
Our sun has risen,
We will not turn back.
Rise, free men!
Rise, Seychellois!
Let us remain in unity and liberty.
With dignity we must cultivate our land,
With determination we must exploit our seas.
Let us for ever march together
To harvest all we have planted.
Let us for ever march together,
Fraternity in our hearts, to the future ahead of us.

FURTHER READING

Apart from the usual books on the Seychelles which you'll find in any well-stocked bookshop, you might like to pay a visit to your local library and see if they can rustle up any of the following early accounts: *More Tramps Abroad* by Mark Twain (1897); *Coconuts and Creoles* by JA Ozanne (1936); and *History of the Seychelles Islands* by JT Bradley (1940).

Also worth searching out are: *Forgotten Eden* by Atholl Thomas (Longman, London, 1968); *The Treasure Seeker's Treasury* by Roy Nevill (Hutchinson, London, 1978); *My World of Islands* by novelist Leslie Thomas (Michael Joseph, London, 1983); *The Seychelles Archipelago* by Claude Pavard (Richer/Hoa Qui, Paris, 1990); *Seychelles: Beyond the Reefs* by William Travis (Arrow Books, London, 1990); and *A Vision of Eden* by Marianne North (Royal Botanic Gardens, Kew, 4th ed. 1993).

For a really splendiferous photographic record that's more than just a coffee table adornment there's *Splendeur des Iles de L'Ocean Indien* by Claude Pavard (Oasis Productions, Sèvres, 1997), which as well as Seychelles also covers Madagascar, Mayotte, Comoros, Réunion, Mauritius and Rodrigues, and Zanzibar.

For foodies *Cuisine Seychelloise* by Eveline Mancham, mother of first president Sir James Mancham, is an interesting introduction to the food of the islands, but you'll probably find the book only in Seychelles. For curiosities from the world's humblest kitchens there's Huguette Couffignal's fascinating compilation *The People's Cookbook* (Pan Books, London, 1980).

For bookshops on Mahé try SPACE, Bookshop Division, Huteau Lane, Victoria (tel 22-4531); and Librairie Ste Fidèle, Olivier Maradam Street, Victoria. For other titles see *Maps and Guides* page 136.

SEYCHELLES: PRACTICAL INFORMATION

 **Getting There**

BY AIR

Seychelles might seem to some like a dot in a faraway ocean, but it's remarkably well served by airlines. In addition to national carrier Air Seychelles, you can get there by British Airways, Air France, Lufthansa (Condor), Emirates Airlines, and Kenya Airways. International gateways to this little archipelago include London, Paris, Frankfurt, Rome, Milan, Zurich, Dubai, Singapore, Nairobi, Mauritius, Réunion and Johannesburg. So far there is no direct commercial air service between the US and Seychelles and the best way to get to there from the US is via London, Paris, Rome or Frankfurt and then by Air Seychelles to Mahé. British Airways, Air France, and Lufthansa also have connecting flights. Flights from London airports cost from around £370-£500 (US$560-750) single or £620 (US$930) return per person, while British Airways operate flights from New York out of JFK and Newark via Gatwick for around $4,750 return, these prices are per person and before airport taxes and can also vary according to carrier and class of ticket. Air France offers particularly good fares if you buy your ticket in Europe. You could even combine your Seychelles holiday with an African safari in South Africa or Kenya, both of which have air connections with Mahé. British Airways flies London/Seychelles and London/Nairobi. A Nairobi/Seychelles hop on Air Seychelles completes a stop-over trip. Qantas flies from Australia to Singapore, from which Air Seychelles flies non-stop to Mahé. There are also air connections through Dubai. On services from Milan, Nairobi, Rome and Réunion Air Seychelles code shares with British Airways, Alitalia and Air Austral. Air Seychelles uses Islanders and De Havilland Twin Otters on inter-island routes.

Duration of non-stop flights to Seychelles:

London	10 hours	Zurich	9 hours
Paris	9^1/2hours	Singapore	7 hours
Rome	8 hours	Dubai	4 hours
Milan	8^1/2hours	Johannesburg	5 hours
Frankfurt	9^1/2 hours	Nairobi	3 hours

Getting to Seychelles will probably be your biggest expense. This has the effect of limiting tourist numbers, which makes the government happy as it is keen to protect the islands unique environment. During low season, January to July, and September to end of November, you might be able to get discounted fares from Air Seychelles, which also gives scuba divers an additional 22 lb (10 kg) luggage allowance for their gear. The normal allowance is 44 lb (20 kg). Try for a window seat when you fly, for some spectacular views as you arrive.

Seychelles International Airport is at Pointe Larue on Mahé, 6 miles (10 km), about 20 minutes, south-east of one of the smallest capitals in the world, Victoria. There's duty-free shopping, banking and currency exchange facilities, vehicle rental, restaurant, bar and lounge (open 8am until the last flight) at the airport. Remember that only foreign currency is accepted. Transport to all points on Mahé

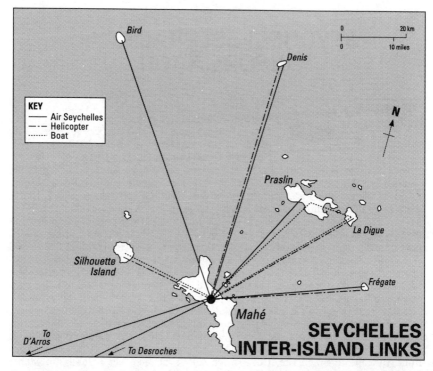

SEYCHELLES INTER-ISLAND LINKS

is available by coach and taxi. When you fly out again you will have to pay a departure tax of US$40 (£25), or its equivalent in hard currency. Children under 12 years are exempt. If you have any flight enquiries you can contact the airport on (tel 37-3001, fax 37-3222; for any onward inter-island reservations tel 38-4405).

AIRLINE OFFICES IN SEYCHELLES

Air Seychelles: Victoria House, Victoria, (tel 22-5300/38-1000, fax 22-5159/22-5933).
British Airways: Kingsgate House (tel 22-2111, fax 22-5596).
Air France: Kingsgate House (tel 32-2414).
Kenya Airways: tel 32-2989/32-2536.

AIR SEYCHELLES OFFICES AROUND THE WORLD

Britain: Premiere House 3, Betts Way, Crawley, West Sussex RH10 2GB (tel 01293-596655, fax 01293-596658).
France: 11 rue de Colisee, F-75008 Paris (tel 1-42 89 86 83, fax 1-45 63 85 12).
Germany: An Der Hauptwache 11, D-60313 Frankfurt/Main, Germany (tel 69-9139 5707, fax 69-9139 5612).
Italy: Viale Allesandro Magno, 282 Casa Palocco, I-00124 Rome (tel 6-509 8413, fax 6-509 1519).
Kenya: Archer's Tours & Travel, Lonrho House, Standard Street, PO Box 40097, Nairobi (tel 2-223131, fax 2-212656).
Singapore: 371 Beach Road, 18-00 Keypoint, Singapore 199597 (tel 395-5399, fax 297-0225, e-mail: info@airseychelles.com.sg).
South Africa: PO Box 2253, Edenvale 1610 (tel 011-453 0655, fax 011-453 0497).

Switzerland: Airpass AG, Flughostrasse 61, CH-8152 Glattbrug (tel 1-816 4524, fax 1-811 0271).

TOUR OPERATORS

A number of tour operators in **Britain** specialise in Seychelles, among them:

Art of Travel: 21 The Bakehouse, Bakery Place, 119 Attenburg Gardens, London SW11 1JQ (tel 020-7738 2038, fax 020-7738 1893).

Discover the World: 29 Nork Way, Banstead, Surrey SM7 1PB (tel 01737-218800, fax 01737-362341).

Distant Dreams: Garrard House, 2-6 Homesdale Road, Bromley, Kent BR2 9LZ (tel 020-8466 7950).

Hayes and Jarvis: Hayes House, 152 King Street, London W6 0QU (tel 020-8222 7800, fax 020-8741 0299).

Holidays for the Barefoot Traveller: 204 King Street, Hammersmith, London W6 0RA (tel 020-8741 4319, fax 020-8741 8657).

Premier Holidays: Westbrook, Milton Road, Cambridge, Cambridgeshire CB4 1YG (tel 01223-516677, fax 01223-516615, e-mail: premier@bptts.co.uk).

Scuba Safaris: PO Box 31, Tenterden, Kent TN30 7ZR (tel 01580-270910, fax 01580-270920).

Seychelles Travel: Suite 14c, Sunrise Business Park, Blandford, Dorset DT11 8ST (tel 01258-450983, fax 01258-450205).

Silhouette Travel: Phoenix House, 2 Upper Teddington Road, Kingston-upon-Thames, Surrey KT1 4DY (tel 0208-255 1738, fax 020-8255 5197, e-mail: lydialarue@aol.com).

Tropical Locations: Travel House, 42-44 Station Road, Harrow, Middlesex HA2 7SE (tel 020-8427 7300, fax 020-8427 7400).

Worldwide Journeys and Expeditions: 8 Comeragh Road, London W14 9HP (tel 020-7381 8638, fax 020-7381 0836).

World Dreams: 3rd Floor, Waterloo House, 11-17 Chertsey Road, Woking, Surrey GU1 5AB (tel 01483-730808, fax 01483-721919).

BY SEA

The days of leisurely pasenger liner voyages to the islands of the Indian Ocean are virtually over, but there are still a few other options open to you. For instance, three container ships of the CMBT Line sail every 2-3 weeks from Antwerp to Felixstowe, then on to Rouen, Montoir, Marseilles, and transit the Suez Canal to Victoria (Seychelles), St Denis (Réunion), Port Louis (Mauritius), and Toamasina (Madagascar). On the return leg the ships call at Mombasa, Port Said, Marseilles, Le Havre, and Dunkirk, arriving back in Antwerp after 60-day round trip. Each ship has only five cabins for passengers and you'll pay anything from £3,000 to £3,800 for the voyage, depending on the cabin and which legs you book.

While there are no scheduled passenger services, cruise liners such as Cunard, Princess, Royal Viking, Pearl, Royal Star, and Renaissance visit Seychelles periodically. Mahé Shipping Company in Victoria is the local agent for some of these cruise ship companies (tel 32-2100). Contact yacht clubs in your own country if you'd like to crew on a yacht and do the trip the long and hard way. If you're already in Seychelles looking for a return passage, try the Yacht Club in Victoria (tel 32-2362), or scout around the Marine Charter Association (tel 32-2126, fax 22-4679). Cargo ships still play an important role in supplying Seychelles. Nedloyd is one major shipping company that is exploring the possibility of using Seychelles for hub and spoke operations within the Indian Ocean region and it's worth contacting their offices or agent to see how these plans are shaping up.

TRAVEL SAFELY

Both the UK Foreign Office and the US State Department have travel information offices which provide regularly updated free advice on countries around the world (see page 24 for their contact details).

Red Tape

ENTRY REQUIREMENTS

PASSPORTS AND VISAS

Your passport should be valid for at least another six months. No visas are required; you receive a visitors' permit on arrival at the airport. This is valid for four weeks, and is subject to your being in possession of a return or forward ticket, pre-booked accommodation and sufficient funds to cover your planned stay. Extensions may be given by the immigration authority for an additional 200 rupees (£25) for up to three months, and 200 rupees (£25) for every three-month extension. For more information contact Immigration and Civil Status Division, PO Box 430, Independence House, Victoria, Mahé (tel 22-5333). If you arrive by yacht, the visitor's permit issued to you will be valid for two weeks, but you can easily get an extension.

From November 1999, all visitors to Seychelles were supposed to buy an obligatory Gold Card for US$ 100 (£62), issued by tour operators or purchased on arrival. The stated purpose was to promote the natural attractions of Seychelles and to enhance the country's position in the world as an ecologically sustainable tourist destination. The tourist authorities said Gold Card holders would not have to pay the airport departure tax and said once the card was purchased it would be valid for the life of the holder. This heavy government imposition, however, next became optional when there was a worldwide tourism industry backlash. The industry, while supportive of the government's stated ideals, was suspicious that the extra revenue it raised might be used for things other than environmental protection. The Association of British Travel Agents, for one, told the Seychelles government that while the environment deserved to be protected the tax was too high, even though an incentive was that Gold Card holders also received free admission to national parks. Although other countries, such as Kenya, add a couple of pounds sterling a week to the hotel bills of tourists to help preserve the coastal environment, the Seychelles was the first country to try to specifically tax tourists to limit both visitor numbers and protect its natural heritage. It seemed to many that what was happening was that an historically leftist government was, in fact, simply intent on soaking capitalist visitors. As a result of the flak the planned tax attracted, the Gold Card has been quietly dropped. Tourism is growing at about 10% a year and the government wants to push the Seychelles more up-market to keep this growth manageable and keep the foreign exchange flowing. Some 140,000 tourists visit the Seychelles every year, mostly from Europe, with UK visitors totalling 20,000. The government says it plans to place a ceiling of 180,000 a year on arrivals to protect the island's as yet unspoilt beaches and unpolluted waters, but current extensive hotel developments could see this protective policy observed more in the breach than in the observance.

HEALTH DOCUMENTS

You don't need any vaccination certificates for Seychelles, provided you have not come from any infected area. If you aim to combine your Seychelles holiday with a stopover in Africa on the way then you should consult your doctor about this. Malaria precautions are then advisable and yellow fever vaccination certificates are required if you arrive in Seychelles from an infected area. The island is free from tropical diseases, but it is advisable to keep your tetanus and polio immunisations up to date. Ask the advice of your doctor before leaving home.

CUSTOMS REGULATIONS

You are not allowed to take firearms, including air pistols and rifles, harpoons and spearfishing equipment, and non-prescription drugs into Seychelles. The import of fruits and vegetables is also prohibited. Pet animals must undergo a minimum quarantine period for six months and can only be imported with written permission of the Chief Veterinary Officer. Generous duty and tax-free allowances are made on items you bring in for personal use. You are allowed 200 cigarettes, or 50 cigars, or 250g tobacco; a litre of spirits and a litre of wine; 125ml of perfume and 250ml of toilet water; and other normally dutiable goods worth up to SR1,000 (£125). Video tapes must be declared but might be confiscated for security reasons. The import of food and other agricultural produce is strictly controlled and subject to licensing.

It is illegal to take any marine animals through customs listed as endangered, including all sea turtles, giant clams, hard corals and black corals. You can help by not buying any jewellery, trinkets, or souvenirs using turtleshell or corals. The law does not cover all the animals and species at risk, because the distribution of many shells and other reef-dwelling creatures in Seychelles is not yet adequately known, but the authorities fully recognise international concern over the exploitation of endangered species and regulate the import and export of threatened marine life in terms of the Convention on International Trade in Endangered Species (CITES). If you want to take home any of the famous coco-de-mer nuts as a souvenir, you must have the proper export certificate. Check with vendors before you buy, as they must supply it.

SEYCHELLES EMBASSIES, CONSULATES AND HIGH COMMISSIONS ABROAD

Austria: Gusshausstrasse 12, A-1040 Vienna (tel 1-505 3215, fax 1-505 1373, e-mail: pisec@pisecgmbh.co.at).

Australia: 23 Marri Crescent, Les Murdie, Perth, Western Australia 6076 (tel 8-9291 6570, fax 8-9291 9154).

Britain: High Commission for the Republic of the Seychelles, 2nd Floor, Eros House, 111 Baker Street, London W1M 1FE (tel 020-7224 1660, fax 020-7487 5756, e-mail sey.ltclon@aol.com).

Canada: 67 Rue St Catherine Ouest, Montreal, Quebec H2X 1Z7 (tel 514-284 3322, fax 514-845 0631, e-mail: Vuesda@cam.org).

Denmark: Solbakken 27, DK-2840 Holte (tel 4242-3079, fax 4566-0899, e-mail: hs@kil.dk).

France: 51 Avenue Mozart, F-75016 Paris (tel 1-42 30 57 47, fax 1-42 30 57 40, e-mail: ambsey@aol.com).

Germany: Oeder Weg 43, D-60318 Frankfurt (tel 69-598262, fax 69-597 0166, e-mail: seychelcon@aol.com).

Italy: Via Francesco Saverio Benucci 9, I-00149 Rome (tel 6-678 0530, fax 6-679 4583).

Madagascar: PO Box 3616, Immeuble SMIDE, Ankorondrano, Antananarivo (tel 226-4203, fax 226-4204, e-mail: comar@bow.dts.mg).

Mauritius: 616 St James Court, St Denis Street, Port Louis (tel 251-0013, fax 238-4526, e-mail: gfok@intnet.mu).

Netherlands: Oud Bussummerweg 44, 1272 PW Huizen (tel 35-694 0904, fax 35-694 9809).

South Africa: 55 Mandeville Road, Bryanston 2021, Johannesburg (tel 11-463 7010, fax 11-462 6110); the High Commission is at 939 Schoeman Street,

Arcadia 0083, Pretoria (tel 12-342 0534, fax 12-342 0362, e-mail: mwhicom@iafrica.com).

USA: Embassy of the Republic of the Seychelles, Suite 400C, 800 2nd Avenue, New York, NY 10017 (tel 212-972 1785, fax 212-972 1786, e-mail: seychelles@un.int).

GETTING MARRIED

Seychelles has become such a popular honeymoon destination that the government even puts out an advisory for anyone whose thoughts turn to marriage while in the islands. In effect, you can get married 11 days after you've found, or brought, a partner. Formalities are few. To get married both parties must be over 18 and they need to have been in Seychelles at least a day before the ceremony, provided the necessary documents have been lodged with the registrar at least 11 days before the wedding date. Civil ceremonies are performed on Mahé, Praslin and La Digue, usually at hotels, between 2pm and 5pm Monday to Friday, except on public holidays. Religious ceremonies are not recognised by the government, but there's no reason on why they cannot be performed after the civil ceremony. For details of churches, contact the Seychelles Tourist Office in London (tel 020-7224-1670). Wedding arrangements are best made through tour operators who co-ordinate them with the hotel and the authorities. To make your own arrangements takes at least two months' advance notice for documents to be prepared and hotel arrangements confirmed. Wedding packages are offered by many hotels and resorts and include, in one convenient fee, all legal processing and handling costs, the registrar's fee and dressing and decoration of the area to be used for the ceremony. On La Digue, decorated ox-carts can be hired for the wedding party. Special tour operator and hotel honeymoon offers range from room upgrades and free dinners to free air flights. So if you're thinking of tying the knot while on holiday contact the Senior Officer at the Civil Status Office, PO Box 430, Victoria, Mahé, and send photocopies of birth certificates, and if applicable, divorce papers (decree absolute), and if widowed previous marriage certificate and death certificate, legal proof if your name has been changed by deed poll and copies of all relevant pages of each party's valid passport. The Civil Status Office is open for business between 8am to noon and 1pm to 4pm Monday to Friday (tel 22-4030, fax 22-5474).

WHAT MONEY TO TAKE

Seychelles can be expensive like out-of-the-way islands everywhere, but that's the price you pay for taking a holiday in paradise. Take your money in sterling or US dollar travellers' cheques. Apart from the safety factor, you get a better rate of exchange. Currency exchange receipts should be kept so that you can re-exchange money on departure. Travellers cheques are widely accepted in all major currencies and rates of exchange are published in the daily newspapers or you can find out what they are at your hotel or at the local bank.

MONEY IN SEYCHELLES

The basic currency of the Seychelles is the Seychelles Rupee (SR), which is divided into 100 cents. Notes come in 10, 25, 50, and 100 rupee denominations and in SR5 and SR1 coins. The smaller stuff comes in 1, 5, 10, and 25 cent coins. You can take in as much foreign currency as you like, but you are not allowed to take out more than 100 rupees in notes and 10 rupees in coins when you leave. Anything over this should be changed at the airport bank, or it could be confiscated.

Exchange Rates

These fluctuate, but it has been around 8 rupees to the pound and 5 rupees to the US dollar for quite some time. If you have access to the internet www.oanda.com/converter/classic is an easy to use and highly regarded currency conversion website which can provide exchange rate information daily.

There are a number of Bureaux de Change dotted around the islands and at the major hotels and there are lots of banks in Victoria, Mahé. Some of the bigger hotels will change money for you, but usually cream off a large commission for doing so. The Seychelles Foreign Earnings (Regulation) Act has been changed to oblige all visitors to pay their hotel bills in some form of foreign exchange when checking out. Acceptable foreign exchange includes credit cards, travellers cheques or foreign currency. The government has done this to get more foreign exchange flowing into the banking system. You will still be able to pay in rupees, but only if you produce the slips and receipts proving conversion from foreign exchange into Seychelles currency with a bank, either locally or overseas. If anything, this emphasises the importance of keeping your currency exchange bank receipts. They are also necessary if you want to change rupees back into your own country's currency at a bank or bureau on leaving Seychelles.

BANKS AND BANKING

The following banks have branches in the Seychelles capital of Victoria, Mahé:

Barclays Bank: Independence Avenue (tel 22-4101). Barclays also has branch offices on the neighbouring islands of Praslin and La Digue.
Bank of Baroda: Albert St (tel 32-3038/32-1533, fax 32-4057).
Banque Francaise Commerciale: Ocean Indien, Albert Street (tel 32-3096).
Central Bank of Seychelles: Independence Avenue (tel 22-5200, fax 22-4958).
Development Bank of Seychelles: tel 22-4471.
Habib Bank: tel 22-4371/22-4372.
Nouvobanq: State House Avenue (tel 22-5011).

The travel grapevine says the most obliging of these is the Banque Francaise Commerciale; the least helpful, the Nouvobanq.

Banking Hours

You'll find several banks outside the arrivals area at the international airport and these usually open to meet all incoming and departing flights. Bank opening hours differ from island to island. Banks in Victoria are generally open between 8.30am and 4pm Monday to Friday, and some banks open on Saturday from 8.30 am to 11am. Praslin bank hours are from 8.30am to 1pm; Baie St. Anne and Grand Anse from 9am to noon Monday to Friday, and 8.30am to 11am on Saturday.

Credit Cards

Most international credit cards, including American Express, Diners Club, Visa, Access and MasterCard, are widely accepted in the larger establishments, but not always in shops, so it's wise to carry some rupees, pounds or dollars. American Express (tel 32-24140); Diners Club, Victoria (tel 22-53030); MasterCard, Victoria (tel 22-5392/22-4101); and Visa, Victoria (tel 22-4101).

Tipping

Most establishments add a 5-10% service charge to their bills. It's a matter of personal choice to tip, but 10% is the usual way of showing your appreciation, or you might round off the bill to the next convenient amount, especially if you are paying in cash.

For general health information see pages 41-44.

Health

MEDICAL SERVICES

State health services are free for all citizens. Seven hospitals maintain a total of 416 beds and most health indicators for Seychelles are comparable to those achieved by developed countries. Medical facilities in Seychelles are limited, especially in the isolated islands where doctors are often unavailable. If you need treatment doctors and hospitals usually expect to be paid immediately for any services rendered.

Hospitals

Victoria Hospital, at Mont Fleuri in Victoria, is a large (373 beds) and well-equipped hospital, and is the main health facility (tel 38-8000). All doctors speak English and/or French. There are also small hospitals on Praslin, at Baie St Anne (tel 23-3333), and on La Digue, at La Passe (tel 23-4255), but anyone needing more than basic medical attention is sent to Victoria. There are also several clinics on Mahé, Praslin and La Digue. Private doctors are available and can be contacted through your hotel reception. If a doctor visits you at your hotel you can ask for his fee to be charged to your hotel bill. Some doctors, however, expect immediate cash payment for their services. Emergency treatment is available to visitors for a flat consultation fee of £13 and there is a 'Tourist Doctor' and 'Tourist Dentist' on 24-hour call (tel 38-8000).

   Prescription drugs can be bought at hospitals, such as the Central Pharmacy at Victoria Hospital, and some pharmacies. There is no pharmacy on Praslin.

Dentists

You can find dentists at Castor Road Dental Clinic, Victoria (tel 32-3100); Le Chantier Dental Clinic, Le Chantier (tel 22-4354); and Specialised Dental Clinic and Medent Services, Aart Chambers, Mont Fleuri (tel 22-5822).

HEALTH HAZARDS

Black wasps are harmless, but the yellow ones should be treated with respect. They live in cone-shaped nests hanging from the trees. Watch out for large centipedes and scorpions when out walking in the bush, and be careful you don't step on cone shells or spiky black sea urchins in lagoons or reefs. **Always wear shoes when walking on coral**. There are no poisonous snakes in the Seychelles.

CLOTHING

What to Wear and When

Casual is the keynote for island wear. Temperatures are generally constant throughout the year so lightweight cotton clothes can be worn. For men, shorts and T-shirts during the day, and slacks for evening wear. Jackets and ties are rarely worn. For business, safari suits are usual. Ties are not worn, except to church. Men must wear long trousers to enter casinos after 7pm. For women, cotton wrap-arounds (*pareos*), or shorts for daytime, and cool dresses for the evening. Sun-hats and good quality protective sunglasses are essential. Take flip-flop sandals to wear when walking on coral reef and rubber flippers when swimming. Trainers or lightweight walking shoes are useful if you intend to explore the islands, otherwise sandals or light canvas shoes are adequate. Swimwear is worn only on the beaches or around the hotel pool; it is not acceptable anywhere else. Women into topless sunbathing will find that this is tolerated on the main tourist beaches, although nowhere else. Sunscreen in the Seychelles is expensive (as is film) so it is advisable to take some with you.

Communications

MAIL

Good links with the rest of the world ensure Seychelles has a fast, reliable postal service. The central post office in Victoria is open from 8am to 4pm Monday to Friday, and 8am to noon on Saturday. Airmail collections are at 3pm during the week and noon on Saturday. An airmailed letter or postcard to Europe takes up to a week to get there. You can also buy stamps (about 40p for postcards) at some shops, and usually most hotels, which will also mail letters and postcards for you. Courier companies such as TNT and DHL are also reliable and even quicker and ensure that parcels and mail are speedily delivered to all parts of the world.

TELEPHONES

Telecommunications are generally good. There are 13,000 telephones on the island, direct radio communications with adjacent islands and African coastal countries, inter-city radio communications between the islands in the archipelago, and an Intelsat (Indian Ocean) satellite earth station for international communication. There is international direct dialling (IDD) to most countries. Cable & Wireless on Francis Rachel Street, Victoria, runs a telephone, fax and telex service between 7am and 9pm. If you need to make a call use their services as hotels are known to impose up to a 100% surcharge on telephone calls. Many of the islands have coin and card public phone boxes. Phone cards (known locally as Phonocards) of various values can be bought at post offices, the airport, and at many shops. Some of the more remote islands do not have telephones, but satellite telephone links are being increasingly installed. Mobile telephones with a world roaming option can be used, as there is now good GSM coverage. The number for the local operator is 100, and 151 for the international operator. The directory enquiries number is 181. Internet and e-mail facilities are also available. The country code for Seychelles is 248 and the outgoing international code is 00. Modular jacks are of the US RJ-11 wire type.

MEDIA

Television

The Seychelles Broadcasting Corporation (SBC) transmits TV broadcasts in Kreol, French and English to the 75%-80% of the population which can receive TV signals. The state-owned SBC, previously closely controlled, was granted more freedom in 1992, and although TV and radio broadcasts continue to show a pro-government bias, material mildly critical of the government does appear in the news programmes from time to time.

Radio

There are about 50,000 radio sets on the island. Seychelles' first 24-hour FM station, 'Paradise FM,' broadcasts to Mahé, Praslin, La Digue, Silhouette, and the many small inner islands. The station has been on the air since May 1997, and is part of the state-funded broadcaster, SBC. It favours a bright new sound in tune with European commercial FM stations, and has established itself as the number one music station in the country. Before Paradise FM came on the air there was only one AM radio station in the country. Paradise FM broadcasts mainly in English, but there is a distinctly Seychellois feel to the station. Kreol music forms part of the daily menu and there are specialist music programmes which cater for French pop and rock, jazz and international music. (Paradise FM, tel 22-4161, fax 32-4015, e-mail: sbcradfm@seychelles.net) Seychelles Broadcasting Corporation

(SBC) broadcasts a full news bulletin in English at 6pm daily on 1368kHz. BBC World Service and Voice of America frequencies change from time to time but can usually be found on MHz 17.88 15.42 11.73 6.005 for BBC, and for Voice of America on MHz 21.55 15.25 9.645 6.035.

Newspapers and Magazines

The government-controlled *Seychelles Nation* is a weekday morning newspaper available in English, French and Kreol. There is also a weekend edition. Independent publications include *The People,* a monthly, and *Seychelles Review,* a monthly news review. *L'Echo des Îles,* a Catholic weekly that touches on current events, is not subject to control and often carries views critical of the government. Since the political liberalisation of 1992 a number of political opposition publications have appeared and continue to appear without government interference. Foreign newspapers and magazines are imported and sold without restriction.

Getting Around

MAPS

Recommended is the laminated Seychelles road map (scale 1:50, 000) published by Berndtson & Berndtson. Brief introductions are given in English, French, German, Italian, and Spanish. You can mark your routes on the map and then erase them on the easy-to-clean surface. There are grid references for points of interest, and for the main hotels. The map is sturdy and folds easily. Globetrotter's Seychelles 1:33,000 map (1997) gives detailed information on all the islands, and includes a Victoria town plan, a map of the Vallée de Mai nature trail, and the Botanical Garden. There's also a Seychelles Holiday Map in Collins Cartographic Series. You can pick up giveaway booklets from your hotel reception area which have maps detailed enough to get you around the place. You can also get them at the local tourist office (tel 22-5313, fax 22-4035, e-mail: dgtmtca@seychelles.net).

GUIDES

You are reading the latest (2000). There's a plethora of others, but for an insider view read the illustrated Odyssey guide *Seychelles* (1996) by British journalist Sarah Carpin, who has lived and worked in Seychelles for many years. For would-be tourists living in southern Africa there's Marco Turco's *Comoros and Seychelles* (Southern Book Publishers, Halfway House 1995). If you are a diver, and can find a copy, you should enjoy Al J Venter's booklet *Underwater Seychelles* (Gordon Verhoef, Cape Town 1972), and his *Where to Dive in Southern Africa and Off the Islands* (Ashanti, Rivonia, 1991), as well as Lawson Wood's *Diving and Snorkelling Guide to the Seychelles* published in 1997. For twitchers, forget the rest and get the illustrated field guide *Birds of the Indian Ocean Islands* by Ian Sinclair and Olivier Langrand (Struik, Cape Town 1998). As well as Seychelles, it covers Madagascar, Mauritius and Rodrigues, Réunion, and Comoros. The Seychelles Island Foundation's *Aldabra – World Heritage Site* is one of the best publications on this remote group of islets and atolls. Contact the Foundation through the Seychelles Tourism Marketing Authority (STMA), Mahé (tel 22-5333). In the capital, Victoria, is a shop called Antigone, which stocks a wide range of books on Seychelles, as well as a selection of local maps. You'll find it in the Victoria House shopping arcade known as the Passage des Palmes (tel 22-5443).

BY AIR

Air Seychelles operates at least 18 return flights between Mahé and Praslin daily, and regular flights operate from Mahé to Frégate, Bird Island, St Denis and Desroches. The Islander, which carries six passengers, and four DHC-6 Twin Otters, which take 20, are used on these routes. Baggage allowance is restricted to 22-33 lb (10-15 kg), and it's is recommended that you use soft-sided luggage for inter-island flights. Baggage may be left behind if flights are full but there is secure storage at the Mahé airport. Make sure you confirm your inter-island flights as they are subject to change right up to the last minute. All flights begin or end in Mahé at the domestic terminal of the International Airport. There are 14 airports throughout the archipelago. Flights from Mahé to Praslin take about 15 minutes. You are allowed 33 lb (15 kg) of luggage. Mahé to Denis flights are on Tuesday, Thursday, Friday and Sunday and take 30 minutes, the baggage allowance is the same as to Praslin. Excess baggage is charged at 62p/lb (£1.24/kg) but again may not be allowed on the flight. Mahé to Desroches takes one hour and there are flights on Monday, Wednesday, Friday, and Sunday. Daily flights (except Monday) from Mahé to Bird are included in Bird Island Lodge rates. Here the luggage allowance is only 22lb (10 kg) and excess baggage costs 62p/lb (£1.24/kg) and again may not be allowed on board. For inter-island reservations contact the airport (tel 38-4405).

There are regular helicopter services only to La Digue and Silhouette, although you can go by charter helicopter to other islands as well. Flights to Bird, Denis and Descroches islands are generally organised in collaboration with the islands' lodges. Island-hopping itineraries can be arranged by local tour companies, among them:

Bunson's Travel: tel 32-2682.   *Premier Holidays:* tel 22-5777.
Mason's Travel: tel 32-2642.   *Travel Services:* tel 32-2414.
National Travel Agency: tel 22-4900.

Helicopter seats can be booked through *Helicopter Seychelles*, which also operates special charter flights, scenic tours and photographic charters from Mahé (tel 37-5400, fax 37-5812, e-mail: victor@seychelles.net). Helicopter Seychelles operates to and from Mahé International Airport, Victoria Helistop, Plantation Helistop, Denis, Frégate, La Digue, Praslin, and Silhouette. In addition to weekday morning transfer services between Mahé and Silhouette, sightseeing flights or private transfer charters can be organised at any these heli-stops. Privately owned Helicopter Seychelles, in a joint venture with Air Seychelles, also provides transport, search and rescue, emergency and survey operations.

Travel to Aldabra is possible by way of a three-hour flight from Mahé which costs about £4,198/US$6376 to charter the plane, and then a three-hour trip by boat to Aldabra, which costs another £2,778/US$4219 to charter. Accommodation is basic, usually a room with bathroom, and is based at the research station on Picard Island, the only one in the Aldabra group with this facility. Basic shelters can be found on the other islands, but these are used for long-term field trips, undertaken by scientists for research purposes. A charge of £309/US$470 per person per week is usual for board and lodging. Food is usually simple fisherman-style cook-ups, with lots of fish and rice.

BY SEA

Island-hopping is a perfect way to explore the islands, each of which has its own unique charm and beauty. Government-run ferries operate on some routes. You can get a handy inter-island ferry schedule from the tourist office, Ground Floor, Independence House, Independence Avenue, Victoria.

FERRIES
A ferry leaves Mahé for Praslin at 5am Monday to Friday and returns at 11am. The trip takes three hours and costs about £6/US$9 one way. Contact *La Belle Praslinoise,* in Praslin (tel 23-3238).

There is also a ferry between Praslin and La Digue five times a day, taking 30 minutes and costing about £4/US$6 one way. Contact Praslin/La Digue Ferry Service in Praslin (tel 23-3229).

The *Cat Cocos,* a fast catamaran ferry leaves Mahé for Praslin at 7.30am, 1pm, and 4pm every day and returns at 9am, 2.30pm, and 5.30pm. The journey takes one hour and costs about £31/US$46 return. Contact Mahé Shipping Company (tel 32-2100).

Travel to other islands from Mahé is all by private charter. A trip to Bird Island will take about 7 hours, Denis 6 hours, La Digue $3^{1}/4$, Frégate 2 hours, and to Round and Moyenne islands, in the St Anne Marine National Park off Victoria, about 30 minutes. Shuttle boats leave Mahé for Cerf at 8am, 9am, midday, 3.45pm, 4.30pm, 6pm, and the last one is at 10.30pm; and Cerf to Mahé at 8.30am, 11.45am, 3.30pm, 4pm, 5.30pm, and 6.30 pm.

Although there are no scheduled services, cruise and cargo ships do call at the main and only deep-sea port at Victoria, and regular connections between Mahé, Praslin and La Digue are provided by privately owned catamarans and motor and sailing schooner ferries which carry cargo and passengers.

To hire a boat, contact the Marine Charter Association, at the harbour near the Yacht Club in Victoria (tel 32-2126). Otherwise you can make arrangements through:

Boat House: tel 24-7898.   *Payet Le Superb:* tel 32-2288.
Brownie Marine Services: tel 34-4827. *Tam Tam:* tel 34-4266.
Game Fishing: tel 34-4266.   *VPM Yacht Charter:* tel 22-5676.
Jumaya: tel 37-8523.   *Yacht MY Way:* tel 22-4573.

The national authority is the Seychelles Yachting Association, PO Box 504, Seychelles (tel 32-2232, fax 32-2790).

CRUISES
The port at Victoria is regularly visited by cruise ships, among them the big three of the cruise industry, RCCL, Princess Cruises and Carnival.

Renaissance Cruises of the US is now the first line to base two luxury cruise ships in Seychelles. Mahé Shipping Company (tel 32-2100), wholly owned by Corvina, handles bookings for these and the majority of other visiting cruise ships.

A leisurely cruise on the *Galileo Sun* around the archipelago is also an option, visiting Mahé, La Digue, Praslin, Curieuse and Aride. The cruise is expensive and available only during the winter months. The *Galileo Sun* is a motor-sailing yacht with accommodation for up to 46 passengers and is designed to navigate in shallow waters and access remote places with accommodation for up to 46 passengers. All cabins are superbly finished with en-suite bathroom and individually controlled air-conditioning. Friendly service and gourmet meals are features of the cruise. There's plenty of free time in port for excursions, shopping or watersports. On-board facilities include a ski-boat and waterskis, windsurfer, snorkelling and fishing gear (in the UK telephone 020-7616-1010).

Scuba-divers and snorkellers can visit Aldabra on one of the cruises of the liveaboard *Indian Ocean Explorer,* which operates between March and April and October to November. Their all-in prices are significantly lower than the air and sea option. The *Indian Ocean Explorer* (tel 34-5445, fax 34-4223) can take you to the Amirantes and the Outer Islands, as well as Aldabra. Once only visited by passing yachts and fishermen, the Outer Islands are now open to all with this locally based and operated vessel. Inner island cruises to the main islands of Mahé, Praslin, La Digue and nearby smaller ones can also be booked. These cruises concentrate on sites not normally visited by day cruises, including the Ennerdale and Brissare rocks, as well as the lesser known, more remote and, arguably, more spectacular places around Les Soeurs, Aride, Trompeuse, Frégate, Denis and other islands. The cost of a cruise is around £154/US$234 per person per day. The islands of Seychelles with their prevailing trade winds are ideal for sailing, particularly since 42 of the most interesting islands and islets within the inner group are all within 40 miles (64 km) of Mahé.

BY ROAD

Taxis

Taxis and buses are available only on Mahé and Praslin. Taxis offer good but expensive service. There are about 200 taxis on Mahé and Praslin which are metered at government-controlled rates. Tell the driver to switch on his meter when you get in. This could save you an argument about the fare when you arrive. Some drivers won't take you to some remote areas where they have to travel on bad roads. Try to negotiate a daily or hourly rate, as many of the drivers make knowlegeable tour guides. Rates on Praslin are 25% higher and there is a surcharge between 8pm and 6am on both islands. Do not expect to be able to hail a taxi anywhere. They can be found at the airport in Mahé, at the Victoria Taxi Rank, in Independence Avenue, Victoria, as well as at the airport on Praslin, and outside larger hotels. Typical fares from Mahé Airport to Beau Vallon, and to Plantation Club is £15/US$22; Beau Vallon to Victoria £4/US$6; Plantation Club to Victoria £22/US$33; Praslin Airport to La Reserve £12/US$18; and to Baie Ste Anne Jetty £9/US$14. You can contact the Taxi Operators Association for up-to-date fares. You will find them at St Claire's School, Victoria, Mahé (tel 32-3895). Otherwise you can order a taxi on Mahé from:

Wilton Albest: tel 32-2518.   *M Alcindor:* tel 32-2515.
AA Leong: tel 32-2763.   *B Otar:* tel 32-2763.
Jean Ponwayne: tel 22-5033.

You should get some memorable photographs on La Digue as taxis are wooden slatted carts drawn by bullocks. You can take one of these ox-carts to get from the island pier to La Digue Island Lodge. It costs about £4/US$6 per person each way.

Buses

There's an efficient daily bus service on Mahé. The Victoria Central Bus Station is in Palm Street. Seychelles Public Transport Corporation (SPTC) buses run on a regular basis on Mahé between the rural areas and Victoria, the capital. There are 26 bus routes, most of which originate in Victoria. Every village and hotel is served by at least one route. Buses run from around 5.30am to 9.30pm except on weekends (Friday and Saturday) when they run until 1.30am. Praslin has one bus route which circles the island in a large reversed C pattern from Anse Kerlan to Anse Boudin. There are about nine runs daily in each direction between 6am and 5pm. These buses are an inexpensive way to get around. They are painted white and bus stop signs are painted on the road surface. Be prepared to wait for buses and hustle for a seat on some of the routes. Many buses are rather run-down, but will get you there eventually. If you want to get off the bus, just shout *Dévant* as loud as you can.

A number of 18-seater coaches operate for airport transfers and excursions. Prices for buses and coaches are reasonable. Various tour companies operate motorcoach and minibus tours around the islands and they also offer a wide selection of tours on Cerf, Round, Cousin and other nearby islands.

Cycling

La Digue is great for cycling and you can hire a bicycle almost everywhere. For bicycle hire on Praslin contact Cote d'Or (tel 23-2071); or Sunbike (tel 23-30330); and on La Digue try Tarosa (tel 23-4250). Pedal power is ideally suited to the pace of Seychelles but beware of the steep, busy and narrow roads.

DRIVING

LICENCES

A valid licence from your own country is required and you should have had it for at least two years. An international driver's licence is not necessary. To hire a car or other vehicle you must be 21 or over.

ROADS

Traffic drives on the **left-hand side of the road**. There are about 214 miles (345 km) of roads of which about 172 miles (277 km) are surfaced. That's not a lot of road for the 7,000 registered vehicles. Most roads are on Mahé and Praslin where they are tarred and generally in good condition. Once outside Victoria roads are unlit at night. The roads are narrow with deep gutters at the side. Don't be alarmed if you see a tree in the middle of the road – it is probably a pot-hole and this is someone's way of marking it. When driving stay alert. Local driving standards can be hair-raising and road discipline sloppy. Pedestrians tend to be careless and at weekends you should watch out for inebriated locals on the road. On the open road the speed limit is 40 mph (65 km/h); in built-up areas and throughout Praslin it is 25 mph (40 km/h). You can whizz along Mahé's coast road – the limit is 50 mph (80 km/h). On the other islands, roads are normally sandy tracks, narrow and winding, but generally well maintained. Exercise caution at all times.

FUEL

The price of petrol is about 30% higher – around 85p/US$1.30 a litre – than in Europe and places to buy it are few and far between. Make sure that your car tank is full when you set out on a jaunt. No place is very far, but steep, twisting roads can take a toll on fuel and on your pocket. Although the islands have metricated, petrol is still sold in gallons (4.5 litres).

VEHICLE RENTAL

Cars can be rented on Mahé and Praslin at the airport and the large hotels. On the other islands the best way of getting around is on foot or by bike. It is advisable to book rental cars well in advance, especially in high season. Hire is usually on an unlimited mileage basis and can range from 330-450 rupees (£38-53/US$58-80) for one day hire of a mini-moke to 2,695 rupees (£317/US$476) for a week's hire of an air-conditioned Suzuki jeep. In addition to the mini-mokes and jeeps offered by all hire firms Hertz can also provide Toyota saloons. Rental prices include Third Party insurance and road tax, but check all the small print before hiring, especially the insurance documentation. Some cars are not in very good condition, so always check the brakes and indicators before you hire a vehicle. Most international car hire firms are represented on the island (in fact Hertz and Avis can arrange hire through their websites) as well as many local operators. Many companies offer a breakdown service. The choice of vehicles ranges from mini to impressive, from luxury to rugged. Chauffeur-driven vehicles are also available. Cars are delivered to and collected from hotels and the airport.

Car Hire on Mahé

Alpha Rent a Car: Victoria (tel 32-2078/32-2954).

Avis: Shalom, Le Chantier (tel 22-4511, fax 22-5193; Website www.avis.com).

Budget Rent-A-Car: Les Mamelles (tel 34-4280/34-4296, fax 34-43830; Airport Kiosk (tel 37-30690; Berjaya Beau Vallon Bay desk (tel 34-4280); Le Meridien Barnarons desk (tel 344-4280).

Eden's Rent-A-Car: Stevenson-Delhomme Road (tel 26-6333, fax 26-6441, after hours tel 37-8307/5038).

Hertz Rent-A-Car: Victoria and at the airport (tel 32-2447/32-2669, fax 32-4111; Website www.hertz.com). Hertz is also represented in Victoria at Reef Hotel, Barbaron Hotel, Sheraton Hotel, Beau Vallon Hotel, Plantation Club Hotel, Fisherman Cove Hotel, Equator Hotel, Auberge Club Hotel, and Northolme Hotel.

Leisure Cars: Revolution Avenue (tel 32-2447/32-2669).

Sunshine Cars: Le Chantier, Victoria (tel 22-4671).

Tropicar: Providence (tel 37-3336, fax 37-6350); Airport Agency (tel 37-3299); Breakdown/After Hours (tel 51-0211).

Car Hire on Praslin

Amitie Car Hire: tel 23-3826.

Austral Car Rental: Baie St Anne (tel 23-2015).

Praslin Holiday Car Rental: Grand Anse (tel 23-3219/23-3325).

Prestige Car Hire: Grand Anse (tel 23-3226, fax 23-3050).

Standard Car Hire: Amitie (tel 23-3555).

Taurus Car Rental: Baie St Anne (tel 23-2406/23-2443, fax 23-2406).

Valle Car Hire: Grand Anse (tel 23-3893).

Mini-mokes are **the** rental cars in the Seychelles, but they are rather expensive. They are built for outdoor driving and very often the outdoors gets inside. You do not pay a per kilometre rate for mokes. The longer you use the vehicle, the lower your daily rate will become. Suzuki open jeeps are also popular and not that much more expensive than mokes.

Accommodation

Seychelles has been a popular tourist destination for little more than 10 years, but it offers a full range of accommodation from self-catering apartments and guest-houses, to luxury hotels, lodges and chalets The government has so far resisted the lure of mass tourism, choosing instead to market the islands as an eco-tourist destination. It is targeting a mere 140,000 tourists a year for the next three years. This does not mean that independent travellers with limited budgets are discouraged by the authorities, but they do not welcome hordes of backpackers either. There are no youth hostels and camping is not allowed. The government's restriction on the number of holidaymakers it allows in at any one time might sound authoritarian but it means you'll never find the islands looking like the south of Spain, Miami at Spring Break or Blackpool on Bank Holidays.

Seychelles has a reputation of being an expensive and slightly stand-offish holiday destination. Well, yes and no. It is expensive if you stay at one of the big hotels and pay the hair-raising prices charged for booze in most bars and restaurants. It is possible, however, to have an affordable holiday by staying at an owner-run guest-house. For people who dislike large hotels, a guest-house really is the best option. Ranging from the comfortable to the downright luxurious, they are homely without the kind of enforced intimacy that makes you feel you are obliged to greet your fellow guests with a fixed smile every time you bump into them. The island might also cure you of any prejudice you might have against a package holiday.

All recently built hotels are well up to international standards and there are a number of large resort hotels equipped with air-conditioning, private bathrooms, swimming pools and full sporting facilities. Older hotels and guest-houses on the smaller islands may lack the same levels of sophistication, but their charming seclusion has long recommended them to anyone looking for tranquillity and privacy. Novelist Somerset Maugham found a quiet place here so that he could write in peace. Many hotels and guest-houses are former plantation houses which have been modernised and are run by resident owners. Thatched-roof chalets and guest-houses, built in the local style, are found mainly on outlying islands. Self-catering units are available on most of the main islands. Careful planning has ensured that the islands have retained the astonishing beauty and quiet charm that attracts tourists in the first place. Right from the start, the government decreed that new buildings could not rise higher than the surrounding palm trees, with the result that big city levels of comfort and convenience have been achieved in idyllic Seychellois settings. The hotels are almost without exception clean and well kept and the food everywhere is something to write home about. There are only 4,500 hotel beds on the islands so it is advisable to confirm your reservations with a deposit, if you are making them yourself, particularly during the high season from December to January, and in July and August. For more information, contact the Seychelles Hotel Association (PO Box 1174, Victoria, Mahé, tel 32-4131, fax 32-4145), or see *Exploring Seychelles.*

If you have deep pockets you might like to rent, or even buy, yourself a piece of island paradise. A German company specialises in this sort of real estate and for US$50 will send you a catalogue of islands available for rent or sale. Contact Vladi Private Islands, Ballindamm 7, D-20095 Hamburg, Germany (tel 4033-0000, fax 4033-0081).

Eating and Drinking

CUISINE

Just as the racial blend of the Seychelles is a salad bowl of cultures, the food of the islands and its preparation provide some dishes that are uniquely Kreol. Forget the stories about curried fruit bat – although it does appear on Kreol restaurant menus as *chauve-souris* – and explore a cuisine that has its origins in French, African, Chinese, and Indian cookery. What makes it special is the delectable blending of spices applied to the fruits of land and sea. Try local specialities such as coconut curries, bouillon bréde, tec-tec soup, la daube, a delicious stew of breadfruit, cassavas, yams, and bananas, and kat-kat banane, a mixture of tuna, coconut milk and bananas. *Macquereau boucaner* is mackerel steamed in banana leaves, and *chatini requin,* a 'chutney' of dried shark, stir-fried with herbs and onions and a savoury fruit called *bilimbi,* and infinitely better than it sounds. The rice which comes with all these dishes is probably the only part of the meal that is not local. It is imported from India and China. Fish is naturally an important part of a Seychellois meal, as it is readily available fresh and of exceptional quality. Typical fish delicacies include succulent red snapper (*bourzwa*), tuna steaks to die for, kingfish, and, if you're lucky enough to find it and can steel yourself to eat such a pretty reef fish, tender fillets of parrotfish. There isn't a great variety of other seafood available. Lobsters are imported as they are scarce in local waters, through crabs and local prawns are readily available. The *tec-tec* is a tiny white shellfish which looks like a small clam and makes a tasty soup with the addition of onions, garlic, ginger and parsley. Octopus curry is virtually the national dish of Seychelles. Its preparation is lengthy and involves beating the washed octopus with a rolling pin for up to 30 minutes before boiling it in water for an hour. The octopus is then finely chopped and simmered for a further half-hour in three cups of coconut cream flavoured with curry powder, pepper, salt, onions, chillies and cinnamon leaves. Served on a bed of rice with a millionaire's salad on the side this is a dish to convert any sceptic. Peppered tern's eggs are also a local delicacy and you can recognise them by both their tiny size and the bright orange of their yolks. Roast pork glazed with wild bee honey is sometimes an enticement on menus in Chinese restaurants. Most beef and lamb is imported and is used nowhere near as much as pork, lobster, octopus, and chicken.

Vegetarian Cooking
If you are a vegetarian you will be in your element in the Seychelles. Not only will you discover vegetables you've never seen before, but the way they are cooked is so innovative that even boring common old veggies become culinary delights. Local fresh vegetables and fruits enhance every meal. A popular starter is *salade de palmiste* for which a whole palm tree has to be felled to get the crunchy heart used in this millionaire's salad. The locals say if you eat Seychelles breadfruit you'll always come back to the islands, so sample it fried like chips, baked, boiled, or mashed like a potato. It has a sweet taste and is the starchy fruit whose collection from Tahiti in 1788 for ultimate transplantation in the West Indies caused Captain William Bligh of the *Bounty* so much trouble. Other local fruits and vegetables include aubergines, bananas, calabashes, patoles, papayas, mangoes, avocados, jackfruit, grapefruit, guavas, lychees, pineapples, melons, limes and golden apples (*frisiters*).

Desserts are not all that exciting and usually consist of fresh fruit and ice-cream or fried bananas and coconut cream. Fresh fruit alone is the perfect way to round off an island meal. For a change you might try corasol, jamalac, jackfruit, papaya, zat, or the more familiar mango, pineapple and granadilla.

Restaurants
International cuisine is always an alternative in most restaurants and hotels and on Mahé there are Chinese, Japanese and Italian restaurants, as well as those specialising in Kreol dishes. Restaurants which belong to the Seychelles Restauranteurs' Association usually quote an average price per person for a three-course meal, which is inclusive of two glasses of wine and a cup of coffee. Advance bookings should be made for groups of four or more people when eating out and should defintely be made for the restaurants on Round and Cerf islands, and for La Réserve restaurant on Praslin.

Self-Catering
If you are self-catering the best place to buy most of your basic supplies is one of the supermarkets run by the Seychelles Marketing Board (SMB). The one with the biggest selection is on Albert Street, Victoria (tel 22-4444).

Other supermarkets include:

Beau Vallon: tel 24-7808.	*Krishna:* tel 32-2594.
Bridge: tel 34-4335.	*Luc:* tel 23-3238.
Chaka Brothers: tel 22-4337.	*Mohan:* tel 34-4290.
Chez Deenu: tel 32-2639.	*Quincy:* tel 32-3273.
Continental Stores: tel 32-3702.	*Temooltjee:* tel 22-4331.
Jivan: tel 32-3310.	*TLC:* tel 26-6426.
Jumaya: tel 37-8523.	*Tristar:* tel 34-4744.

If your order is big enough some of them might deliver.

DRINKING

Soft Drinks

There's a reasonable choice of alcoholic and non-alcoholic beverages available. A wide range of fresh fruit juices are sold and drunk around the clock. Fresh lime juice and soda is especially popular and one of the best-all round thirst quenchers. You should also try the popular local tea, *citronella*, which is made by pouring boiling water on to lemon grass and is a recommended remedy for indigestion. Coconut juice served in the nut is a refreshing drink not to be missed. One-litre bottles of Eau de Val Riche water are sold in shops at around £1.15 to £1.50; in restaurants and hotels it can cost up to £2.10. If you are a caffeine addict you might have difficulty finding a decent cup of coffee.

Wines and Beers

All wines have to be imported, usually from South Africa, France, or Greece, and so they are quite expensive. If you like to drink wine South African labels are good, and are likely to be less expensive than other imports. Seychelles Breweries says the best beer on the islands is Eku Bavaria, but they would, they brew and bottle it under licence from Bavaria's Erste Kulmbacher Actienbrauerei. They also brew what local beer drinkers say is the best drop, a German-style lager called Seybrew, as well as producing Guinness under licence. The chilled Irish stuff is especially favoured by the older generation of islanders. As well as in hotels and restaurants, you can buy beer in supermarkets and cafés, and even from street vendors. Hotels and restaurants generally double the shop price for the drinks they serve. The average price for a bottle of wine in a restaurant is £15 to £20 and a bottle of beer costs £2 or more. A point for budget travellers to remember is that all glass drink bottles carry a small refundable deposit.

Spirits

Unlike other Indian Ocean islands there's no strong local tradition of rum making and drinking, and the brands you get in bars usually come from Barbados. Interesting, and illegal, local drinks are a variety of toddies and other moonshine brews which rely on coconut palms, pineapples and sugarcane as the detonating ingredients in these explosive concoctions. If you become really friendly with villagers you might be invited to quaff some of their brews. North-west Mahé, Praslin, and the hills of La Digue are the hot spots for drinkers with an inquiring turn of mind. Another, legal, Seychelles drink is the local aphrodisiac, Coco d'Amour, a creamy tropical liqueur that comes in a novel bottle shaped like the legendary erotic anatomy of the coco-de-mer. You'll find it in hotels, boutiques and shops everywhere.

Licensing Hours

If you are a hotel resident you can be served with alcohol at any time of the day and night. Other bars are open from 11.30am to 3pm and 6pm to 10pm. It is allegedly illegal to drink alcohol in the street or in public, but as far back as 1883 a visiting lady botanical artist disapprovingly recorded: 'At night we heard singing and raving all round; it was like an island of lunatics, and we barred all the windows well before going to bed: to sleep was impossible.'

Entertainment

You don't go to Seychelles for the nightlife, which is just as well as there's not much of it. While it's undeveloped and largely unsophisticated, there is a fair sprinkling of venues and events to be enjoyed in the evenings. Many hotels have evening barbecues and dinner dances, **theatre productions** are often staged in Kreol, French and English, and there's a cinema and a couple of casinos. **Deepam's cinema** is on Albert Street, Victoria, although due to a lack of variety – screenings are mainly kung-fu films – videos seem to be more popular with local movie-goers.

Casinos
An added attraction to Mahé's natural appeal for some. You'll find them at Berjaya Beau Vallon Bay Beach Resort & Casino Hotel, Beau Vallon (tel 24-7141, fax 24-7943), and the Plantation Club Resort and Casino, in the south-east at Baie Lazare (tel 36-1361, fax 36-1333). On Praslin is the super-duper Casino des Îles (tel 23-2500). All offer the usual slot machines, poker, blackjack and roulette tables. Anyone can play at the casinos, the only stipulation is that you must be smartly dressed. They usually open the tables for business at 7.30pm or 8pm and go on until the small hours.

DANCING
There are also a few popular discos on Mahé, such as Katiolo Club (tel 37-5453), on the main eastern coastal road not far from the airport; Mahé's most popular night spot, the Lovenut (tel 32-3232), and the Barrel (tel 32-2136), are both in Victoria. The larger hotels have bands on some nights and often put on their own discos, especially at the weekend. Traditional music, dancing and singing are specialities at some Mahé and Praslin hotels. Seychellois love to dance and are drawn naturally to the beats and rhythms that excited their African and Madagascan forefathers. Both the *sega* and their *moutia*, the most famous of the island dances, are still part of island culture. Where the *sega* is the main dance everywhere else in the Indian Ocean the Seychellois have made the *moutia* their own distinct music and dance form. The songs used are actually prayers that the old slaves turned into work chants and the dance itself is performed to African and Madagascan rhythms, accompanied by throbbing drums. This popular communal dance in its purest expression is usually performed around a fire at night. A true *moutia* is quite a sight. At one time it was regarded as licentious and banned by the colonial authorities. Something else you'll come across in the islands is *kamtolet* music, which is an exhilarating mix of rhythms whose European influences can be seen in the *contredanse,* which can be traced back to the heydey of French Sun King Louis XIV, and the *mazok* and *kosez* which are echoes of the later European waltz and quadrille.

Music
Music, introduced to the islands by the European settlers and played on violins or accordions, is now melded with the beat of the African drums. Local instrumnets include: the *makalapo,* a stringed instrument whose tin sound-box is buried in the sand while it is being played, the *bonm,* a bowed instrument, the *kaskavel,* a seed-filled container shaken like Caribbean maracas, and the *zez,* a Madagascan stringed instrument capable of four notes, all brought to Seychelles by early slaves and immigrant races. You'll find a wide selection of Kreol music on CD and cassette at Ray's Music Room, on Albert Street, Victoria (tel 32-2674, fax 32-4009).

FLORA AND FAUNA

FLORA
There's much to enchant and stir you to wonder here, and even staid natural historians have long been enthralled by some of the island's more unusual trees,

flowers, animals and reptiles. Nothing, however, has been so romanticised and embedded in legend as the **coco-de-mer**. This 'nut of the sea' is also known to Seychellois as the love nut, because of its highly suggestive shape and the strange stories associated with the male and female trees. Victorian warrior General Gordon, later of Khartoum fame, firmly believed that the Vallée de Mai in Praslin, with its towering coco-de-mer palms, was the site of the biblical Garden of Eden. 'The female fruit, the heaviest in the vegetable kingdom, shaped uncannily like a female pelvis, and the phallic catkin of the male palm, must be absolute testimony to the fact that this was where Eve tempted Adam,' he wrote to the Royal Botanic Gardens at Kew in England. 'As we generally believe that there was a tree of Knowledge of Good and Evil, and a tree of Life, actual trees, set aside for a time to be imbued with mystic powers, there is no reason why these trees should not exist now...' Seychellois certainly agree with Gordon on the palm's mystical abilities. They say that at night when the male tree moves over to the female the whole valley shudders, and if you should be there to witness their joining you'll turn into a black parrot. When these erotically shaped double coconuts first washed ashore on the coast of India centuries ago their origin was a mystery. Many believed that the nuts must have grown on the seabed, as no one had ever seen the nut growing on a palm. The sweet jelly contained in the nut was believed to be a sovereign cure-all for disease and was highly regarded as an aphrodisiac. Villagers beachcombing on the Maldives and Malabar coasts received thousands of rupees from rajahs and rulers for each sea nut they found. Only when the French landed on the Seychelles in the middle of the 18th century and found coco-de-mer palms growing plentifully in the wild on Praslin was the mystery of their origin finally solved. An enterprising Frenchman, Brayer du Barré, then sent a shipload to India hoping to make a killing on a credulous market. Instead, he ruined the market forever, although coco-de-mer nuts are still sold to tourists. Islanders cut the nuts in two and use them as dishes and plates. It takes 25 years for the coco-de-mer seed to germinate and grow into a full-sized, fruit-bearing tree. As the palm was once thought to grow under the sea off the Maldives its Latin name became *Lodoicea maldivica*. When Seychellois conservationists later tried to rename it *Lodoica seychellensis* the botanical world was horrified and dismissed the proposal. The fact remains that these trees are found growing in the wild only in Seychelles, mostly on Praslin, with a few on nearby Curieuse island, in the Victoria Botanical Gardens, and in the gardens at State House. There are coco-de-mer nuts mounted in gold in the museums of Paris, Vienna and Jakarta, and there are some vivid paintings of the palms by botanical artist Marianne North in the gallery at Kew Gardens. The tallest of the palms on Praslin is 115 ft (35 m) high and 400 years old, although it's believed they can live for 800-1,000 years. Today the collection of coco-de-mer is strictly controlled by law and the government has a monopoly on their legal sale, which is why you need an official export permit if you buy one.

As a result of their historical isolation, the islands are rich in rare plants which flourish nowhere else. Lush vegetation holds more than 2,000 species of tropical plants, of which 81 species are unique survivors from the even more luxuriant tropical forests that once covered the islands. In the high mossy **cloud forests** of Mahé the hills are populated by some extraordinary plants, among them the nectar-filled hollow tubes of the **pitcher plant** that are deadly traps for insects. If you watch long enough you might see one of these carnivorous plants snap up and snack on an unlucky insect. At Grand Anse, on the west coast of Mahé, is the **Medusae gynae,** a plant with a reproductive system so obscure it's said to have a death wish. It is also so rare that when it was discovered a new botanical family had to be created to categorise it. It is not, however, necessary to go trekking around all the islands to see interesting plants. Many of them can be viewed in comfort in Victoria's **Botanical Gardens**.

The national flower of the Seychelles, the **wild vanilla orchid** or **tropic bird orchid**, can often be found growing in the crooks of tree trunks. This is named after the white-tailed bird that can be seen soaring on thermals over the mountains of Mahé. The granitic islands still have plenty of forest on their mountain slopes; the coral islands are also densely covered with the scrub vegetation more characteristic of sandy soils. The most common trees are the **coconut palm** and **casuarina**, as well as **banyans, screw pines, tortoise trees** and **takamaka**, an indigenous tree whose wood is extensively used for making furniture and for boat-building.

Without doubt the coconut palm is king of the islands and, more than the legendary coco-de-mer, is the real tree of life. Palms reach maturity after 13 years and bear fruit for at least 50 years. They then begin to decline and die in their eighties or nineties. At any given moment in its life the coconut palm provides 12 different products. A five-month-old coconut contains two big cups of sweet, crystal-clear liquid, rich in vitamins and minerals. During World War Two, US and Japanese military doctors used this sterile liquid as a glucose solution for intravenous injections. Once the coconut flesh hardens the flesh can be grated, soaked, and squeezed to produce coconut milk for cooking. Heated, the flesh gives oil for cooking, lighting and, mixed with ash, soap. At the top of the tree the cabbage-like bud can be harvested as heart of palm, although this kills the tree. Coconuts take about 10 months to grow to maturity if the flowers of the palm are not used for other purposes. When unopened flowers are bent back up to eight litres a day of sweet sap flows. The sap ferments rapidly, changing within a few hours into a tangy alcoholic drink. After a few weeks it also turns into an excellent vinegar. When boiled the amber liquid crystallises into a red sugar. After soaking, the fibres covering of the nuts and known as coir can be woven into cloth, twisted for rope, or used for insulation or stuffing cushions. Copra is made by drying halves of the shelled nuts. Copra oil can be extracted from the copra, the residual material going to enrich animal feed. Nothing from the coconut palm is wasted. Baskets and brooms are made from the ribs of the leaves, mattresses and pillows are stuffed with the fibre, hats are woven from the split fronds and the trunk can often provide a few usable planks. Locals also use the husks to polish their floors. Instead of kneeling to scrub and polish, one foot is placed in a husk and slid around the floor in movements not unlike those of the traditional *sega* dance. Palm roots can be chewed for dental hygiene, or their extracts used in dyes and stomach medicines. Where there are coconut trees there are usually tree-climbing crabs. These climb the trunk, snip a nut free with their pincers and then shake the stem to make the coconut drop and burst. To catch a crab, tie a belt of grass high up around the trunk. When the crab is coming down it lets go on touching the grass, thinking it has reached the ground. The fall stuns or kills the crab.

FAUNA

As well as the black parrots and other birds found in the Vallée de Mai, the white-tailed **tropic bird** can often be spotted soaring on the thermals rising around the mountains of Mahé. The Vallée de Mai is also home to Seychelles' only two indigenous mammals, the endemic **flying fox**, or fruit bat, which roosts in the reserve, and the **sheath-tailed bat**, which can be regularly seen at dusk. The hedgehog-like insect-eating **tenrec** introduced from Madagascar is also common. There are more than 3,000 species of insect. Reptiles include the endemic **chameleon**, Seychelles house and **mole snakes**, and the introduced **blind snake**. There are green and bronze **geckos**, skinks, and one endemic frog – at half the size of a thumbnail the world's smallest – which lives in the misty hills of the Morne Seychellois National Park on Mahé among the ferns and lichens.

BIRD-WATCHING

Virtually all the endemic birds of the Seychelles can be seen on Mahé and the other granitic islands of Praslin, La Digue, Cousin and Aride. Bird and Aride are in particular the places for spectacular sightings of tropical seabirds such as **wedge-tailed** and **Audubon's shearwaters**, red-tailed and white-tailed **tropicbirds**, greater and lesser **frigatebirds**, sooty, bridled, roseate, white, greater crested, and common and lesser noddy **terns**. It's estimated that two million sooty terns alone nest each year on Bird. Among the **birds endemic to Seychelles** are the kestrel, blue pigeon, black parrot, scops owl, swiftlet, bulbul, magpie robin, brush warbler, paradise flycatcher, white-eye, sunbird and the Seychelles fody. The two most difficult species to locate are the **scops owl** and the **white-eye**, and you'll need knowledgeable locals to help you spot these. Concentrate your search in Mahé's Souvenir area for the little owl and on Mahé and Conception island for the white-eye. You'll make rewarding trips to La Digue for the **paradise flycatcher**, to Praslin and Curieuse for the **black parrot**, and Aride or Cousin for both **magpie robin** and **Seychelles fody**.

The other outlying islands are largely covered in coconut palm plantations, are virtually birdless as a result, and anyway can be reached only by charter boat or by charter air flight. Some islands of the Amirante and Farquhar groups are home to magnificent seabird colonies, but to visit these islands requires special permission. The Aldabras are exceptionally rewarding but access is very difficult, expensive and it takes many days to get there by charter boat. Another, expensive, way to see the birds on these exceptional islands is on a cruise ship. Among Aldabra's many attractions are its breeding seabirds. Massed colonies of **red-footed boobies** and greater and lesser **frigatebirds** make memorable spectacles. White-tailed and red-tailed tropicbirds, and greater-crested, bridled, black-naped and white terns also breed there.

Endemic birds of the Aldabra islands include the Aldabra flightless rail, brush warbler, Abbott's sunbird, Aldabra fody, and the drongo. The drongo and fody can be spotted quite easily within a short walk of the research station on Picard Island, and you might even see a **white-throated rail** there, the only flightless bird left in the Indian Ocean. Its ill-fated counterparts in Mauritius, Réunion and Madagascar did not survive the arrival of man. To see rails in any significant numbers, however, you will have to visit the islets of Malabar or Polymnie where they are much more common. Rarer is the **brush warbler**, which was recorded in only a small area of Malabar but has not been seen there since 1983.

Abbott's sunbird is common on Cosmolédo, Astove, and Assumption and a visit to one of these islands should guarantee you sightings of this lovely metallic-hued bird.

RARITIES

Seychelles has its fair share of rarities among the 206 species so far recorded in the archipelago. Some, such as the stunning black **Seychelles paradise flycatcher** and the **Seychelles scops owl**, measuring all of 8 inches (20 cm), are difficult for all but the most dedicated twitcher to find. The endangered black paradise flycatcher is found only in stands of mature trees on La Digue island. In 1988, there were 60-75 of these beautiful birds on the island, but since then the area of their preferred habitat has dwindled in size and flycatcher numbers have accordingly fallen alarmingly. Outside of the 20-acre (8 ha.) reserve of La Veuve, which has been set aside for the last 50 breeding pairs of flycatchers, their habitat is under threat from man, increasing development, and other birds; the bulbuls regularly steal their eggs. The flycatchers breed throughout the year, but fewer than one in five eggs results in a fully fledged chick. Locally this bird is called *veuve*, which literally means 'widow,' referring to the bird's streaming black tail feathers, which give islanders the impression of a mourning woman. Its nest is an extraordinary construction held together by silk from spiders' webs.

Described in a recent Red Data Book as 'declining inexorably towards extinction for reasons unknown,' the **Seychelles white-eye** is found in only two areas of Mahé. There were only 100 birds or so in the mid-1970s; the population is now down to about 25. The cause of their decline is a mystery that scientists are still exploring.

One bird that apparently came back from the dead is the little **scops owl**, which was discovered in 1880 and believed only 70 years later to have become extinct. It was again recorded in 1960. This little-known bird lives only in the Souvenir area of Mahé, high up in remote, misty forest belt, although a scops owl nest has yet to be found. This secretive and almost exclusively nocturnal owl was down to an estimated 80 pairs in the 1990s.

The once endangered **Seychelles warbler** is one of the more heartening of local conservation stories. Not too long ago the total world population of these birds was down to 26, and these were found only on Cousin. Since the island was proclaimed a nature reserve in 1968 the warbler population has reached what BirdLife International believes is the maximum that Cousin can sustain, and recently Cousin warblers have been translocated to Aride, with encouraging results.

Magpie robins have in turn been translocated to rat-free Cousin from Frégate island where there were only 12 remaining birds in the mid-1960s. The Cousin magpie robins are now breeding more successfully than their forebears on Frégate, although the original dozen have also increased dramatically thanks to a recovery project sponsored by the World Bank and implemented by BirdLife International.

Planning a Visit

Twitchers come from all over the world in the hope of seeing some of the rarest birds on earth among the 15 endemic species found only in Seychelles, and many new species were, in fact, first noted by hawk-eyed visiting birders. The **best bird-watching time** is from April to May, which is the beginning of the breeding season for most seabirds. If you want to see migrant birds, October is better. Rare migrants sometimes fly in from as far afield as Siberia and the Antarctic, providing twitchers with occasional but exciting sightings of these vagrants.

Adrian Skerrett, resident author of books on the flora and fauna of Seychelles has created specialist bird-watching itineraries for 7° South. Contact them at Kingsgate House, PO Box 475, Victoria (tel 32-2682, fax 32-1322, e-mail: 7south@seychelles.net).

CONSERVATION, NATIONAL PARKS AND RESERVES

After only two decades of active conservation Seychelles entered the new millennium by announcing that it was dedicating itself to preserving this little corner of the planet for future generations. To protect its wealth of rare plants, birds, and marine species Seychelles has turned nearly half of its total land area of 176 sq miles (455 sq km) into national parks and reserves, as well as designating several hundred protected sensitive areas. Two of these areas, **Aldabra Atoll** and **Vallée de Mai**, are World Heritage Sites, and protected under international law as unique natural areas of world importance. In addition to Aldabra, two other islands, **Aride** and **Cousin**, have been are proclaimed in their entirety as nature reserves. **Marine national parks and reserves** have been established at Silhouette, Curieuse, Aride, Cousin, St Anne, and at two locations off Mahé's east coast, **Baie Ternay** and nearby **Port Launay**. Virtually all fishing is prohibited within these sanctuaries. Spearfishing is banned and all corals, shells and other marine life is protected. One shell in particular, the huge **Triton's Trumpet**, is completely protected throughout all the islands. Boats are not allowed to anchor in certain areas and park rangers are employed to ensure that all rules and regulations are observed. You might wonder about all these restrictions when you see corals and shells on sale in Seychelles, but many of these have been imported, usually from the Philippines. As a responsible tourist you'll naturally ignore these in favour of other less environmentally damaging souvenirs.

Until fairly recently, huge numbers of turtles were killed each year, not for food but for their carapaces, and it was possible to buy trinkets and curios made from their shells. This slaughter has been stopped and there are now hefty fines and even jail sentences for offenders. Artisans who once made their living selling tortoiseshell artefacts have been retrained to produce eco-safe products with the help of World Bank funding. Seychelles is the only place on earth where hawksbill turtles come up beaches to nest by day. This habit, which evolved countless years ago when no natural predators prowled the beaches, has cost them dearly during two centuries of contact with humans. Protective legislation means there is now more hope for the hawksbill's survival here than almost anywhere else on earth. The ocean around the Seychelles is a whale sanctuary, and these giant mammals cannot be hunted or disturbed for any reason.

With international help, Seychelles has also been successful in its efforts to safeguard its birds and increase the numbers of its rare and endangered species (see *Bird Watching*). In 1968, 67-acre (27 ha) Cousin island was bought and turned into a nature reserve by the Royal Society of Nature Conservation (RSNC), and has since been managed by BirdLife International, whose conservation programmes there and elsewhere have enjoyed some spectacular successes in the restoration of disturbed habitats and the regeneration of depleted bird populations. The entire island of Cousin is a reserve, with seven breeding seabird species, nesting beaches for hawksbill turtles, and its pride – 400 or so brush warblers rescued from the brink of extinction. Even centipedes are protected here. The designation of islands as reserves has helped to recreate a window on a world that existed undisturbed probably from the dawn of time. Climb to the summit of Aride and you can look down on a vista as it must have been before the first human footsteps imprinted its sand. Apart from its 10 breeding species of seabird, Aride (French for barren) has two plants – **Wright's gardenia** and **Aride peponium** – which are found nowhere else on earth.

Far to the south-west of the archipelago is Aldabra which accounts for nearly one-third of Seychelles' land mass and is a sanctuary for almost 90% of the world's giant tortoises – 150,000 of them – and a variety of unique island birds and plants, including the last surviving flightless bird of the Indian Ocean, the Aldabra rail. Uncountable numbers of frigatebirds breed in the mangroves along the northern perimeter of the massive lagoon encircled by Aldabra's limestone cays. It became a World Heritage Site in 1982, and a plaque stands there with the simple message in English and French: 'Aldabra, wonder of nature, given to humanity by the people of the Republic of Seychelles.'

Conservation measures on **Aldabra**, the world's biggest atoll, have protected the world's largest population of giant tortoises, the only surviving flightless bird in the world, and one of the few known breeding sites for the pink greater flamingo. Aldabra's waters also provide refuge for one of the world's biggest collections of sea turtles. The atoll's thousands of mushroom-shaped islets harbour significant populations of sea birds. Sunbirds and the bright red Madagascar fody hover among the blossoms of rare flowers such as the Aldabra lily, with its spike of scarlet flowers, and fragrant Aldabra jasmine. Aldabra is a UN-designated World Heritage

Site and a milestone for living museum conservation efforts, especially for its preservation of giant land tortoises, of which there are now an estimated 150,000. These slow-moving terrestrial turtles, some weighing up to 500 lb (225 kg), often move no further than a couple of metres a day while grazing on the lawn-like tortoise turf, so it's little wonder some of them live to be 150. These tortoises were once found on many other Indian Ocean islands, but were ruthlessly hunted by the crews of passing ships, who regarded them as the perfect fresh food source on long voyages. As a result of this they became extinct everywhere except on Aldabra, where rocky shores were a landing hazard, and on the islands of Galapagos on the other side of the world.

An interesting account survives relating to five giant tortoises taken from Aldabra to Mauritius in 1766. In 1828, Admiral Sir Henry Keppler saw one of them in the grounds of Government House in Port Louis and wrote that it could move 'with six men on its back, three each side, standing on the edge of its shell, holding hands across.' This tortoise died nearly 100 years later, after falling and breaking its neck. British officers said it committed suicide on hearing that Fort George was to be manned by the local Volunteer Force. A refugee male Aldabra tortoise named Esmerelda still lives on Bird Island. It is estimated to be more than 200 years old and weighs 705 lb (320 kg).

You might not be able to find the time and funds for a trip to Aldabra, but on no account go home without seeing the Vallée de Mai National Park on Praslin. This is the home of the magnificent coco-de-mer and five other species of palms unique to Seychelles. It is also the favourite haunt of the last surviving 120 black parrots, Seychelles' national bird. A small fee is charged by the Seychelles Islands Foundation for entry to Vallée de Mai. For the past few years, exotic species have been gradually removed and much of the valley has been replanted with endemic plants. Access within the reserve is restricted to a carefully designed system of paths. Since 1989 Vallée de Mai has been managed by the Seychelles Islands Foundation, which seems to be having difficulty in effectively patrolling the reserve. Poaching of coco-de-mer nuts has become a serious problem and there is also a considerable fire hazard, although all smoking and use of fire is prohibited within the reserve. Rats and feral cats have established themselves in the area and are threatening endemic birds. Special rat-proof nesting boxes have been installed to protect the reserve's endangered black parrots.

Tours. These can be organised for groups or individuals, accompanied by knowledgeable local guides. Guided tours can be booked through: Bunson's Travel (tel 32-2682); Mason's Travel (tel 32-2642); National Travel Agency (tel 22-4900); Premier Holidays (tel 22-5777); and Travel Services (tel 32-2414).

For more information contact:
Seychelles Island Foundation: PO Box 853, Victoria, Seychelles.
Division of Environment: Ministry of Foreign Affairs, Planning and Environment, PO Box 445, Victoria (tel 22-4644, fax 22-4500).
Nature Protection Trust of Seychelles: PO Box 207, Mahé.

Global warming has become a serious threat to coral reefs around the world and is the subject of scientific study in Seychelles, where already warm waters have increased in temperature recently to as high as 91°F (33°C), posing the threat of widespread bleaching of the reefs. You can do your bit to protect these coral reefs from damage. Do not touch, stand on, scrape, of kick sand on living corals. A careless kick of your fin when snorkelling or diving can break off a section of coral which might have taken decades to grow. Don't remove or destroy any natural feature, living or dead, corals, plants, animals, fish or shells. Each organism is part of an eco-system that is vital to the reef's survival. Anchor your hire boat on a mooring buoy where possible, or else on a sandy bottom, so that you don't damage any coral reef. Take all your litter with you, especially plastics and styrofoam, which do not biodegrade.

SPORT AND RECREATION

The Seychelles islands have lots to offer in the way of recreational activities, but they are especially renowned for scuba-diving and snorkelling, deep-sea big-game fishing, sailing, nature walks and bird-watching. The clean, clear waters around the islands and atolls dotting the ocean are a haven for more than 900 species of fish, as well as 100 types of coral, and diving on and around the coral reefs is the main attraction for underwater enthusiasts. In view of their popularity with both divers and local fishermen Austrian pioneer underwater photographer Hans Hass investigated their impact on Indian Ocean marine life. He found that there had been no noticeable detrimental effect, in distinct contrast to other areas in the world where the use of harpoons and even dynamite had damaged the environment beyond all hope of recovery. Spearfishing is absolutely forbidden in Seychelles, and the fish seem to know this, so the reefs teem with life. Near-perfect visibility most of the year makes for excellent underwater photography and reef rambling. There's a wide variety of sites and excursions available for both scuba divers and snorkellers, and one of the great pleasures of diving in the islands is the feeling you get that no one has ever been there before you in this most pristine of underwater worlds.

The Best Time for Diving

Diving is possible all year in these waters but there are seasonal changes in visibility, water temperature, and the state of the sea. The best time to go to the islands for calm seas and visibility up to 150 ft (46 m) is in April and May and the months of October and November. Seas are calmer during these periods, and the water temperature can reach 84°F (29°C). Other times, however, make up for possibly lower underwater visibility by offering other attractions, such as the periodic visits of monster, but harmless, whale sharks. The south-easterly trade winds blow from June to September and the sea can be rough except in sheltered bays such as Beau Vallon Bay on Mahé. Water temperature can fall as low as 75°F (24°C). From December to February the wind blows from the north-west, so that the Victoria side of Mahé is sheltered. A 3mm wetsuit is recommended for all dives.

SCUBA TRAINING

Even if you can't dive when you arrive it doesn't take long to get your underwater passport. Most of the diving centres are members of the local Association of Professional Divers of Seychelles (APDS) and are approved by the international Professional Association of Diving Instructors (PADI). If you are over 12 and can meet certain basic medical criteria, you can enrol at any APDS/PADI dive centre for a scuba-diving course. There's no upper age limit. You don't need any equipment, the dive centre will provide you with full scuba kit and wetsuit and other bits and pieces. You can become a certificated Open Water Diver after just five confined water and classroom sessions and four sea dives, or get your Advanced Open Water Diver qualification, which takes you through five exploratory dives to increase your diving skills. First open water dives are always made in water no deeper than 10-13 ft (3-4 m) at spots free from worrisome currents or surge. Once you feel comfortable underwater you start to explore with the instructor. Dives on inshore reefs vary between 33 and 66 ft (10 and 20 m) and you won't be allowed to dive deeper than a maximum 98 ft (30 m) on APDS outings. Staged decompression dives are not allowed, even though there is an emergency twin-lock recompression 'pot' in Victoria. This is used only as a transit chamber to get a bent diver to the nearest full recompression facility at Mombasa on the Kenya coast.

The two largest dive operators are Island Ventures (tel 24-7141, fax 24-7433, e-mail: ivdivsey@seychelles.net) and Underwater Centre Seychelles (tel 24-7357, fax 34-4223, e-mail: divesey@seychelles.net or uwc@sey.net). The PADI 5 Star Seychelles Underwater Centre has resident British professional instructors and is affiliated to the British Sub Aqua Club. It operates modern, safe dive boats from dive shops at the Coral Strand Hotel and the Reef Hotel and Golf Club on Mahé and at the Paradise Sun Hotel on Praslin. They offer introductory scuba lessons as well as complete certification and advanced courses. All the diving centres arrange a variety of diving activities, including night dives, wreck and adventure dives. Other diving contacts include:

Jules Verne Undersea Walk: Anse Royale, Mahé (tel 37-1171).
La Digue Dive Centre: tel 23-4232.
Le Diable de Mer: Beau Vallon Beach, Mahé (tel 24-7104).
Octopus Diving: Anse Volbert, Praslin (tel/fax 23-2350).
Pro Diving: Victoria (tel 36-1361/37-6377).
Savuka Dive/Fishing Centre: Anse Bois de Rose, Praslin (tel 23-3900, fax 23-3919).

BEST DIVE SPOTS

With so many to choose from it's difficult, and contentious, to recommend as best any particular spots, but you can't go wrong off the coast of Mahé, Praslin, and La Digue centrally and the Amirantes and Aldabra for far out trips. A popular site for beginners is in the Marine Park at Baie Ternay, where you'll be led over a white sandy sea floor to one of Seychelles' most beautiful coral gardens. Among the best sites around Mahé are St Anne Marine National Park (from a boat) and Port Launay (from the shore); the rocks at the Northolme Hotel; Anse Soleil; Petite Anse and Ile Souris. Chauve Souris Island near Praslin and Petite Soeur island north of La Digue are also good dive sites.

SNORKELLING

If you are looking at the water anywhere in the islands you can be sure you are looking at excellent snorkelling areas. Many of the snorkelling spots are close to the beach, although the best spots are usually off rocky shorelines. Most of the larger hotels on beaches have snorkelling equipment – mask, snorkel and fins – available on a complimentary basis for guests or for hire. They'll also advise you on where to find a boat if you want to snorkel offshore. Wear something for protection against coral cuts and grazes.

LIVEABOARD DIVING

If you'd like to combine your diving with cruising and get to some of the really fabulous but distant diving the Underwater Centre offers from 7 to 14 night cruises on the 70 ft (21 m) *Indian Ocean Explorer*. This will take you to the northern islands as well as to the virginal diving sites of the Aldabra islands group, more than 700 miles (1,127 km) to the south-west and nearer to Madagascar than to Seychelles. The high point for all visiting divers is the adrenalin pumping drift diving through the channels into Aldbara's vast lagoon.

The *Indian Ocean Explorer* is the first scuba diving liveaboard vessel to stay in Seychellois waters all year round, visiting all of the prime diving destinations in the country, among them the Inner Islands, the Amirantes and Aldabra. Four times a year it makes two-week diving trips from Mahé to Aldabra. There are also a number of whale shark expeditions undertaken in conjunction with the Whale Shark Institute. The *Indian Ocean Explorer* is a converted oceanographic research ship fitted out for 16 divers with eight air-conditioned double cabins with en-suite bathrooms, and spacious air-conditioned lounge and dining areas. The liveaboard boasts one of the finest diving facilities in the Indian Ocean, with a large rear dive deck and platform, individual equipment storage lockers, Nitrox and E6 processing facilities. Itineraries range from £154-£200/US$235-300 a day (for more information e-mail explorer@sey.net).

BIG-GAME FISHING

This is a relatively new sport in Seychelles, but the abundance of fish has already made the islands popular with anglers. Black, blue and striped marlin, sailfish, yellowfish, dogtooth tuna, wahoo and barracuda are just a few of the fighting fish found in these tropical waters. Dogtooth tuna have set world records here, including the all-tackle record. Traditionally, strip bait is used but live bait is available and tag and release is increasingly encouraged. Night fishing for barracuda is an adventure all of its own, and bonefish have become a popular quarry, with rewarding catches off Desroches, Denis, Bird, and North islands.

Best Time for Fishing

Fishing, like diving, is governed by weather conditions. From May to September, the trade winds blow from the south-east; and from November to February, from the north-west. Unless you are happy out on fairly choppy seas during the south-east monsoon, which blows between the months of April and October, the best time for enjoyable fishing is between October and April, when the sea can sometimes resemble an enormous calm lake and offers good bottom fishing, which can result in giant red snapper, grouper and Jobfish. Trolling brings in red-meat fish (tuna, jackfish and dorado). May to September is recorded as the best time for the really big-game fish.

Hire

Many liveaboards are equipped for the sport or a purpose-built vessel from the Marine Charter Association (MCA) can be hired to take you to the rich banks around Mahé, Frégate, Bird and Denis. Pre-book your fishing in good time because the popularity of this sport sometimes means a lot of anglers chasing too few well-equipped boats. If you don't want the expense of hiring a boat for yourself, MCA often knows of other visitors who want to make up a fishing party. Four is a good number to go for if each angler wants a reasonable length of time in the fighting chair. A wide selection of boats is on offer from the MCA and these are usually hired out on a daily, overnight or half-day basis, and come with skipper. Rates usually include drinks and a light lunch.

A favourite boat with visiting anglers is the *Tam Tam* which is specially designed for all types of fishing and is available for fishing expeditions ranging from a day trip to a week or more offshore, visiting almost any island within 250 miles (402 km) of Mahé.

There are well-monitored fishing centres on the islands of Bird, Denis – which has the distinction of providing record catches of sailfish and blue marlin – and Desroches in the Amirantes. MCA can put you in touch with these. Prices vary, but an average half-day outing with a charter company starts from £400/US$605, with full-day from £530/US$800 per boat. Four days will cost from £820/US$1250 per person for a four-person charter.

Useful Addresses:
Marine Charter Association: PO Box 204, Victoria, Mahé (tel 32-2126, fax 22-4679).
Tam Tam: to book ahead (tel 34-4266; e-mail tamtam@sey.net).
Boat House: Beau Vallon, Mahé (tel 24-7898, fax 24-7898/24-7955).
La Digue Island Cruising: Anse Reunion (tel 23-4299).
Payet Conrad: Mahé (tel 32-2288).
The Optimist Charter: Praslin (tel 23-2329, fax 23-2374).
VPM Charter: tel 22-5676.
Yacht 'MY Way': tel 22-4573.
There are also other independent big-game fishing specialists. For more information contact the Tourism Trade Association (PO Box 1109, Victoria, Mahé: tel 32-4131, fax 32-4145).

SALTWATER FLY-FISHING
This type of fishing on island flats is exhilarating, especially with a guide who knows the local waters. Guides are expert and usually inexpensive. You fish either by wading or from a small pirogue. The fishing categories fall generally into flats, surf, inshore reefs, and deep-sea. All the flats fishing, with the exception of the main granitic islands, means lots of wading. On the flats, floating or intermediate lines are best, but from the beaches, if the surf is rough and the currents strong, a fast sinking line will be needed for using below-surface flies. On the reefs around the islands pelagic species such as tuna, dorado, wahoo and sailfish are found inshore as well as out in the blue water. Bonefish, pompano, trevally, barracuda and milkfish are almost as common on the flats as they are in the surf. Bonefish seem only too pleased to take whatever flies you want to try. However, as a general rule you should match the basic colour of the fly to the area you are fishing in, and the flats are mainly white sand with occasional darker areas. Bear in mind that there is no shelter from the sun when you are out fishing the flats, so make sure you don't become dehydrated or sunburnt. A good pair of sunglasses not only protects your eyes, they also make fish spotting easier. What you wear on your feet is also important. Even a small cut can become infected, so wear comfortable waders.

Alphonse island, south of the Amirantes, offers world-class saltwater fly-fishing for bonefish and trevally and nearby St Francois island is virtually unexploited. Bonefish of up to 15 lb (7 kg) can be caught and even half-hearted fly fishermen have caught 50 fish in a day. Several world records have already been claimed, four of them within the space of a week.

FISHING CALENDAR

Species	Jan	Feb	Mar	Apr	May	Jun	Jul	Aug	Oct	Nov	Dec
Marlin	*	*	*	**	**	**	*	-	**	**	**
Sailfish	*	*	*	**	**	**	**	**	**	**	**
Yellow Tuna	*	*	*	**	**	**	*	-	**	**	**
Wahoo	*	*	*	**	**	**	*	-	**	**	**
Dorado	*	*	*	**	**	**	*	-	**	**	**
Bonefish	**	**	**	**	**	**	*	-	***	***	**

Key   ***=Very Good   **=Good   *=Average

Fishing Competitions

During the game-fish season there is a number of fishing competitions open to all under the watchful eye of the local representative of the International Game Fishing Association (IGFA) who is on hand to arbitrate between anglers as to who caught what. Seychelles has more than 280 species of fish that can be taken with rod and reel, and around 100 are recognised for IGFA record purposes. There are a few shops in Victoria where you can buy fishing equipment, but if you are keen you'll bring your own. Get local opinion on where to fish in various weather conditions.

SAILING

This is an all year round sailing location, and as Seychelles lies outside the Indian Ocean cyclone belt there is no better way to explore the nooks and crannies, beaches and lagoons of the 115 islands which stretch over an oceanic patch twice the area of Texas and well over twice the size of France. Yachting is not only for the experienced sailor, it is possible to hire expert local crew who can show you favourite island hideaways while you sit back and relax. You can charter a crewed yacht, power-boat or cabin cruiser for fishing, diving, or leisurely exploration, or a combination of all three activities. For the more adventurous, bare-boat charters are available and there is an excellent selection of yachts, sailboats and catamarans to choose from for hire by the week or longer. Half-day and full-day yacht charters, with captain, and sometimes crew, can be booked in advance or simply call in at the Marine Charter Association at the harbour in Victoria (tel 32-2126, fax 22-4679).

Silhouette Cruises operates two old-style sailing ships for Seychelles cruises. They are *Sea Pearl* and sister ship *Sea Shell*. They offer cruises that combine old-fashioned charm and elegance with all mod cons. *Sea Shell,* a Dutch sailing vessel built in 1910, began cruising in local waters in 1997. Interest grew so rapidly that by 1999 it could no longer meet the demand. The *Sea Pearl,* an almost identical vessel, was brought from the Caribbean in August 1999.

Silhouette Cruises: 7° South, Kingsgate House, PO Box 475, Victoria (tel 32-2682, fax 32-1322).

WALKS AND TRAILS

If you prefer to explore this natural paradise at ground level, guided walking tours will introduce you to the islands' exotic flora and fauna and can be arranged through most hotels or local tour operators. You can strike out on your own and there are, for instance, excellent marked trails on Mahé, Praslin, Silhouette and Aride. You can get an experienced guide to walk you through the tropical forests, explaining the flora and fauna along the way. Even though it is advisable to walk early in the morning it will still be warmer than most northern hemisphere visitors are accustomed to, so you should carry plenty of water. Trails are conveniently graded into easy, medium and difficult walks. Some pre-walk planning is recommended: choose the difficulty level best suited to your ability; wear sturdy shoes, pack a hat, snacks and drinks, and a plastic bag to take out your litter. Be careful during the rainy months, especially December-February, when the mountain paths can be slippery. The best time to explore is from May to September. If you like rock climbing and you like a challenge, Praslin and La Digue are the places for you. The tourism office has excellent brochures with information on hiking routes, points of interest, and fauna and flora. These are available for a small charge from the Ministry of Tourism (PO Box 92, Mahé, Seychelles). In Victoria, you can get them from the Tourist Information Centre in Independence Avenue.

Other Sports

Windsurfers, canoes, dinghies, can be hired on the more popular beaches, such as Beau Vallon Bay on Mahé, and paragliding and hang-gliding are available at some of the resorts, which also hire out equipment. There are also opportunities for golf, squash, tennis and badminton, although the heat and humidity makes these pastimes pretty draining. Seychelles has never been known for its water-skiing and, for environmental reasons, does not encourage it.

Opening Hours

Shops are generally open from 8am or 9am to 5pm Monday to Friday (lunch is from noon to 1pm), and 8am to noon on Saturday. Some shops also open on Sunday mornings.

Gifts and Souvenirs

As the capital, Victoria naturally has the greatest variety of shops and it's the best place to search for souvenirs. There are also boutiques and general merchandise stores all over the island and most of the larger hotels have their own boutiques. Good buys include pottery and batiks, clothes and handicrafts. You can take home memories from a wide range of locally crafted gold and sea-shell jewellery, artworks, and handicrafts such as basketware, tablemats, hats, and wood carvings. Jewellery made from green snail shells, orchids dipped in gold, and the island's trinkets made from mother-of-pearl are popular. The **local liqueur** known as Coco d'Amour will remind you of the island when you are back home. **Local tea** can be bought in the shops or when visiting the tea factory on Mahé, where many blends of tea may be sampled at the Tea Tavern, at the tea estate off the road from Victoria to Port Glaud. **Vanilla** is cultivated as a climbing plant around the base of trees, as pollination can be done by hand, and their fragrant dried pods can be bought in shops. **Cinnamon** grows wild on all the islands and it can be bought as oil or as quills of dried bark.

Near Mahé's main taxi rank on Albert Street is **Camion Hall** and one of the **Compagnie pour le Développement de L'Artisanat** (Codevar) shops known as Artizan de Zil. This organisation promotes traditional craft industries and its shops sell a wide variety of craftwork, including *vakwa* bags and hats made from vacoa palm fibre, as well as some innovative creations such as ceramic and coconut jewellery. All these souvenirs are made to a high standard from Seychellois raw materials and designs. Camion Hall houses several other **craft shops**, including Seychelles Creations, which sells jewellery, buttons and hair clips made of natural fibres, and Kreol d'Or, which produces 18-carat gold jewellery using such Seychellois motifs as palm trees, coconuts and fish. The Premier Building office block, opposite Camion Hall, has several modern boutiques. Further along the road is the largest supermarket in Seychelles, belonging to the Seychelles Marketing Board (SMB), as well as a number of old stores offering a wide variety of goods for both locals and tourists.

Jivan Imports on the corner of Albert and Markets streets is better known locally than the rest, simply because its proprietor, Kantilal Jivan Shah, is well known throughout the island. Kanti is an amateur biologist, historian, anthropologist, masseur and cook. His promotion and support of efforts to protect and preserve the Seychelles' natural environment has earned him a silver medal from the Royal Norwegian Society of Sciences and Letters, as well as a UN Environment Protection 'Global 500' award.

On Market Street, Sunstroke Designs is a boutique selling innovative **clothing and accessories**, all locally designed and hand-printed. On nearby Church Street,

Brijals will print you a **personalised T-shirt**, shirt or cap using any photograph you give them. The Victoria House shopping arcade, known as Passage des Palmes, is close to the Clock Tower in the centre of town. For model boats and objects to do with sailing and historic ships try La Marine, at La Plaine, St Andre, Mahé (tel/fax 37-1441). At **Kreol Fleurage Parfums**, at North East Point in Mahé (tel 24-1329), you can sniff some delightful Indian Ocean fragrances.

There are mini-markets everywhere selling everything from make-up and garden equipment to French champagne.There is a **duty-free** facility at the Berjaya Beau Vallon Hotel, where you can collect your purchases immediately on production of your air ticket. For more information contact SMB Duty Free (tel 22-4444, fax 22-4735). Seychelles International Airport's duty free shops are ideal for buying that last-minute souvenir or present.

ART GALLERIES

Art is flourishing in Seychelles and you can get a leaflet listing local artists from the Association for Visual Arts (tel 22-4777). Christine Harter, with painter Michael Adams, is one of the best-known and most sought after Seychellois artists. Her land and seascapes and portraits of Creole subjects are in museums and homes around the world. She studied art and design in Britain. The Cote d'Or, Praslin, where she opened a gallery and a small restaurant, the Café des Arts, exhibits her work (tel 23-2131). Christine is primarily a watercolour artist, working occasionally in pencil, pen and ink, and oils. Her mural of the coco-de-mer forest in the Vallée de Mai is in the reception area of the Beau Vallon Bay Hotel, and it featured on a Seychelles stamp. Michael Adams has his studio on the south-west coast at Anse aux Poules Bleues. If you plan to visit him it's a good idea to phone first (tel 36-1006, fax 36-1200). There are several galleries on Mahé, among them Alexis Gerard, St Claire Building, Victoria (tel 32-2375); Antigone Trading, Victoria House (tel 22-5443); South African Ron Gerlach's Batik Studio, at Beau Vallon (tel 24-7875); Banane Joel (tel 37-6295), and Bauscher Carina (tel 37-5474), which are both at the Codevar Craft Village, Anse Aux Pins (tel 37-6100).

Kaz Zanana, in a restored old colonial house on Revolution Avenue, Victoria, exhibits works by leading Seychelles artists. Try its delicious pastries with tea or coffee after browsing. It's open daily except Sundays (tel 32-5150). Visit the **Seychelles Potters Co-operative Society** (Seypot), at Les Mamelles (tel 34-4080) and check out silkscreen prints, limited editions and original paintings at **Studio de Voud** (tel 34-4148).

CAUTION

Turtle shells and most hard corals, especially the red and black coral used for jewellery, are listed as endangered species. Turtleshell products – often sold as tortoiseshell – or any of these endangered corals are illegal in almost every country in the world. If you even unknowingly buy a turtleshell souvenir it could be confiscated by customs as you leave or on your return home, and in some countries you could face prosecution.

Crime and Safety

Petty crime has become fairly common in the islands in recent years and it is the worm in the apple of this Eden. Violent crime involving visitors, however, is rare. Be sensible. Never leave your valuables unguarded; keep them in room or hotel safes and close and lock any windows in your room at night. It is risky, especially for women, to swim alone at isolated beaches. Opportunist thieves often target boats left unlocked while moored in Victoria harbour. If you lose or have your passport stolen report it immediately to local police and to your nearest embassy or consulate. Police officers are the ones in dark blue trousers or skirts, with white short-sleeve shirts and epaulettes. The central police station on Mahé is in Revolution Avenue, Victoria. The main emergency number throughout the country for police, fire and ambulance is the easy-to-remember 999. On remote islands law is maintained by a circuiting police officer. If you are found in illegal possession or transporting shells, corals, preserved fish, or turtles, or any other endangered species, these items will be confiscated and you can be sure of a fine. Drinking on any road or in public places is illegal, although you'd never know it. Possession, use of or trafficking in any drugs (including cannabis) is illegal, and can get you a sentence of up to 15 years' in jail. Useful numbers are the Central Police Station (tel 32-2011); Beau Vallon Police Station (tel 24-7242); Praslin Police Station (tel 23-3251); and La Digue Police Station (tel 23-4251).

TOURIST INFORMATION CENTRE
Seychelles Tourism Marketing Authority (STMA): Independence House, Independence Avenue, Victoria, Mahé (tel 22-5313, fax 22-4035, e-mail: dgtmtca@seychelles.net).

SEYCHELLES TOURIST OFFICES AND REPRESENTATIVES ABROAD

United Kingdom, Eire, Netherlands, Scandanavia: 2nd Floor, Eros House, 111 Baker Street, London W1M 1FE (tel 020-7224-1670, fax 020-7486-1352, e-mail sto@seychelles.uk.com).

France, Belgium, Luxembourg and Switzerland (French-speaking): 32 Rue De Ponthieu, F-75008 Paris, France (tel 1-4289 9777, fax 1-4289 9770).

Germany, Austria and Switzerland (German-speaking): An Der Hauptwache 11, D-60313 Frankfurt, Germany (tel 69-292064, fax 69-296230, e-mail: Seyinfo@aol.com).

Italy: Via Giulia 66, I-00186 Rome (tel 6-686 9056/686-8075, fax 6-686 8127).

Japan: Berna Heits 4-A3, Hiroo 5-4-11, Shibuya-Ku, Tokyo 150 (tel 3-5449 0461, fax 3-5449 0462).

Kenya: Jubilee Insurance Exchange Building, 3rd Floor, Kaunda Street, PO Box 30702, Nairobi (tel 2-221335/226744, fax 2-219787, e-mail coa@africaonline.co.ke).

Singapore: 11 Cavenagh Road, #01-10, Holiday Inn Parkview, Singapore 229616 (tel 835-1200, fax 834-1500).

Spain & Portugal: Gran Via, 6-4 Planta, E-28013 Madrid, Spain (tel 91-524 7426, fax 91-524 7476, e-mail: stomad@ibm.net).

South Africa: PO Box 782551, 5th Floor, Sandton City Tower, Sandton 2146 (tel 11-784 6706/6707, fax 11-784 6442, e-mail: crol@icon.co.za).

USA & Canada: 235 East 40th Street, Suite 24A, New York, NY 10016, USA (tel 212-687 9766/7, fax 212-922 9177, e-mail: sto@sto-americas.com).

EMBASSIES AND CONSULATES

In Seychelles you'll find the **British High Commission** on the 3rd Floor, Victoria House, Mahé (tel 22-5225, fax 22-5127, e-mail: bhcsey@seychelles.net). The US closed its embassy in the Seychelles in August 1996 and transferred consular responsibilities to the **US Embassy in Mauritius**, at 4th Floor, Rogers House, on President John F Kennedy Street, Port Louis (tel 208-9764-69, fax 208-9534). The consular agency in Seychelles provides limited services, such as the distribution of forms and information. US citizens should register at this agency, which provides updated information on local travel and security. The agency is located at 1st Floor, Room 112, Victoria House, Victoria, Mahé (tel 22-5256, fax 22-5189, e-mail: usoffice@seychelles.net).

Other diplomatic representatives:
Belgium: tel 26-1455.
France: tel 22-4523/4590.
Germany: tel 26-1212.
Italy: tel 22-4741.
Netherlands: tel 26-1111.

DISABLED TRAVELLERS
Most of the excursions in the islands could be fairly gruelling for disabled travellers. A beach holiday in bungalow accommodation might be the safest option. Bird island makes provision for visitors in wheelchairs.

BUDGET TRAVEL
The cost of living is pretty high for low-budget travellers and La Digue island is the best bet. As mentioned elsewhere, the Seychelles government wants to encourage middle to upper bracket visitors, but don't let this put you off if you are a backpacker and can afford the air fares and the island cost of living.

USEFUL INFORMATION

Time Zone
Seychelles time is 4 hours ahead of GMT (3 hours ahead of British summer time). The islands are nine to 15 hours ahead of US time; $7^1/2$ to 13 hours ahead of Canadian time; 8 hours behind New Zealand; 4-6 hours behind Australia; 4 hours behind Singapore; 2 hours ahead of South Africa; $1^1/2$ hours behind Indian standard time; and an hour ahead of Madagascar. Daylight saving is not observed.

Electrical Appliances
Power supply on the islands is 240 volts AC 50 Hz. Plugs are the square English type three-pin. Adaptors are usually available at hotels but it is a good idea to take a universal adaptor with you. A torch is a useful item to carry as power cuts occur fairly regularly and there are few street lights. The country's Public Utilities Corporation produces, manages and distributes electricity to most parts of the main islands. The present installed capacity is just over 30 megawatts and annual consumption is below 150,000 kWh.

Useful Addresses and Telephone Numbers:
Air Seychelles: Victoria House, Mahé (tel 22-5300/38-1000).
Nature Protection Trust of Seychelles: PO Box 207, Mahé.
Police, Fire Brigade and Ambulance Emergencies: dial 999.
Seychelles Bird Records Committee: c/o Adrian Skerret, PO Box 336, Mahé.
Seychelles Hotel Association: tel 32-4131.
Tourist Dentist and Tourist Doctor: tel 38-8000.
Meteorological Office: tel 37-3377.

Public Holidays

New Year	January 1
Public Holiday	January 2
Good Friday,	
Easter Saturday, Sunday and Monday	March/April
Labour Day	May 1
Liberation Day (Anniversary of 1977 coup)	June 5
Corpus Christi	May/June
National Day	June 18
Independence Day	June 29
Assumption Day (it's a festival on La Digue)	August 15
All Saints' Day	November 1
Immaculate Conception	December 8
Christmas Day	December 25

Calendar of Events

Each village celebrates its own Saint's Day. Although these celebrations are not public holidays, they are colourful occasions and well worth attending if you are in the area. Every April the **National Fishing Competition** is held. If you want to participate, make sure to join a group or charter a boat well in advance. If you are into scuba-diving, the big event of the year is **Subios** (Sub-Indian Ocean Seychelles), an annual underwater festival usually staged over three weeks in November on Mahé and Praslin islands. Highlights include underwater films and talks by world-renowned diving, conservation and photographic experts. A popular underwater photography contest is held during the festival. During the last weekend of September the two-day **Beau Vallon Regatta** is held. The regatta includes a yacht race, swimming competition (underwater treasure hunt), beach tug-of-war and eating and drinking contests. Evening entertainment offers live music and magic shows. In September La Digue plays host to the **Annual Regatta**. The last week of October marks the biggest cultural event of the year – the **Kreol Festival**. Kreol artists gather from countries with similar cultures to the Seychelles (including Mauritius and the Caribbean). The main purpose of the festival is to help mould a sense of national identity. Victoria is colourfully decorated for this festival and entertainment includes dances, concerts, plays and processions.

EXPLORING
SEYCHELLES

The 115 islands of the Seychelles archipelago, scattered over a boundless stretch of the Indian Ocean below the equator, combine their icing-sugar white beaches, magnificent coral reefs, clean, crystal waters, and luxuriant tropical vegetation to make-up one of the world's most intriguing and enticing holiday destinations. It's truly a dream vacation spot, the sort of place you have in your mind's eye when you go off to other, nearer, places only to find the reality rather a shock when you get there. Anyone who has been to the Seychelles islands will tell you that they are Technicolor picture postcards come true. They are incomparable but, if you insist, the well-travelled will speak with nostalgia of the islands of the Caribbean before they were discovered – not by Columbus, but by the tourist industry 30 or 40 years ago. It's by no means cheap to get to Seychelles, but once there you won't find a great deal to spend your money on except for island-hopping planes and boats to enable you to enjoy the things that matter and what Seychelles epitomises: lots of sand on which to do nothing except listen to the palm trees rustle, and lots of clear blue sea to swim in, dive under and sail over. For those into something more strenuous there's walking, bird-watching, fishing, and perhaps a bit of treasure-hunting in this most famous of old pirate lairs. Oh yes, and the Kreol food; that's something to write home about on your postcards. If all this sounds like hyperbole it isn't, it's because that's the only way to talk about Seychelles.

VICTORIA

One of the smallest national capitals in the world – with a population of about 28,000; it is the economic and administrative centre, as well as the only commercial port. Lying in a well-sheltered natural harbour and protected by the islands of the offshore St Anne Marine National Park, the town sits between the sea and an impressive mountain barrier. Look up from Victoria and you'll see Morne Seychellois; the three peaks to its right are the *Trois Frères* ('Three Brothers'). A British East India Company vessel recorded the first visit to what is today Victoria in 1609. Victoria was first settled in the late 18th century, when it was known as *L'Etablissement de Roi* ('King's Settlement'). In the early days, the settlers had to contend with thick mangrove swamps full of crocodiles. By 1841 the crocs were long gone and the town was renamed Victoria in honour of England's reigning monarch. Marianne North, the English botanical artist who visited Victoria in 1883, was more impressed by the red-legged turquoise crabs scurrying over the mud and sand than by the town itself. The **Clock Tower**, or *l'horloge*, in the town's bustling centre was paid for by public subscription and erected to mark Seychelles separation from Mauritius and its new status as a British Crown Colony in 1903. The Kreol remark *il n'a pas vu l'horloge* ('he hasn't seen the clock') is used to refer to a country bumpkin. The best way to get a feel for Victoria is to walk around it. It doesn't take long. The clock tower is a good starting point, but walk either in the early morning or late afternoon to avoid the worst of the heat. Use the street map printed in *Seychelles Rendezvous,* the free magazine published by the Ministry of Tourism.

Running north from the clock is Albert Street, named after Queen Victoria's husband. On this street is Mahé Trading Building which houses Travel Services Seychelles, one of the main travel agents and tour operators on the islands. Cross the St Louis River – which is little more than a drain – and the main taxi rank is on your right. The taxi rank is the starting point for the Beau Vallon-Victoria nature trail and walk. Also on Albert Street is **Deepam's Cinema**, the only one in the

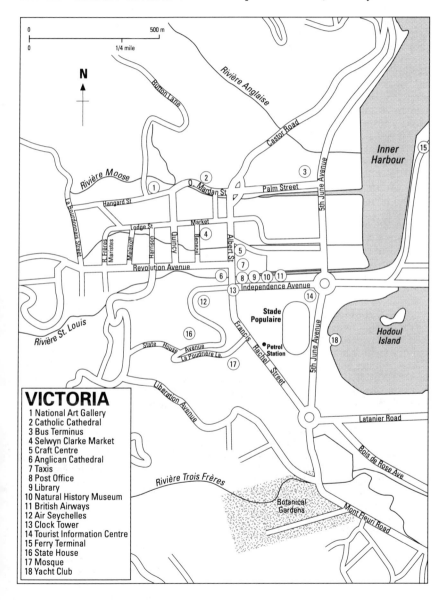

VICTORIA

1 National Art Gallery
2 Catholic Cathedral
3 Bus Terminus
4 Selwyn Clarke Market
5 Craft Centre
6 Anglican Cathedral
7 Taxis
8 Post Office
9 Library
10 Natural History Museum
11 British Airways
12 Air Seychelles
13 Clock Tower
14 Tourist Information Centre
15 Ferry Terminal
16 State House
17 Mosque
18 Yacht Club

country. Near the cinema on Oliver Maradan Street is the **Catholic Cathedral of the Immaculate Conception**, built in 1898. The cathedral has a famous clock which until recently chimed the hour twice, just before and then again on the hour. No one seems quite sure why. Next to the cathedral is the **Capucin Seminary**, built in 1933 and now a national monument. A beautiful stone building next door to the Seminary houses the Seminary's printing works. Walk along Hangard Street and you'll be in one of the town's oldest residential areas, dotted with typical Seychellois houses and stores. Along Quincy Street, named after Chevalier Jean-Baptiste Queau de Quinssi (he anglicised his surname to please the British after they made him administrator of Seychelles), is **Christy's art gallery**, which stocks works by local artists, including those of Michael Adams, Serge and Elizabeth Rouillon, Christine Harter, Donald Adelaide and Egbert Marday. **Market Street** is one of the busiest streets in Victoria, mainly because of the market there, named after British colonial governor Sir Selwyn Selwyn-Clarke. The market is full of numerous stalls selling souvenirs and local produce. It's open every day except Sunday from 5.30am, but the best time to visit is early on Saturday. The markets will give you a good idea of indigenous island food. Familiar veggies lie next to more exotic offerings, such as *patole*, which is like a hollow cucumber. Fish stalls are piled with mackerel, tuna, barracuda, red snapper, parrotfish, octopus and shark. You'll also find the chutneys and spices to accompany them. Try the fiery local chillies preserved in vinegar or minced into chilli sauce to add real Kreol zest to your home cooking. A favourite is *mazavarou*, red peppers seasoned with garlic and ginger.

On Revolution Avenue, near the central police station, is Mason's Travel, a major tour operator. As Anglicans are a minority in Seychelles, **St Paul's Anglican Cathedral** on Revolution Avenue is small by European standards. One of Mahé's most popular nightclubs, the Lovenut, is on the ground floor of the Premier Building, opposite the cathedral. Between the police station and the cathedral is an alley leading to State House Avenue. **State House**, an impressive example of colonial architecture, is closed to the public. You can, however, get permission to visit the **State House Cemetery** which is a national monument. Several important historical figures are buried here.

On Francis Rachel Street, near the only petrol station in town, is the restored building which houses the **Seychelles People's United Party (SPUP) Museum**. Further along, housed in a traditional Kreol mansion, are the **National Library**, and the **National Archives**. The **Botanical Gardens** to the south of the town, near Victoria Hospital, are an excellent place to cool off during your walk. The 15-acre (6 ha) gardens were laid out in 1901. Not all the trees, shrubs and plants in the gardens are labelled, although a brief explanatory pamphlet is available from the kiosk at the entrance. Several species of palm flank the driveway, including a small endangered talipot palm. In front of the giant tortoise pen in the gardens is a female coco-de-mer palm. You can see vanilla orchids, and if you are not up to scrambling in the mountain forests, which is their natural habitat, you'll find the unique pitcher plant. In the gardens is a bust of Pierre Poivre ('Peter Pepper'), the Frenchman who introduced spices to the islands and classified many of the floral species found in the Seychelles. For refreshment there's a small thatched cafeteria called *Le Sapin*, where you can get simple snacks and drinks.

The **Seychelles Yacht Club** is a popular local watering-hole off 5th June Avenue. The club says it offers temporary membership but be warned, you're not made to feel all that welcome and you can't get a drink in the bar unless you have the requisite vouchers. Instead, go next door to the **Marine Charter Bar** where you'll be welcomed – as long as you are wearing a shirt. The Marine Charter Association represents owners and skippers with boats available for big-game fishing, day cruises or longer charters. Along 5th June Avenue is a roundabout which features the national **Bicentennial Monument**, designed by Italian artist Lorenzo Appiani, and known locally as *Twa Zwazo* ('Three Birds'), which was erected to mark 200 years of settlement. It symbolises the three ethnic strands of the Seychellois, Europe, Africa and Asia. Another Appiani sculpture is at the other roundabout on the same avenue. Near the first roundabout is Independence House, which houses several government departments and, on the ground floor, the Tourist Information Office. Also on the ground floor, is a survey office where you can buy good ordinance survey maps of the various islands.

From the monument, the road runs one way into Independence Avenue and the other way to **Long Pier** and the **Inter-Island Quay**. This is the point from which local schooners leave to take cargo and passengers to Praslin and La Digue. **Le Marinier** restaurant is at the pier and a good place to relax and watch port comings and goings. The **National Museum** on Independence Avenue displays examples of local cultural and natural history, along with shipwreck artefacts, coral, voodoo implements, stuffed tortoises, old musical instruments, household objects, and various relics of the pirates who once roamed these waters. There's a particularly interesting display depicting the history of spice cultivation. The cannon at the entrance were discovered in 1971 and carry the royal coat of arms of Portugal. The Possession Stone, laid in 1756 by Irish Captain Corneille Morphey to proclaim French sovereignty over the islands, can be seen in the entrance hall of the museum. Victoria's **post office** is next door. Seychelles stamps are extremely popular souvenirs and even if you don't collect them they are worth buying simply for their design and beauty.

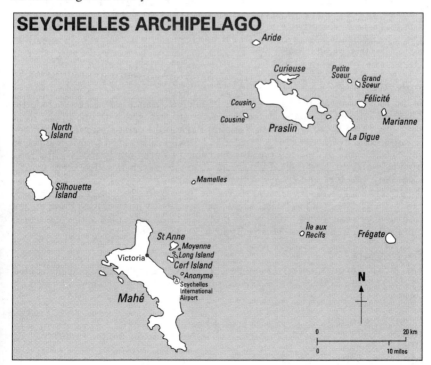

SEYCHELLES ARCHIPELAGO

MAHE

Mahé is the largest and most important island in Seychelles and the principal island on which most visitors start their holiday and from which they do their island-hopping. One lure is that Mahé has more than 70 beaches, each with a different character, around its 58 sq miles (150 sq km). The island is 17 miles (27 km) long and 8 miles (12 km) wide and is home to some 65,000 people, 80% of the total population. The island has a rugged mountainous backbone. The highest point, Morne Seychellois, is 2,969 ft (905 m) above sea level, in Seychelles' biggest national park of the same name. The airport, on the east coast, south of Victoria, is built on reclaimed land and flying in is an interesting experience, with dreamy views of the island and coastline.

TREASURE

Mahé is reputedly a treasure island and one of the interesting sites is the treasure dig on the west coast at Bel Ombre. Local legend has it that French pirate Olivier le Vasseur (*La Buse,* or 'The Buzzard') buried his treasure here. When La Buse was about to be hanged by the French in 1730 he tossed a scrap of parchment into the crowd of onlookers, shouting that whoever could decipher its markings would find his buried treasure. Regardless of the tales and plenty of pick and shovel work by various fortune hunters over the years nothing has ever been found, except for the odd silver coin, a shoe buckle and a flintlock pistol. In the neglected **old cemetery** to the west of Victoria at Bel Air one of France's most famous corsairs lies buried. On his tombstone under a banyan tree is the inscription: 'Here lies Jean Francois Hodoul, former captain of corsairs. Born June 15, 1765. Died January 10, 1835.' The gravestone was originally decorated with a picture of his ship, *Apollon,* the vessel he used to wreak havoc on British merchantmen at the height of his legalised piracy, but this, like the inscription, is badly weathered. Nearby is the long grave of the 9 ft (3 m) 'Giant of Mahé' who was poisoned by fearful settlers in 1874.

Port Glaud

In the foothills of Morne Blanc. Places of interest around Port Glaud include **Ile Thérèse**. Trips to this uninhabited island can be arranged with one of the local fishermen. **Port Launay Marine National Park and Forest Reserve** is 2.5 miles (4 km) from Port Glaud and is a wonderland of wild flowers and forests, with clear views across the marine reserve to uninhabited Conception Island. On the road from Victoria to Port Glaud you can visit the **Seychelles Tea and Coffee Company's factory** and estates. A tour around the estate gives you an insight into the production process for tea and shows you how coffee is roasted and packaged. There is a tea tavern at the estate, where you can buy a variety of teas. From the tea plantation you can follow a trail which takes you through tea plantations and scenic rain forests up to the top of **Morne Blanc** at 2,188 ft (667 m).

Baie Lazare

This area has many small coves and beaches and while in the area you can visit the **Val D'Andorre Pottery**, which produces some beautiful glazed and unglazed art pieces.

Anse aux Pins

This area is great for snorkelling and scuba-diving. Nearby are the **Codevar craft village,** which is a good place to buy curios and watch local artists at work. The village is a collection of craft shops grouped around a restored colonial building and restaurant. The **Coconut Museum** is in a palm-frond building in a coconut grove and can tell you everything you've ever wanted to know about coconuts but been afraid to ask.

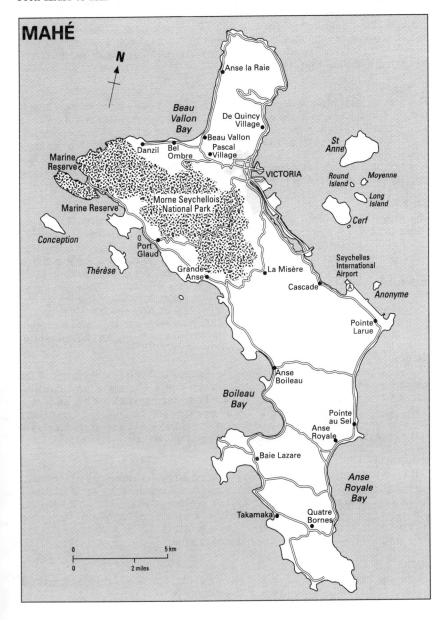

MAHÉ

N

Anse la Raie

Beau Vallon Bay

De Quincy Village

Beau Vallon

Danzil Bel Ombre Pascal Village

St Anne

Marine Reserve

VICTORIA

Round Island Moyenne

Morne Seychellois National Park

Long Island

Marine Reserve

Cerf

Conception

Port Glaud

Thérèse

Grande Anse La Misère

Seychelles International Airport

Cascade

Anonyme

Pointe Larue

Anse Boileau

Boileau Bay

Pointe au Sel

Anse Royale

Baie Lazare

Anse Royale Bay

Takamaka Quatre Bornes

0 5 km

0 2 miles

ST ANNE MARINE NATIONAL PARK

Lying off Victoria, across the Cerf Passage channel, this was one of the first (1973) national marine parks in the Indian Ocean and is the most accessible of all the protected marine areas in the Seychelles. It holds six islands, St Anne, Cerf, Round, Moyenne, Long and Cachée. The 6 sq mile (15 sq km) marine park protects fragile marine ecosystems and provides safe habitats for the hundreds of species that need them for their survival. The park area extends to enclose all six islands and the plants, corals, fish and other animals living in the sea, on the seabed and along the shore.

St Anne

This was the first place Europeans settled in 1770. St Anne provided easy access and good anchorage, as Mahé was surrounded by mangrove swamps and crawling with crocodiles. During the time it was administered by the British, a whaling station was established on St Anne and the moorings for slaughtered whales and a blubber boiler can still be seen. During World War Two St Anne was used as a seaplane depot and petroleum storage facility by the British, and old gun emplacements still stand near the shoreline.

Cerf

This lush island is named after the frigate *Le Cerf,* which claimed the islands for France in 1756. It is 15 minutes by boat from Mahé. Cerf is ringed by dazzling beaches and the north coast has a superb coral reef which makes it ideal for snorkelling and scuba diving. The island is home to **giant tortoises** and **fruit bats** (flying foxes) as well as to South African blockbuster novelist Wilbur Smith who uses it as an occasional retreat. The island has a population of only 40 people. You can get a fish-eye view of the underwater world in a semi-submersible. Worth investigating are two small **chapels**, and the **bat colonies** in the inland woods. There's a bar and restaurant serving excellent Kreol food as well as fresh plain grilled fish and it's open every day. Offshore is the little nature reserve islet of **Cachée,** where you are not allowed to land.

Round

This island is barely 164 yards (150 m) in diameter and is the headquarters of the Marine National Park, with an informative **visitors' centre**. The snorkelling is excellent here, with the possibility of sighting the **rare green turtles** which use the island as a nesting place. Shellfish and starfish abound near the sandy beaches. The **Chez Gaby** restaurant (tel 32-2111) on the island is popular with locals and tourists alike and is in a converted chapel which once ministered to lepers quarantined on the island.

Moyenne

This is owned by former East African journalist Brendon Grimshaw and is open to visitors only on certain days. Visitors must be accompanied by an official tour operator. You can explore the forest and tiny beaches on foot. Elephant Rock gives great views of Coral Cove and the beaches of south-east of Mahé. Pirates are believed to have buried treasure on Moyenne island, which makes lunch at the **Jolly Roger** bar and restaurant a fitting end to a tour.

Long

Unless you have had your collar felt you are unlikely to visit Long island. It is off limits to tourists, as it is the site of a low-security prison.

HOW TO GET THERE

Visits to the park can be arranged by tour operators in Victoria or you can go by boat. Tour operators visiting the marine park include Masons, National Travel Agency and Travel Services Seychelles. Private charters can be arranged through the Marine Charter Association, Victoria. You are allowed to swim in the park, snorkel, sail, enjoy the beaches, and take a cruise in a glass-bottom boat or semi-submersible. Fishing, and shell and coral collecting is, of course, forbidden. There are Kreol restaurants on Moyenne, Cerf and Round Islands. There's an information centre on Round Island where you can learn all about the park's amazing variety of marine life. For safety's sake you should ask your guide to show you the few organisms on the reef which can be painful or dangerous, such as sea-urchins, fire coral, and stonefish. Watch for swimmers and snorkellers if boating, protect your skin from sunburn, and keep a sharp eye on currents, winds and tides.

BEACHES
The east coast of Mahé has long beaches such as **Anse Royale** and **Anse Marie-Louise**. In the north-west is **Beau Vallon**, to many the best of all, a huge two-mile-long (3 km) curve of white sand with crystal clear waters. As this is Mahé's main tourist area it is also the choice of the people thronging the many up-market hotels and resorts, so it can be busy. To avoid the crowds try the smaller beaches, such as **Port Glaud** and **Barbarons**. Off Port Glaud is a really tiny beach on **L'Islette**, where there's a popular restaurant, and on the larger nearby **Île Thérése** is a beach well-equipped for various water activities. Loners might prefer **Anse Takamaka** in the south-west or next door **Anse Intendance** where the sand is like talcum powder and the water is an unbelievable turquoise, but you should be careful when swimming here, especially between May and September.

ACCOMMODATION

Premier Hotels
Most, but not all, up-market hotels and resorts on Mahé cluster in the Beau Vallon Bay area of the west coast.

Best Western's *Berjaya Beau Vallon Beach Resort and Casino* (tel 24-7141, fax 24-7943, e-mail: bbhfc@seychelles.net), has 182 air-conditioned rooms, mini-bar and satellite TV, two boutiques, a hairdressing salon, and duty-free shops. *The Parrot* is the main restaurant with bar, *Le Canton* serves Chinese cuisine, there's a beachside pizzeria, poolside grill, casino, diving centre and watersports.

Berjaya Mahé Beach Resort (tel 37-8451, fax 37-8517, e-mail: bmbfc@seychelles.net), another Best Western at Port Glaud on the west coast, 20 minutes from the airport. This seven-storey high-rise is on a granite outcropping set in 20 acres (8 ha) of tropical gardens. All rooms have a bath or shower, and satellite TV. There are main and poolside restaurants, with watersports available at nearby Thérèse (a short boat ride away), tennis and squash courts, and a swimming pool.

Le Meridien Barbarons (tel 37-8253, fax 37-8484, e-mail: merbbh@seychelles.net) is one of two Meridien hotels on the west coast. 20 minutes from Victoria, this hotel has 125 up/down split-level rooms with private balconies. There's a swimming pool, two restaurants, two bars, and entertainment evenings featuring fashion shows.

Le Meridien Fisherman's Cove (tel 24-7247, fax 24-7742, e-mail: merbbhl@seychelles.net) at Bel Ombre, is built in traditional timber and palm thatch and has 48 rooms, all with access to the beach, two restaurants, swimming pool, tennis courts, pool bar, games room and boutique.

The Plantation Club Resort and Casino (tel 36-1361, fax 36-1333, e-mail: resatpc@seychelles.net), which was once a coconut plantation is 35 minutes from the airport in the south-west of Mahé. It has 200 split-level air-conditioned rooms, all facing the sea or the freshwater lagoon, stretching along a kilometre of white sand beach. *The Terrace* serves light meals; the *Frangipani* serves a full tropical breakfast and themed buffet dinners; *Lazare's* is a gourmet restaurant, *Coco-de-Mer* is a poolside snack bar, and there are three other bars. Complimentary sports include windsurfing, sailing, snorkelling, canoeing, pedalo, volleyball and tennis. The dive centre caters all year round to both beginners and experienced scuba divers. There is a sauna, jacuzzi, massage and exercise room at the health centre, and the Turtle Club is for children 3 to 11.

The *Reef Hotel and Golf Club* (tel 37-6251, fax 37-6296, e-mail: reefsey@seychelles.net), 10 minutes from the airport, is set in a coconut grove close to the fishing village of Anse aux Pins. It has 150 air-conditioned rooms with private balcony overlooking the ocean and backed by a nine-hole golf course. There's a restaurant and bar, swimming pool, tennis, outdoor badminton, boat cruises, a fully-equipped dive centre, glass-bottomed boats, and fishing.

The Spanish-style *Sunset Beach Hotel* (tel 26-1111, fax 26-1221), built on a headland on the north-west coast, has 25 air-conditioned rooms, a swimming pool carved out of rock and a private beach. Large model ships decorate the lounge and restaurant, which serves international and local cuisine. Children under 12 are not accepted.

Vista Bay Club (tel 26-1333, fax 26-1061), on the north-west coast of Mahé, has 37 air-conditioned rooms staggered along a sloping site, with a bridge linking the rooms to the restaurant and sundeck above the sea, two restaurants, bar, swimming pool.

Le Northolme (tel 26-1222, fax 26-1223), on the west coast, was long a favourite haunt of British writers, who found it offered the charm of a home from home. Ian Fleming, Somerset Maugham, and Noel Coward have watched red sunsets from its terrace bar. They say even if you can afford only a single G&T it's worth the trip to savour the view from the terrace. It's in a secluded cove, 10 minutes from Victoria, and 25 minutes' drive from the airport. Twenty air-conditioned rooms, gourmet restaurant, and grounds with winding paths, and interesting nooks and crannies. There's also an underwater centre.

Chateau d'Eau (tel 37-8577/8339, fax 37-8388), is set on a semi-private beach, on the west coast. It has an authentic Creole-style plantation atmosphere, five luxurious double rooms, each with own bath and shower.

Mid-range Hotels

Auberge Club des Seychelles (tel 24-7550, fax 24-7703), on the north-west coast near the fishing village of Bel Ombre, has 40 bungalow-type rooms with bath or shower, air-conditioning, swimming pool, restaurant and poolside bar, offshore snorkelling and diving.

The 60-roomed *Equator Hotel* (tel 37-8228, fax 37-8244), is a member of Royal Hotels and is situated on the west coast on granite sloping to the ocean, a few minutes walk from Grand Anse beach. It has four restaurants, tennis courts and a swimming pool. The Royal Card entitles guests to shopping, watersports and restaurant discounts.

Coral Strand Hotel (tel 24-7036, fax 24-7517, e-mail: coralfc@seychelles.net), is on Beau Vallon beach, with 102 air-conditioned rooms with bath or shower. Facilities are set in a half-circle around the swimming pool, there is also a bistro, poolside bar, piano bar, disco, boutique, watersports and diving centre. Wheelchair accessibility.

Vacoa Village (tel 26-1130, fax 26-1146), has one and two-roomed suites in an 11 apartment, Spanish-style hotel, surrounded by frangipani, bougainvillaea and palm trees, just north of Beau Vallon beach. Restaurant and bar, swimming pool.

Budget Accommodation

Within a short distance of popular Beau Vallon beach are:

Coco D'Or (tel 24-7331, fax 24-7454), which has 22 air-conditioned rooms and five suites, two restaurants featuring Kreol and international specialities, and a swimming pool.

Villa de Roses (tel 24-7455, fax 24-1208), a three-bedroomed villa with lounge, dining room, patio and one self-catering unit with a double room and fully-equipped kitchen. Bed and breakfast, meals on request.

Beau Vallon Bungalows (tel 24-7382, fax 24-7955), eight fully-equipped self-catering units, B&B and dinner on request, boat, fishing and diving trips to nearby islands, free bus service to the casino at Beau Vallon.

Panorama Relais des Iles (tel 24-7300, fax 24-7947) is a small hotel with panoramic views of the northern coastline, B&B only, bar, close to grocery shops, with accessible transport.

At Mont Fleuri, south of Victoria, is the *Sunrise Hotel* (tel 22-4560, fax 22-5290) with 16 rooms, three with fully-equipped kitchen, each with antique furniture. Chinese and Kreol cuisine.

Further south at Anse Royale is *Auberge de Bougainville* (tel 37-1788, fax 37-1808), originally built in 1927 as a planter's house. It has 11 rooms and almost all the original panelling and timber flooring has been retained. An interesting feature is the collection of shells in the dining room.

Auberge D'Anse Boileau (tel 37-5660, fax 37-6406), is a nine-room hotel in the south-west, overlooking the picturesque fishing village of Anse Boileau. All rooms have a sea view. There's a restaurant, watersports and deep-sea fishing.

Guest-houses

Beaufond Lane (tel 32-2408, fax 22-4566), a family-run establishment with five air-conditioned rooms, situated within walking distance of Victoria. The restaurant specialises in Kreol and Chinese cuisine.

Bel Air (tel 22-4416, fax 22-4923), close to Victoria and a 10-minute drive from Beau Vallon beach, colonial-style accommodation, personalised service, en-suite bathrooms, fully air-conditioned rooms, local and international cuisine.

Carefree (tel 37-5237, fax 37-5654) is a four-bedroomed hotel facing the sea on the east coast. Restaurant serves international and Kreol cuisine, and specialises in seafood.

Casuarina Beach (tel 37-6211, fax 37-6016, e-mail: pierrejg@seychelles.net), on the beach front at Anse aux Pins, has 20 air-conditioned rooms, The main building, with pillars made from takamaka tree trunks and a ceiling of braided coconut leaves, houses the reception area, bar and restaurant, which serves continental and Kreol cuisine. There's a games room and a jacuzzi for eight people.

Chez Jean (tel 24-1445, fax 26-6340) is a family-run, five-room guest-house, on the north coast, B&B other meals prepared on request.

Harbour View Guest House (tel 32-2473), on the outskirts of Victoria, has eight rooms, restaurant serves Kreol cuisine.

Hilltop Guest House (tel 26-6555, fax 26-6505), with 11 rooms, is on a hillside on the outskirts of Victoria. Restaurant serves international and Kreol cuisine.

L'Islette (tel 37-8229, fax 37-8499) is on a little island a stone's throw off the south-east coast. It has four rooms overlooking a secluded beach. The restaurant serves Kreol specialities.

La Desirade (tel 22-5714, fax 22-5736) is on the south-east coast, 4 miles (6 km) from the airport and 16 miles (25 km) from Victoria. All air-conditioned apartments have sea views and fully-equipped kitchenettes.

Lalla Panzi (tel 37-6411, fax 37-5633), opposite a golf course, is a four-room house in a tropical garden, on the beach at Anse aux Pins, air-conditioning is optional, serves Kreol cuisine.

La Louise Lodge (tel/fax 34-4349) is a family run establishment with nine rooms, on a hillside overlooking the Marine Park. Restaurant serves Kreol and continental cuisine.

La Roussette (tel 37-6245, fax 37-6011), chalet-type hotel at Anse aux Pins with 10 air-conditioned terraced rooms and a restaurant serving Kreol specialities.

Le Niol (tel 26-6262) is on the edge of a tropical forest reserve high on the hillside overlooking Beau Vallon Bay. It has four rooms and a restaurant serving Kreol and continental cuisine.

La Tamarinier Guesthouse (tel 24-7611, fax 24-7711), on the north-west coast, has 13 rooms, some with air-conditioning, Kreol and seafood restaurant, complimentary bus to casino, lounge with TV, and indoor games room.

Manresa Guest House (tel/fax 24-1388), five-roomed guest-house, is in the north-east close to Victoria and to Carana Beach. Air-conditioned rooms with balconies overlooking the sea, restaurant serving continental and Kreol cuisine, bar, small boat which, on request, will take you to nearby islands.

Maxim's Jade House (tel 24-1489, fax 24-1409), six-room guest-house at Ma Constance on the east coast road north of Victoria, Chinese restaurant.

Pension Bel Air (tel 22-4416, fax 22-4923), colonial-style hotel with seven rooms, air-conditioning optional. Restaurant serves international and Kreol cuisine, six-minute walk from Victoria.

Residence Bougainville (tel 37-1334/37-1788, fax 37-1808), old plantation house with seven rooms set in tropical gardens overlooking a secluded beach on the east coast. Restaurant specialises in Kreol cuisine, facilities include fishing and sailing.

Sea Breeze Chalets (tel 24-1021, fax 24-1198), small family-run modern chalet complex, six air-conditioned rooms with terraces, restaurant serving Kreol cuisine, facilities include TV and video.

Tec-Tec Hotel (tel 37-6430, fax 37-5050), secluded in a lush tropical garden, restaurant serves Kreol and international meals.

Villa Madonna (tel 24-7403), two minutes' walk from Beau Vallon Beach, a two-bedroomed establishment with a homely atmosphere. Serves Kreol cuisine.

Villa Napoleon (tel 24-7133), a short walk to Beau Vallon Beach, has accommodation in two houses, each with three rooms, sitting room and dining-room, meals prepared on request.

Self-Catering

Sun Resort (tel 24-7647), is a few minutes walk from Beau Vallon beach. It has a small restaurant and swimming pool.

The 10 double-room colonial-style *Allamanda Hotel* (tel 36-6266, fax 36-6175) is at Anse Forbans, which was once a pirate hideout along the south-east coast. It's ideal for sunbathing and snorkelling, depending on the tides, and has a restaurant and bar.

Lazare Picault (tel 36-1111, fax 36-1177) is perched on the hillside above historic Baie Lazare where French explorer Lazare Picault is said to have landed in the 18th century (he didn't). There are 14 simple, rustic cottages with panoramic views of a bay where dolphins can often be seen surfing the waves. Climbing the hill to and from the rooms could be a strain for the sedentary. There's a restaurant and bar, and facilities include equipment for snorkelling, windsurfing and fishing.

North Point is as far north as you can go. *Carana Beach Chalets* (tel 24-1041) has 16 spacious log-cabin type chalets here. Each chalet has its own kitchen integrated within the lounge, a spacious bedroom and adjoining bathroom, and private paths meander through tropical gardens to both of the hotel's beaches. The Royal Hotel group's *Auberge Louis XVII* (tel 34-4411, fax 34-4428) sits high on a hill in the middle of Mahé, near *Les Mamelles* and overlooking Victoria and the St Anne National Park. Four bungalows and four rooms, all air-conditioned, a swimming pool, and reportedly one of the best gourmet restaurants on the island. *Mountain Rise Hotel* (tel 22-5145, fax 22-5503), high in the hills 10 minutes from Victoria is a rustic family-run property with five rooms. It's an old colonial home with antique furnishings, spreading down a hill overlooking Anse Louis Beach on the south-west coast, restaurant and bar, swimming pool, hikes into the mountains, a good place for solitude.

EATING OUT

You won't find a British fish-and-chipper, but you can get almost anything else, from traditional Kreol and French cuisine to Indian, Chinese, Japanese and Italian. In addition to hotels and restaurants, there are take-aways in Victoria and you can buy snacks from street and market vendors. Before you try anywhere else you must drop into the **Pirate's Arms**, not just for the restaurant, but because it is the central social watering hole and gossip shop where you can find out about virtually anything you want to know. The *Pirate's Arms* is on Independence Avenue in Victoria near the Clock Tower (tel 22-5001). If you feel like splashing out, try to book a table for dinner at *La Scala Restaurant*, at Bel Ombre (tel 24-7535, fax 24-7902). Run by an Italian master chef and his wife, the restaurant specialises in authentic Italian and international cuisine. The menu is wide, ranging from fresh fish marinated in lime juice, seafood platters, clams stuffed with garlic, butter and poached in white wine, cream of shellfish soup, to a variety of prawn dishes. La Scala's reputation for Chateaubriand and various tenderloin dishes is a byword in Mahé, so too are the freshly made pastas. The chef is a keen fisherman, so the restaurant is naturally noted for its fresh fish. La Scala is open for dinner only, and it's closed in June for the whole month. Down at Baie Lazare, at the side of the road near a bus-stop, is the *Splash Café* (tel 36-1500) run by Sandra Benatton, who before she married her Seychellois husband was Sandra Hanks of the USA. She has the same eyes and the identical smile of her brother – film star Tom Hanks. The food is simple and reasonably priced. The *Marie Antoinette* (tel 26-6222) restaurant on Serret Road, Victoria, has a Kreol buffet that will set you back about £8 (US$12), but you probably won't be able to eat for another three days. Smoked fish, coconut salad, Kreol chicken curry, fried aubergines, ginger and pumpkin salad, are just some of the filling dishes. Further down the road is the *Kaz Zanana* (tel 32-5150). The *Kaz Kreol Restaurant* (tel/fax 37-1680) is the only beachfront pizzeria and Kreol restaurant at Anse Royale. Popular with the diving fraternity is the beachside bar at the *Coral Strand Hotel* (tel 24-7036) at Beau Vallon, which has one of the finest sunset views in the Indian Ocean. Divers who can't seem to get enough of fish usually end up at the *Boat House* (tel 24-7898) at Beau Vallon for their fish suppers.

Other restaurants well worth checking out if you are in their area are *Le Corsaire* (tel 24-7171), on the beach at Bel Ombre near the treasure excavation site where the pirate known as *La Buse*, ('The Buzzard'), allegedly buried his loot; the *Sundown Restaurant* (tel 37-8352), at Port Glaud, for seafood; *Le Vieux Creole* (tel 37-8228, fax 37-8244), at the Equator Hotel, Grand Anse; *Chez Plume* (tel 37-6660), at Anse Boileau; and *Lazare's* (tel 37-1588) for a gourmet feast at the Plantation Club, Baie Lazare.

The *Turtle Beach Restaurant* (tel 22-5536, fax 32-2269) on Cerf island, in the middle of the St Anne Marine National Park, has a reputation for good Kreol barbecue and buffet. The owner is the representative of the Belgian Association of

Master Chefs (*Queux de Belgique*). There's a complimentary taxi-boat ride to the island from Victoria. Reservations are recommended. Sharing the beach is another, smaller, restaurant called the *Kapok Tree* (tel 32-2959).

DIVING AND SNORKELLING

For many, **diving** in Seychelles means diving around the main islands of Mahé and Praslin, which are accessible from land-based dive centres. While these areas do have some excellent diving spots, they represent only a fraction of the diving opportunities in the archipelago. Having said that, Mahé is a good place to start your diving, as it has been extensively researched and the sites are well known. Both diving and snorkelling sites are plentiful but you should get local advice before donning mask and fins. On the eastern coast, the northern end of Anse Royale has some good coral formations and marine life. The outer reef at Anse aux Pins is too far offshore for all but the keenest, fittest snorkellers. The southern end of the island has some idyllic coves and beaches, but they are exposed to heavy surf and strong currents. At the north-west tip of the island is **L'Ilot**, little more than a few granite boulders crowned by a coconut palm, but underwater it's a maze of gullies, walls, arches and a wonderland of fish and soft corals at depths of up to 60 ft (20 m). Up to 14 **whale sharks** have been spotted here in a single day. These monsters are usually around in July and August, and again in November and December. If you want to find out more about them and fancy joining them in the briny, contact the Shark Research Institute, which runs a whale shark tagging programme.

North-West Bay

There is good snorkelling from L'Ilot to Sunset Beach Hotel, where the rugged granite coast provides lots of hiding places for fish. This is an interesting spot for diving, with some **fine soft coral formations**. There are other submerged granite outcrops off **Petite Blanche Bay** and *Sunset Beach Hotel*, which are also good dive sites. A fringing reef extends from the Sunset Beach Hotel to Beau Vallon Beach, and snorkellers should concentrate on the reef front to avoid wave action that might drive them on to the coral. **Fisherman's Cove**, to the west of Beau Vallon, has good snorkelling among granite rocks.

St Anne Marine National Park

This reserve covers the islands offshore to the east of Victoria. Snorkellers should head for reef patches to the north of Cerf island and the fringing reef to the north and east of Moyenne island. Scuba-divers should make for **Beacon Island**, a popular diving site, especially during the north-west monsoon; its granite outcrops are pierced by interesting archways frequented by masses of fish.

Baie Ternay Special Reserve

The fringing reef at Baie Ternay is one of the best areas for live coral around Mahé. Maximum depth is 60 ft (18 m). It is separated from the shore by a shallow lagoon up to nearly a half-mile (800 m) wide, where coral formations are found as shallow as 15 ft (95 m). Anemones are found in profusion at the end of the underwater terrace. The shallow inner reef is cut by lots of surge channels and that makes it a favourite spot for snorkellers, as well as glass-bottomed boats.

Port Launay

Cut off from Baie Ternay by the intervening headland of Cap Matoopa, this marine national park has narrow fringing reefs off the rocks at either end of the beach. The best way to get there is by boat from Beau Vallon. Diving centres, glass-bottom and charter boats all run regular half and full day excursions to these marine sanctuaries.

Conception Island

This island lies off Port Launay on the west coast and has three good dive sites, ranging from the deepest at 66-92 ft (20-28 m) to the boulders at South Point. There are a few resident **Napoleon wrasse**, as well as visiting **pelagic fish** and cruising **reef sharks**. A site for qualified divers only.

Brisarre Rocks

These granite outcrops off the north-east coast are covered in places in wonderful **fire coral**. The reef provides exciting fish-watching outings for scuba-divers and snorkellers. **Giant Napoleon wrasse** live here, as do large **bumphead parrotfish**, snappers, groupers, sweetlips and dense shoals of fusiliers. Whitetip reef and other **sharks** can often be found sleeping in the larger caves, and you might also see **eagle rays. Caution:** snorkellers should attempt this site only if the sea is calm, as the area is noted for a powerful surge.

Shark Bank

Five miles (8 km) to the north of Mahé, in the direction of Silhouette island, is the shallowest point of a granite bank rising to within 66 ft (20 m) of the surface. There are stunning **white fan corals** here and large **stingrays** and pelagic fish are frequent visitors. For experienced divers only.

Wreck

The *Ennerdale* was a Royal Fleet Auxiliary tanker which struck an uncharted rock about 8 miles (12 km) off the north-eastern point of Mahé in 1969. As a hazard to shipping, she was sunk in 1970 by the Royal Navy, and now lies in 15 fathoms of water. Fish life is abundant round the wreck, which shelters some whopping **moray eels** and a resident 5 ft (1.5 m) **black grouper** which often acts as an underwater escort. Most dives are on the stern of the vessel, which is one of the three sections still relatively intact. **For experienced divers only.**

Danzilles

A shallow shoreline granite reef to a maximum depth of 39 ft (12 m) with many overhangs and archways. Often used for colourful night dives. A coral reef slopes seaward to a depth of 46 ft (14 m) with **finger and table corals**, as well as anemones. This site is suitable for all divers.

WALKS AND TRAILS

Danzilles to Anse Major

The trail follows part of the rocky north-west coastline and leads to a small secluded beach at Anse Major. Much of the trail lies within the boundaries of the 11 sq mile (29 sq km) **Morne Seychellois National Park**. The trail is **graded as easy** and it follows the contours of the land, passing spectacular rock slopes and native vegetation typical of drier areas. It should take you no longer than 1¹/2 hours to reach Anse Major. It's quicker on the way back and along the same route. An early start is recommended as there is very little shade along the way.

Glacis to Anse Etoile

This trail follows minor roads across the northern hills. These eroded hills are covered in coconut palms and vegetation. From Glacis there is a fairly steep climb to the hamlet of La Gogue and a gentler descent to picturesque La Gogue Reservoir. A choice of two routes is then available to Anse Etoile. This trail is **graded easy**.

The walk takes about 3 hours and should be started early in the day. Buses are frequent from Anse Etoile.

Victoria/Beau Vallon

This walk can be done in either direction. Part of the way is along the main road. The rest is along minor roads which take you through an historical part of Victoria. Several small shops sell refreshment along the way. **The walk is designated easy**, but there is one steep section whichever direction you walk. Allow 1½ hours. Local buses and taxis are frequent along the main roads.

Les Trois Frères

The Trois Frères path leads through a section of the Morne Seychellois National Park to the summit of the mountain overlooking Victoria. This is a spectacular walk among some of the most beautiful forest anywhere in the islands, with views to match. It is **not an easy walk** and is very steep in places. It takes about 2 hours to reach the summit (2,293 ft/699 m) and around an hour to get back. Take care not to stray from the path as it's easy to fall among the boulders or even to get lost in the dense undergrowth.

Tea Factory to Morne Blanc

This is a spectacular walk in the Morne Seychellois National Park. Apart from a short steep section at the start of the trail this is a shaded and steady climb that should take you only about an hour to reach the summit of Morne Blanc, 2,188 ft (667 m) above sea level. Along the way you'll see many of the exotic and diverse plants unique to Seychelles. **The walk is graded as medium.** An early start is recommended to avoid both morning sun and afternoon mountain mist.

La Réserve and Brulée

La Réserve contains one of the last areas of palm forest left on Mahé. Five of the Seychelles' six endemic palms grow along this **medium grade walk**. A backdrop of granite cliffs and boulders add variety to the tropical forest. Several different routes are available, marked by different colours of paint. The walk takes 2-3 hours, depending on the route you take.

Val Riche to Copolia

Although most of the walk is through shady forest the summit of Copolia is exposed to direct sun at 1,631 ft (497 m). There are great views from the summit overlooking the east coast and on a clear day you should be able to make out up to 14 other islands. As some stretches of the walk are slightly difficult and require a bit of climbing, it is designated **a medium grade walk**. Allow 2 hours to reach the summit and then return.

Anse Royale to Anse a la Mouche

This is an **easy grade walk** right across a narrow part of the island through small settlements and scattered houses, allowing you a glimpse of rural life. It will take 3-4 hours to do the walk, depending on the route you take, and you can visit an old chapel and two old cemeteries on the way. Local buses are available at the end of the walk.

HANG-GLIDING

Some precipitous granite slopes, steady, predictable winds, and strong thermals are particularly good for take-off and make Mahé an ideal place for this airborne sport, which is taking off in a big way. The downside is that the slopes usually have a thick forest cover, with few roads and even fewer launch sites. Aborted launches can be dangerous over the forest canopy. From **November to April** northerlies are ideal winds and the launch site at Beau Vallon should be your target; **April to October** brings easterlies and you should try Copolia and other sites in that area.

Beau Vallon Bay is at the north-west tip of the island and has a launch site that is a flat area cut into the side of the mountain above the bay. It's accessible only by four-wheel drive but there's lots of room to set up. There's also plenty of parking, but you'll need someone to take your vehicle down to where you plan to land. Good landing sites are on the beach, next to the Beau Vallon Hotel, and the Danzilles village school-yard.

Copolia is a large granite mountain top above Victoria. The hike to the site makes it suitable only for paragliders. To get there take the well-marked nature trail to Copolia, about 4 miles (6 km) from Victoria. You should reach the launch site in about 30 minutes. The best launch faces east, but as this is from a cliff it can be dangerous. Ideal winds blow directly from the east. There are strong thermals, so don't get whipped up and blown out to sea. There are several landing sites around Victoria. In an emergency there's also a hospital there.

Hang-gliding information is scarce, but try asking at the dive centre at Berjaya Beau Vallon Bay Hotel (tel 24-7141, fax 24-7107). You can buy a trail guide at the tourist information centre in Victoria.

OTHER SPORTS

Many of the bigger hotels have tennis and squash courts. The Reef Hotel, Anse aux Pins, south of the international airport, has a nine-hole golf course. Visitors can arrange temporary membership and hire equipment at the clubhouse. There is also a miniature golf course at Le Meridien Barbarons Hotel, on the west coast near Grand Anse. Horseback riding is available at a stable across the street from this hotel.

PRASLIN

Praslin is most people's idea of the perfect tropical island. Old French navigators, impressed by its lush vegetation, called it 'palm tree island.' Its present name was given to it in 1768 by French Captain Marion Dufresne in honour of Gabriel de Choiseul, Duke of Praslin. The second largest island of Seychelles, Praslin has an area of only 6.5 miles (10.5 km) by 2 miles (3.7 km), and is about 25 miles (40 km) from Mahé. It is a 15 minute flight or 2¹/₂ hours by boat. The island has a population of 5,500, who live mostly in two hamlets facing Mahé: **Baie St Anne**, the docking point in the south-east, and **Grand Anse**, with its airport, 2 miles (3 km) away on the southern coast. Praslin is not as mountainous as Mahé – the highest point is only 1,082 ft (330 m) – but it has similar granitic outcrops surrounded by beautiful beaches and a coral reef enclosing crystal-clear waters. **Anse Volbert**, also known as Côte d'Or, to the east of the island, is particularly beautiful, with its powdery white sand beach. Near the northernmost tip of the island, **Anse Lazio** is **the** beach and excellent for swimming and snorkelling. If you are there at the weekend get there early in the day. Grand Anse, on the west coast, has an equally beautiful beach for lazing about, but the water is sometimes full of drifting seaweed and, as it is shallow over the coral, swimming can be difficult when the tide is out. Some interesting walks start from Grand Anse. **Anse Marie Louise**, **Anse Consolation** and **Anse Bois de Rose** are all on the western side of the island, and have good stretches of beach, with excellent scuba-diving and snorkelling. Round the corner from Baie St Anne, at the far side from the docking point you'll find another secluded beach, Anse la Blague. **Baie St Anne** in the south has a natural harbour where inter-island boats land. The view as you sail in is strikingly picturesque. The village is a must for boat enthusiasts, where you can see fishing vessels being built in the traditional way. Model ships and curios are on sale at Atelier de Maquettes.

Praslin is perfect to explore on foot as it is criss-crossed by a network of walkways. If you wish to drive, there is a limited number of cars for hire and it is wise to book ahead, particularly during the busy season, which is roughly from December to January and July to August. There are petrol pumps at Grand Anse and Baie St Anne. There is a taxi rank at the airport, with around 20 vehicles. These can be called by telephone from hotels and the airport (tel 23-3214). Fares increase slightly at night. There is a bus service between 5.30am and 7pm, with a special Sunday service. Bicycles can be hired at the *Hotel Marechiaro*, Grande Anse (tel 23-3337), and at the *Indian Ocean Lodge* (tel 23-3324). Boats can also be hired from the Indian Ocean Lodge, as well as the *Maison des Palmes*, Grande Anse (tel 23-3411), and Bernard Camille, Anse Volbert (tel 23-2148).

For souvenir shopping there are boutiques in all main hotels. **Barclays Bank** is at Baie St Anne (tel 23-3344), with a branch at Grande Anse which opens from Monday to Friday from 8.30am to 12.30pm.

There are regular boat excursions to smaller islands such as **Chauve Souris island**, and behind it **St Pierre**, a tiny rocky islet on the edge of Curieuse Marine National Park, with a coral reef full of colourful marine life. This is an area that is particularly good for amateurs who want to try out their underwater photography. Trips can be booked through hotels or local tour operators.

THE VALLÉE DE MAI

The main reason people visit Praslin is for the island's own Jurassic Park (minus the dinosaurs), the **Vallée de Mai.** In effect, this is a sanctuary within a sanctuary, as the 48 acre (19.5 ha) reserve is in the greater (800 acres/324 ha) national park. The **home of the famous coco-de-mer** and the **endangered black parrot**, it lies in a well-watered valley in the low-lying central hills of the island. From its discovery in the late 18th century the area remained untouched until the 1930s and still retains some palm forest in a near-original state. The forest canopy reaches up to 98-131 ft (30-40 m). There are no inhabitants in Vallée de Mai, other than a national park forestry settlement. The entrance is on the road from Baie St Anne to Grande Anse. Access to the valley is on foot along marked trails from the road, which divides the national park in two. Guided tours are available. There is an information centre and a small shop at the entrance. You can use three separate well maintained and clearly indicated trails, along which you'll see **rare ferns**, the fabulous **coco-de-mer** and other varieties of **palms** and **tropical plants**, while you try to spot the endangered black parrot. This World Heritage Site is open from 8am to 5.30pm.

CURIEUSE MARINE NATIONAL PARK

Named after the French ship whose captain discovered the island in 1768, Curieuse lies about a mile (2 km) to the north-east of Praslin. The island is only about a mile (2 km) long and half a mile (800 m) wide and has more **giant tortoises** (120) than people living on it. It is one of the prettiest of the granitic inner islands and while small enough to be explored in a day it is sufficiently interesting to make you want to stay longer. The entire island is part of a national park. It became a tourist attraction in 1978 when it was selected as a breeding springboard to reintroduce giant tortoises to the main islands, where they were once abundant. At that time far-off Aldabra was the only remaining natural refuge of these prehistoric creatures.

The following year, to protect the island's flora and fauna and its marine environment, Curieuse and its surrounding waters were designated a marine national park. The tortoise conservation programme got off to a disappointing start. Between 1978 and 1982, 245 adult tortoises were transferred from Aldabra to Curieuse. Since then half of them have disappeared, presumably poached. The Marine Parks Authority has introduced electronic monitoring measures to follow the movements of the tortoises, and it has stepped up its anti-poaching measures. With the tortoises free to roam all over Curieuse, you are not likely to see many on a brief visit, as they are shy creatures and during the heat of the day seek shade in the undergrowth. Forage is regularly put down near the ranger headquarters at Laraie Bay to encourage them to stay in the area. Here you can also see how tortoises grow during their first few years. As part of the conservation programme, the young are kept in separate pens until they are five years old, when they are released. The **mangrove swamp** is a prominent feature of Curieuse and is the habitat for six of the seven types of mangroves found in Seychelles. A refurbished boardwalk built on pilings goes through the mangrove swamp fringing Laraie Bay to Anse St José, on the island's southern coast. The narrow causeway across Laraie Bay was built in 1911 to enclose an area for the rearing of hawksbill turtles. The project was abandoned in 1914 but if you walk across the lagoon you might still see the odd turtle. Today covered in lush vegetation and huge **takamaka trees**, Curieuse was once covered with **coco-de-mer palms**. They were virtually all destroyed in 1771 when locals attempting to harvest them set the island on fire. In 1828, during the early days of the British administration, government agent George Harrison was worried that the coco-de-mer might be on the road to extinction and suggested that Curieuse should be replanted with young palms. At the same time he proposed that the island should also become a settlement for lepers from Mauritius and Seychelles. The administration thought both ideas excellent and the island became both a haven for coco-de-mer palms and for unfortunate lepers. Today the coco-de-mer palm is protected, and to ensure its survival the Seychelles government is still following Harrison's advice and has an ongoing planting programme. The stone ruins of the old leper settlement (1833-1965) can still be seen on the south coast, a short walk from the turtle pond causeway. An old building known as the Doctor's House has been restored with financial help from France and is used as a **reception centre** for visitors, as well as exhibitions and displays of aspects of Curieuse's history. A **ramblers' path** around the island has almost been completed.

ACCOMMODATION

With the exception of major hotels Lemuria, the Paradise Sun, and Berjaya Praslin Beach Resort, most of the hotels on Praslin are medium to small in size. There are also a number of guest-houses and self-catering apartments.

Premier Hotels

The environmentally integrated resort of *Lemuria* (tel 32-2682, fax 32-1322, e-mail: 7south@seychelles.net) opened in the north-west at the end of 1999. It has three beaches, including Anse Georgette, voted the second best beach in the world by readers of German travel magazine *Reise & Preise*. The resort's 88 suites are furnished in teak and granite with marble floors, and there is a choice of four bars and three restaurants, offering international, Mediterranean and Kreol cuisine. Among its facilities are saunas, tennis courts and three swimming pools, one cascading into another over granite boulders. The resort also has an 18-hole 70-par championship golf course, the first in Seychelles. The grounds cover more than 297 acres (120 ha) and are rich in wildlife. Regular nature walks are organised and a replanting programme aims to extend the area covered by endemic palms and trees to encourage birdlife.

Third of the Best Western's hotels in the Seychelles is at Anse Volbert on Praslin. This is the *Berjaya Praslin Beach Hotel and Casino* (tel 23-2222, fax 23-2244), on a most beautiful stretch of beach at Côte d'Or. All 77 rooms are air-conditioned and equipped with all amenities, satellite TV and mini-bar. There are six food and beverage outlets, and a pool and cocktail bar, swimming pool, a children's pool, jungle trekking, sea sport facilities and a tennis court.

La Réserve (tel 23-2211, fax 23-2166) overlooks a secluded bay at Anse Petite Cour on the north-east coast, 25 minutes from the airport, and offers a mix of colonial-style villas and thatched-roof bungalows, as well as a mansion house perched atop a huge boulder, ceiling fans, gourmet restaurant with al fresco dining on the jetty, tennis, snorkelling, diving and fishing.

Coco de Mer Hotel (tel 23-3900, fax 23-3919), has 40 spacious sea-facing rooms set in a tropical garden bordering a palm-tree lined beach. Amenities include a restaurant and bar, swimming pool, boat excursions, deep-sea fishing, diving centre, snorkelling, tennis and squash, hiking trail and fitness centre.

Black Parrot Hotel, perched on a hillside overlooking the ocean, is a favourite of the rich and famous. It has only 12 rooms, a restaurant, bar, games room, swimming pool, a deck with excellent views, private nature trails, tennis and squash, and non-motorised watersports. Book through Coco de Mer Hotel (tel 23-3900, fax 23-3919).

Paradise Sun Hotel (tel 23-2255, fax 23-2019), offers traditional-style accommodation in 80 chalets, with a main restaurant and bar, themed evening entertainment, diving, watersports, and fishing.

The *Chauve Souris Island Lodge* (tel 23-2003, fax 23-2133), on the island of Chauve Souris, off Anse Volbert, has three bedrooms in a villa with individualised décor, and two bedrooms in a bungalow, all air-conditioned, ceiling fan, and refrigerator. This is all you will find on this tiny, rocky island a few hundred yards offshore, and it's just the place for those who want privacy. 'Naufrage' is the most isolated, smallest, romantic and requested room. It is in a separate building, far from everyone, built between the rocks and the sea, with an open-air jacuzzi. There is a restaurant solely for residents, serving Kreol, Italian and international cuisine.

For those seeking luxury, *L'Archipel Hotel* (tel 23-2040, fax 23-2072, e-mail: archipel@ila-chateau.com), set in a large private estate at the end of Anse Volbert beach, has ocean-facing rooms laid out in amphitheatre of coconut trees and flowers. There are 24 air-conditioned rooms and private suites, with bathroom and shower, TV, on either single or split-level. There are two restaurants and cocktail lounges on the beach and in the main building, where the Kreol fish buffet is a memorable tuck-in. There's windsurfing, deep-sea fishing, diving, snorkelling, cruises or visits to other islands on a private catamaran.

Côte d'Or Lodge (tel 23-2200, fax 23-2130) is run as private Italian club hotel where reservations might be possible. It's a 38-room beach resort, with restaurant and bar, nightly entertainment, disco, and a well-equipped watersports centre.

The *Emerald Cove Hotel* (tel 23-2323, fax 23-2300) faces the channel between Praslin and La Digue, with 40 air-conditioned rooms, restaurant and bar, swimming pool, tennis and diving centre.

Mid-Range Hotels

Hotel Acajou (tel 23-2400, fax 23-2401), on the east coast at Côte d'Or, is named after the mahogany used to build this 28 air-conditioned room hotel. There's a restaurant, bar, cocktail lounge, swimming pool and beach bar.

Hotel Marechiaro (tel 23-3337, fax 23-3993, e-mail: merkler@seychelles.net), on Grand Anse beach, is a 13-room hotel with stone walls and wooden shutters and covered swimming pool, on Grand Anse beach. It's convenient for the airport and only six minutes from the Vallée de Mai National Park. The restaurant specialises in Italian and Kreol cuisine, bar, and entertainment.

Chateau de Feuilles (tel 23-3031/3316, fax 23-3916, e-mail: info@chateau.com.sc), at Baie St Anne, is a quaint 12-roomed thatch-roofed hotel on a hilltop. The restaurant specialises in fish dishes, with bar, swimming pool, weekly entertainment by local groups, fishing and boat excursions.

Maison Des Palmes Hotel (tel 23-3411, fax 23-3880) has thatched bungalows with showers, a restaurant serving Kreol specialities, swimming pool, tennis, table tennis, sailing, windsurfing, boat excursions to surrounding islands, game-fishing, yacht charter and tennis.

Budget Accommodation

Le Duc de Praslin (tel 23-2252, fax 23-2355), has three double-room whitewashed bungalows and a main reception/dining area, set between fabulous Anse Volbert beach and the granite mountains, next to Paradise Sun with its dive shop and beach. B&B, meals on request Monday to Friday, bar, laundry service.

Indian Ocean Lodge (tel 23-3324/3457, fax 23-3911), at Grand Anse on the southern coast, is a 16-room lodge with rustic bungalows, thatched restaurant building, rooms are basic but neat and clean, with kingsize four-poster beds, good budget value.

Guest-Houses

La Cabane des Pêcheurs (tel/fax 23-3320), a six-roomed guest-house, close to the airstrip on Grand Anse beach, B&B only.

Bodamyen (tel 23-3066, fax 23-3159), eight Kreol-style chalets with sea view, located on a secluded corner of Anse Marie Louise's sandy beach, restaurant serves Kreol food.

Britannia (tel 23-3215, fax 23-3944), family-run establishment with 10 spacious bungalows in the shade of frangipani, flamboyant and apple trees, four minutes from Grande Anse beach, restaurant serves Kreol specialities.

Casa de Maestro Hotel (tel/fax 23-3847), family-run hotel at Grand Anse, six rooms with balconies overlooking beach, freshwater swimming pool, and a restaurant serving a variety of continental and Kreol food.

Le Colibri (tel/fax 23-2302) a family-run guest-house, with nine air-conditioned rooms all facing the sea on the hillside overlooking harbour at Pointe Cabris, with 10-minute walk to Baie St Anne jetty.

La Cuvette (tel 23-3219/23-3005, fax 23-3369), is a family-run hotel with four rooms with en-suite showers, mini-bar, ceiling fan and one family bungalow comprising three rooms, en-suite bath and shower, mini-bar, ceiling fan. B&B, meals on request, private swimming pool, bar, restaurant, laundry, car hire, bicycle hire, island visits.

Grand Anse Beach Villas (tel 23-3445), eight-room palm thatched chalet-style hotel on the beach front, B&B, other meals on request.

Orange Tree (tel 23-3248), five-roomed house close to Baie St Anne jetty, serves Kreol cuisine.

On the north-west coast at Anse Kerlan is the *Islander Guesthouse* (tel 23-3224, fax 23-3154), with six double/triple rooms and two family apartments of two bedrooms each, own kitchen/lounge, shower, bathroom and veranda, secluded beach, offer self-catering, B&B or half board, restaurant serving Kreol and seafood dishes.

La Vanille (tel 23-2178, fax 23-2284), at Anse La Blague, with three bungalows, B&B, meals on request, restaurant and beachside bar.

Villa Flamboyant (tel/fax 23-3036), Anse St Sauveur, two-storey building with six rooms each, with surrounding veranda, and studio where you can watch the owner painting watercolours.

Self-Catering

Chalets Côte Mer (tel/fax 23-2367), six split-level chalets with an excellent view of Baie St Anne and Anse La Farine. Each unit has a sitting room and veranda, bathroom with hot water, ceiling fans, and fully-equipped kitchen. Additional four rooms without kitchen.

Le Grand Bleu (tel/fax 23-2437), two independent villas (four bedrooms) overlooking the channel between Praslin and La Digue. Each villa has ceiling fans and en-suite bathrooms, fully-equipped kitchen.

Le Tropique Villa (tel 23-3027, fax 23-3969), situated in the quiet residential hamlet of l'Amitié, not far from the airport, two bungalows of two apartments, air-conditioning and fan, lounge, patio and equipped kitchenette.

Villas de Mer (tel 23-3972, fax 23-3015), five minutes from the airport, two chalets with a total of six units, each chalet has one bedroom with hot shower, ceiling fan, lounge, private veranda and equipped kitchenette.

EATING OUT

Praslin is hilly with coves and beaches around every corner and some good beach restaurants where you can eat palm-heart salad, seafoods and Kreol curries. The beachside restaurant/bar at *Paradise Sun Hotel* (tel 23-2255), at Anse Volbert, seems to have a regular following. There are some other good restaurants on the island if you feel like a meal away from your own hotel. There is first-class Kreol cuisine at *Le Britannia* (tel 23-3215), and *Coco Bello* (tel 23-3320), both at Grande Anse. The *Black Parrot* (tel 23-3900) at the *Hotel Coco de Mer*, at Anse Boise de Rose, is noted for its carvery, buffet and for its helpings. At Anse Lazio beach car park in the north-west is the *Bonbon Plume* (tel 23-2136), specialising in fresh seafood and Kreol dishes. It's cheaper at lunchtime than at night. Gourmet foodies should enjoy the evening spread at *L'Archipel's* restaurant (tel 23-2040) at Anse Volbert. Another gourmet Kreol spot, but at more affordable prices, is the *Café des Arts* (tel 23-2131), at Côte d'Or.

DIVING AND SNORKELLING

Praslin has a fine selection of dive sites, among them:

Trompeuse Rocks

Towards the northern end of Praslin, these granite pinnacles just break the surface. They harbour an impressive diversity of marine life, including **stingrays** and **reef shark**. You'll see schools of fusiliers, mackerel and jacks. This is a comfortable dive in calm conditions, to a maximum depth of 75 ft (23 m). However, in any sort of swell, the granite reef turns the surface into white-out conditions.

Booby Rocks

These are closer to Praslin and are known for a **classic drift dive** and for the resident schools of **bumphead parrotfish** and other more bizarre fish life. This granite rock island with its boulder-strewn reef also attracts many semi-pelagics, such as blue-fin carangue and barracuda, as well as the odd patrolling reef shark. Shoals of jackfish, barracuda and mackerel often surround divers. It is a favourite place for night dives. Maximum depth is 66 ft (20 m).

Ave Maria Rocks
This is a favourite spot for dive centres from both Praslin and La Digue and is one of the better known sites in this area. A series of huge granite boulders surround the small island, dropping down in dramatic vertical walls and swim-throughs to about 49 ft (15 m). The maze of protected gullies and bays are home to a prolific fish population, including stingrays, **Napoleon wrasse** and **reef sharks** and are also visited by **turtles**. The site tends to be exposed to currents, but there is almost always a calm area.

White Bank
Right next to Ave Maria Rocks, and less known but every bit as interesting, this series of rocks is the gathering place for schools of **unicornfish, jackfish, snappers** and **batfish**. In the crevices and tunnels **lobster, octopus** and **scorpionfish** lurk. Maximum depth is 66 ft (20 m).

Pointe Chevalier
These granitic and coral reefs off the island's northernmost point provide good diving and some fairly deep snorkelling among clouds of small fish. Further to the south, near La Réserve Hotel, is **Anse Petite Cour**, which has a small fringing reef with some interesting staghorn and branching coral formations

The entrance to **Baie St Anne** is marked by a granite rock outcrop. This area provides some interesting diving with a number of small caves and some large groupers. Don't stray into the busy channel used by inter-island ferries and other boats.

St Pierre Islet
Off Anse Volbert, this is an interesting snorkel or shallow dive. The granite rocks rise from the sea-bed at about 26 ft (8 m); coral is sparse but fish are plentiful.

Coral Gardens
The local Anse Volbert reef may be shallow but it has some interesting corals and attracts lots of fish, and is an **ideal dive site for beginners**, as well as an excellent spot for underwater photography and night dives. Maximum depth is 46 ft (14 m).

Channel Rocks
These are in the middle of the narrow channel between Praslin and La Digue and their cracks and corals are a magnet for fish and invertebrate life. A series of interesting gullies and holes provide shelter not only for shoals of small reef fish, but also for larger groupers and snappers. Maximum depth is 66 ft (20 m).

Curieuse Island
The island has a shallow fringing reef running across south-east-facing **Laraie Bay**. The inshore areas have little live coral but plentiful fish life; the outer slope of the reef is more productive, but watch out for **stinging fire coral**.

Red Point
The submarine rocks at the east end of Curieuse are covered by a wide diversity of coral, attracting an equally exciting range of coral fish species. **Sharks** and **rays** are frequently seen here and **turtles** are also fairly common. Maximum depth is 59 ft (18 m).

Grand Soeur

Pinnacles of granite reach to the surface from the sand at 66 ft (20 m) forming impressive underwater spires and canyons. These provide shelter for Napoleon wrasse, jackfish, parrotfish and a multitude of other **colourful reef fish**. Maximum depth is 85 ft (26 m).

Sister Rocks

These rocks between Grand Soeur and Félicitè start at just 10 ft (3 m) below the surface and are a natural focus for swirling schools of jackfish and mackerel. Reef sharks and bumphead parrotfish are also frequently seen. Maximum depth is 85 ft (26 m).

To the west of Praslin, the twin islands of **Grand Soeur** and **Petit Soeur** provide a tropical backdrop for a series of drift dives, either close to their shores or on one of the outlying submerged reefs.

OTHER ACTIVITIES

FISHING

Bonefish found on the small flats around Praslin are similar in size and numbers to those on the flats of Mahé. Pompano are common on the Praslin flats, which have more of them than any other main group island. Barracuda and trevally can also be caught here. Praslin sees good runs of **yellowfin tuna**, dorado and **sailfish** in its waters, and for offshore fishing you can charter a boat from the Indian Ocean Angling Club (tel 23-3324).

WALKS

Vallée de Mai National Park

This is the most famous of all the walks in Seychelles. It takes you through one of the most unspoilt and richest tropical forests in the world. Home to the famous coco-de-mer palm and its legendary double nut, this is a walk that no visitor to Praslin should miss. It's **graded as easy** and is a fascinating walk through what some might agree with General Gordon is the site of the biblical Garden of Eden, although it's difficult to swallow the surmise that the fruit Eve used to tempt Adam was one of the 55 lb (25 kg) coco-de-mer nuts, the heaviest of all known fruits. A small charge is made to enter the park. Walks can take 45 minutes to 2 hours, depending on which of the paths you take through the reserve.

COUSIN

A few kilometres off Praslin, this fascinating 67-acre (27 ha) islet is owned by the Royal Society for Nature Conservation (RSNC) and has been administered by the International Council for Bird Preservation (ICBP) since it was turned into a nature reserve in 1968. It can be visited on Tuesdays, Thursdays and Fridays, but allows only a maximum of 20 visitors at a time. The **best time to visit** is April or May and a full tour takes only 1-2 hours. Dedicated ornithologists come here to see the **Seychelles fody**, the melodious **magpie robin** (called the *pie chanteuse* locally, the singing magpie), and the **Seychelles brush warbler**. There are also sooty terns, brown noddies, lesser noddies, Malagasy turtle doves, Audubon's shearwaters and Seychelles sunbirds, as well as the fairy tern, the symbol of Seychelles, which is seen on the livery of the national airline. More than a quarter-million seabirds breed here every year and there are major nesting beaches for **turtles**. There are also interesting reptiles, **geckos** and **giant tortoises** which were introduced from Aldabra. All visits to the island must be made as part of an organised tour. Local rangers act as guides and accompany visitors on their tour of the island. A popular day trip leaves Praslin every Tuesday morning, taking in Curieuse as well, with time for a swim and a barbecue, arriving back at Praslin around 4pm. Check with your hotel or tour operator.

DIVING
There are good areas for snorkelling around the Roche Canon rocks at the western end of this island nature reserve, where the granite reef is encrusted with a variety of coral formations.

COUSINE

Cousine is an island between Mahé and Praslin, and not to be confused with nearby sister island Cousin. Cousine is only 185 acres (75 ha) in size and can accommodate a maximum of 10 people at any one time. Cousine is privately owned and **open to visitors** from October to the end of April. There's a breeding programme on the island to boost numbers of the magpie robin, one of the world's rarest birds. Hundreds of thousands of noddies and terns nest on Cousine from May onwards, and tropicbirds, Seychelles fodies, brush warblers, and shearwaters can also be seen. As well as birds, the island has wonderfully secluded beaches.

DIVING
There's superb diving and snorkelling on the untouched surrounding reefs. Cousine is a 25-minute helicopter flight from Mahé, or a short boat trip away, weather permitting, from Praslin. A long granitic offshore ridge rises to within 23 ft (7 m) of the surface, and is covered with both hard and soft corals. It shelters shoals of small fish and these in turn attract **turtles, dolphins** and occasional reef sharks. This is also one of the best sites to give if you fancy a swim with **whale sharks**. Maximum depth is 62 ft (19 m).

ARIDE

This is the most northerly of the granitic Seychelles islands and was bought by the Royal Society for Nature Conservation in 1973. It is second only to Aldabra in importance as a nature reserve. On Aride there are more breeding species of seabirds than on any other island in the region, together with the only breeding sites in the granitic islands for **red-tailed tropicbirds**, and **roseate terns**, and holds the world's only sooty tern colony that's not on a coral island. The world's largest colony of lesser noddy and possibly white-tailed tropicbirds enhance Aride's reputation as the seabird citadel of the Indian Ocean. Aride has also recently become a home for the endangered Seychelles magpie robin. Twenty-nine rare brush warblers introduced from Cousin in September 1988 have multiplied many times over. The island's warden will guide you along breathtaking cliff tops, where hundreds of huge **frigate birds** soar above the turquoise sea. If you are lucky, you will glimpse **hawksbill turtles** and **dolphins** in the waters below.

Aride is also a botanical treasure house. There are several endemic species of flowers and it is the world's only site for the magnificent **Wright's gardenia**, known in Kreol as *bwa sitron*, and a species of *peponium* so new to science that in the botanical world it still officially lacks a description and a name. As well as all this Aride has the highest density of lizards anywhere on earth. Visits can be arranged from most Praslin hotels, but landings can sometimes be difficult. Take plenty of film if you are an avid twitcher, as well as sturdy shoes and a bottle of water.

DIVING

The island is renowned as a birdlife nature reserve, but the underwater life can be just as spectacular. It is difficult to land here, but worth it for the dramatic snorkelling and diving round the west point. Below the sheer northern cliffs there are large expanses of staghorn coral scored by deep channels. Schools of dolphin are frequently seen swimming among the coral gardens and fish and turtles are also common. Maximum depth is 72 ft (22 m).

LA DIGUE

This is the fourth largest island in Seychelles, but without doubt the most popular with visitors. If reputed to be the most photographed, especially the superb beach at **Anse Source D'Argent** whose dazzling white sands, palm trees, sculptured pink granite rocks and translucent waters have made it a familiar backdrop to fashion magazine spreads – as well as soft porn movies. It is a half-hour boat trip from Praslin, about three hours by schooner from Mahé with a following wind, or a 20-minute flight with Helicopter Seychelles. The island lies 27 miles (43 km) east of Mahé, and measures 3 miles (5 km) by 2 miles (3 km). About 2,000 people live on La Digue, whose pace of life is slow, about the same as their traditional mode of transport by ox-cart. Most parts of the island can be reached in under an hour. There are few cars on the island and bicycles are the most popular way to get around. They can be hired near the Inter Island pier at La Passe harbour, where ox-carts, and the couple of local taxis are lined up on one side, bicycles on the other, or at Anse La Réunion.

La Digue is named after one of the vessels of the French expedition to Seychelles in 1768 which claimed the island for France. French officer Charles Ogar who visited in 1770 left a document in a bottle beneath a stone cairn formally annexing La Digue to the French crown. The first attempts at settlement were failures. Eventually, a party of political deportees from Réunion arrived, after hijacking the ship that was taking them to India. With nowhere else to go, they stuck it out on La Digue and accidentally laid the foundations for what has become the most prosperous Seychelles island after Mahé. There are graves of some of these colonists at Pointe Cap Barbi. La Digue is noted for some **grand colonial-style architecture**. A stroll along the coastal road from the jetty at La Passe, or a bicycle ride, takes you past many of these. A prominent landmark on the seaward side of the road is a cross and a small lighthouse above granite rocks rising from the shallow water. Along the road running parallel with the beach are **art galleries** and **craft shops**. The main public coastal route peters out into a loose sandy track at L'Union Estate. Near the estate, through a line of trees, is an old cemetery. There is a small charge for entering the estate, but you won't get better value for your money anywhere on the island. The entrance fee includes a fresh coconut full of juice and an opportunity to see a **working coconut plantation**, copra factory and an oil press, which uses La Digue's traditional source of power, the ox. A bullock still walks in circles crushing the de-husked coconuts to extract the valuable oil. Opposite the grinding mill are the drying houses, kilns, storerooms, and gigantic mounds of coconuts. There's also a vanilla plantation, and on the lawns of the estate guest-house (used in one of the controversial soft porn *Emanuelle* films) quills of vanilla are dried on long trestle tables. You can even feed the **giant tortoises** and check out the estate's **curio shop**, which sells crafts, bottles of coconut oil, vanilla, spice essences and T-shirts, before strolling on to what is arguably La Digue's greatest attraction, the stunning picture-postcard beach at **Anse Source D'Argent**, background to scores of glossy ads, including some for Bacardi rum and Bounty chocolate. Anse Source d' Argent and **Anse Patate** at the northernmost point of the island are famous for their colossal **granite rocks**, looking like petrified beached monsters on the white sand. The rocks change colour as the day progresses, from pink to black and ochre.

The beaches at Grand Anse, Petite Anse and Anse Cocos with their pink-tinged sands are beautiful, but beware of dangerous currents and underflow. Good beaches in the south-west for swimming, snorkelling, windsurfing are Anse Pierrot, Anse aux Cedres and Anse Bonnet Carré.

VEUVE RESERVE
About a hundred or so jet-black paradise flycatchers live on La Digue, and they are found nowhere else the world. The male bird's feathers reflect a glorious bluish butterfly-wing sheen as it flits among the takamaka and Indian almond trees. The female paradise flycatcher is dowdy by comparison, chestnut above, white below, with a black hood. The island is also one of the last havens of the Seychelles magpie robin. This reserve, originally established by UK conservationists Christopher Cadbury and Tony Beamish, is situated in a narrow strip of forest and has clearly marked trails for walkers. Entrance is free.

ACCOMMODATION
La Digue has some more affordable accommodation than many other places in the islands. It has a score or so places to stay, ranging from simple, family-run guest-houses to comfortable beachside villas, although *La Digue Island Lodge* (tel 23-4232, fax 23-4366, e-mail: lilodge@seychelles.net), at Anse La Réunion, is a glamorous and more expensive exception. This is the largest resort hotel on the island, built with local woods, with several types of accommodation from beachfront suites and A-frame cottages to luxury rooms in a restored plantation house, known as the Yellow House. There is a dive shop here, next to the pool and beach, restaurant, poolside café, lounge bar, two boutiques, bicycle hire, watersports, fishing and boat excursions. There's a minimum stay of three nights.

Guest-Houses
Bernique Guest House (tel 23-4229, fax 23-4288), in the heart of La Passe, has 12 rooms in standard and bungalow-style accommodation. Its restaurant is known for its excellent Kreol cuisine, there is also a bar, entertainment, bicycle hire, and boat excursions to nearby islands on request.

Calou Guest House (tel 23-4083), named after the local toddy obtained from tapping the sap of the coconut palm, is inland at La Passe. It has three Kreol-style bungalows, showers with cold water, ceiling fans and veranda, restaurant, bar, bicycle hire, and excursions on request. Half-board is usual.

Choppy's Beach Bungalows (tel 23-4224, fax 23-4088), at Anse La Réunion, on the beach not far from the jetty, has 10 rooms: two bungalows with two double rooms, two of which are on the beach, plus a villa complex of six garden-view rooms, all with hot showers. Half and full-board, B&B by request only. There's also a beachside restaurant and bar, local bands and other entertainment weekly, bicycle hire, excursions to other islands. For what it is worth, Beatles star George Harrison thought the Kreol food here the best on the island.

Hotel L'Ocean (tel 23-4180, fax 23-4308) overlooks the secluded cove of Anse

Patate and has a great view of the islands surrounding La Digue. It's on an unsurfaced single track street which means no traffic. Restaurant and bar.

Patatran Village (tel 23-4333, fax 23-4344) is built on the rocks at picturesque Anse Patate, and the reception has been moulded around a huge granite boulder. The view from the hotel is stunning. Sheltered from the prevailing winds it is also an excellent spot for snorkelling and swimming. There are 12 cliffside bungalows, a restaurant with regular traditional shows, and it offers snorkelling equipment, bicycle hire and excursions to nearby islands on request.

Le Tournesol (tel 23-4155, fax 23-4364), in the centre of La Passe, has three double bungalows, with a large rustic restaurant and bar. The beach is less than a three-minute walk away. B&B on request, restaurant and bar, weekly entertainment, excursions and fishing trips on request, bicycles to rent. This is ideal for budget travellers and families.

A short detour on the road inland from La Passe will take you to the old vanilla plantation house of *Chateau St Cloud* (tel 23-4346), home to one of La Digue's oldest families and now refurbished as a pleasant medium-priced hotel.

Self-catering

Quaint *Paradise Flycatcher's Lodge* (tel 23-4015, fax 23-4015), across the road from Anse La Réunion beach, and within a short walk of l'Union Estate, is for those on a budget who like to be close to a beach. Four wooden bungalows, each with two large bedrooms, fridge and mini-bar. Each bungalow shares a common kitchen. The middle of the building is a large combination sitting area and kitchen. There's a small beach about 100 paces away. Breakfast and dinner served.

EATING OUT

There are not many restaurants on La Digue, as most visitors are expected to eat at their hotels or guest-houses. Two which seem to have stood the test of time are *Chez Marston* (tel/fax 23-4023) restaurant, at La Passe not far from the hospital, which serves reasonably priced traditional cuisine and specialities which the owner says are made according to ancestral recipes, and *Zerof Restaurant* (tel 23-4439), at Anse La Réunion, near the Veuve Reserve, which has a locally acclaimed Kreol and international menu at reasonable prices.

DIVING AND SNORKELLING

The west coast of La Digue is bordered by a well-developed fringing reef, with the exception of the harbour area at La Passe. Although the reef top is shallow enough for snorkelling, the coral is in poor condition because of silting. The fringing reef in the north off **Anse Sévère** is in better condition, with colourful live coral colonies along the reef front.

Anse Marron Rocks

A long granitic backbone here supports an **impressive coral reef** which has become the happy hunting ground of several small reef sharks. The end of the reef has a series of interesting caves and swim-throughs which harbour a diversity of shyer fish. Maximum depth is 85 ft (26 m).

Shark Rocks and Caiman Rocks

These two granite reefs have large coral formations which are frequently visited by **schools of barracuda** and jackfish as well as being foraging grounds for turtles, stingrays and reef sharks. Maximum depth is 79 ft (24 m).

OTHER ACTIVITIES

FISHING

La Digue has some spectacular flats along its western shore, where you can fish for **pompano, snapper** and **trevally**. **Best fishing** is from April to November, when the south-easters blow. This area of La Digue is extravagantly scenic and you might have to share the beach with photographers and models in various stages of undress, as this is a popular location with international high-fashion photographers. This can distract all but the most dedicated angler. At D'Argent you can also watch local artisans building traditional island boats on the beach where the movie *Robinson Crusoe* was filmed.

WALKS

La Passe to Grand Anse

This stunning walk through some of La Digue's fascinating and varied scenery will take about two hours and is **graded as easy**. You can branch off the trail early on near Chateau St Cloud to take a path up to La Digue Island, an odd name for the highest point at 1,093 ft (333m), where you'll enjoy some excellent views of the island and its surrounds. The main trail can be followed on foot or by bicycle and passes several old houses built in the architectural style of the French colonial era before entering woodlands and a marsh. The trail ends at the spectacular beach of Grand Anse. This is a dangerous beach for swimming, but a great spot for experienced body surfers. Dense fern and bamboo forests inland in the area are populated by **flying fox fruit bats**, the ones with the huge wings like patent leather. The return walk leads you through a couple of villages and past the endemic black paradise flycatcher reserve.

SILHOUETTE

You'll be told on Mahé that Silhouette gets its name because of the striking profile Mt Dauban presents to watchers on Beau Vallon beach as the sun sinks behind it. Not so. The island is named after some now forgotten 18th century French dignitary. Silhouette is the third largest island in Seychelles and is considered by conservationists to be one of the most **important biodiversity hotspots** in the Indian Ocean. Unlike neighbouring islands, Silhouette is of volcanic origin. It has a population of just over 250 and although only 19 miles (30 km) from Mahé it had few visitors until recently as outlying coral reefs made it difficult to land boats. Most visitors now arrive by helicopter. Helicopter Seychelles runs transfers on Sunday, Wednesday and Friday morning (tel 37-5400, fax 37-5277).

There are no roads, only sandy paths and tracks, and this makes it an ideal place for walkers. It is a mountainous little island, with highest peak **Mt Dauban** rising to 2,460 ft (750 m), above an island covered with lush vegetation, palm trees, plantations of tobacco, coffee, cinnamon and avocados. Bigarades, a sharp-tasting fruit similar to an orange, are also grown. If you are a serious walker you can take one of two paths across the island through **equatorial forests** linking La Passe and Grande Barbe. It will take you a day to walk there and back. Don't forget to take plenty of water and wear sturdy shoes, not sandals. There are many traditional Kreol houses still around and an old plantation house near **La Passe** is one of the finest in Seychelles. Nearby is the Dauban planter family's tomb, an ornate mausoleum in the classical style, looking at odds with its surroundings. On the east coast at **Anse Lascars** (Kreol for arabs) are some sea-worn graves, cited as possible evidence that these islands were known to Arab traders long before the arrival of the first Europeans. Islanders will tell you that notorious 18th century corsair Jean Francois Hodoul used Silhouette as a base and buried his treasure here.

Since 1983 the island has been leased by the Islands Development Company (IDC) which has experimented with various forms of agriculture. In 1987, the waters around Silhouette were declared a **Marine National Park** and in 1994 the IDC invited The Nature Protection Trust of Seychelles (NPTS) to help with the conservation management of the island. In 1997, NPTS established its Silhouette Conservation Project, which aims to protect the forests of Silhouette and restore them to a near-natural state. The NPTS's Seychelles giant tortoises conservation project (see *Curieuse* page 178) is also based on Silhouette. NPTS has an office on the island. For more information contact IDC in Victoria, Mahé (tel 22-4640, fax 22-4467).

ACCOMMODATION

There is only one, expensive, hotel on the island and a dive centre of sorts where you can hire snorkelling and diving gear as well as water sports equipment.

Silhouette Island Lodge (tel 22-4003, fax 22-4897) is situated in a grove of takamaka trees, tropical shrubs and flowers, and has 12 sea-facing wooden, thatched bungalows, with veranda, shower and hot water, ceiling fan, and mini-bar, as well as two superior bungalows with sitting room and bath. In addition to it's restaurant and bar the hotel can arrange hiking, game fishing, bottom fishing, snorkelling and boat trips around the island. One of the best swimming spots on the island is in front of the lodge. For more information and reservations you can also contact the head office on Mahé (tel 34-4154).

Diving

There is not much coral around this beautiful palm-clad mountainous island, but there are some good diving spots and underwater granite rock outcrops shelter some large fish. Although the island is fairly large in Seychelles terms, there is not much boat traffic, so pelagic game-fish are often seen in the shallow coastal waters.

SMALLER ISLANDS

FÉLICITÉ

This island lies 2.5 miles (4 km) north-east of La Digue. The main attraction of the island is its **primary forest** and stretches of **unexplored coral reef**. Most of the island is planted with coconuts. The highest point of the central ridge is only 699 ft (213 m) above sea level and there are no roads to speak of and not too many tracks. There's one decent stretch of beach at the north-west tip which is where you'll find the only accommodation on the island.

Félicité Island Lodge (tel 23-4323, fax 23-4100, e-mail: lilodge@ seychelles.net), where 25 cottages nestle among palms halfway between the small airstrip and a bird colony. Each cottage has a king-size bed, shower and terrace. Central facilities include restaurant, lounge with billiards, and a library. Snorkelling, deep-sea fishing, and birdwatching are the main pastimes. There are daily flights – except Sunday – which take 30 minutes to and from Mahé, but these are restricted to guests. There is a minimum stay of three nights.

NORTH

North island is 4 miles (7 km) to the north of Silhouette and as it is large and inhabited by fewer than a hundred people, it has been chosen as the place most suitable for the relocation and restocking of critically endangered island species. The aim is to rehabilitate the island and take it back 200 years in time by eradicating all alien and invasive fauna and flora. Once this has been achieved, many of the archipelago's rare and endangered species will be reintroduced to North island to breed, and turtles, tortoises, birds, hardwoods, corals and reef fish will be among those given the chance to recover their old lifestyle in this haven. The island rehabilitation programme is being partly funded by the Royal Society for the Protection or Birds (RSPB) of the UK, aided by a low-volume tourism programme. Day visitors are being encouraged between October and April and eventually 20 beds in (still to be completed) private villas will offer guests 'barefoot luxury.' All this in the future when the island is hopefully once more looking as it did in 1609 when a passing English sea captain noted in his ship's log that it seemed to be an earthly paradise 'except for the allagartes'.

FRÉGATE

This tiny island, the most easterly and isolated of the granitic islands, is less than a square mile (2 sq km) in area, but the *Sunday Times* of London called one of its five beaches, **Anse Victorin** on the north-west coast, 'the world's best beach.' The island is 35 miles (56 km) or 15 minutes by air from Mahé. The most striking features of Frégate are the two hills which dominate the island. The highest point is **Signal Rock** at 410 ft (125 m), but a climb to the top of either of the two hills is worth the effort for the magnificent views you'll get. Some old graves on the island have given rise to the belief that the island was a refuge for pirates in the 17th and 18th centuries and, naturally, that somewhere in its sands lies buried untold wealth. The real treasures are the island's abundant and varied flora and fauna. The island is covered in takamaka, casuarinas and Indian almond trees, along with mangoes, banyans and breadfruit. There are nearly 50 species of birds, as well as geckos, reptiles, and 100 **giant land tortoises** introduced from Aldabra nearly 50 years ago. They can usually be spotted munching away in the cashew thickets. The island is also the last refuge of the giant flightless tenebrionid beetle, which looks like a miniature rhinoceros and is generally found dining under dry bark. Most important of all its natural treasures is the **Seychelles magpie robin**, which is found only here and on the islands of Cousin, Cousine and Aride. There are only 40 or so of these rare birds and they are best spotted on the eastern coastal plateau. There's no traffic on the island so it's a paradise for walkers, with **canopied paths** leading through groups of bamboo and avocado and citrus plantations, and a nature trail you can follow from the Plantation House hotel, near the airstrip, round most of the island.

Accommodation

Plantation House (tel 32-3123, fax 32-5169), once a coconut plantation owner's home, is the only place you can stay on Frégate. It has 16 luxury suites of rooms in garden chalets near one of the island's half a dozen incomparable beaches, and a restaurant specialising in Kreol fish and spicy seafood. Deep-sea fishing expeditions can be arranged and you can get basic snorkelling gear. Like most other hotels on the small islands this is an expensive place to stay, but if your pockets are deep...

Diving

Some of the **best hard coral formations** imaginable can be found off Frégate island, where **eagle rays** and **devil rays** swim among dense shoals of fusiliers. There is some **excellent snorkelling** and scuba diving around the rocks to the right of the landing area. The fringing coral reef itself is usually too rough for diving or snorkelling, although a wonderful diving spot is **Chimney Rocks** when visibility is good. The abundance of large fish in the area tends to attract oceanic predators.

BIRD

If you'd like to share a small island with more than a million sooty terns, then Bird Island between April and September is the place for you. That's when the terns breed, and that's one of the things that makes Bird Island really special. When the terns are nesting they are so tame you can get almost within touching distance of them. Sharing the breeding grounds with the sooty terns are noddies, cardinals, ground doves, mynahs, crested terns and plovers. This 130-acre (53 ha) flat coral island is right at the northern edge of the Seychelles archipelago, a location making for a second ornithological wonder. When winter grips the northern hemisphere, rare migrant birds and other wind-blown vagrants arrive at this, the first landfall in Seychelles. Many species new to Seychelles have been seen here, giving visiting twitchers an opportunity for unrivalled bird-watching. Bird Island is also the home of **Esmerelda**, a giant tortoise said to be between 150 and 200 years old and the largest in the world, with a shell more than 6 ft (1.8 m) in length. Officially weighing in at 298kg (25 kg more than London Zoo's Marmaduke), Esmerelda has made it into the *The Guinness Book of Records*. Esmerelda, incidentally, is a male turtle, but no one realised that when he was named nearly two centuries ago. There are other giant tortoises living on the island and they can occasionally be seen making use of the many footpaths that traverse the island. A **beach walk** around the entire island takes a human about two hours. Bird Island also hosts endangered green and hawksbill breeding turtles, the latter unusually laying their eggs in daylight on the beach between October and March. The island is covered in palms and ringed by a white coral beach which makes it ideal for sun worshippers, divers, snorkellers, swimmers, and windsurfers. It lies on the edge of the Seychelles Bank, 61 miles (98 km) north of Mahé, where the Indian Ocean precipitously plunges into the big blue to around 1,000 fathoms (2,000 m) and its location at the edge of the continental shelf makes it a favourite destination for deep-sea big-game anglers.

A trip from Mahé to Bird Island takes six to eight hours by boat (not really recommended) or 30 minutes by air. Flights are daily, except for Monday. To visit the island you have to make use of a tour operator and flights are restricted to guests of the only accommodation on the island. The idea is to offer a holiday where guests can live in a real nature reserve with comfort, but without putting the wildlife in jeopardy. Guests have to carry torches after dark to find their way back to their bungalows, as lighted paths could attract birds, causing them to fly into buildings. Guests can also help management in their research by helping to tag birds and hawksbill turtles.

Accommodation

Bird Island Lodge (tel 32-3322, fax 22-5074) has 25 thatched cottages by the sea each with a kingsize four-poster bed, hot water shower, ceiling fan and terrace. Central facilities include a restaurant serving buffet-style local cuisine, a boutique, big-game and bottom fishing, and snorkelling.

DENIS

Ten miles (16 km) from Bird Island is another tiny coral island for serious escapists. You can walk around it in less than an hour. Inland, you go through groves of palms and ferns; walk along the beach and it's silver sands and swaying movie-set coconut palms. Denis Island was named after explorer Denis de Trobriand, who claimed its 350 acres (142 ha) for France in 1773.

Like Bird Island, Denis is on the edge of the continental shelf and is a mecca for deep-sea anglers. Many world record fish have been caught here. The island holds several international game-fish records, including five for dog-tooth tuna, and hosts numerous international fishing competitions. Barracuda, sailfish, dorados and bonitos can be caught year-round; marlin is usual from October to December. Two boats operate from Denis, the six-passenger *Mako* and *Commodore*, which can take four. Picnic lunches are provided for full-day fishing trips and all soft drinks and bottled water are complimentary.

There is not a great deal on Denis, a little village, a couple of abandoned prisons, a disused copra plant, a lighthouse built in 1910, and an ecumenical chapel that is the only one of its kind in Seychelles. The vegetation is rich, even by Seychelles' standards, as the result of centuries of guano deposits. There are four flights a week from Mahé every Sunday, Tuesday, Thursday and Friday. The 25-minute flight leaves Mahé at 12.45pm and the return flight leaves Denis at 1.20pm.

Accommodation
Denis Island Lodge (tel 32-1143, fax 32-1010), the Seychelles Coconut Estates company owns the island and runs the lodge, which is the only accommodation on the island. There are 4 air-conditioned chalets right by the beach, showers with hot water, ceiling fans, a restaurant and bar, fishing and diving centres, swimming pool, canoeing, windsurfing, sailing, volleyball, tennis, billiard table, games room, TV room, boutique, and even golf practice on the airstrip. They don't stand on formality at the lodge. Although long trousers or *pareos* (sarongs) are the preferred evening attire, shoes are not compulsory. To discourage day trippers, a stay of three nights is the minimum.

Diving
The island's lagoon is surrounded by coral with a reef dropping sharply to depths of 49-98 ft (15-30 m) and offering some interesting dives. Boats are available to take divers further afield.

AMIRANTES GROUP

The islands of Amirantes, named by Portuguese admiral Vasco da Gama in 1503, lie 186 miles (300 km) south-west of Mahé, and include 25 islands and atolls. Main islands in this scattered archipelago are Desroches, D'Arros, and the more southerly Alphonse group. Most of the islands of the Amirantes are privately owned, although their owners are keen to build up their tourist trade. Desroches is the most visited and developed island in the group and Air Seychelles has three weekly flights there from Mahé. It is possible to arrange boat excursions from Desroches to the neighbouring islands of D'Arros, Poivre and the northerly African Banks. The coral islands of the Amirantes chain are low-lying, which means the **best times to visit** them are in April-May and October-November. Desroches was the first Amirantes island to develop a pukka tourist lodge.

DESROCHES
The island is only 3 miles (5 km) long and a few hundred yards wide and it's covered in casuarina trees and coconut plantations from the old colonial days. They say the loudest noise on the island is the sound of coconuts hitting the ground. The island is just under an hour by air from Mahé and a magnet for twitchers, scuba-divers and salt water anglers, and is a good base from which to explore the other islands of the Amirantes.

Accommodation
Desroches Island Lodge (tel 22-9003, fax 32-1366; for reservations tel 32-2414, fax 32-2401, e-mail: tssez02@seychelles.net) is popular with visitors looking for romantic solitude and some superb diving and fishing. It has 20 air-conditioned

suites with bath/shower and hot water, ceiling fan, kingsize beds, mini-bar, hair-dryers, lounge areas and patios facing the gardens and the sea. If it's any attraction, it is the only remote island with a swimming pool and floodlit tennis courts. There's a main restaurant and bar, swimming pool, non-motorised water sports, a first-class dive centre, fishing centre, bicycle hire, and boat excursions to other islands in the Amirantes. There is usually a special offer on a minimum seven-night stay.

Diving

Desroches has magnificent beaches, but the island's main attraction is its scuba-diving and fishing. Experts say that the coral around the island offers some of the **best diving in the Indian Ocean**. The diving on the outer sites is little short of amazing, and large pelagic fish and sharks are regularly seen. Desroches also has the advantage of sheltered snorkelling and diving inside the lagoon when it's rough outside. The African Banks in the north of the group have a remarkable coral reef to the west, which has a variety of fragile hard coral colonies, and has good sites for both snorkellers and scuba-divers.

Fishing

Flyfishing for bonefish is great in the shallows and flats around Desroches and neighbouring Poivre and D'Arros, 60 minutes away over the horizon by deep-sea fishing boat. Americans, Argentinians and South Africans are regarded as the main exponents of bonefishing, flying anywhere in the world to find this fighting fish. The Amirantes islands are now high on their list of rewarding destinations. The attraction lies in the stalking of this near-transparent fish, which when hooked can run at speeds of up to 50 mph (80 km/h). There's excellent bone-fishing on nearby St Joseph's Atoll, and even further south, down in the little-known Alphonse group of islands.

D'ARROS

This large island in the middle of the group is covered in coconut palms in a plantation split by a small air strip and is about an hour by air from Mahé. Discovered in 1771 and named after French administrator Baron D'Arros, it has opened to visitors only recently as a secluded retreat able to take only a limited number of visitors. The accommodation (tel 32-3960, fax 32-4011) comprises a main villa with three rooms and two adjoining chalets, each with two bedrooms. There's a common dining-room, swimming pool, home-style entertainment, library, video library, board games, tennis court, cycling, fishing and snorkelling. Rooms have bath/shower with hot water, ceiling fan, and refrigerator.

ALPHONSE

Alphonse Island Resort opened its doors for the first time in December 1999 to open up an island previously too remote and spartan for all but a few dedicated travellers. The new resort has 25 individual chalets, five senior suites, and a presidential suite. For reservations contact *7° South* in Victoria (tel 32-2682, fax 32-1322).

Diving and Fishing

The wall dive off Alphonse where the rim of the atoll plummets into the blue abyss is said to be unforgettable. For fishermen there is the choice of traditional big-game fishing or fly-fishing. The atolls of Alphonse, Bijoutier and St Francois offer what Indian Ocean angling guru Charles Norman describes as 'the ultimate fly-fishing available on the face of the planet.' He says that as the tide starts to flood the flats you'll find bonefish and trevally following the rising tide and feeding in water barely deep enough to cover them. These are fish that have never seen a human; stand still and they swim around you, bumping into your legs; cast a fly and they push each other out of the way to get at it, world-record big-eye trevally in the 15 lb (7 kg) range, as well as milkfish up to 7 ft (2 m) long in shoals 50-100 strong.

FARQUHAR GROUP

This group of islands is about 435 miles (700 km) south-west of Mahé. Scattered within an enormous reef, they are the most difficult of all the Seychelles islands to reach and ideally you need either your own boat or you have to charter one. The few island families there live on fish, coconuts and vegetables. We haven't been there – and don't know anyone that has – but we've been advised that a unique experience awaits the truly adventurous who can get to these islands, which were discovered and named in 1504 by Portuguese navigator Juan Nova. They were given their present name during the heydey of British rule in the Indian Ocean in honour of Sir Robert Farquhar, governor of Mauritius.

The main coral islands making up the group – **Farquhar** atoll itself, **St Pierre** and **Providence** – are even more difficult to get to than far-off Aldabra, although Air Seychelles occasionally flies in supplies, and carries the odd passenger to a rudimentary landing strip on tiny **Ile du Nord**. For more information contact the airline in Victoria, Mahé (tel 22-5220, fax 22-5159), or the Island Development Company in Victoria (tel 22-4640, fax 22-4467).

Farquhar is popular with ocean-roving yachtsmen because of easy access from the sea to an invitingly sheltered lagoon. They also like to relax after the ocean rigours on **Twenty-Five Franc Beach**, a seemingly unending stretch of blinding white sand.

ALDABRA

This is the largest and most famous coral atoll in the world. Remote and lovely, 684 miles (1,100 km) from the main Seychelles group, it is a horseshoe atoll with a land rim some 60 miles (97 km) in circumference surrounding a huge shallow central lagoon over 50sq miles (130 sq km) in extent, whose shores are covered in mangroves. The atoll has a total area of 86,487 acres (35,000 ha), larger in area than Mahé and one-third of Seychelles' total land area. The group comprises four main island clusters, none of them rising much more than 33 ft (10 m) above sea level. These coral limestone island clusters are **Aldabra** and **Assumption** (the westerly group), and **Cosmolédo** and **Astove** (the easterly group). They lie between Madagascar and the main Seychelles islands in what is the driest part of the Indian Ocean, with an annual rainfall of less than 39 inches (1,000 mm).

Aldabra has been protected from undue human interference by its isolation and by the fact that landing here from the sea can be a dangerous business. With only four openings to the sea in the ring of islands, the pressure of the ebb and flow of the tide causes raging tidal steams which make entry by boat impossible. As a result Aldabra has become a refuge for an estimated **152,000 giant tortoises**, the world's largest population, and a UN-designated World Heritage Site. The Aldabra atoll is administered by the Seychelles Island Foundation and is probably the most famous of all natural heritage sites. As well as being a tortoise sanctuary it is also home to the flightless **white-throated rail**, a distant relative of the long extinct dodo of Mauritius, and a dozen other species of terrestrial birds. There are about 5,000 flightless rails left, and about 1,500 **Aldabran drongos**, which is also an endemic

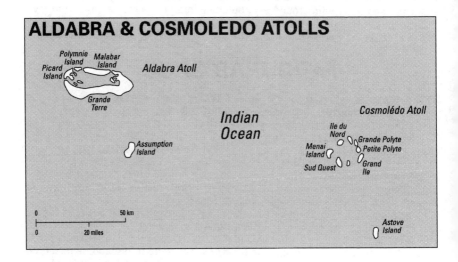

species. Growing in Aldabra are some 178 species of indigenous flowering plants, of which about 20% are believed to be endemic, with many of them considered to be under threat. The mangroves and populations of turtles, fish and tortoises all seem to have recovered from past exploitation. **Dimorphic egrets** (found only here and Madagascar) wade in shallow water with the **Aldabra sacred ibis** and a host of terns. **Dolphins** and **whales** are often spotted offshore and some 2,000 **green turtles** breed here every year. Aldabra's main islands are Picard, Grande Terre, Polymnie and Malabar, encircling the largest lagoon in the world. At low water more than 80% of the lagoon is dry. Mushroom-shaped pinnacles of honeycombed limestone known as *champignons* dot the lagoon, carved into these strange shapes by rushing currents created by a tidal rise and fall of more than 10 ft (3 m).

There is no accommodation in Aldabra; a day trip is possible from Assumption island, which although opened to tourists only recently is already one of the world's foremost eco-tourism destinations. There is an airstrip on the island, and full-day boat trips will take you to Aldabra, about 4 hours away. Trained guides from the foundation escort visitors. Although there are no permanent settlements on Aldabra, a research station was established there by the Royal Society in 1971, and donated to the Seychelles Islands Foundation in 1980, which now maintains it. The Seychelles government also has a meteorological station there. Accommodation and a network of field stations are available for up to five scientists, but visitors are not encouraged to stay.

For more information about this fascinating place write to the Seychelles Islands Foundation. PO Box 853, Victoria, Mahé, Seychelles, or contact the Information Officer, World Conservation Monitoring Centre, 219 Huntingdon Road, Cambridge CB3 0DL, England (tel 27-7314, fax 27-7136, e-mail: info@wcmc.org.uk). E-mail for World Heritage enquiries is jim.paine@wcmc.org.uk.

Diving
Diving on Aldabra's terraced walls is dramatic and you can expect to see lots of **green turtles**, but the diving highlight is the **stunning drift-diving** through the channels into Aldabra's vast lagoon. You can join shoals of snappers, **surgeonfish**

and **stingrays** and drift effortlessly into the lagoon at speeds of up to six knots. The main channel into the lagoon is the **Grand Passé**, virtually a large river flowing by turn into and out of the sea. More than half of the lagoon water drains out through this channel making it ideal for a rollercoast drift dive. Visibility in the channels, however, is often murky. About a mile (3 km) along the north coast, beyond Grand Passé, is a smaller channel called **Passé Gionnet**, but popularly known as Passé Johnny. This is a narrow but exciting island-filled channel with some good diving. There are 185 species of fish to be seen within a mere square mile (3 sq km) of reef, with the **emperor angelfish** and the **regal angelfish**, two of the most beautiful but rarely seen examples of the angelfish family, common in the shallow waters of the atoll. A good way for divers to get to Aldabra from Mahé is on the *Indian Ocean Explorer* which does regular live-aboard cruises to the group of islands (see *Getting Around* page 138).

ASSUMPTION

On Assumption island most of the plants and birdlife were wiped out long ago by guano diggers, but underwater life remains a wonder. When French aquanaut Jacques Cousteau visited the island on his research vessel *Calypso* he wrote that he had never seen anything approaching the vistas offered by Assumption reef. Cousteau and his team planned a quick dive; they stayed more than a month and became so friendly with the giant rock cod that they had to pen some of them underwater to prevent them from getting in the way while they were filming.

COSMOLÉDO

The Aldabra group's Cosmolédo is an atoll that graphically demonstrates what relentless ocean pounding can do. Around the atoll the waters are so gin-clear that if you are fishing there you can look down and actually choose the size and colour of the fish you intend to catch. How's that for a fisherman's tale? Horse-shaped **Astove Island** to the south is regarded by all who have seen it as the perfect atoll, with a lagoon that has only one major access and exit channel to the sea. The western side has some incredibly sheer drop-offs, with seawalls running the whole length of the island. Divers say this is without doubt one of the Indian Ocean's most dramatic seawalls, dropping to depths of 1,640 ft (500 m) not far from the shore.

Réunion

Waterfall at
Cirque de Salazie

The days of dirt-cheap holidays are long gone. The nearest these days is a package tour – but what you might save in cash you more or less pay for in regimentation and a limited choice in where you can go and what you can do. If you are more of a free spirit and prefer to make your own arrangements you should look for a destination where you'll pay more or less what you would pay at home – same B&B, hotel, food, drink, car hire, and petrol prices – then the only real expense you'll face will probably be the flight. Desert islands beckon in the imagination, but they're usually full of mosquitoes and sand fleas, and the plumbing is not up to scratch. The island of Réunion is a place that offers the delights of the tropics combined with the comforts and mod cons of Europe. Réunion really is a little bit of France plonked down in the Indian Ocean, and an added attraction is that it is still a relatively undiscovered holiday destination, with none of the hordes of tourists you'll find in Spain, Portugal, Greece and other popular destinations around the Mediterranean. While there are some excellent beaches – the one at Boucan Canot is superb – the real attraction of the island lies in its central highlands, where the spectacularly rugged peaks of dormant or extinct volcanoes cradle huge natural amphitheatres, *cirques*, and offer unrivalled high-level hiking trails and climbs. You can even trek inside a live volcano and live to wear the T-shirt. Réunion really is waiting to be discovered. Only 400,000 people a year visit this island wonderland, 1,500 from the UK. Don't wait for it to become like you know where...

GEOGRAPHY

Réunion is geologically the youngest of the trio of islands which make up the group known as the Mascarenes. The others are Mauritius and Rodrigues. The island is about 7,000 miles (11,265 km) from most of the capitals of Europe, 1,305 miles (2,100 km) from Johannesburg, 500 miles (804 km) east of Madagascar, and 124 miles (200 km) west of Mauritius. It is a volcanic island 45 miles (72 km) long and 40 miles (64 km) wide with an area of 942 sq miles (2,512 sq km), slightly smaller than Rhode Island or Luxembourg. The islands of Tromelin, Juan de Nova, the Iles Glorieuses, Bassas da India and Europa are dependencies of Réunion. Tromelin is in the Indian Ocean to the north-west of Mauritius, and the others lie in the Mozambican Channel between Madagascar and the African mainland. These serve primarily as meteorological stations, and have no accommodation for tourists. Their economic value is important as they give France access to a wide area of territorial waters and useful fishing rights. As well as being a French military base, Réunion is also a supply base for France's Austral and Antarctic territories.

Topography

The island is dominated by two mountainous massifs, the central Piton des Neiges (Snow Peak), at 10,069 ft (3,069 m) the highest mountain in the Indian Ocean, and the volcano Piton de la Fournaise (Furnace Peak), rising in the south-east corner of the island to 8,632 ft (2,631 m). This volcano, one of the most active on earth, last erupted on 9 March 1998 and the coulée, or hardened lava flow, can be seen in many areas of the south-east coast. These two mountainous areas are separated by two plains, the Plaine des Palmistes – the palms have all been chopped down over the years to make heart of palm salad – and the Plaine des Cafres. Other startling features and among Réunion's greatest attractions are the deeply gouged valleys and wild gorges of three cirques, or enormous natural amphitheatres, named Cilaos, Salazie and Mafate. The latter is inaccessible by vehicle and can be reached only on foot or by helicopter. The three cirques have collapsed around the inactive volcano of Piton des Neiges in a huge ace of clubs formation and all are accessible only through deep canyons formed by the rivers which cascade through them to the sea. Salazie faces east in the direction of the warm trade winds which help, with the innumerable waterfalls of the cirque, to make it a luxuriant wilderness and great for walking. Cilaos faces south and is drier, and its many exposed rock faces make it a magnet for climbers and canyoners. The rugged interior of Mafate is the most spectacular of the three and offers by far the most exciting – and strenuous – trails. The rim of the cirque reaches in places to 9,514 ft (2,900 m). The seascape varies a lot around the island. In the west, the mainly black and scattered white sand beaches of the 129 mile (207 km) coastline become rocky shores in the wilder south, and the island's contrasting micro-climates are the result of this unusual

REUNION

topography. The main towns of St Denis, the capital, St Gilles les Baines, St Leu, Etang Salé les Bains, St Pierre, and St Benoit lie along the coast. Little villages dot the lowlands and nestle high in the mountains and cirques.

CLIMATE

Generally, the island has a tropical climate and, due to the influence of trade winds, its temperatures are moderate, but vary according to season and altitude. The cool, dry season, or the equivalent of winter, is from May to October and is the **best time** to visit the island, with average temperatures ranging from 77°F (25°C) on the coast to 54°F (12°C) in the mountains. Evenings are much cooler. The hot, humid season, or summer, runs from November to May, with average temperatures ranging from 86°F (30°C) on the coast to 66°F (19°C) in the mountain region. Temperatures are cooler in the hills; from July to November the temperature at high altitude can fall to 50°F (10°C) during the day and 43°F (6°C) at night. It can even drop to freezing point at night.

Cyclone Season

This is from January to March. Tropical cyclones are monitored by satellite and warnings are broadcast several days in advance of their expected arrival. When they come, they usually bring short but heavy rains. The rest of the year the sky is clear blue.

Summer cyclones don't affect Réunion very often; and when they do they last only for a few days. For information about south-west Indian Ocean depressions (intensity, travelling speed, path, distance, state of alert status), tel 083-665-0101.

Weather Forecast

Réunion has a 24-hour advance weather forecast (tel 083-668-0000) which can provide **hourly updates** (tel 083-668-0202); essential for paragliders, canyoners, hikers and all other outdoor enthusiasts.

Hours of sunshine a day: East coast (windward) 6 hours; west coast (leeward) 7 hours; and high ground 4,921 ft (1,500 m) 6 hours. The average annual rainfall varies from about 25 inches (64 cm) in the north to 160-315 inches (406-800 cm) in the south. The warmest, wettest months are from November to April, but rainfall is usually intermittent and of short duration. There is very little rain during the cooler and dryer season from May to October, but this is no cause for worry if you are holidaying on the west coast, as this is where the best beaches are. The sea is always a warm 70-80°F (21-27°C).

Temperatures

Month	Maximum	Minimum
January	90°F (32°C)	70°F (21°C)
February	90°F (32°C	72°F (22°C)
March	86°F (30°C)	68°F (20°C)
April	84°F (29°C)	65°F (18°C)
May	82°F (28°C)	63°F (17°C)
June	81°F (27°C)	61°F (16°C)
July	79°F (26°C)	57°F (14°C)
August	81°F (27°C)	59°F (15°C)
September	81°F (27°C	61°F (16°C)
October	82°F (28°C)	63°F (17°C)
November	86°F (30°C)	65°F (18°C)
December	92°F (33°C)	68°F (20°C)

HISTORY

The Portuguese

Portuguese seafarers had been stumbling across unmapped islands and atolls in the Indian Ocean ever since the ships of Vasco da Gama were first blown round the foot of Africa into the area in 1498. They found them, named them, lost them, found and renamed them, time and again. They didn't regard them as places of settlement, but rather as watering spots and useful signposts on the spice route to the east.

Early in 1507 Diego Fernandez Pereira, first pilot in the fleet of Tristan da Cunha, wandered off on his own and found an island that was not marked on his charts. The volcanic island was known to earlier Arab navigators as *Dina Margabin*. Pereira didn't know this and named the island Santa Appolina, after the saint on whose feast day it was at the time. In 1513, Pedro Mascarenhas called at Rodrigues, Mauritius and Santa Appolina on his way home to Portugal from India and renamed Pereira's island Mascareigne. This name didn't stick either, although the three islands are known collectively to this day as the Mascarenes. The next passerby was Captain Gaubart, whose ship *St Alexis* visited Mascareigne in 1638. He nailed the royal fleur-de-lys to a tree to claim the island for France. One of the main obstacles to the colonisation of the island was its lack of a natural harbour or any kind of sheltered port for visiting vessels. This, however, had to be disregarded after the Compagnie Francais de l'Orient was formed and the body established to govern French trade with the east decided it needed a refreshment station for its ships in the Indian Ocean.

The French

In March 1642 Sieur Jacques de Pronis was despatched to choose a suitable place for such a way station. De Pronis and his party first landed at Santa Appolina and immediately renamed the island Bourbon, in honour of the French royal family. Although the island was perfect in every other respect the absence of a harbour led de Pronis to discount it and move on and he eventually established a settlement at the south-eastern tip of Madagascar, which he named Fort Dauphin in honour of the French Crown Prince. Far from the comforts of home it was not long before the complaints of the settlers on Madagascar flared into outright mutiny. Governor de Pronis was clapped in irons by the mutineers and spent six months in detention until saved by the arrival of a French ship. De Pronis immediately banished the 12 leaders of the settler insurrection to the uninhabited island of Bourbon and had them dumped on the beach at a place not far from where in 1642 he himself had reclaimed the island for France. This point is still known as La Possession. In this way, in 1646, Pronis gave Réunion its founding fathers and set a precedent later followed in other parts of the world where colonies were initially stocked by convicts and social misfits. Bourbon's first inhabitants were left ashore near present day St Paul with no provisions or shelter and only a handful of Madagascan women for solace. They quickly found that life in a climate much healthier than Madagascar's, with rivers teeming with fish and forests full of game, was not as bad as de Pronis had obviously hoped. The exiles passed three congenial years, living in seaside caves which are still to be seen and now proudly referred to as the *Grotte des Premiers Francais* ('Cave of the First Frenchmen'). The exiles were eventually taken off and apparently left with regret. A few years later, in 1654, more malcontents from Fort Dauphin were exiled to Bourbon. These, seven Frenchmen and 66 Madagascans, with the handful of volunteers who joined them, founded the present town of St Paul. They stuck it out until 1658 before joining a visiting English ship and sailing off to India.

First Settlers

When the first group of free and permanent settlers arrived on the island in 1662 they found it once more deserted, and the shacks at St Paul abandoned. The leader of Réunion's first true settlers was Louis Payen, who with his French servant, seven Madagascan men and women, had stolen a boat in Fort Dauphin and set sail for Bourbon in search of a more peaceful and healthier life. By the time the first official Commandent of Bourbon, Etienne Regnault, arrived with a further 20 settlers in 1667, Payen and his domestic servant were the sole inhabitants of St Paul; the Madagascans had taken to the hills and inaccessible mountainous cirques to live a less irksome life, relying on wild fruit and game rather than hoeing and planting. They were the first of what was to become a future problem colony of *marrons* – from the Spanish term *cimarron*, meaning runaway slaves or wild men. Over the next few years more and more disgruntled French left Fort Dauphin to join the Bourbon settlement, their only complaint the shortage of white women.

The Pirates

By 1690, Bourbon had degenerated to the point where it had become a byword in the Indian Ocean and in the seafaring world for wanton licence, a haven for pirates and freebooters whose activities were condoned by a succession of venal governors. One of the most infamous of the pirates was English renegade Captain John 'Long Ben' Avery, who took to freebooting at a time when William III was granting a commission in England to Captain William Kidd to chase and capture known pirates operating in the Indian Ocean. How Kidd fulfilled his commission is well known. He became the most famous pirate of them all and ended his career only four years later at the end of a rope in London's Execution Dock. Avery began his career by seizing the ship on which he was mate while the master was sleeping off an overdose of punch. Avery and his cut-throats pulled off their greatest feat in 1695 when they captured and ransacked two ships of India's Great Mogul, which were on their way to Mecca and carrying his daughter and a fortune in gold, silver and jewels. Avery and his crew were warmly welcomed in Bourbon when they sought refuge there to share out their plunder. According to the *General History of Robberies and Murders of the Most Notorious Pyrates* published in 1726 by an unknown Captain Charles Johnson, Avery then returned to England with his share, but was swindled out of it by respectable merchants and died a pauper in Devon. All the pirates in Johnson's history came to well-deserved sticky ends and the tales are without exception cautionary ones about comeuppance for evil-doers.

The Slaves

It took more than the best part of three decades for Bourbon to shake off its unsavoury reputation, years during which the island survived various epidemics, simmering settler discontent and, in 1730, a mass slave revolt put down with severity and considerable bloodshed. On the credit side, agriculture changed from a subsistence to a prosperous activity, particularly after the introduction of coffee trees from Arabia in 1715, and plantings of spices and cotton. Bourbon was finally set on the road to stability by that remarkable French renaissance man, Mahé de Labourdonnais, who was appointed Governor-General of the Mascarene islands in 1735. During his 10 years' tenure Bourbon flourished as a satellite of Mauritius, which though smaller had the advantage of a fine harbour. Labourdonnais went off to fight the British in 1746 and never returned to his island post. In 1764 the virtual owners of Bourbon, the French East India Company, went bankrupt and had to relinquish control of the island to the crown. The early 18th century saw sugar become a staple crop, and one whose intensive cultivation resulted in the importation of more and more black slaves. The slave population rose steadily to reach 60,000 in 1848, when slavery was legally abolished. In January 1790 news of the French Revolution reached the Mascarenes, but it was not until February 1793 that ultra-revolutionaries on Bourbon got together with like-minded associates on Mauritius and celebrated this political reunion by abolishing the royal name of their island and renaming it Réunion. Just to underscore the change they also erected Réunion's first guillotine. In 1806, on the second anniversary of Napoleon Bonaparte's elevation as Emperor of France, islanders proclaimed their loyalty by renaming their home yet again, this time as Ile Bonaparte.

The British

As a preliminary to their planned invasion and occupation of Mauritius, the British made probing raids on Bourbon to test French strength and resolution. In August 1809, they attacked St Gilles and devastated the neighbourhood; the following month they did the same to St Rose. Then, on the 21 September 1809, they launched a major raid on the west coast and the town of St Paul was taken by a force of 604 men. Three French warships lying in the bay with their prizes were also taken. The British forces withdrew on the 7 October leaving the French governor in such despair that he committed suicide. On the 7 July 1810, the British returned in full force landing nearly 5,000 men on the beach on either side of the capital St Denis. After some skirmishing the French capitulated on 9 July 1810. Using Bourbon as their launch pad the British then bore down on the troublesome island of Mauritius on the 29 November 1810 and early in December accepted the French surrender. The British remained in Mauritius for the next 158 years; in the island once more renamed Bourbon they stayed in occupation for less than five years.

French Return

The British left once the Treaty of Paris on 15 October 1814 ratified the cession of Mauritius, Rodrigues and Seychelles to Britain, returning Bourbon to France. The apocryphal story has it that Bourbon was returned to France through ignorance. The British delegates thought that the island was in the West Indies and regarded it as unimportant. When France resumed possession of Bourbon the island was populated by 16,500 Europeans, 3,500 mixed-blood Creoles, and 70,000 slaves, living on the fertile coastal terrace around the island and relying principally for an income on cotton and, increasingly, sugar, which eventually ousted the former crop as the staple. There were insufficient slaves to work the fields as agriculture expanded and by 1829 paid labour was allowed in from India. Slavery was finally, officially, abolished in 1848, the year the French monarchy was overthrown and a new republic proclaimed. That year the island also resumed its old name of Réunion, this time for good. Within the space of 20 years Réunion was no longer a strategic pawn on the sea route to India and therefore of little interest to the European powers, even though a harbour had been developed on the west coast at Le Port, near La Possession. The opening of the Suez Canal in 1869 put an end to any last shred of geographical importance the island might have had. In 1871, Réunion experienced dramatic internal social change. Universal suffrage had been extended to all by France's Third Republic and for the first time the descendants of slaves forming the majority in the population were handed political power, not that they could do much with it. With Mauritius hogging most of the limelight Réunion bumbled on through periods of prosperity and periods of pestilence, volcanic and cyclonic batterings, which set back agriculture until the outbreak of the First World War. Some 14,000 islanders left to fight in Europe, adding to the economic woes that reliance on a monoculture is apt to bring. Plantations staggered along for the next 20 years, still keeping the landed class affluent but leading to impoverishment in general. The years of World War 2 saw a German-blockaded Réunion sitting on mountains of sugar, but teetering on the brink of famine. When the war ended France took stock and was shocked by the deterioration in its Indian Ocean colony. On 19 March 1946 Réunion became a *Département Francais d'Outre Mer*, a French overseas department and to all intents and purposes a territorial extension of metropolitan France. A *préfet* replaced the former governor and numerous departmental directives gave the island a strong corps of civil servants. Large infrastructural projects were started in an attempt to bring about the rapid transformation of this neglected island, with the result that Réunion today is probably the most modern island in the entire Indian Ocean.

POLITICS

As an overseas département of France, Réunion is governed in terms of the French Constitution of 1958. The President of France is head of state and is represented on the island by a Prefect, who is appointed by the president in consultation with the French Ministry of the Interior. The Prefect administers island affairs through a General Council of 47 elected members, and a Regional Council of 45 elected members, established in 1974 to co-ordinate Réunion's social and economic development. The presidents of these two councils are elected by council members, voting along party lines. Main political parties active are the Gaullist-oriented Rally for the Republic (RPR), the centre-right Union for French Democracy (UDF), Communist Party of Réunion (PCR), France-Réunion Future (FRA), Socialist Party (PS), Centre of Social Democrats (CDS), Union for France (UPF), the Free-DOM Movement, and National Front (FN). For the purposes of local government the island is divided into four *arrondisements* or administrative districts, 24 communes and 47 cantons. Réunion sends five deputies and three senators to the French National Assembly (and an island soccer team plays in French Cup matches every year). The Communist Party vies with the PS for dominance in the General Council but loses out to UPF and the Free-DOM Movement in Regional Council affairs. Politics in Réunion have tended to revolve around the continuance of ties with France, and their substance, and differences with the metropole over discriminatory allocation of welfare benefits. Réunion did not share the metropolitan minimum wage structure until 1996, and lower welfare payments have been a source of discontent for some time. The gulf in Réunion between the affluent, usually white and Indian, and the poor, usually Creole, is responsible for persistent social tensions. The disadvantaged groups bear the brunt of the serious unemployment and suffer the poverty typical of nations on the African continent. The outbreak of anti-government rioting in February 1991 which left 8 dead illustrates the seriousness of these socio-economic tensions. A rapid lowering of the unemployment figure is a priority for the administration in its bid to reduce these tensions, and tourism is seen as the principal means to achieve this.

THE ECONOMY

Agriculture
The economy of Réunion has been based on agriculture in one form or another since first the island was settled. Sugarcane has been the primary crop for more than a century and in some years sugar, which uses nearly half of all the island's arable land, has accounted for as much as 85% of total exports. Other important crops include tobacco, tropical fruits, vegetables, maize, lentils, beans, onions, garlic, vanilla, and plants used to produce base essences for European perfume manufacture – principally geranium and vetiver. Although their overall contribution to the economy is relatively minor, exotic plants such as vanilla, geranium, and vetiver have a special place in island lore. The vanilla orchid, for instance, was once hailed as a plant that would supplant sugarcane as a major source of income. Unfortunately, it didn't reproduce easily on Réunion because the insect vital to its pollination was not present to do the job. Then one day in 1841, in the island vanilla capital of St Suzanne on the east coast, a slave called Edmond Albius discovered that after piercing them with a sliver of bamboo, the flowers could be pollinated by a simple wave of the hand. From that day on vanilla production took off. In 1848, some 110 lb (50 kg) of vanilla was exported to France. In 1895, a record 200 tons was reached. In 1951, the Réunion Vanilla Planters Co-operative was established and today deals with 93% of all the island's vanilla production. In 1981, more than 150 years after his discovery, Albius got his reward; the municipality of St Suzanne erected a stele in his memory.

Essential oils are produced for the perfume industry from the leaves and stalks of geraniums grown along the road to Piton Maïdo and around Le Tampon, and from the roots of vetiver, an aromatic grass introduced from India and grown on a small scale in the south. The island's economy is moving away from its traditional agricultural base with the surge in growth of the tourism industry, and an expanding manufacturing sector. Tourism now brings in more money than sugarcane, vanilla, geranium and vetiver oils put together.

Manufacturing

This sector is mainly made up of sugar processing, rum and molasses, construction materials, metal goods, textiles and electronics.

Imports

Major imports include motorcars, motorcycles and bicycles, petroleum products, pharmaceuticals, manufactured goods, food, beverages, tobacco, machinery and transportation equipment.

Exports

Milled sugar – an average of 180,000-200,000 tons a year – accounts for about 65% of Réunion's exports and by-products such as rum and molasses account for much of the rest. Langouste has also been a useful export, but this crustacean's contribution has been tailing off every year since 1995.

Most of Réunion's trade is with France, which with other European Union member countries accounts for close on 90% of all imports and exports. Per capita gross domestic product (GDP) is estimated at US$4,800 (1998) and this is growing annually by about 3.8%. There's an active labour force of nearly 300,000 (1998), but unemployment is running at 40%. Réunion relies heavily on continued financial assistance from France for its economic well-being.

THE PEOPLE

Réunion is another good Indian Ocean example of a trade entrepot that became a racial melting pot. Today, you'll find every human hue and a mix of religions and cultures there that gives the lie to Kipling's old line 'East is East, and West is West, and never the twain shall meet'. It's taken nearly three centuries for the population to grow from 734 inhabitants in 1707 to the present 707,200, and with nearly 750 people to the square mile (280 per sq km) it has one of the highest population densities of all French regions. The population is growing at an estimated 2% a year, and 48% of all islanders are under 25. This is the age group generally hardest hit by Réunion's widespread unemployment, running at 40.2% among an economically active population of nearly 300,000. Although job creation is higher than in France, the population growth makes it difficult for the administration to make a dent in this staggeringly high unemployment, or to save on the income support (*Revenu Minimum d'Insertion*) it is obliged to pay 57,000 claimants every month. Most of the islanders (68%) live in urban areas, which means in the towns and villages on the narrow coastal plain around the island, leaving the mountainous interior sparsely populated. At 125,000 people, the capital St Denis has the largest urban population. Women outnumber men slightly; women statistically bear 2.64 children each; and life expectancy for all is 75.73 years.

The Smiths, Browns and Whites of the island are the Payets, Grondins, and Hoaraus, common surnames belonging to families tracing their descent from a blend of the early French, Madagascan and other settlers. Multi-coloured families are numerous and make up more than a third of the island's total population, which encompasses French, African, Madagascan, Comorian, Chinese, Pakistani and Indian communities. Over the years since they arrived on the island different communities have come to dominate or be identified with various trades and business activities. The Chinese are largely store and food outlet owners, the

Indians have taken over the clothing and textile trade, the French are dominant in the service and hospitality industry and form the core of the civil service, although Creoles have recently made inroads here and in the professions. The majority of Creoles – the ones with jobs – are the backbone of the labour force.

LANGUAGES

The two main languages on the island are French, which is the official language, and Creole. Montagnards, living in the mountainous interior, speak an archaic highland form of French. Creole in Réunion sprang from 18th century French and a mixture of the languages spoken by slaves, who needed a common language to communicate with each other. It is quite different from the Creole spoken on other Indian Ocean islands. There is no recognised spelling, no real conjugation, and few grammatical rules. Creole is rarely used in literary works, except in comic or satirical pieces, as it is generally regarded as inferior to French. Most of the 90% of the population speaking it, however, admit that they feel more comfortable using Creole in their everyday life. Colloquial Creole terms are commonly used to describe Reunionese of different origins. Blacks with African features are known as '*cafre*', Hindu Indians are '*malbar*', Muslim Indians are '*zarab*', and the poor of inderterminate colour living in the upper reaches of the island are known as '*yab*'. English are known as '*Zanglais*'. Very few of the local people understand English, although you'll have no problem in hotels, restaurants, the larger stores and any businesses dealing regularly with tourists. Having said that, a pocket French/English dictionary is a useful thing to carry. The French-based patois of Réunion is quite different from the Creole spoken in Mauritius and the Kreol used in Seychelles. Just how different it is from the other islands, and from French, can be judged from the following Creole words and phrases when compared to those listed on pages 26 and 124:

Creole	French	English
Allons batt'carre	viens te promener	come for a walk
Cari d'sous d'riz	faire quelque chose	do something on the sly
(the meat is hidden under the rice)	en catamini	
Faire dentelle		
(to make lace, to attract attention)	faire des manières	to be fussy
Car y amuse		
(the bus is joking)	le car est en retard	the bus is late
La peau du bois (skin of the tree)	l'écorce	the peel/bark
Mon femme lé gênée		
(my wife is embarassed)	femme enceinte	pregnant woman
Faire son gros zef		
(to be a big egg or show-off)	faire son malin	to be clever
Carie la faiblesse (a weak meal)	cari sans viande	curry without meat
Travailler clair d'lune		
(a moonlight worker)	voleur	thief
Mi	je	I
Vi	vous	you (polite form/plural)
Zot	toi	you (second person)
Li	lui	he
Moins nana	j'ai	I have
Moins le	je suis	I am
Mi di a ou	je vous dis	I am telling you
Mi ca va	je m'en vais	I am leaving
Skisse à moin	excusez-moi	excuse me

Guette à li	regarde-le	look at him
Mi aime à ou	je vous aime	I love you
Mi gagne pi	je n'en peux plus	I cannot take it any longer
Fénoir (pitch-dark)	la nuit	night
La di la fé		
(say what has been done)	commérages	gossip
La loi (law)	les gendarmes	the police
Marmailles	enfants	children
Mon caze	ma maison	my home
Moucater	se moquer	make fun of
Nénère (fiancée)	amoureux	in love
Effet (to hang over)	planer, avoir l'effet	to float/to glide
Quo ça? (What's that?)	qu'est-ce que c'est?	what is this?
Tantine (a chick)	fille	daughter/girl
Totocher (to fight)	frapper	to hit or to strike
Train (a date)	j'ai un rendez-vous, faire sa vie	I have an appointment, it's my life
Ralé-poussé (push and pull)	bousculade, provocation	rush, provocation
Arzent	argent	money
Comment y pète, le Caf?	comment vas-tu?	how are you?
Conserves (cans)	lunettes	spectacles
Zoréole	enfant né d'un(e)	Child born of a
(from Zoreil and Creole)	ressortissant(e) français(e) de métropole et d'un(e) Créole	French national and a Creole

A lot of the Creole used is even more colourful and expressive, for instance:

Zoreilles ou métros (*gens de la métropole* or people from metropolitan France), literally means 'ears,' the reference being to people from France who don't understand Creole, so they are all ears.

Chauffe galet (*fainéant*/lazy) means someone who is warming up a stone by sitting on it.

Travail gros doigt (*travail mal fait*/badly done work) is work done with big fingers.

Un femme manze la corde (*une femme vagabonde*/a wandering woman) means a woman who is chewing the rope.

Gardien volcan (*rouquin*/redhead) is a volcano watchman with burnt hair.

Gratteur de fesses (*paresseux*/lazy) means bum-scratcher.

La pluie y farine (*crachin*/drizzle) means the rain is like flour.

Argent braguette (*allocations familiales*/child benefits) is zipper money.

Bonbon la fesse (*suppositoire*/suppository) means bum candy.

RELIGION

Christianity is the dominant religious faith and it is estimated that about 95% of Réunion's people are Catholic, the result of energetic proselytising over the past two hundred years which influenced all newcomers to the island, whether black slaves, Europeans or Indian contract workers.

Réunion's Catholics celebrate the feast days of a host of saints and roadside shrines and odd volcanic nooks and crannies house makeshift altars dedicated to many of them. The most curious of these is probably the most popular, certainly with the island's Creoles. These are the startling red altars dedicated to St Expédit, a saint tolerated rather than acknowledged by the Catholic church. An old Creole woman we spoke to as she was placing some dubious offerings at a St Expédit shrine said she did not always ask good things of the saint, and some of the odd offerings looked more appropriate to a voodoo shrine. The story of how St Expédit joined the more recognised saints is told with humour in Réunion. Some years ago the local fathers apparently asked the Vatican to send them some religious icons and saintly relics and a box arrived in due course with the word *Expédit* written on it. This instruction to despatch quickly was misunderstood and a chapel, it is said, was duly consecrated to the new St Expédit. The more serious will tell you that St Expédit was really an historical figure, a Christian Roman legionary officer who fought on the frontier of the empire against the Hungarians and suffered martyrdom in AD 303. This explains why the little plaster statues of St Expédit in the wayside shrines are of a Roman soldier, dressed in a red cape, cuirass, and holding a crucifix. The head is often missing, and this is said to be in recognition of his death by decapitation. Creoles, however, say this is what happens to statues of St Expédit when he has not been expeditious enough in answering someone's prayers.

Réunion's second most practised religion is Hinduism. It came with the indentured Indian labourers who replaced the slaves after they gained their freedom in the mid-19th century, and most of the oldest temples are still to be found in the sugarcane plantation areas, vividly decorated temples to a pantheon of gods. There is a large Hindu ashram in St Louis (an Indian spiritual retreat) which welcomes visitors, and might even offer you a meal and a bed for the night. You can visit Hindu temples if you leave your shoes and any leather garments at the entrance.

The Tamil people originally came from the Coromandel coast and Madras in India. Most of them are Catholic as well, since they were converted to this religion on their arrival on the island. Being a practising Tamil as well as a practising Catholic does not trouble them as their religion is polytheistic. Tamil religious festivals are awe-inspiring, with firewalking displays (usually in January) and religious penitents who at *Cavadee* walk with their skin pierced by needles, carrying heavy wooden altars bedecked with flowers.

Islam is more exclusive and it is rare for non-Muslims to be allowed to watch their religious observances, such as the Sacrifice of Abraham. The mosques of St Pierre, St Denis, St Andre or St Louis have been built by Indian Muslims originally from Bombay and Gujarat and can be visited provided you are respectful and obey certain rules, such as leaving your footwear at the door. Muslims have for the past few years been turning more to fundamentalism and have returned to the old dress code: austere clothing for women and long white kaftans (*gondoura*) for men.

Chinese Taoism is not practised as a religion, but it is still very much alive, nurturing deep roots within this community, especially their bonds with their ancestors. They see no conflict in following these old practices while going to mass in the Catholic church and baptising their children Christians. The Chinese pagodas in St Denis and St Pierre cannot be visited without permission.

The **national anthem** and **flag** used are those of metropolitan France.

FURTHER READING

For what it was like in the old days check your local library for *Trip to Réunion* by FJ Mouat (1852); *Six Months in Réunion* by P Beaton (1860); *La Réunion* by G Manes (1913); and *La Réunion* by P Herman (1923). For more up-to-date coverage: *Histoire des îles Mascareignes* by Auguste Toussaint; *Histoire résumée de la Réunion* by Gabriel Gerard; *Le Réunion du Battant des lames au sommet des montagnes* by Catherine Lavaux (Pacifique); *La Réunion* by Daniel Vaxelaire (Gérard Doyen); *Contes et légendes de l'île de la Réunion* by Isabelle Hoarau (Orphie et Azalées) and Gîtes de France's *Complete Guide to Réunion*.

Réunion From the Air by Catherine Lavaux, photography by Guido Alberto Rossi (Gallimard), gives a bird's-eye view of remote villages buried in mist-swathed mountains, and other entrancing aspects of this little-known bit of France in the Indian Ocean, while *Cases Creoles de la Réunion* by Christian Barat, photographs by Christian Vaisse (Albin Michel), is a fascinating look at Creole vernacular architectural styles in Réunion.

Serious foodies should look for: *Du bonheur dans votre assiette* by Brigitte Grondin (éditions Quatre Epices), a cookbook of 290 local recipes which sells in Réunion for about £16; *La cuisine réunionnaise* by Louise et Caroline; *Le grand guide de la cuisine réunionnaise* by Marie-France et Ivrin and *Les meilleures recettes de la cuisine réunionnaise* by G Gay and C Huc.

If you can't find any of the French titles locally they are available in Paris from Librairie Itinéraires, 60, rue Saint-Honoré, 75001 Paris, tel 4236-1263.

Highly recommended for birdwatchers is *Birds of the Indian Ocean Islands* by Ian Sinclair and Olivier Langrand (published by Struik, Cape Town 1998). It's the first field guide covering the Mascarene islands (Réunion, Mauritius and Rodrigues), as well as Comoros, Seychelles, and Madagascar.

For insight into what makes Réunion tick economically there's nothing better than *Tableau Economique de la Réunion 2000* (TER) published by the Institut National de la Statisque et des Etudes Economiques (INSEE) in Réunion. It costs 70 francs (£7).

RÉUNION: PRACTICAL INFORMATION

Getting There

BY AIR

Regular airlines operating from all major European cities offer special pre-routing fares for passengers to and from Réunion. This is the case with Air France's flights from Europe to Réunion via Paris. The Reunion Tourist Office website links to Air France and lists several airlines serving Réunion, return fares will cost between FF3480-5340 (£330-510/US$495-760). Some French companies have signed preferential trade agreements with foreign airlines to service Réunion (eg AOM with Swissair, Sabena and Austrian Airlines, Air Liberté with British Airways). Some airlines offer flights from Europe to other islands in the Indian Ocean – Comoros, Mauritius, Madagascar, Seychelles – and these islands provide air links to Réunion. Dates and times change according to the airline and the season and ticket prices will vary by route and availability; a flight from Seychelles to Réunion may cost around £200 (US$300), while one from Mauritius may be as low as £60 (US$90). There are no direct flights from any European capital other than Paris, but connections can be organised by your travel agent.

The **best way** to get to Réunion from the UK is from London to Paris and then by Air France or one of the other airlines offering direct flights to the island. Six airlines operate flights with varying frequencies to Réunion from France. They are Air France (9 weekly flights), AOM (daily flights), Air Liberté (4 weekly flights), Corsair (3-6 weekly flights, Aerolyon (1 weekly flight), and Jet Ocean Indien (6 weekly flights). The non-stop flight to Réunion from Paris takes 11 hours or up to 13 hours with stops en route. There are also flights from Lyons, Marseilles, and Toulouse on certain days and periods of the year. Prices depend on travelling dates, and there are often attractive promotional fares. From South Africa, Air Austral has two weekly flights and a code share agreement with Interair. If you opt for a stop-over in Africa or another Indian Ocean island on your way to Réunion you can complete your trip on an Air Austral connecting flight. For more information, contact your travel agent or get in touch with the airlines.

AIRPORTS

Réunion has two airports, the Roland Garros International Airport 8 miles (12 km) from St Denis, and Pierrefonds Airport, between St Pierre and St Louis, on the south-west coast. Gillot is the old name for Roland Garros airport, and even though it was renamed in 1997 road signs still say Gillot. Try to arrive with some small change, as you'll need a 10-franc coin to unlock a trolley. You can, however, get coins at a desk near the trolleys, and the coin pops out when you return and lock the trolley again. Roland Garros is a modern, efficient airport. There are shops and a bookstore in the main public hall and in the boarding lounge; shops in the departure lounge; a well-stocked duty-free shop; snack-bars and restaurant; and telephones. You will also find a Post Office (tel 28 25 52); and a bank and foreign exchange counter (tel 48 80 55). ATMs dispense French francs, US dollars, pounds sterling, and Mauritian rupees.

Airport Telephone Numbers:
Check-in and luggage transport: tel 55 33 77.
Information desk: tel 48 80 68.
Immigration control: tel 48 81 31.
Customs: tel 48 81 25.
Airport police: tel 93 00 38.
Emergencies: tel 48 80 68.
Arrival and departure times: tel 28 16 16, or Minitel 3615 RUNTEL code HORA.
Passenger information: tel 48 81 81.
Parking information/lost and found: tel 48 80 19.
Airport e-mail agrcom@guetali.fr.
Buses: tel 41 51 10
Taxis: tel 48 83 83
For car rentals see *Getting Around.*

Call the airline to ascertain facilities for disabled passengers. Before you leave, pick up a copy of the airport information booklet. You'll find this on the rack next to the Information Desk in the main concourse.

Pierrefonds Airport is 3 miles (5 km) from St Pierre. It has been in operation since 20 December 1998 and runs at least two daily connections to SSR Airport (Plaisance), Mauritius. Regular bus services go from Pierrefonds Airport to St Pierre, Tampon, St Louis, Entre-Deux, Avirons, Etang-Salé, St Leu, St Philippe, Petite Ile, St Joseph, and Cilaos. There are hire cars at the airport, as well as taxis.

Getting to Town
From the air terminal, you can make use of the shuttle bus service which links Roland Garros Airport to St Denis city centre and stops either at the bus terminal or at Le St Denis hotel. *Cars Jaunes* (Yellow Coaches) run 13 times a day between the airport and St Denis bus terminal (Gare routière); off Boulevard Joffre (tel 41 51 10), starting at 6.30am. Last departure is at 8.30pm. The fare is FF25. There are also taxi ranks in front of the airport. The fare to St Denis should be FF100-150. This increases after 8pm, on Sundays and public holidays.

AIRLINES SERVING RÉUNION
Air France: Number of weekly flights: 9, of which 7 are non-stop flights Orly Ouest/Réunion, 2 non-stop Charles de Gaulle/Réunion on Friday and Saturday. Reservations tel 0802 802 802.

Contact address in Britain: 1st Floor, 10 Warwick Street, London, W1R 5RA (tel 0207-474 5555; Website www.airfrance.fr/).
Contact address in France: 119 Avenue des Champs Elysées, F-75384 Paris Cedex 08 (tel 1-42 99 23 64).
Contact Address in USA: 120 West 56th Street, New York, NY 10019, USA; tel 1-800-237 2747 (reservations).
Contact address in Réunion: 7 Avenue de la Victoire, St Denis (tel 40 39 00); Reservations (tel 40 38 38, fax 40 38 40); Agency: 10 rue François de Mahy, St Pierre (tel 40 38 38); Roland Garros Airport (tel 48 80 86).

AOM (Aire Outre Mer): Number of weekly flights: 7, of which 5 are non-stop Orly-Sud/Réunion, 2 with stop-overs in Lyons (Wednesday), and Marseilles (Sunday).
Contact address in France: Bàt 363 BP 854, F-94551 Orly Aérogare Cedex (tel 1-

08 03 00 12 34);
Orly Airport (tel 1-49 75 24 95);
Agence Opéra France, 45 Avenue de l'Opéra, F-75002
Paris (tel 1-53 45 48 00).

Contact address in Réunion: 7 rue Jean Chatel, St Denis (tel 94 77 77, fax 20 07 16);
St Pierre Agency: Angle des rues Francois de Mahy et
Four a Chaux, St Pierre (tel 96 17 00);
Roland Garros Airport (tel 48 80 99).

Air Liberté: (also agent for British Airways) Number of weekly flights: 4 flights
direct from Orly Sud, on Mondays and Sundays, and 2 with stopover in Marseilles
on Tuesdays, and in Toulouse on Fridays.

Contact address in France: Parc d' Affaires SILIC, 67 rue de Monthléry, Rungis
(tel 1-49 79 23 00).

Contact address in Réunion: 13 rue Charles Gounod, St Denis (tel 94 72 00, fax 41
68 00);
Roland Garros Airport (tel 48 83 83, fax 48 83 86).
British Airways is at the same address in St Denis
(tel 94 72 10, fax 41 68 00).

Corsair: (Nouvelles Frontières): Number of weekly flights: 3-6 direct flights from
Paris.

Contact address in France: 2 Avenue Charles Lindbergh, 94528 Rungis Cedex
(tel 1-49 79 49 79, fax 1-49 79 49 68; Information
0803-33 33 33).

Contact address in Réunion: Nouvelles Frontières, 20 rue Labourdonnais, St Denis
(tel 21 54 54, fax 20-2637);
St Pierre, 1 rue Désiré Barquisseau, St Pierre (tel 35
27 17, fax 25 46 93);
Roland Garros Airport (tel 48 82 48, fax 48 83 23).

Aerolyon: Number of weekly flights: 1 from Lyons on Sunday, 1 from Nantes and
Toulouse.

Contact address in France: Aerolyon BP136, F-69125 Lyon Satolas (tel 4-72 22
73 00, fax 4-72 22 73 10).

Jet Ocean Indien: Number of weekly flights: 4 Paris/Réunion, 1 Marseilles and 1
Toulouse. It also connects with flights in Nantes, Bordeaux, Toulouse, Perpignan,
Montpellier, Marseilles, Toulon, Nice and Strasbourg.

Contact address in France: 4 rue Monge, F-75005 Paris (tel 1-44 07 20 04/20 06,
fax 1-43 25 69 94).

Contact address in Reunion: 55 rue Labourdonnais, St Denis (tel 21 47 21, fax 41
49 37).

INDIAN OCEAN AND AFRICAN LINKS WITH RÉUNION

There are regular **Air Austral** connections with:
Kenya (Nairobi 1 weekly flight); Zimbabwe (Harare 1 weekly flight); South Africa
(Johannesburg 2 weekly flights); Seychelles (Mahé 2 weekly flights); Mauritius
(SSR/Plaisance 20 weekly flights); Mayotte (Dzaoudzi 7 weekly flights);
Madagascar (Majunga 2 weekly flights; Tamatave 1 weekly flight; Antananarivo 3
weekly flights; Nosy Bé 2 weekly flights); and Comoros (Moroni 3 weekly flights).
Flights between Réunion and Mauritius are also available at Pierrefonds airport
(one daily flight with Air Austral and Air Mauritius).

Air Austral. Since it was established in 1990 Réunion-based Air Austral has been the dominant air carrier in the south-west Indian Ocean, and is the only airline flying from Réunion to 11 destinations in the region. Its fleet of Boeing 737s has two classes: Comfort Class with 23 seats at the front of the aircraft, with five seats abreast instead of six; and Leisure Class, which is economy class with international standard comfort and a 32-inch pitch.

Contact address in France: 2 rue de l'Eglise, F-92200 Neuilly sur Seine (tel 1-92 01 33, fax 1-92 01 37).
Contact address in Réunion: 4 rue de Nice, St Denis Cedex, (tel 90 90 90, fax 90 90 91 bookings);
Roland Garros Airport (tel 48 80 20);
St Pierre, 14 rue Archambaud (tel 96 26 96, fax 35 46 49);
Pierrefonds Airport (tel 96 80 20, fax 96 80 19).

Air Mauritius: 13 rue Charles Gounod, St Denis (tel 94 83 83, fax 94 13 23);
Roland Garros Airport (tel 48 80 18, fax 48 18 60);
St Pierre, 7 rue Francois de Mahy, St Pierre (tel 96 06 00, fax 96 27 47);
Pierrefonds Airport (tel 96 80 18, fax 96 80 17).

Air Madagascar: 2 rue Victor MacAuliffe, St Denis (tel 21 05 21, fax 21 10 08). Also has a few Réunion/Madagascar flights.

TTAM (Transports et Travaux Aériens de Madagascar): Operates flights between Réunion and Madagascar (Nosy-Bé/Diégo Suarez/Majunga/Fort Dauphin/Tulear/St Marie/Tamatave).
Contact address in Réunion: 3 rue de Nice, St Denis (tel 94 38 48, fax 94 39 49); Airport (tel 48 83 60, fax 48 83 62).

TOUR OPERATORS

Australia
Beachcomber Tours: 10 Stirling Highway, Nedlands, WA 6009, Perth (tel 8-9442 3356, fax 8-9442 3365).
Paradise Island Holidays: 200 Adelaide Terrace, WA 6000 Perth (tel 8-9221 8999, fax 8-9221 8998).

Britain:
Cosmos Distant Dreams: Tourama House, 17 Homesdale Road, Bromley BR2 9LX (tel 020-8464 3444, fax 020-8466 0699).
Solo's Holidays: 54-58 High Street, Edgware HA8 7EJ (tel 020-8951 2800, fax 020-8951 1051, e-mail travel@solosholidays.co.uk).
Sunbird Travel: 341 Kensington Road, London SE11 4QE (tel 020-7582 5353, fax 020-7793 0407).
Sunset Travel: 306 Clapham Road, London SW9 9AE (tel 020-7622 5466, fax 020-7978 1337).
Voyages Jules Verne: 10 Glentworth Street, London NW1 5P4 (tel 020-7616 1000, fax 020-7723 8629).

Canada
Club Voyages: 4 place Ville-Marie, Montréal (tel 514-871 0209).
Inter Voyage: 1095 rue de l'Amérique-Française, Québec (tel 418-524 1414).

Nouvelles Frontières: 1001 rue Sherbrooke Est, Bureau 720, Montréal (tel 514-526 6774).

France

Accor Tour: 31 rue du Colonnel Pierre Avia, F-75015 Paris (tel 1-41 33 69 33, fax 1-41 33 69 49).

Akaloa: 16 rue des Quatre Cheminées, F-92100 Boulogne Billancourt (tel 1-41 41 90 33, fax 1-41 41 91 31).

Austral Voyages: 29 rue du Puits Mauger, F-35000 Rennes (tel 2-99 85 94 94, fax 2-99 30 66 77, e-mail: austral-resa@wanadoo.fr).

Aventures et Volcans: 73 cours de la Liberté, F-69003 Lyon (tel 4-78 60 51 11, fax 4-78 60 63 22, e-mail aventurevolcans@yahoo.com).

Climats du Monde: 14 rue Beauvau, F-13001 Marseilles (tel 4-91 15 70 20, fax 4-91 15 70 21).

Fram: 1 rue Lapeyrouse, F-31008 Toulouse Cedex (tel 5-62 15 16 17, fax 5-62 15 17 17, e-mail: question@fram.fr).

Look Voyages: 12 rue Truillot, F-94204 Ivry-sur-Seine Cedex (tel 1-45 15 15 00, fax 1-45 15 15 88).

Nuances du Monde: 61 rue Faubourg-Montmartre, F-75009 Paris (tel 1-49 70 68 68, fax 1-49 70 68 69).

Terrien: 1 Allée Turenne, BP 20324, F-44003, Nantes Cedex 01 (tel 2-40 47 72 95, fax 2-40 35 67 57).

Tibo Tours: 15 rue Jean-Roisin BP 159, F-59027 Lille Cedex (tel 3-20 14 56 40, fax 3-20 14 56 44).

Tourinter: 30 rue Ferrandiére, F-69002 Lyon (tel 4-72 56 44 44, fax 4-78 37 80 92, e-mail: tourinter@tourinter.com).

South Africa

Africa and Island Tours: PO Box 1399, Halfway House 1685, Constantia Square Suites 9 & 10, 16th Street, Midrand, Johannesburg (tel 11-315 9300, fax 11-315 8216).

Sun & Sandals: PO Box 2513, Edenvale 1610, 4 Banksia Avenue Oriel, Bedfordview 2008, Johannesburg (tel 11-616 7705, fax 11-616 7716, e-mail: sunsand@pixie.co.za).

Unusual Destinations: PO Box 11583, Vorna Valley 1686, 13 Gustav Preller Street, Vorna Valley, Johannesburg (tel 11-805 4833, fax 11-805 4835, e-mail: unusdest@global.co.za).

BY SEA

Two boats operate between Mauritius and Réunion. They are *MV Mauritius Pride*, a passenger/goods ship, and *L' Ahinora*, a 260-passenger catamaran taking only 4 hours to make the trip. Between them they carry 40,000 arriving and departing passengers a year. While you are making the crossing you can make international telephone calls, buy stamps and postcards, handicrafts, change money, and even organise car rental. For *MV Mauritius Pride* contact Scoam at 4 Avenue du 14 Juillet 1789, Le Port (tel 42 10 45, fax 43 25 47, e-mail: postmaster@scoam.fr). The adult fare depends on the season and travelling class (seat or berth). A return ticket costs FF740-1,300 and a one-way ticket FF444-780. There are discount rates for children, teenagers, and the elderly. For *L'Ahinora* contact Blue Line Shipping Agency at 67 rue de St Paul, Le Port (tel 55 23 25, fax 55 23 26). A return ticket costs from FF850, children under 12 FF435, children under 2 FF103. The catamaran departs from Réunion on Mondays and Wednesdays at 8am, and Fridays and Saturdays at 3pm. It returns to Réunion on Sundays at 2.30pm, and Tuesdays,

Thursdays and Saturdays at 1.30pm. You can also buy tickets in Réunion at *Atlas Voyages* (tel 33 02 20), *Papangue Tours* (tel 30 45 45); and *Réucir Voyages* (tel 41 55 66). Reunion's passenger terminal for arrivals by sea is at Port Est, 9 miles (15 km) from St Denis (tel 43 10 93). Outside office hours, call the Port Authority's switchboard operator (tel 42 90 00). The terminal is open at arrival and departure times of inter-island ferries and catamarans. Getting a passage on a cargo ship these days is largely a matter of luck. The *Mediterranean Shipping Company* runs regular services to the Mascarene islands and it might be worth contacting them: **Paris.** MSC France SA, 23 Avenue de Neuilly, F-75116 Paris (tel 1-53 64 63 00, fax 1-53 64 63 10); **Le Havre.** MSC France SA, Centre Havrais de Commerce International Quai George V, F-76600 Le Havre (tel 2-35 19 78 00, fax 2-35 18 78 10; and **Réunion.** MSC France SA, 49 rue E de Parny, Le Port Cedex (tel 42 78 00, fax 42 78 10). A cruise ship is another way of getting there. They bring nearly 7,000 visitors a year to Réunion. Passenger liners – the majority French – use Pointe des Galets as their port of call.

TRAVEL SAFELY
Both the UK Foreign Office and the US State Department have travel information offices which provide regularly updated free advice on countries around the world (see page 34 for their contact details).

Red Tape

ENTRY REQUIREMENTS

PASSPORTS AND VISAS
If you can enter France without any red tape you can also enter Réunion. All French and European Union nationals need is a valid identity card or passport, but nationals of non-European Union countries must be in possession of a valid passport, a visa, if required (as for South African passport holders) and a return or onward ticket. You could be asked where you intend to stay in Réunion.

HEALTH DOCUMENTS
No specific inoculations or vaccinations are required to enter Réunion, unless you are arriving from countries with endemic diseases, such as cholera and yellow fever, in which case you'll have to produce an International Certificate of Vaccination. This does not apply to children up to a year old.

CUSTOMS REGULATIONS
Tobacco. If you smoke you can take in 200 cigarettes, or 100 cigarillos, 50 cigars, or 250g of tobacco.
Alcohol. For your personal consumption you are allowed 2 litres of still wine, 1 litre of alcohol over 22%, or 2 litres of alcohol under 22%.
You are also allowed 50g perfume, 250ml of eau de toilette, 500g of coffee, 200g of coffee extract and essence, 100g of tea, and 40g of tea extract – whatever that is.
Pets. Quarantine regulations could make this a no-no. Check with Direction des Services Vétérinaires de la Réunion, Poste d'Inspection Frontalier, Le Port Cedex (tel 42 09 97, fax 42 05 83).
Plants. Think again if you intend to take into Réunion any fresh plants or parts of same, bulbs, rhizomes, flowers, vegetables or fresh fruit. All these things are prohibited. You can, of course, mail or freight them by air or sea, but they will require approval from the Service de Protection des Végétaux (the Ministry of Agriculture's Plant Protection Agency) (tel 48 61 45).

There are no restrictions on your camera equipment, and you are allowed a reasonable amount of film for personal use (film is expensive, so take lots). For further information contact the Local Customs Services, 7 Avenue de la Victoire, St Denis Cedex (tel 90 81 00, fax 41 09 81).

WHAT MONEY TO TAKE

Local Currency

The basic unit of currency in Réunion is the French Franc (FF), which is divided into 100 centimes. Banknotes come in 500, 200, 100, 50, and 20 franc denominations; coins in 20, 10, 5, 2 and 1 francs and in 50, 20, 10 and 5 centimes. The import and export of local and foreign currency is unrestricted, although you are obliged to declare amounts of FF50,000 and over.

Exchange Rates

These are the same as in Europe and can be checked daily at any bank or hotel reception, but a rough guide is around 10 francs to the pound sterling and about 6 francs to the US dollar.

Banks and Banking

The following banks are in St Denis, but most of them have branches in towns throughout the island:
Banque de la Réunion: 27 rue Jean Chatel (tel 40 01 23).
Banque Francaise Commerciale: 60 rue Alexis de Villeneuve (tel 40 55 55).
Banque Nationale de Paris Intercontinentale (BNPI): 67 rue Juliette Dodu (tel 40 30 30).
Banque Regionale D'Escompte et de Depot (Bred): 33 rue Victor MacAuliffe (tel 90 15 60).
Caisse D'Epargne Ecureuil: 55 rue de Paris (tel 94 80 00).
Credit Agricole: 18 rue Felix Guyon (tel 90 91 00).
Hours. Most banks are open Monday to Friday from 8am to 4pm.

Credit Cards and ATMs

All major credit cards are accepted in Réunion, including Visa, MasterCard, Diners Club, Eurocard, Carte Bleue, and American Express. Holders of some foreign bank cards (MasterCard, Visa, Eurocheque, Cirrus) can withdraw cash in francs at automatic teller machines (ATMs). Most shops, restaurants, and businesses accept credit cards, but naturally it's wise to check first.

Tipping

Imagine you are on holiday in France, and tip accordingly – usually 10% to 15% of the bill in restaurants, especially if the menu says *service non compris.* The French word for tip is *pourboire,* which literally and without equivocation means 'for a drink.'

For general health information see pages 41-43.

MEDICAL SERVICES

There are good health services on the island, which conform to French metropolitan standards. There are 1,346 doctors and 17 hospitals and clinics scattered throughout the island, all equipped with modern, state-of-the-art equipment, so if you need any treatment you don't have to worry about the quality of the healthcare you'll receive. There are also 284 pharmacies on Réunion, and 337 dental surgeons.

HEALTH HAZARDS
There is no danger from malaria in Réunion; it was eliminated in 1952.

Altitude Sickness
Yes, you could suffer from this, also known as mountain sickness, if you go up into the central mountains, which top out at more than 10,000 ft (3,048 m). As you climb to higher altitudes from sea level the air pressure gets lower, so it becomes harder to breathe enough air into your lungs to keep the oxygen in your blood at the right level. Many people begin to feel the effects of altitude sickness at 8,202-9,843 ft (2,500-3,000 m). One cause is dehydration. The higher you go the drier the air becomes, so you should drink as much liquid as possible as you climb. Mountain sickness can range from a mild feeling of discomfort to a fatal attack, and it has nothing to do with your fitness level. The best thing to do is to descend as fast as you can to a lower altitude, where you'll get more oxygen. To avoid the problem in the first place climb slowly, to give your body time to acclimatise and adjust to the thinner atmosphere.

CLOTHING

What to Wear – and When
The best clothing for men and women is lightweight cotton or linen summer wear, although you should pack some warm clothing if you are planning a trip into the mountains. A woollen sweater is ideal for the evenings. Don't forget to take a strong pair of walking shoes or boots if you are heading for the heights. A lightweight rain jacket is also advisable, as is a hat to protect you from the sun – and the rain.

If you are doing a lot of walking you are more likely to suffer from the normal hiking problems – chafing, blisters, cuts and grazes – so make sure you carry plasters and disinfectants in your pack.

MAIL
You pay the same tariff for stamps in Réunion as in France, FF3 for a letter of 100g. For all other countries of the European Union the tariff is FF5.20 per 100g.

Post Offices. There is a post office in just about every town on the island but you can contact the main office at 62 rue du Maréchal-Leclerc, 97400 St Denis (tel 40 17 17, fax 20 01 06), for information on the post office nearest to where you are staying. There are also a few courier companies, among them Courier Express International, 94b Avenue Leconte Delisle, St Clotilde (tel 97 15 00, fax 97 07 08); and DHL International, 8 rue de la Rivière des Pluies (tel 48 43 80). When you see Cedex in an address it stands for *courier d'enterprise à distribution exceptionelle*, and means a service for bulk postal users.

TELEPHONES
Réunion's telephone network is entirely automatic and linked to metropolitan France and the rest of the world by satellite. The international code for Réunion is 262. To call Réunion by international direct dialling (IDD) from anywhere other

than France, dial the international code (generally 00) + 262 + the local six-digit number. From metropolitan France, dial 0262 + the local six-figure number. To call countries other than France from Réunion dial 00 + country code + town code and/or number. To call France from Réunion: Paris region: 01 + 8 digits, north-west: 02 + 8 digits, north-east: 03 + 8 digits, south-east: 04 + 8 digits, south-west: 05 + 8 digits.

To call Réunion from:
Britain: 00 262 + area code (less the 0) + 6 or 8-digit number
Switzerland: 00 262 + 8 figures
Belgium: 00 262 + 6-digit number
South Africa: 09 262 + 6-digit number
If you have any problems you can contact France Telecom in St Denis (tel 20 60 39, fax 99 00 04 0).

Mobile Phones

Réunion has a cellphone (mobile) network (SFR), and with partnership agreements between cellphone companies users from other countries can use their cellphones in Réunion if they are subscribers to any of the following:

Australia: Vodafone	**Italy:** Telecom Italia Mobile
Belgium: Mobistar	**Seychelles:** Cable and Wireless
Britain: Vodafone, Cellnet	**South Africa:** Vodacom, MTN
France: Itineris-SFR	**Spain:** Telefonica Movilles
Germany: Mannesmann	**Switzerland:** Swisscomm

Subscribers of the companies listed above should get more information from their providers before leaving. If they give you the green light, your cellphone should connect directly to the Réunion SFR network on calling. Otherwise, enter Réunion's network code number (64710) manually in the cellphone menu. If you have a problem, contact the SFR subscriber service at 062-29-7400 or 900 on your cellphone. Services available for cellphone users are:
Emergency calls: tel 112 (free).
Phone enquiries: tel 222 (for rates and information call SFR).
Subscriber services: tel 900 (local call rate).

Areas covered by local cellphone company SFR of special interest to visitors include Volcano, Mafate, Rivière des Remparts, and Cilaos.

MEDIA

Television
You can watch television beamed direct from Paris by satellite. The two national channels are Télé Réunion, broadcasting programmes from TF1, F3, Arte, and La5; and Tempo which broadcasts programmes from France 2. The private TV channels are: Antennae Réunion, Canal+, Canal Réunion, Canal Satellite, and Parabole Réunion.

Radio
There are 13 FM and 3 AM stations broadcasting to an estimated 200,000 radio owners on the island. Radio Free-Dom broadcasting on 97.4 MHz has the biggest audience after Radio Réunion/RFO on 88.9Mhz.

Newspapers and Magazines
There are several newspapers and magazines. Most French daily newspapers and magazines are for sale in Réunion. Three daily newspapers are published locally: *Le Quotdien* (tel 92 15 15), *Journal de l'Île* (tel 90 46 00), and *Témoignages* (tel

21 13 07). The four weekly magazines are *Visu* (tel 90 20 60), *Télé Mag* (tel 94 77 50), *Télé Zap*, and *Stars Top TV*. There are also a number of economic reviews and newspapers available, one of which is *L'Eco Austral* (tel 41 32 14), and a couple of bi-monthlies, such as *Leader Réunion* (tel 41 20 66).

MAPS

The *Carte Touristique* is a free colour map handed out by the Comité du Tourisme de la Réunion through its offices and agencies, and through such other handy collection points as car hire companies and hotels. It has a scale of 1:180, 628 (about 1.8 km to the centimetre, or roughly 2.8 miles to the inch) and is good enough to orient yourself or drive around the island. For more detail you can get an IGN (Institut Géographique National) La Réunion tourist map with a scale of 1:100,000 (1 km to the centimetre, or about half a mile to the inch) from any good bookstore on the island for FF65.90. The IGN 1:25,000 series covers the entire island in six maps, from 4401 RT to 4406 RT. These also cost FF65.90 and at a scale of 1cm to 250m (just under half a mile to the inch) these are the best for walkers. You'll definitely need the IGN Piton de la Fournaise sheet (4406 RT) if you plan to hike inside or outside this amazing volcano. You can also buy Trotet town plans for FF26 each, but as all the municipal and town tourist offices hand their own out free there's really no need to spend money on these.

GUIDES

Albert Trotet also produces a *Tourist Guide to Réunion Island* in English, although we could never find a copy. His French edition is readily available. One of the first things you should do on arrival is ask around for a copy of *RUN*. This is the free guide published by the Comité du Tourism de la Réunion, and is an exceptionally informative and professional production. They also produce a *Practical Guide* and a series of illustrated booklets on various aspects of island life culture, sports and hotels. They are all free and available in English. Réunion's tourist authorities are undoubtedly the most efficient of all the main tourist destinations in the Indian Ocean. If your French is up to it an excellent little compilation is the Petit Futé *La Réunion* guide, which also has a small section on French sister island Mayotte. This costs FF84.20 (£8/US$12). Not really a tourist aid but an invaluable reference for businessmen and anyone keen to know more about the nuts and bolts of Réunion is *La Réunion Annuaire International*, which costs FF170 (£16/US$25).

BY AIR

If you are, foolishly, making only a quick trip to Réunion as an extension of a beach holiday in Mauritius you'll want to see as much as possible in the time you have available. One way is to hire a car and whizz right round the island on the coastal road, but this way you'll miss Réunion's crowning glory, its cirques and mountains; the other option which gives the best views of the island is to fly.

Helicopters

For a bird's-eye view a helicopter flight is unbeatable. Most local travel agencies can organise this or you can make direct reservations with the helicopter companies. You can book for a *circuit complet*, which takes about 45 minutes and leaves early in the morning. On this trip you fly over the three cirques, go down the Trou de Fer, surrounded by waterfalls, fly over the vertiginous gorges of Maïdo, Rivière des Remparts, Grand Bassin, the moonscape craters of the Plaine des

Sables, and back to St Gilles over the beautiful beaches. The pilot gives you a running commentary during the flight through individual earphones. You can even have a Creole *cari* lunch inside the Mafate cirque. The complete tour of the island costs about FF1,300 (£125/US$190). These are also shorter flights, taking in two and three of the cirques. These cost about FF850-1,100, depending on the time you spend in the air. The helicopter flight with the Creole lunch option costs about FF700 (£67/US$102).

Helicopter Services and Charters:
Heli Réunion: Roland Garros Airport, St Denis (tel 93 11 11, fax 29 51 70); and St Gilles heliport (tel 24 00 00). Bookings Monday-Friday 7am to 8pm, Saturday 7am to 6pm, Sunday 7am to noon. Flights only in the morning.
Helilagon: (departure from Eperon and the airport) Altiport de l'Eperon, St Gilles les Hauts (tel 55 55 55, fax 22 86 78). Bookings Monday-Sunday 6.30am to 8pm. Flights only in the morning.
Héli-Blue: Helistation de l'Hermitage RN 1, 85 Chemin Bruniquel, Saint Gilles les Bains (tel 24 64 00, fax 24 16 13).

Light Aircraft
There are also sightseeing flights in light aircraft over Réunion. Air Evasion, based at Pierrefonds airport, between St Louis and St Pierre, has a specially designed plane for such excursions. The entire cabin is made of glass and the wings are partly see-through. The pilot gives you a running individual commentary through headphones as you fly. Air Evasion says that one advantage of their plane over similar helicopter excursions is that it can cruise at much lower speeds (56-62 mph/90-100 kmh) to give passengers more time to appreciate the views. Prices range from about FF900 (£86/US$130) for a 60-minute flight over the three cirques and the volcano, to about FF300 for a 20-minute flip along the coast. Cost is about FF700 for 40 minutes over the three cirques.
Air Evasion: 35, Chemin des Pêcheurs, Aérodrome de Pierrefonds, St Pierre (tel 25 19 72, fax 25 93 34).

For inter-island trips and flights further afield regional airline *Air Austral* flies from Réunion to the following destinations: Kenya (weekly); Madagascar: Antananarivo (4 flights a week), Majunga (2 flights a week), Tamatave (weekly), Nosy Bé (weekly); Mauritius (2-3 daily flights); Mayotte (daily); Comoros: Moroni (3 flights a week); Seychelles (2 flights a week); South Africa (2 flights a week); Zimbabwe (weekly).
Air Austral: 4 rue de Nice, 97400 St Denis (tel 90 90 90, fax 90 90 91); Roland Garros Airport (tel 48 80 20, fax 48 18 79).

BY SEA
The Blue Line Shipping Agency's *L'Ahinora* catamaran, which links Réunion to Mauritius by sea, also has mini-cruises on Sunday afternoons: Le Port Est/St Gilles/St Denis/Port Est. The cruise costs FF130 (£12/US$18) for adults and children under 12 pay FF65. Contact Blue Line at 67 rue de St Paul, Le Port (tel 55 23 25, fax 55 23 26). For yacht rental and cruises, try Planch'Alizé at Saline les Bains, fees on request (tel 24 62 61).

BY ROAD

Buses
The bus service is adequate for getting about in the towns and along the coastal roads. Only the yellow buses (*Cars Jaunes*) go right round the island.

This is the bus network serving all Réunion towns:

St Denis/St Pierre (Express) Line A: Operating from 4.30am (first departure from St Pierre) to 5.45pm (last departure from St Denis). Trip takes 1 hour 35 minutes.

St Denis/St Louis (Coast road) Line B: Operating from 4.50am (first departure from St Louis) to 7.10pm (last departure from St Denis). Trip takes 1 hour 35 minutes.

St Denis/St Pierre (High road) Line C: Operating from 4.15am (first departure from St Pierre) to 6.45pm (last departure from St Denis). Trip takes 2 hours 20 minutes.

Chaloupe St Leu/St Denis Line D: Operating from 5am (first departure from Chaloupe St Leu) to 6pm (last departure from St Denis). Trip takes 2 hours.

Chaloupe St Leu/St Pierre Line E: Operating from 5.15am (first departure from Chaloupe St Leu) to 4.50pm (last departure from St Pierre). Trip takes 1 hour 50 minutes.

St Denis/St Benoit (Express) Line F: Operating from 5.30am (first departure from St Benoit) to 5.35pm (last departure from St Denis). Trip takes 1 hour.

St Benoit/St Denis Line G: Operating from 5am (first departure from St Denis) to 7pm (last departure from St Benoit). Trip takes 1¹/₂ hours.

St Benoit/St Pierre via les Plaines Line H: Operating from 6.35am (first departure from St Benoit and St Pierre) to 5.35pm (last departure from St Benoit). Trip takes 2¹/₂ hours.

St Benoit/St Pierre via St Philippe Line I: Operating from 6.35am (first departure from St Benoit) to 5.30pm (last departure from St Pierre). Trip takes 2¹/₂ hours.

St Andre/Salazie Line J: Operating from 5.30am (first departure from Salazie) to 5.45pm (last departure from St Andre). Trip takes 30 minutes.

Cilaos/St Pierre Line K: Operating from 5am (first departure from Cilaos) to 5.15pm (last departure from St Pierre). Trip takes 1 hour 40 minutes.

St Pierre/Entre-Deux Line L: Operating from 5.55am (first departure from Entre-Deux) to 6pm (last departure from St Pierre). Trip takes 30 minutes.

For further information about buses, contact:

St Andre: tel 46 80 00; St Joseph: tel 56 03 90;
St Benoit: tel 50 10 69; St Paul: tel 22 54 38;
St Denis: tel 41 51 10; St Pierre: tel 35 67 28;
Client service: tel 94 89 49.

Taxis

There are 24-hour taxi ranks in the city centre, or you can telephone for one: Roland Garros Airport taxi (GIE): tel 48 83 83. Taxis Express: tel 41 78 90. Taxis GTD: tel 21 31 10. Taxis Paille-en-Queue: tel 29 20 29. Taxi Plus: tel 28 37 74. Place du Jardin de l'Etat taxi rank: tel 41 43 31. Super U supermarket (rue Maréchal Leclerc) taxi rank: tel 41 43 32.

St Paul:

Taxis St Paulois: tel 24 08 83. Taxis de St Paul (rue du Commerce rank): tel 45 58 28. Taxis la Buse: tel 45 64 34. Service Taxis du Lagon: tel 24 04 73.

St Leu

Taxi rank (avenue de Châteauvieux): tel 34 83 85.

St Pierre

Taxis St Pierrois: tel 38 54 84.

Le Tampon
Taxi rank (Rue du Père Rognard): tel 27 11 69.

St Suzanne
Taxis Niagara: tel 52 14 70. Taxi rank: Place de l'Eglise.

St Andre
Taxis Léopard: tel 46 00 28. Taxi rank: bus terminal.

St Benoit
Taxis des Marsouins: tel 50 55 28. Calling booth (place Edmond Albius): tel 50 15 70.

Taxi Fares GTD Taxis (tel 21 31 10, fax 94 39 67) list the following fares outside their rank in St Denis. All are from the city centre. To the airport FF90, St Gilles FF300, St Pierre FF700, Volcano FF800, and Salazie FF400. A tour of the island along the coast will cost FF800 by taxi; a half-day excursion is FF600, Piton Maïdo is FF600, and a full day excursion costs FF800.

BY RAIL
Réunion used to be the only French overseas département with a railway, but this gave way in 1976 to better roads and the advance of road transport. The 135-mile (217 km) line of rail was built in 1882 to link a number of towns with the artificially constructed port at Pointe des Galets and was a remarkable engineering feat, at one point tunnelling through a mountain for 6¹/2 miles (11 km), at that time the third largest tunnel in the world. Today, train buffs have resuscitated rail travel in a small way and, if you can make up or join a party of 10-20 people, you can take an excursion on a steam train with *Ti-Train* (tel 44 73 84/45 60 87).

DRIVING

LICENCES
A French *permis de conduire* or an international driver's licence is necessary to hire and drive a vehicle in Réunion. As in France, you drive on the right and follow the same highway code.

ROADS
On the whole the roads are good. However, traffic is on the increase – there are 235,000 licensed vehicles – and residents tend to drive fast. Avoid driving during the rush hour. Traffic is heavy around 8am and again at 4pm, from Monday to Friday, particularly between St Denis and St Andre to the east, and between St Denis and Le Port on the west coast road to St Pierre. Take your time when only one out of the four (two each way) lanes on the coastal road is open, due to bad weather or repairs. Parking is generally difficult to find in the capital, and in some of the larger towns, such as St Gilles and St Pierre.

There are about 311 miles (500 km) of *routes nationales* (main roads), and nearly 1,243 miles (2,000 km) of *routes départementales* (smaller secondary roads) all surfaced and in good condition. The circular 149-mile (240 km) main road going round the island is the N1 from St Denis to St Pierre, then it becomes the N2 along the south and east coast back to the capital. Allow a full day to do this drive. It doesn't take that long to cover the distance, but you'll want to stop a lot along the way to visit points of interest.

To plan a day's outing check the following **distances** and average **drive times**:
From St Denis to:
West coast beaches: 25-50 miles (40-80 km), 30-35 minutes.
Hell-Bourg: 34 miles (55 km), 1 hour 10 minutes.
The Piton de la Fournaise volcano: 93 miles (150 km), 2¹/₂ hours.
Cilaos: 70 miles (113 km), 2 hours.
Roland Garros airport: 8 miles (12 km), 10 minutes.

From St Gilles to:
Hell-Bourg: 62 miles (100 km), 1¹/₂ hours-2 hours.
Piton de la Fournaise volcano: 62 miles (100 km), two hours.
Cilaos: 47 miles (75 km), 1¹/₂ hours.
Roland Garros airport: 32 miles (51 km), 30 minutes.

From St Pierre to:
Hell-Bourg: 60 miles (96 km) via les Plaines, 2 hours.
West coast beaches: 25-34 miles (40-54 km), 30 to 45 minutes.
Piton de la Fournaise volcano: 44 miles (70 km), one hour.
Cilaos: 29 miles (46 km), 1¹/₂ hours.
Roland Garros airport: 57 miles (91 km), 1 hour 15 minutes.

From Cilaos to:
Hell-Bourg: 84 miles (135 km), 3 hours.
West coast beaches: 41-47 miles (66-75 km), 1¹/₂ hours.
Piton de la Fournaise volcano: 33 miles (102 km), 2 hours 15 minutes.
Roland Garros airport: 79 miles (127 km), 2 hours 15 minutes.

From St Philippe to:
Hell-Bourg: 81 miles (130 km), 2 hours.
West coast beaches: 25-56 miles (40-90 km), 1¹/₂ hours.
Piton de la Fournaise volcano: 63 miles (101 km), 2 hours to 2¹/₂ hours.
Cilaos: 53 miles (86 km), 2 hours 15 minutes.
Roland Garros airport: 56 miles (90 km), 2 hours.

FUEL
Petrol suppliers are Elf, Shell, Esso, Caltex, and Total. Prices are the same at all
petrol stations and similar to those in metropolitan France. Unleaded (*sans plomb*)
Super costs FF6.90 (60p/US$1) a litre, and diesel about FF4.70 a litre.

CAR HIRE
If you don't want to drive yourself there are plenty of transport and excursion
companies to choose from, including:
Adret: 137 Route du Volcan, Plaine des Cafres (tel 59 00 85).
Etti Nicolas Augustin: 61 Chemin Neuf, Boise de Nefles, St Paul (tel 44 39 65).
Indian Ocean Excursions: Les Terrasses de Boucan, rue du Grand Hotel, St Gilles
    les Bains (tel 24 28 10, fax 24 33 27).
Kreolie 4x4: 63 Grand Fond Intérieur, Entre-Deux (tel/fax 39 50 87), daily tours
    from 8am-8pm.
Marionnette Tours: 10 rue E Delauney, Bois de Nefles, St Paul (tel 44 18 21, fax
    44 31 13).
Mooland Trans-Evasion: ZI Bel-Air, St Louis (tel 91 39 39, fax 91 39 38),
    excursions around the island daily from 7am to 7.30pm, Sunday 7am to noon.
Moutoussamy: 49 Route de Domenjod, St Clotilde (tel 53 54 65).

Réunion Nature Sauvage: 1 Venelle d'Archery, St Leu (tel 34 89 46, fax 33 07 81).
Sud Bat' Kare: 60 rue Alverdy, Le Tampon (tel/fax 59 92 92).
Voyage Fabrice Zaneguy: 89 rue Medard, Grand Montee, St Marie (tel 53 65 65, fax 53 74 25).

SELF-DRIVE CAR HIRE

There are more than 100 car hire companies and agencies to choose from, with nearly a dozen at Roland Garros Airport alone. Cars are hired either on a daily basis plus mileage, or with unlimited mileage and average FF250-350 (£23-34/US$35-50) per day or FF1,600-2,500 (£152-238/US$228-357) by the week. Some companies have special discount packages – weekend, demonstration cars – and on the whole, rental charges are lower than in metropolitan France (VAT is 9.5%). Our advice is to hire a small car (roads in the interior can be extremely narrow) and insist on air-conditioning. It's well worth the extra. Remember to ask what fuel you should use. The main international and local car rental companies are members of the French National Car Syndicate (CNPA) and can be identified by their logo. They provide reliable vehicles and standard rental contracts.

CNPA car hire companies include:

AMC: 81 rue Léopold Rambaud, St Clotilde (tel 28 86 87, fax 28 70 37); Le Tampon (tel 57 57 74, fax 27 21 22); St Gilles les Bains (tel 24 51 0, fax 24 09 33).

Au Bas Prix: 35 rue Suffren, St Paul (tel 22 69 89, fax 22 54 27); Airport tel 48 81 89.

Budget: 2 rue Pierre Aubert, ZI du Chaudron, St Clotilde (tel 28 92 00, fax 28 93 00, e-mail: budget.reunion@wanadoo.fr); Airport (tel 28 01 95, fax 48 81 86); St Gilles les Bains (tel 24 50 52, fax 24 07 26); St Pierre (tel 25 45 40, fax 35 14 96); Le Port (tel 42 06 49, fax 43 04 58).

Erl: 128 rue Général de Gaulle, St Gilles les Bains (tel 24 02 25, fax 24 06 02); Airport tel 48 81 88.

Europcar Réunion: hires out cars and 4x4s. Cars are three to five doors, almost all are air-conditioned. Unlimited mileage, full insurance, state tax 9.5%. Minimum rental is 24 hours. Vehicles are supplied with a full tank of fuel and you must return it like that. A charge is made for delivery to your hotel. Central reservations (tel 93 14 15, fax 93 14 14); airport (tel 28 27 58, fax 28 36 36); St Clotilde (tel 28 83 37, fax 93 14 14); St Gilles (tel 24 51 15, fax 93 14 14).

Hertz Locamac: 82 rue de la Republique, St Denis (tel 53 22 50, fax 53 26 34 Website www.hertz.com); Reservations (tel 21 06 14 and 21 22 52, fax 21 07 87); Airport (tel 28 05 93; fax 41 39 42).

ITC Tropicar: 207 Avenue Général de Gaulle, St Gilles les Bains (tel 24 01 01, fax 24 05 550).

National-Citer: rents out small cars, vans, and 4x4s from outlets around the island. Airport (tel 48 83 77, fax 48 83 99); St Denis (tel 48 87 87, fax 48 87 99); Le Port (tel 42 92 92, fax 42 92 99); and St Pierre (tel 35 75 75, fax 35 75 99); Salazie (tel 47 71 19); St Louis (tel 26 25 80, fax 26 18 83); Le Tampon (tel 57 62 51, fax 57 61 54); St Paul (tel 45 53 00, fax 45 22 00); St Andre (tel 46 73 45), St Benoit (tel 50 11 70, fax 50 35 03); and St Joseph (tel 56 65 85, fax 56 37 92). Prices from FF290 (£28/US$42) per day for 1-3 days to FF140 a day for a one-month hire for a Citroën; and FF700 (£67/US$102) a day for 1-3 days for a 4x4, to FF390 a day for month's hire.

Pop's Car: Hotel Apolonia Paladien, St Leu (tel 34 72 10, fax 34 62 98); Airport tel 48 81 78.

SGM-Avis: 83 rue Jules Verne, ZI No 2, Le Port (tel 42 15 99, fax 43 95 13); Airport tel 48 81 82.

Sixt Euronet: 45 Avenue de Lattre de Tassigny, St Clotilde (tel 28 85 85, fax 28

86 00); Airport tel 29 79 79.

Transports Souprayenmestry (STS): 1 rue Auguste Rodin, Rivière des Galets, Le Port (tel 42 38 69, fax 42 40 09).

CAMPER VANS
Can be hired through:
Creoline: St Denis (tel 96 98 08).
Évasion Tropicale: 58 Chemin des Fougères, St Francois, St Denis (tel 30 03 21).
Imac Vacances: 10b Chemin des Fougères, St Francois, St Denis (tel 30 02 54).
Réunion Caravane: St Leu (tel 34 74 10).
Réunion Evasion: La Possession (tel 44 61 50).

MOTORCYCLE HIRE
If you fancy a cheaper mode of transport you can hire a motorbike (called a *moto*), moped or a bicycle, but make sure you do this during the drier months. To hire a 50-125cc scooter will cost you about FF90 (£9/US$14) a day and a 50-650cc motorbike from FF125 a day.
Locascoot: 4 rue du Général de Gaulle, St Gilles les Bains (tel 85 88 30, fax 33 98 99).
Max Moto: 10 Avenue G Monerville, St Denis (tel 21 15 25, fax 21 45 66); St Leu (tel 34 70 80, fax 34 86 77).
Moto 2000: 338 rue du Maréchal Leclerc, St Denis (tel 21 15 640).
Moto Rencontre: 84 rue Archambaud, St Pierre (tel 25 09 35).
Top Moto: 2 rue du Général de Gaulle, St Gilles les Bains (tel 24 24 22, fax 24 29 54).

BICYCLES AND MOUNTAIN BIKES
To hire a bike will cost you about FF110 (£10/US$16) for a full day and FF80 for half-day.
Matouta Bike Centre: 44 Route de Matouta, St Joseph (tel 37 20 27).
Parc du Maïdo: Maïdo 1500, Route du Maïdo, Petite France (tel 22 96 00).
Rando Bike: 100 Route du Volcan, Plaine des Cafres (tel 59 15 88).
Run Evasion: 23 rue de Père Boiteau, Cilaos (tel 31 83 57).
Vélos des Cimes: Chemin des Trois-Mares, Cilaos (tel 31 75 11).
VTT Découverte: Place Julius Benard, St Gilles les Bains (tel 24 55 56); 53 rue du Four-à-Chaux, St Pierre (tel 35 16 25); and 37 rue Juliette Dodu, St Denis (tel 41 35 35).
World Bike: Rue des Seychelles, St Gilles les Bains (tel 33 00 44).
More mountain bike hire centres are listed under *Mountain Biking* in *Sport and Recreation* on page 237.

HAZARDS AND HINTS
The surface of the coastal road round the island is superb; but in some towns along the way there are potholes. On the national road nobody seems to keep to the speed limit, as frequent dead animals testify. Watch out for deep culverts at the side of roads, particularly in the hill villages, they're like tank traps.

Seat belts must be worn at all times. Driver and passenger must both buckle up. Offending locals lose points on their licence, and if they lose seven points they must sit the licence test again. The fine for not wearing a seatbelt is FF130.

There are lots of walkers and cyclists on the roads, especially in residential areas. Unemployment and social benefits tend to combine to put inebriated pedestrians on the road at all hours of the day and night.

The drive up into the cirque of Salazie is spectacular, and nerve-wracking. The road is extremely narrow, with few places where vehicles can squeeze past each other, and there is a constant downpour on the road from the cliffs and cataracts above. It's probably the only place you'll ever see a cautionary road sign saying *Pisse en L'Aire* – which we don't think requires any translation.

 There are 55 hotels in Réunion situated in major towns and villages. They are classified according to metropolitan French standards and range in accommodation capacity from 10-200 rooms which, with other island accommodation, offer a total of nearly 5,000 beds. As well as hotels, there are other accommodation options, from a tent on a camp site, rural gîtes and B&B guest-houses, to pensions, chambres d'hôte, youth hostels, and family vacation villages (VVF Réunion).

HOTELS
Hotels are expensive, about 20% more than in Europe, but standards are high and service comes with a smile. They are without exception clean and comfortable.

The major hotel chains on the island are:

Accor, with three hotels. Accor Group Reservations (Resinter) London (tel 020-7724 1000); Paris (tel 6077-2727).

Anthurium Group, with 17 hotels, (10a Chemin des Fougères, St Denis; tel 30 19 29; fax 30 36 89; e-mail: anthurium@guetali.fr).

Apavou, with six hotels (Alizéa, 56 Avenue des Thermes, F-75017 Paris; tel 1-55 37 20 40; fax 1-55 37 20 41).

Best Western, with one hotel (2 rue Doret, St Denis Cedex; tel 21 80 20; fax 21 97 41).

Logis de France, with four hotels. The head office in Réunion is at *Hotel le Baril* (tel 37 01 04, fax 37 07 62).

Paladien (or Nouvelles Frontières Group), with one hotel (Boulevard Bonnier, St Leu; tel 34 62 62; fax 34 61 61).

Protea, with one hotel (Boulevard Hubert Delisle, St Pierre; tel 25 70 00; fax 35 01 41; e-mail: sterne@guetali.fr).

The *Hotellerie Creole* is an organisation of some 30 family hotels around the island. For information about them contact the Réunion Hotel Industry's Trade Union (UMIH), Centhor, 1 Route de l'Eperon, St Gilles les Hauts (tel 55 37 30, fax 55 37 29).

CHEAPER ACCOMMODATION
Réunion has 100 country lodges, 248 B&B places, with 48 also providing other meals, 15 inn farms, 15 mountain lodges, three family holiday villages, 110 furnished tourist flats, and three youth hostels.

Country Lodges
Rates range from FF1,000-3,000 (£96-288/US$145-435) per week (accommodation for 2-14 people). B&B rooms are about FF150 (£14/US$22), and tables d'hôte meals from FF80. Contact Reservation Loisirs Accueil Nature et Campagne, 10 Place du Barachois, St Denis (tel 90 78 90, fax 41 84 29). Open Monday to Thursday 9am to 5.30pm, Fridays until 4.30pm. On Saturday 9am to 4pm.

Farm Inns
For more information about these contact Relais Agriculture et Tourisme, 24 rue de la Source, St Denis Cedex (tel 21 25 88, fax 21 31 56).

Mountain Lodges
The 15 mountain lodges are located on extensive marked trails all around the island. For more information and bookings contact Maison de la Montagne, Loisirs Accueil Nature et Campagne, 10 Place du Barachois, St Denis (tel 90 78 78, fax 90 78 70, fax 41 84 29, e-mail: nature@oceanes.fr).

Family Holiday Villages
Bookings for all Villages Vacances Famille (VVF) can be made at St Gilles reservation centre (tel 24 29 29, fax 24 05 77). It is open Monday to Friday from 8am to 5pm. You can also contact the villages direct.

In Saint-Gilles:
VVF '*Le Lagon*', 129 self-catering studio flats with two twin beds, dining area and veranda. Tariff in low season from FF290-440 (£28-42/US$42-58), high season from FF360-500 (£35-48/US$52-73). There is an extra charge for half-board in any season. Adults FF130 per person per day (drinks not included); FF150 per person a day (wine and coffee included), children 2-11 pay FF85. 90 Avenue de Bourbon, St Gilles les Bains (tel 24 29 39, fax 24 41 02).

In La Saline:
VVF '*Le Macabit*', 12 rooms with 4, 6 and 7 beds for group accommodation. From FF285-460 per room on a one week basis, 8 rue des Argonautes, St Gilles les Bains (tel 24 60 10, fax 24 66 33).

In Cilaos:
VVF '*Fleurs Jaunes*', 10 rooms with two beds, 10 rooms with 4 beds, and 10 flats with 6 beds, 4 *pavillons* (small detached houses) with 14 beds each and 4 with 20 beds each. Half-board rates for a room for two people on a one-week basis. Rates from FF215-400, rue Fleurs Jaunes, Cilaos (tel 31 71 39, fax 31 80 85).

Tourist Furnished Flats
These are all graded from 1 to 4 stars and cost an average of FF1,500-2,000 (£142-192/US$218-290)a week for two people. Information can be obtained from the Réunion Federation of Tourist Offices and Tourist Information Centres (FROTSI), Résidence St Anne, 18 rue St Anne, St Denis (tel 21 73 76, fax 21 84 47, e-mail: frotsi@wanadoo.fr). Ask them for a copy of *Le Guide des Meublés de Tourism,* which lists all the officially approved flats, villas and studios with full details and a colour photograph of each entry.

Youth Hostels
There are three youth hostels, all in the highlands, at Hell-Bourg (tel 47 82 65); Bernica (tel 22 89 75); and Entre-Deux (tel 39 59 20). The Réunion Federation is affiliated to the French Youth Hostels League (LFAJ). You have to be a member to use a hostel but membership cards can be bought at all youth hostels or at the Réunion Federation of Youth Hostels, 42, rue du Général de Gaulle, St Denis (tel 41 15 34, fax 41 72 17). Daily rates are reduced according to length of stay and number of persons:1-4 people: half-board from FF135 (£13/US$20), full-board from FF180 (£17/US$26); 5-15 people: half-board from FF130, full-board from FF175; 16-29 people: half-board FF125, full-board from FF170.

Camping
The number of municipal camping sites has dwindled steadily over the years and there are now only a couple left, at Etang-Salé, rue Octave Bénard (tel 91 75 86),

and at Hermitage les Bains (tel 24 42 35). If you want to camp in the countryside you must get the permission of the farmer or landowner. For information about farm camp sites contact the Chambre d'Agriculture in St Denis (tel 21 25 88, fax 21 31 56).

Other Types of Accommodation

Some of these might be unfamiliar to English-speaking holiday-makers.

Mountain Gîtes. These are mountain cabins or lodges on hiking trails. There are 15 of them around the three cirques. You can't stay for more than two nights.

Rural Gîtes. These are furnished private houses or lodges that can be rented for self-catering holidays. Price for 2-14 people is FF1,000-3,000 (£96-290/US$145-435) a week.

Chambres d'Hote. These are furnished and equipped B&B establishments run by island families. Rates are FF150 (£14/US$22) and up for a single or double, including breakfast.

Chambre d'Hote de Prestige. This is a prestige B&B. Rooms are decorated with genuine antique Creole-style furniture. Breakfast highlights local specialities and is included in the room rate.

Le Chalet Loisirs is a chalet resort comprising 3-25 chalets in a rural area, with accommodation for 4-6 people. Facilities include a living room, kitchen area, bedrooms, and bathroom. This option includes accommodation and leisure activities.

Pensions de Famille. This is a type of boarding house and is a good budget option, although the standard can vary from excellent to poor.

Gîtes d'Etape et de Séjour offer stop-over and holiday accommodation for groups and hikers. Equipment and facilities are more basic than in rural gîtes. They cost about FF60-160 a night per person. Breakfast is not always included.

Eating and Drinking

CUISINE

As with its island neighbours, Réunion's cuisine is as mixed and varied as its population. All the ethnic communities have contributed to the mélange, but the cuisine of France still reigns supreme in most upmarket hotels and restaurants. Available everywhere is the ubiquitous Indian Ocean dish called *cari*, prepared with meat, poultry, fish or seafood and seasoned with varying combinations of garlic, onion, tomatoes, turmeric, cloves, ginger and chillies. There are a hundred different ways to make cari in Réunion and you'll find that a chicken cari with corn cooked on a wood fire in the mountains is quite different from the same cari served at the coast; only the rice is a constant. Traditional Indian cuisine offers hot, highly flavoured *massalés*, served on and eaten directly from a banana leaf. Muslim cuisine, even though from the same sub-continent, is quite different and relies more on the exotic flavours of cinnamon, cloves, and nutmeg. Try *briani*, a saffron rice mixed with meat and vegetables and a triumph of Muslim cooking. The Chinese arrived in the island towards the end of the 19th century, and brought with them their woks and culinary expertise. As most of them were from Canton, a region renowned for its cooking, this is the cuisine you will usually find in the island's Chinese restaurants. If you still hanker for steak and chips, a hamburger, some fried chicken, a pizza or some spaghetti bolognaise you'll also find these.

If you are really serious about food Réunion's Flavours and Fragrances Group, affiliated to the Guild of French Provinces Restaurateurs, guarantees quality. Group members own the following top restaurants: Les Geraniums (Plaine des Cafres), Le

Manapany (Manapany les Bains), Hotel des Thermes (Cilaos), St Alexis (St Gilles les Bains), Relais des Cîmes (Hell-Bourg), Le Mangoustan (Plaine St Paul), Stella (St Leu), Retro (St Pierre), Saladiere (St Denis), Hotel des Plaines (Plaine des Palmistes), and Bouvet (St Benoit).

In rural areas you might come across *cari tangue* which you'll be told is *hérisson* (hedgehog), but is really a member of the rat family, and even wasp larvae, fried to a crisp or mixed in a spicy sauce. Spicy concoctions of chicken or goat are the commonest caris on offer, although there seems to be very little that cannot be turned into a savoury cari. A speciality cari is octopus (*zourite*), which is delicious. Brèdes, a green vegetable somewhat like spinach and which can be the leaves of any number of plants, is often served with Creole dishes, and so is chou-chou, the spiky light green hand-grenade that is the local staple vegetable. This is known in Europe as custard marrow or chayote, and in the US as mirliton. Another common accompaniment is rougaille, made from tomatoes, garlic and chillies, which is a hot sauce similar to Mexican salsa. Rougaille is also served with a spicy sausage, beans and rice, with cups of steaming vanilla tea and slices of sweet potato cake to follow. Regional specialities include the famous lentils and sweet wines of Cilaos, one made from litchis; the trout of Hell-Bourg; *bichique*, tiny young fish used in coastal cari (they cost up to FF300 (£29/US$43) a kilo); *baba figue* a cari of banana flowers; and *zambrocal*, a spicy Creole dish that combines elements of all the island's ethnic groups – rice cooked with beans and *boucané*, smoked pork, believed locally to be the origin of the word buccaneer.

As eating well and cheaply is as difficult in Réunion as it is anywhere else these days you should always first look at the menu and prices, usually displayed at the door or in the window. You can keep costs down by ordering the *plat du jour*, which is usually enough to share between two people because of the amount of bread and rice you get. If you are budget-conscious buy bread, cold meats, cheese, pâté, yoghurt, fresh fruit, and wine or beer in supermarkets such as *Score* and *Champion*. You can cook at youth hostels, vacation villages, gîtes de montagne and camp sites, so this can reduce the cost of your holiday. Creole food is often cheaper in restaurants than haute cuisine dishes, principally because it is bulked up with masses of rice and/or beans.

Vegetarians should note that, amazingly for a tropical island, fruit and veg is expensive. Bananas cost FF20/kg (£2/US$3) and a coconut will be weighed and sold to you for FF20/kg.

Fast-Food

Eating on the run is a cheap way to survive, if your stomach can take it. Street snack bars and caravan eateries seem to be everywhere, particularly in the coastal towns. You can get a filling ham or cheese baguette sandwich for FF8-10, a hamburger for FF15, and chicken and chips for FF18. A cup of coffee costs FF4, Coca-Cola and other soft drinks FF5-8. At lunchtime you'll see most office workers buying a box of take-away cari. It comes with plenty of rice and costs about FF25 (£2.40/US$3.60).

DRINKING

Bottled water, still and carbonated, is available everywhere in restaurants, bars, snack-bars, supermarkets, stores and costs around FF8 in a small corner shop for 1.5 litres. Bagatelle is the cheapest water and costs only FF3.50 in a large supermarket such as *Score*, compared to FF4.50 for Edena. Coca-Cola is FF7.25 a litre and the infinitely preferable Orangina is FF7.27 a litre or FF10.90 for 1.5 litres.

Beer and Wine

Drinking in hotels and bars is expensive, usually at least double the retail price, and the best thing to do if you are counting your cash is to buy your alcohol and soft drinks from a retail outlet, preferably a large supermarket such as *Score, Champion,* or *March-U*. The most popular local beers are *Bourbon* (known locally as Dodo), made by Brasseries de Bourbon in St Denis, and *Fischer*, made by Brassée la Réunion in St Louis. A 330ml bottle of 5% Bourbon costs FF3.96 (38p/57 cents) a bottle if you buy it in a pack of 12 at the supermarket, and a 330ml bottle of 5.5% Fischer a few centimes more. If you buy a beer in a corner café or snack bar to drink on the premises you can get a wonderfully chilled 250ml glass of *pression* (draught) Bourbon for about FF7.

You can buy a good bottle of French champagne for about FF150 (£14/US$22) a 750ml bottle, white table wine for FF14 a bottle, and FF25 for a fair bottle of red. Spirits are generally cheaper than in Europe; a decent Scotch costs FF90-120 a bottle.

Rum

A bottle of common or garden island rum costs about FF40 ($£4/US$6). A well-known brand of local rum is *Rhum Blanc Charrette*, a charrette being the cart the cut sugarcane used to be hauled around in. You can drink it in punch, in cocktails, and in *rhum arrangé*. It's also used in Creole cuisine and in local cakes and confections. Another good white rum is *Rhum Isautier*, which also comes in a variety of fruit punches. One of Réunion's most popular liqueurs is *Paul et Virginie*, which comes in a variety of pleasant fruit flavours.

If you're ever invited into a local home in Réunion you'll probably notice large glass containers on the kitchen shelf, full of herbs, leaves and discoloured fruit steeping in a dark liquid. This is *rhum arrangé*, a traditional home-brew pick-me-up that goes back to the old days when a *canon*, a shot or tot of this, was considered a cure-all for just about any ailment. Today, the blending and maceration of the fruit are family secrets, like recipes for pickled onions in English homes, and every family prides itself on its own arrangement. The appeal lies in the taste and the exclusivity of each preparation. Choice of ingredients is of prime importance, as a badly balanced arrangement produces undrinkable firewater. This old curative is now a digestive, and in Creole etiquette a small glass is usually offered after a meal. If you're not lucky enough to be invited home by a family there's a restaurant owner in St Bernard, high above St Denis near La Montagne, who can show you close to 500 different blends. The oldest – 10-year-olds – are real nectar. **Le Saint Bernard** restaurant is at 146 Chemin Du Pére Raimbault, St Bernard (tel 23 62 90, fax 23 52 77).

DANCE AND MUSIC

The most popular music on Réunion is a curious blend of traditional *sega* and *maloya* with a heavy reggae influence, the sort of mix that in neighbouring Mauritius is known as *seggae*. When it is further mixed with *maloya* on Réunion it becomes *malogue*. *Sega* is itself a cocktail of 19th century European quadrilles and polkas and the primitive rhythms that came with the early Madagascan and African slaves. *Maloya*, is Réunion's other traditional dance, the result of a long evolution of African music, mixed with slave songs, in much the way that the blues of American negro plantation workers developed. The music played in night-clubs is largely a mix of all these styles. The island's best known music groups are Ousa Nousava, Granmoun Lélé, Baster, Ti Fock, Ziskakan, Zong, and Tropicadéro.

AFTER DARK

For its size, Réunion has an intense cultural life. Barely a week goes by without a show being staged at one of the island's cultural centres, and quite a number of internationally renowned artists perform in Réunion. Local theatre, dance, music and humorous production companies are highly creative. There are three theatres in St Denis, one in St Gilles and one in Le Tampon (see *Exploring Reunion*). Theatre and concert prices are usually FF60-100 (£6-9/US$9-15). Cinemas cost about FF15, although at some you get two films for the price of one. To find out what's on check *Saison*, a free booklet put out by the Office Départmental de la Culture in St Denis, which details theatre, cinema, music, dance and other events for months ahead at the Théâtre de Champ Fleuri and the Théâtre de St Gilles. St Denis also has the most cinemas, fashionable bars, night-clubs and discothèques.

GAMBLING

There are three casinos on the island. The Casino de St Denis is at Place du Barachois (tel 41 33 33 0); at St Gilles is the Casino de St Gilles, Les Filaos (tel 24 47 00); and in St Pierre there's the Casino de St Pierre, 47 Boulevard Hubert Delisle, Front de Mer (tel 25 26 96).

For more information on night-life on the island see *Exploring Réunion*.

FLORA AND FAUNA

FLORA

Tropical vegetation is lush all over the island, with the exception of the scorched areas around the volcano in the south-east. Adding to the natural flora 18th and 19th century botanists introduced exotic plants and flowers from other tropical islands all over the world – from the bougainvillaea of Tahiti to the cabbage-tree palm of Brazil. Zealous French botanist Pierre Poivre often had more success here with his spices and food plants than on neighbouring Ile de France (Mauritius), due to Réunion's greater variety of micro-climates. Réunion is a fascinating place for botanists, gardeners and all lovers of the outdoors. It is like a vast garden, with a bewildering variety of trees and flowers. The forest of Bébour, near the Plaine des Palmistes, with its countless towering tree ferns and carpets of wild flowers, looks like something out of a child's fairy story. In spring both the Plaine des Palmistes and the adjoining Plaine des Cafres are a blaze of wild flowers, yellow épinard, white aubépine, bright yellow mimosa and fields full of geraniums. Among the many flowers and trees brightening the island landscape are gladioli, dahlias, vanilla orchids, geraniums, nasturtiums (used by Creoles to make fritters), digitalis, bamboo, tamarind, flamboyants – trees whose beautiful red blossoms cascade from the branches around Christmas – bougainvillaeas, mimosa, daisies, marguerites and fuschias in the winter. There are also common tropical fruits such as bananas, coconuts, papaya, guavas, mangoes, litchis, and pineapples. As these appear at different times of the year you can eat delicious tropical fruit all year round.

Vanilla. This is the seed pod of the climbing orchid *Vanilla planifolia*. As early as the 14th century the Aztecs of Mexico were using it to flavour their favourite drink of *chocólatl*. In the 16th century, vanilla was introduced into Spain and France. Vanilla lianas arrived in Réunion in September 1822, but it was not until 1841 when a young slave in St Suzanne, Edmond Albius, discovered how to pollinate vanilla artificially that the plantations flourished and brought wealth and prosperity to many.

FAUNA

In 1649, Etienne de Flacour of the French East India Company penned this lyrical description of the scene around the site of the first settlement: 'The banks are covered with beautiful trees of all kinds, latanias, palm trees and others. They teem with pigs, with very large water and land tortoises, lots of wood pigeons and doves, the most beautiful parrots on earth and all kinds of other birds. The first inhabitants on Bourbon Island could not have found a better place for their settlement, paradise-like surrounding, an open-air pantry and plenty of clear-water springs.' Once the settlers found that tortoise flesh tasted just like beef and that they had especially delicious enormous livers it was not long before the teeming tortoises began to disappear. The birds, however, were the true glory of the island, incredible in their variety and as tame as those on Mauritius. As the tortoises dwindled so did some of the larger and tastier species of the bird population. The *oiseaux bleus*, the blue birds of Bourbon, and the local relative of the Mauritius dodo were the first to become extinct. The island still has a number of its original endemic birds, as more original forest remains intact in Réunion than on any other island in the Indian Ocean (see *Bird-Watching* below).

There are no dangerous animals on the island; in fact, there are not many wild animals at all. The most common are hares, the odd introduced deer, tenrecs, a small hedgehog-like rodent which often finds its way into Creole cari, and chameleons, although there are not many of these useful reptiles islanders call *l'endormi*, ('the sleeper') around. There are trout in some of the higher rivers, originally introduced in 1940 from Madagascar. There are also lots of freshwater shrimps. In pools and ponds around St Paul and St Benoit there are eels which grow up to 44 lb (20 kg). These are small fry if travellers tales are to be believed. In the early 19th century Bory St Vincent wrote of seeing 20 ft (6 m) eels in island lakes and a hundred years after this innkeepers in the Salazie area were serving up steaks from local eels as thick as a man's thigh.

BIRD-WATCHING

You can spot common birds such as **moorhens, red cardinals, martins, quail, bulbuls, mynahs,** and *l'oiseau de la Vierge* (a bird with flowing red tail plumes, believed by Creoles to have seen the Virgin Mary), all over the island. The **Mascarene swiftlet** and **Mascarene paradise flycatcher** are found on Mauritius and Réunion. The former is easily seen on both islands, but Réunion is a better place to spot the flycatcher.

The Roche Ecrite area above St Denis is particularly rewarding if you are a twitcher in search of such Réunion specials as the rare *merle blanc*, or **cuckoo shrike,** the stonechat, the grey white-eye and the raptor *papangue*, or **Réunion harrier.** Roche Ecrite has a well-marked hiking trail. If you start out at first light you'll avoid the inevitable late morning and early afternoon rain and mist. Follow the trail for 2-3 mile (3-5 km) and you should see all the endemics of the perching group. You'll probably see the most elusive, the Réunion cuckoo shrike, in forest close to the trail at the 2 mile (3 km) mark.

Really ardent birders will want to spot both **Barau's** and **Mascarene black petrels.** For this you will have to hire a deep-sea craft for the afternoon and early evening from either St Gilles or St Pierre and cruise 6-12 miles (10-20 km) offshore. If you are lucky you'll see both species as the sun goes down. Barau's petrel might also be seen from the beach at St Pierre around sunset. You'll need birding binoculars to watch these birds offshore beyond the surf zone, or flying high overhead.

Easier to see is the protected *paille en queue*, the smallest and most graceful of the tropicbirds, which nests on cliff ledges. Réunion's fishermen are particularly fond of this white-tailed seabird as they can be fairly sure of finding *espadon* (swordfish) wherever they see it diving for fish in the right season. Other seabirds to look out for include wedge-tailed, **Audubon's** and **Mascarene shearwaters**; lesser noddy; and sooty, bridled and common terns. For more information contact the Société d'Etudes Ornithologiques de la Réunion, Musée d'Histoire Naturelle, rue Poivre, St Denis (tel 20 02 19, fax 21 33 93).

SPORT AND RECREATION

Réunion is an island of jagged mountains and deep valleys, green plains and lava moonscapes, tinkling streams and raging torrents, crystal lagoons and beaches washed by a tumbling ocean. When it comes to sport and recreation there's very little you can't do, from walking trails and climbing to yachting, deep-sea fishing, surfing, water-skiing, snorkelling and scuba-diving, windsurfing, sailing, hang-gliding and parasailing, horse-riding, golf, mountain biking, tennis, gliding, abseiling, and canyoning, to mention but a few activities.

RAMBLING AND HIKING

Réunion is a paradise for ramblers and hikers, with spectacular scenery, rugged terrain and numerous trails, and you don't need to be super-fit to make the most of it. The choice of routes is extensive and great for weekend ramblers as well as scramblers and high-peak climbers. The wildest, most strenuous hike is through the Mafate cirque. There are nearly 620 miles (1,000 km) of marked paths, including two major tough trails known as *Grande Randonnée*, as well as more than 50 different itineraries for walks. **Maison de la Montagne** is the name here for advice in choosing routes. They'll give you practical advice and recommend mountain guides where necessary. They also organise horse and pony treks, mountain-biking, 4x4 outings, hang-gliding and paragliding, canyoning, mountain climbs, and various other leisure activities.

Maison de la Montagne is also a booking office for *Gîtes de montagne* (rest huts or guest-houses), and can help you to plan guided or unguided hiking tours for one to 13 days, which means no worries about transport to and from the trails, accommodation, meals, for guided parties. For reservations and more information contact Maison de la Montagne, 10 Place Sarda Garriga, Barachois, St Denis (tel 90 78 78, fax 41 84 29); Maison de la Montagne de Cilaos, 2 rue MacAuliffe, Cilaos (tel 31 71 71, fax 31 80 54). Several Réunion Federation of Tourist Offices and Tourist Information Centres (FROTSI) and *Syndicats d'Initiative* (SI) offices are also part of the reservation network run by the Maison de la Montagne, including: l'Ouest (tel 24 57 47); St Philippe (tel 37 10 43); Bras Panon (tel 51 50 62); St Pierre (tel 25 02 36); Etang-Salé (tel 26 67 32); Salazie (tel 47 50 14); La Possession (tel 22 26 66); Hell-Bourg (tel 47 83 25). Reservations can be made up to eight months in advance by phone, fax or mail. Early reservations are recommended for the April-December period. Full payment must be made 15 days prior to arrival to avoid cancellation. Limited numbers of late reservations are occasionally accepted due to last-minute cancellations.

Information centres for mountain hiking trails (*Cimes Réunion*) are located in St Denis, near the airport, and in Cilaos in the heart of the mountain cirques. These centres provide topographic guides and maps, information about accommodation, the state of hiking trails, available itineraries, transport, hiking tours organised by state certified guides or escorts, and other mountain leisure activities, such as mountain biking, canyoning, abseiling, paragliding, and white-water rafting.

If you are doing your own organising, dinner and breakfast can be ordered from *gîtes* or hotels, and for picnics you can buy food at local village *boutiques* (grocery stores). You can pick up supplies en route from village grocery stores at La Nouvelle, Marla, Roche Plate, Grand Place les Hauts, Ilet à Bourse, Ilet à Malheur, and Aurère. Hiking in other areas you'll find grocery stores at Brûlé, Dos d'Ane, Grand Ilet, Hell-Bourg, Cilaos, Plaine des Palmistes, Bourg Murat, Entre-Deux, and Grand Coude. Isolated areas with no stores include Bélouve, Roche Ecrite, Piton des Neiges, Volcano, Rivière des Remparts, Basse-Vallée, Dimitile, Grand Bassin, Pavillon, and Ilet Haute. Village grocery stores are usually closed on Sunday afternoons and Monday mornings.

ACCOMMODATION FOR HIKERS

Gîtes de Montagne (Mountain Huts) offer dormitories with bunk beds. Mountain huts are the most widespread and often the only type of accommodation in the hiking areas. They are found in isolated and rugged locations. The only water supply at the Piton des Neiges hut comes from rainwater, with no shower facilities or hot water. The Roche Ecrite hut is located in an area with higher rainfall but during a prolonged dry spell water may be scarce. Showers and hot water depend on the season. The Volcano mountain hut relies on a local reservoir or on tanker/trucks for its water, cold showers are available, you pay for hot showers. Other mountain huts will all have hot showers, with power provided by solar heating. All the mountain huts have year-round caretakers. On arrival you get two sheets, two blankets, kitchen utensils and a gas cooker (ask the caretaker for the kitchen utensils). The caretakers will be happy to cook you Creole-style dinner and breakfast (reserve in advance). On average it costs about FF80 per person per night. Breakfast is an extra FF30, and dinner FF100. For meals, caretakers take reservations by phone at least two days in advance. Meals must be paid for on the spot.

Gîtes Nature (Rest Huts). These are found in remote locations but some, such as Roche Plate, Rivière des Remparts, Volcano and Basse Vallée mountain huts, are accessible by 4x4 or other vehicles. Access to vehicles is closed during popular visiting periods, usually from Friday noon to Monday at 7am.

Gîtes D'Etape (Guest-Houses). These are usually in villages and display the *Gîtes de France* logo. They offer better facilities and service than other *gîtes*, which are not inspected. Dinner and breakfast are prepared by the host (no self-cooking facilities are available).

Refuges (Shelters). These are in remote areas of cirques such as Mafate. They offer basic facilities and are looked after by their owners, who will prepare dinner and breakfast on request. No self-cooking facilities are available.

Chambres d'Hotes (B&Bs). These are rooms for one or two persons in private homes. Most of them display the *Gîtes de France* sign and provide adequate comfort. They offer dinner on request. No self-cooking facilities are available.

Camping. Camping is prohibited in state forests, although they may make an exception in Cilaos. Check with the Forestry Office there (tel 31 71 40). You can often camp in the cirques if you first get permission from the landowner.

Gîtes de Montagne

Basse-Vallée/M Benard: two huts with 28 beds (tel 37 00 75).
Bélouve/Mme Rosset: 39 beds (tel 41 21 23).
Piton des Neiges/M Dijoux and Morel: 39 beds (tel 51 15 26).
Roche Ecrite/M Bonald: 36 beds (tel 43 99 84).
Roche Plate (Rivière des Remparts)/M Begue: 31 beds (tel 59 13 94).
Volcan/M Picard: three huts with 57 beds (tel 21 28 96).
In Mafate:
Marla/M Hoareau: 21 beds (tel 43 78 31).

Grand Place Cayenne/M Thomas: 16 beds (tel 43 85 42).
Ilet à Bourse/M Thomas: 16 beds (tel 43 43 93).
La Nouvelle/M Begue Andre: 42 beds (tel 43 61 77).
Roche Plate/M Thiburce: 24 beds (tel 43 60 01).

Shelters

Aurère/Boyer Georget: tel 43 28 37.
Ilet Orangers/Yoland Louise: tel 43 50 90.
La Nouvelle/Begue Serge Paul: tel 43 99 48.
La Nouvelle/Begue Sylvain: tel 43 82 77.
La Nouvelle/Cuvelier Edouard: tel 43 99 51.
Marla/Giroday: tel 43 83 13.
Marla/Hoareau Expédit (Marla): tel 43 78 31.
Roche Plate/Thiburce: tel 43 60 01.

Organisations offering outdoor and hiking services include:
Altitudes Australes: Rés Ixora, 196 RN1, L'Hermitage les Bains (tel 33 84 93, mobile 0262-65 60 09, e-mail: onery@guetali.fr).
Anne le Garrec: 73 Allée des Roberts, St André (tel/fax 58 37 44, mobile 0262-85 93 06).
Austral Adventure: 11 rue des Myrtiles, St Gilles les Hauts (tel 55 69 55, fax 87 55 50, e-mail: austraven@oceanes.fr).
Francois Lauthier: 6a Chemin Anse les Bas, Petite Ile (tel 31 24 29).
Gie Maham: Place Artisanale, Hell-Bourg, Salazie (tel/fax 47 82 82, mobile 0262-86 50 67).
Jacaranda: 4a Résidence les Oreades, La Montagne (tel 23 82 58, fax 23 82 58).
La Réunion Sport-Natur-Kultur: specialises in German visitors, 60a rue Lucien Gasparin, St Denis (tel 26 60 65, fax 26 60 61).
Magma Rando: 41b Ligne Berthaud, St Gilles les Hauts Fleurimont (tel/fax 55 72 22, mobile 0262-85 94 92).
Olivier Thevenot: Appartement 2, Résidence Philibert, 5 Rue Philibert, St Denis (tel/fax 94 35 24, mobile 0262-85 83 04).
Rando Run: 2 Impasse des Acacias, Etang-Salé les Bains (tel/fax 26 31 31).
Réunion Sensations: Place Paul Julius Bénard, Galerie Amandine Bât 1, No 2a, St Gilles les Bains (tel 24 57 00, fax 24 56 57); and 28 rue de Pére Boiteau, Cilaos (tel 31 84 84, fax 31 84 85).

HORSE TREKKING

Horse and pony trekking is another way to explore the island, and you don't need to be experienced to ride the gentle Mérens horses, which come from the French Pyrenees. The Plaine des Cafres and Volcano region is the place for this sort of trekking.

There are horse trekking centres at:
Alti Merens: 49 Route de Notre Dame de la Paix, La Petite Ferme, Plaine des Cafres (tel 59 18 14, mobile 0262-68 59 04).
Centre Equestre de L'Etalon Blanc: 263 Chemin Rural du Maniron, Le Maniron, Etange-Salé (tel 26 55 65).
Centre Equestre du Maïdo: 350 Route du Maïdo, Le Guillaume St Paul (tel 32 49 15, fax 32 43 10).
Centre Equestre de Pont Neuf: 59b, CD11, Les Avirons (tel/fax 38 09 40).
Eldorado la Diligence: Bourg-Murat, Plaine des Cafres (tel 59 06 71).
Ferme Équestre du Grand Etang: RN3 Pont Payet, St Benoit (tel/fax 50 90 03, mobile 0262-86 88 25).

Poney Vert: St Gilles les Hauts (tel 22 80 67).
Ranch Kikouyou: Grand Fond, Entre-Deux (tel 39 60 62).

HORSE-RIDING CENTRES:
Centre D'Équitation du Colorado: Chemin Couilloux, St Bernard, La Montagne, St Denis (tel 23 62 51).
Club Hippique de L'Hermitage: Zac Hermitage, Chemin Ceinture, St Gilles les Bains (tel 24 47 73).
Criniere Réunion: 42 rue Henri Cornu Cambaie, St Paul (tel 45 19 37).

MOUNTAIN BIKING
Mountain bikes are known simply as VVT (*vélo tout-terrain*). There are seven special trails providing demanding, but safe, mountain-biking. These trails total more than 870 miles (1,400 km) and comply with the French Cycling Federation's safety regulations. The trails are 'Geranium Station' in Maïdo, 'Entre-Deux Station', 'Cilaos Station', 'Goyavier' and 'Volcano' in Hautes Plaines, 'Vacoa' in St Philippe, and 'Vert-Bleu' in St Rose.

You can hire mountain bikes from:
Austral Aventure: 11 rue des Myrtilles, St Gilles les Hauts (tel 55 69 55, fax 87 55 50).
Jacaranda: 4a Résidences les Oreades, La Montagne (tel 23 82 58, fax 23 82 58).
Parc du Maïdo: Route du Maïdo, La Petite France (tel 22 96 00, fax 32 52 52).
Pic des Sables: Parc Hotel du Maïdo, La Petite France (tel 22 96 00, fax 32 52 52).
Rando Bike: 100 route du Volcan, La Plaine des Cafres (tel 59 15 88).
Réunion Sensations: 28 rue du Père Boiteau, Cilaos (tel 31 84 84, fax 31 84 85).
Run Evasion: 23 rue du Père Boiteau, Cilaos (tel 31 83 57, fax 31 80 72).
Telenavette: 35 rue de la Baie, St Paul (tel 69 30 00, fax 45 45 95).
VTT Découverte: Place Julius Benard, St Gilles les Bains (tel 24-5556, fax 24 51 79).
VTT Loisirs Maïdo: Ravine Fleurie, 35 Route du Maïdo, Le Guillaume (tel 32 49 15, fax 32 43 10).
VTT Passion: 30 Chemin du Piton. Montgaillard les Hauts, St Denis (mobile 0262-86 32 88, fax 23 76 10).
VTT Station Elf: RN2, St Rose (tel/fax 47 32 76).
There are also pick-up points at:
53 rue Four à Chaux, St Pierre (tel 35 16 25).
37 rue Juliette Dodu, St Denis (tel 41 35 35).
World Bike; rue des Seychelles, St Gilles les Bains (tel 33-0044).
When you hire a VTT ask for a mountain-bike map. This details all the best trails and grades them like ski runs in the French Alps, from very easy and easy, to difficult and very difficult.

4x4 OUTINGS
The island's road network gets you to the most remote areas by ordinary car, but the mountains are ideal for 4x4 excursions. Contact:
Evasion 4x4: Ile de la Réunion, 187 RN3, Bourg Murat, Plaine des Cafres (tel 59 34 12, fax 59 24 46).
Indi Aventure Et Indi 4x4: 14 rue des Lanternes, St Gilles les Bains (tel 24 23 87, fax 24 27 62 0).
Kreolie 4x4: 63 Grand Fond Intérieur, Entre-Deux (tel/fax 39 50 87, mobile 0262-86 52 26).

GOLF
Réunion has three golf courses; the oldest course is near Etang-Salé. Above St Denis is Colorado with a wonderful view of the Indian Ocean. For golfers who like technical difficulties, the Bassin Bleu course at St Gilles les Hauts is regarded as the island's most technically and physically challenging.

Contact:

Golf Club de Bourbon: 140 Les Sables, Etang-Salé (tel 26 33 39, fax 26 38 40).

Golf du Bassin Bleu: Villèle, St Gilles les Hauts (tel 55 53 58, fax 22 78 21).

Golf du Colorado: Zone de Loisirs du Colorado, La Montagne (tel 23 79 50, fax 23 99 46).

AERIAL SPORTS
Best hang-gliding and **paragliding** spots are at Maïdo, Colimacons above St Leu, St Paul Heights, and from the top of Piton des Neiges. Known locally as *parapenting,* parasailing was born in the French Alps when parachutist Jean-Claude Betemps decided to save time by using a mountain slope instead of an aircraft as a launching site. Betemps now spends eight months of the year in Réunion, which says something for the island's thermals. Parasailing, hang-gliding and other airborne sports have a wide following on the island. The St Leu region especially offers ideal conditions – moderate winds, numerous hillside take-off slopes, as well as a dreamlike touchdown strip on the shores of the lagoon. At a speed of 19 mph (30 kmh) and an altitude of 656 ft (200 m) you can wing across the sky. International hang-gliders come to Réunion for the exceptional flights over the central peaks.

Hang-gliding, paragliding, and delta-wing
Azurtech: Trois-Bassin (tel 85 04 00, fax 33 91 36).

Bourbon Parapente: 1 rue Terre Tabaillet, St Leu (tel 87 58 74).

Parapente Réunion: Pente-école, 4 CD 12, Montée des Colimaçons, St Leu (tel 24 87 84, fax 24 87 15).

Microlight
Air Intense: Aerodrome de Pierrefonds, St Pierre (tel 66 18 51, fax 31 26 58).

Felix Ulm Run: Base ULM du Port, rue A Artaud, Le Port (tel 43 02 59, fax 45 63 08).

Les Passagers du Vent: Base ULM, rue A Artaud, Le Port (tel 42 95 95, fax 42 22 34).

Volulm: Aérodrome de Pierrefonds, St Pierre (tel 97 30 38, fax 57 46 66).

CANYONING
Canyoning fanatics go for the challenge of precipitous mountains, otherwise inaccessible gorges, and waterfalls considered hairy in the extreme. Professional instructors keep an eye on you as you drop down high cliffs into deep canyons. You don't have to be in tip-top physical condition, just have a yen for an adrenalin rush.

Ric a Ric: 12 Avenue de Bourbon, St Gilles les Bains (tel/fax 33 25 38, mobile 0262-86-5485, e-mail: ricaric@chez.com).

Also:

Austral Aventure: 11 rue des Myrtilles, St Gilles les Hauts (tel 55 69 55, fax 55 83 32, mobile 0262-87 55 50).

Jacaranda: 4a Résidences les Oreades, La Montagne (tel 23 82 58, fax 23 82 58, mobile 0262-66 81 81).

Kalanoro: Bras-Panon (tel 51 71 10, fax 51 72 94, mobile 0262-65 14 21).

Réunion Sensations: Place Paul Julius Benard, Galerie Amandine Bât 1, No 2a, St Gilles les Bains (tel 24 57 00, fax 24 56 57).

SAILING AND WATERSPORTS

If you are not in the mountains and cirques, the sea is where it all happens, whether it's sailing, water-skiing, or surfing and body-boarding (see *Exploring Réunion*).

Blue Cat: 2 rue des Brisants, Zone Portuaire, St Gilles les Bains (tel 24 32 04, fax 24 22 38).

Compagnie des Alizes: Hnoss, 1 rue Berthier le Forban, Le Port (tel 65 60 00, fax 33 91 36).

Grand Bleu Croisieres and Découvertes: St Gilles Yachting Harbour, St Gilles (tel 33 28 32, fax 33 25 89).

Planch'Alizé: Plage de la Saline, La Saline les Bains (tel 24 62 61, fax 24 68 95).

Ski Club de St Paul: 1 rue Croix de l'Etang, St Paul (tel 45 42 87, mobile 0262-85 14 96).

Thim Location: jet-ski and boat rental (tel 33 03 74, mobile 0262-85 14 96).

Visiobul Réunion: Port de St Gilles, St Gilles les Bains (tel 85 23 46, fax 24 45 34).

SCUBA-DIVING

Any diving of consequence is centred at St Gilles, where dive clubs operate at a highly professional level, with good boats and equipment, and with French-qualified CIMAS divemasters who are all sticklers for correct procedures. You won't get a dive if you cannot produce a recognised certificate, nor will you get your aqualung filled. Good air is available at all diving clubs, and you can dive deep with little fear of serious consequences in the event of a minor recompression problem. There is a government decompression chamber at St Pierre, and the French Navy runs an efficient emergency back-up service on the island with three-man chambers and helicopter airlifts. There are also doctors on the island trained in diving medicine.

DEEP-SEA ANGLING

Blue marlin, sailfish, blue-fin tuna and **sea bream** are the quarry here for deep-sea fishermen. The **best time** is from October to May. As recently as the 1997-1998 season the French record for the best sailfish landed was beaten, and so was the world record for the best kingfish. Recently, a world record was recognised by the International Game Fishing Association (IGFA) for a superb pompano caught off the coast.

Réunion Fishing Club: (IGFA member), 5 rue du Grand Large, St Gilles les Bains (tel 24 36 10/34 74, fax 55 34 03).

OPENING HOURS

Shopping hours: 8.30am to noon and 2.30pm to 6pm Monday to Saturday. Shops and stores in the bigger towns also stay open through lunchtime. Some are open on Sunday mornings, mainly food stores. Score supermarket, for example, is open on Monday from 2.30pm to 8pm, Tuesday to Thursday 9am to 12.30pm and 2.30pm to 8pm, Saturday 9am to 8pm, and Sunday 8.30am to 12.30pm.

GIFTS AND SOUVENIRS

Gifts and souvenirs are often a problem when travelling, as they can be too big, too expensive, or simply non-existent. You won't get decision neurosis on this score in Réunion, which has plenty of souvenirs you can eat or drink and more durable ones that you'll be dusting off or wearing for years to come. The towns are full of boutiques, galleries, stores, and markets selling everything from 'been there, done that' T-shirts to rum, liqueurs, vanilla, honey, spices, preserves, chocolates, flasks of vetiver and geranium oils, and handicrafts such as lace embroidery, patchwork bedspreads and travel rugs, carved wood and volcanic rock, engravings, wickerwork, music and lavish photographic books.

Caution: Turtle shell in various forms is on sale in some places. The shell is really beautiful – but it is even lovelier when it's still on the turtle. Don't encourage this trade by buying it, even if you are told the shell comes from turtles bred in captivity on the island.

Handicrafts

Handicrafts are on sale in St Denis at:

Boutique Artisanale: (Association Lacaze), 10 Place Sarda Garriga. Open Monday to Friday 9am to 12.30pm and 1.30pm to 6pm, Saturday 9.30am to 12.30pm and 2pm to 6pm (tel 21 55 47).

Arts Malgaches: 62 rue Jean Chatel (tel 20 17 96).

Bijouterie Kalidas: corner of Jean Chatel and de la Compagnie streets (tel 20 03 50).

Comptoir d'Asie: corner of Jules Auber and Victor MacAuliffe streets (tel 21 74 62).

Cristoflor: 3 rue Gilbert des Molières (tel 21 91 61).

Galerie des Mascareignes: 5 rue de Nice (tel 21 89 87).

Mineral Gallery: 20a rue Jean Chatel (tel 21 53 78).

Rose de Chine: 46 rue Alexis de Villeneuve (tel 21 22 38).

Studio Universal: rue Alexis de Villeneuve (tel 21 37 84).

Trésors Créoles: 39 Impasse Triolet, St Clotilde (tel 29 02 23).

Handicraft Gallery: Escape Continent, 75 Route du Karting, St Clotilde (tel 29 56 66).

Zoma: 19 rue St Anne (tel 20 11 14).

The **best place for basketwork** is the market (Grande Marché) on rue Maréchal Leclerc, in St Denis. It's open from 8am to 6.30pm (tel 21 09 02).

If you have a sweet tooth try Mascarin chocolates while you are in Réunion before you buy a box or two to take home. They come in flavours such as guava, pineapple, and litchi. There's also a bitter black (*noir amer*) version.

Music

The group Okilé celebrated the 150th anniversary of the abolition of slavery with an album called *Bob's Solo*, which is a mélange of traditional maloya music and dance, with other local cultural inputs; island songstress Michou has some evocative numbers on a CD called *Piments bien forts* ('Strong Peppers'); a popular CD of local music is *mon île*, and *Granmoun Lélé* by Dan Ker Lélé is regarded as the best compilation of island maloya music. The CD *La Réunion des Plus Belles Chansons* should make a good gift for a musical auntie or uncle.

Books

There are about 60 bookshops in Réunion. Probably the best three are in St Denis. They are the *Librairie Papeterie Gerard*, 5b rue de la Compagnie (tel 20 08 15); the *Librairie l'Entrepôt*, which is across from the Ritz cinema at 82-88 rue Juliette Dodu (tel 20 94 94), which also has a cyber café; and the *Trésors de l'Ile de la Réunion*, 122 rue Juliette Dodu, (tel 41 25 25). The latter specialises in beautifully illustrated books on all aspects of the island, from guidebooks to Creole cookbooks, as well as videos, calendars and T-shirts. Book prices range from FF49 to FF260 (£25/US$38). Open Monday to Friday 8am to 12.30pm and 1.45pm to 6.30pm, Saturday 8.30am to 12.30pm and 2pm to 6.30pm.

For that last-minute buy there is a souvenir shop at the airport that has every conceivable knick-knack made of lava from the Piton de la Fournaise volcano. You can get clocks, pendants, games, pen-holders and other lava souvenirs, each with the inscription *Coulée 1998*, the date of the last eruption.

Statistics show that the people of Réunion are a fairly law-abiding lot. In 1998 (the latest available figures) nearly 26,000 crimes and offences were reported to the police. Most of these (17,264) were thefts of one sort or another, mainly from caravans and burglaries of residential property. There were 57 murders and attempted murders and 43 armed robberies. There are the usual petty crimes, pick-pocketing and bag-snatching, but apart from these irritants it is a pretty safe destination as far as visitors are concerned unless, of course, you are a caravanner. Worst areas (44-62 crimes and offences per 1,000 inhabitants) are the adjoining communes of St Denis, La Possession and Le Port. The most crime-free (10-20 per 1,000) are the coastal areas of St Joseph, Petite Ile, St Louis, Trois Bassins, and St Suzanne, as well as the inland communes of Salazie, Cilaos, and Entre-Deux.

POLICE

The law is evident in the shape of the *gendarmerie*, the military police who operate in rural areas and small towns, state police and municipal police.

DRINK, DRUGS AND THE LAW

Alcoholism is a social problem in Réunion, probably because of the availability of cheap drink and the high rate of unemployment, but the police tend to turn a blind eye to drunks, so long as they are quiet, and don't get behind the wheel of a car. Réunion has been preserved from the menace of hard drugs for a long time but not from *zamal* (marijuana), which grows in the interior of the island. You can be arrested for growing and selling this, but not for smoking it. It's usually grown in remote areas of the cirques and this is where people from the capital go to buy their supplies. Infractions of the laws governing what the French call *stupéfiants* (drugs/narcotics) saw 230 delinquents charged by police in 1998 and of these 88 were foreign visitors, presumably dealers rather than users.

TOURIST INFORMATION CENTRES

You will find the highly efficient and extremely helpful Réunion Tourist Board (Comité du Tourisme de la Réunion) at Place du 20 Décembre 1848, BP 615 87472 St Denis Cedex (tel 21 00 41, fax 21 00 21, e-mail: ctr@guetali.fr). Other tourist offices are scattered throughout the island and the following are members of FROTSI (Réunion Federation of Tourist Offices and Tourist Information Centres), Résidence St Anne, 18 rue St Anne, St Denis (tel 21 73 76, fax 21 84 47, e-mail: frotsi@wanadoo.fr).

North Coast

La Possession Tourist Office: 27 rue Waldeck Rochet, La Possession (tel 22 26 66, fax 22 25 17). Information and bookings for mountain lodges, camping equipment rentals. Open Monday to Friday 8.30am to 12.30pm and 1.30pm to 5.30pm, and Saturday 8.30am to 12.30pm and 2pm to 5pm.

West Coast

West Coast Tourist Office: Galerie Amandine, St Gilles les Bains (tel 24 57 47, fax 24 34 40, e-mail: tourist.information@wanadoo,fr). Information, mountain lodge (gîtes) and ticket bookings. Open Monday 9am to noon and 1pm to 6pm, Tuesday to Friday 8.30am to 12.30pm and 1pm to 6pm, Saturday 9am to 5pm.

South Coast
Etang-Salé Tourist Office: 74 rue Octave-Bénard, Etang-Salé les Bains (tel 26 67 32, fax 26 67 92). Information and mountain lodge bookings. Open Monday to Friday 8.30am to noon and 2.30pm to 6pm, and Saturday 9.30am to noon and 3pm to 6pm.

Entre-Deux Tourist Office: 9 rue Fortuné Hoareau, Entre-Deux (tel 39 69 80, fax 39 69 83). Open Monday to Friday 9am to 3pm, Saturday, Sunday and Bank holidays 9am to 3pm.

St Pierre Tourist Office: (South Region), 17 Boulevard Hubert Delisle, St Pierre (tel 25 02 36, fax 25 82 76). Information and mountain lodge bookings, Summer (November to April): Open Monday to Friday 9am to 5.45pm, Saturday 9am to 3.45pm. Winter (May to October): Open Monday to Friday 8.30 am to 5.15pm and Saturday 9am to 3.45pm.

St Philippe Tourist Office: 69 rue Leconte de Lisle, St Philippe (tel 37 10 43, fax 37 10 97). Information and bookings for mountain lodges, and visits to the spice and fragrance garden. Open Monday to Saturday 9am to 5pm, Sundays and public holidays 9am to 2.30pm.

East Coast
St Marie Tourist Office: Centre Commercial Cora Duparc, St Marie (tel 53 30 00, fax 53 91 00). Mountain lodge booking. Open Monday 2pm to 7pm, Tuesday to Saturday 8.30am to 12.30pm and 2pm to 7pm, Sunday 9am to noon.

St André District Tourist Office: 66 Centre Commercial, St André (tel 46 91 63, fax 46 52 16). Open Tuesday to Friday 8.30am to noon and 1.30pm and 5.30pm, Saturday 8.30am to noon and 1.30pm to 4.30pm.

Bras-Panon Tourist Office: 21 Route Nationale, Bras-Panon (tel 51 50 62, fax 51 75 47. Open Monday to Friday 8.30am to noon and 1.30pm to 5pm.

St Benoit Tourist Office: Centre d'Affaires Agora, Route des Plaines, St Benoit (tel 50 21 29, fax 50 88 49). Open Monday to Friday 9am to noon and 2pm to 5pm, closed on Saturday afternoon and Sunday.

High Plains
Country Tourist Information: Domaine des Tourelles, rue de la République, Plaine des Palmistes (tel 51 39 92, fax 51 45 33).

The Cirques
Cilaos Tourist Office: 2a rue Victor MacAuliffe, Cilaos (tel 31 78 03, fax 31 70 30). Open Monday to Saturday 8.30am to 12.30pm and 1.30pm to 5.30pm, Sunday and Bank holidays 9am to 1pm.

Salazie Tourist Office: rue Georges Pompidou, Salazie (tel 47 50 14, fax 47 60 06). Open Monday to Saturday 9am to 3pm and Sunday 9am to 11am.

Information Offices (*Syndicats d'Initiative*) can be found at:

The Mairie St Denis: rue Pasteur (tel 21 33 12).

Office Municipal du Tourisme de St Andre: 88 Centre Commercial (tel 46 91 63).

Salazie: Mairie annexe, rue Georges Pompidou (tel 47 50 14).

Bras-Panon: 21 Route Nationale (tel 51 50 62).

St Benoit (Region Est): 44 rue Amiral Bouvet (tel 50 10 65).

Plaine des Palmistes: Place de la Mairie (tel 51 32 57).

St Philippe: Mairie de St Philippe (tel 37 00 12).

St Pierre: 27 rue Archambaud (tel 25 02 36).

Cilaos: 4 rue des Ecoles (tel 31 78 03).

Entre-Deux: 2 rue Fortune Hoareau (tel 39 50 50).

Etang-Salé: Old railway station building, rue Octave Benard (town hall tel 26 32 44).

L'Ouest: Galerie Amandine, St Gilles les Bains (tel 24 57 47).
La Possession: tel 22 52 52.

RÉUNION TOURIST OFFICES AND REPRESENTATIVES ABROAD

Australia: French Tourist Bureau, 25 Bligh Street, Sydney NSW 2000 (tel 2-9231 5244, fax 2-9221 8682, e-mail: french@ozermail.com.au).

Britain: French Tourist Office (Maison de la France), 178 Piccadilly, London W1V 0AL (tel 020-7491 7622, fax 020-7493 6594, e-mail: piccadilly@ mdlf.demon.co.uk).

Canada: French Tourist Office, 1981 Avenue McGill College, Suite 490, Montréal Quebec H3A 2W9 (tel 514-288 4264, fax 514-845 4868, e-mail: mfrance@passeport.com).

France: Réunion Tourism Board (Comité du Tourisme de la Réunion), 90 rue la Boetie, F-75008 Paris (tel 1-40 75 02 79).

South Africa: French Tourist Office, 196 Oxford Road, Illovo 2196, PO Box 41022, Craighall 2024 (tel 011-880 8062, fax 011-880 7772, e-mail: runint@frenchdoor.co.za).

FOREIGN EMBASSIES AND CONSULATES

Belgium: 72 Avenue Eudoxie Nonge, St Clotilde (tel 29 16 64, fax 97 99 10).

Germany: 9c rue de Lorraine, St Denis (tel 21 62 06, fax 21 74 55).

India: 266 rue Maréchal Leclerc, St Denis (tel 41 75 47, fax 21 01 70, e-mail: congendia@guetali.fr).

Italy: Residence les Lataniers Appt. 111, 12 rue Rouget Delisle, La Possession, (tel/fax 22 28 89).

Madagascar: 77 rue Juliette Dodu, St Denis (tel 21 66 00, fax 21 10 08).

Norway: 44 rue Paul Verlaine, Zic 2, Le Port Cedex (tel 43 30 48, fax 43 22 48).

Switzerland: 107 Chemin Crève Coeur, St Paul (tel 45 55 74).

USEFUL INFORMATION

Time Zone

Réunion time is four hours ahead of GMT. In the northern hemisphere winter, Britain is 4 hours behind Réunion and 2 hours behind in summer. France is 3 hours and 2 hours respectively, and Germany, Switzerland, Italy and Belgium, are the same as France. South Africa is two hours behind Réunion in both winter and summer. Australia, depending where you are Down Under, is 4-6 hours, and the USA, likewise depending on the seaboard, is 9-12 hours behind Réunion.

Electrical Appliances

Power supply is 220 volts AC, at 50 cycles Hertz. Plugs are mainly European round two-pin. A universal electrical adaptor is a good thing to carry, no matter where you travel.

Weights and Measures: As a département of France, Réunion naturally adheres to the metric system of weight and measures.

USEFUL ADDRESSES AND TELEPHONE NUMBERS

Air Austral: 4 rue de Nice, St Denis Cedex (tel 90 90 90, fax 90 90 91).

Customs Service: 7 Avenue de la Victoire, St Denis Cedex (tel 90 81 00, fax 41 09 81).

Police: Hôtel de Police, 5 rue Malartic, St Denis Cedex (tel 90 74 74).

Port Passenger Terminal: tel 43 10 93.

Réunion Tourist Board: Place du 20 Décembre 1848, St Denis Cedex (tel 21 00 41, fax 21 00 21).

Roland Garros Airport Information desk: tel 48 80 68.
Taxis: tel 48 83 83.
Volcano Observatory: 14 RN 3-27e km, Plaine des Cafres (tel 27 52 92, fax 59 12 04).
Weather Forecast: tel 083-66 80 00 0.

PUBLIC HOLIDAYS

New Year	1 January
Easter Holidays	March/April
Labour Day	1 May
Victory Day (1945)	8 May
Ascension Day	1 June
Pentecost	12 June
Bastille Day (1789)	14 July
Assumption Day	15 August
All Saints' Day	1 November
Armistice Day (1918)	11 November
Abolition of Slavery	20 December
Christmas Day	25 December

CALENDAR OF EVENTS
January
Fire-walking in various parts of the island.
Cavadee Tamil procession in St André.
'*Miel Vert*' handicraft and agricultural show, Plaine des Cafres.
Tevelave festival.

February
Chinese New Year (Chinese dancing).
Wine harvest in Cilaos.
Deep-sea fishing contest in Le Port-Pointe des Galets.

March
Fire-walking at Gillot St Marie.
Tradition and Nature Festival at Grande Chaloupe.

April
Tamil New Year (Indian dancing).
Deep-sea fishing opens (8th and 9th) at Le Port-Pointe des Galets.

May
Piton des Neiges cross-country race (mountain race).
Chou-chou (local vegetable) and fishing festival in Hell-Bourg.
Billabong Pro Junior Surf Contest at Trois-Bassins.

June
Tourism, Languages and Leisure Fair in St Denis.
International tournament of Sevens rugby.
Réunion surf contests: Rip Curl Réunion pro-am in St Gilles les Bains; and Yop
    Réunion Pro in St Leu.
Music festival all over the island.
Goyavier (guava) festival at Plaine des Palmistes.

Bras-Panon Agricultural Fair.
Heritage Day (Creole gardens).

July
Fire-walking at St Rose.
'Rando Gadiamb' (mountain race).
Mountain triathlon at Cilaos.
Cilaos festival.
National festival.
White-water festival at St Benoit.

August
'Fait Main' handicraft exhibition in St Pierre.
Embroidery Day in Cilaos.
Pandanus and palm festival in St Philippe.
'Expo Bois' woodwork exhibition in Rivière St Louis.
'Trancimasa' (mountain race).
Réunion tour (car rally).

September
Heritage Day (Creole gardens).
Eco-tourism festival at St Rose.
Flower Show at St Denis exhibition centre.
Food festival at Le Port exhibition centre.
Sea-mountain combined weekend in St Rose (*weekend vert-bleu*).
Garlic festival in Petite Ile.
'Green-Blue' triathalon in St Rose.

October
Dipavali: Light Festival of the Tamil community in St André and other towns.
Paragliding World Cup pre-selection.
'Floriléges' flower show in Tampon.
Freshwater Festival in St Benoit.
Creole Week in St Denis.
Embroidery Day in Cilaos.

November
'Grand Raid' (mountain race).
Maïdo Run (international paragliding competition).
International cross-country race in St Denis.
International Pétanque (bowls) Tournament.
International deep-sea fishing competition in Le Port.
White-water festival at St Benoit.
'Régal' in St Denis.
Curcuma (saffron) festival in Plaine des Grègues.

December
Celebrations all over the island on 20 December to commemorate the freeing of slaves in 1848.
Trans-Dimitile (mountain race).

Dates of these events can change and you should contact the local or regional tourist office for the latest information.

EXPLORING REUNION

ST DENIS AND THE NORTH COAST

ST DENIS

The city is situated on the banks of the Rivière St Denis at the northern tip of the island and has been the capital of Réunion since 1738, when island governor Mahé de Labourdonnais decided to move the administration here from St Paul and build a port nearby. One claim to fame is that it is the largest of all overseas French département cities (130,000 inhabitants, 30% of them in the central area), but it's not too big to get a good feel for it by exploring on foot. The **best place to start** is from the seafront at the **Barachois**. From the Barachois, the **Avenue de la Victoire** takes you right through the centre of the city to the Place de Metz and the Jardin de l'Etat (State Gardens). On either side of this artery – it becomes the rue de Paris along the way – are most of the city's main places of interest. Take this walk and you will in effect traverse the entire history of the capital, from the sea where it was born, past genteelly decaying but still impressive Creole houses and colonial mansions, to the commercial centre, the industrial zone, and then, by car, the heights which now house wealthy city escapees in the elegant residential suburbs of Le Brûlé, St Francois and La Montagne. The picturesque winding road to La Montagne was the only route to the island's west coast until 1963, when the coast road south from St Denis was opened. It gives you a splendid view of the capital, especially at sunset.

The city is laid out grid fashion, with its heart bounded by rue de Paris and rue Charles Gounod, and includes main shopping throughfares Jean Chatel, Juliette Dodu, Jules Auber, and Maréchal Leclerc, the commercial pulse of the city. The St Denis *Syndicat d'Initiative* (tourist information office) organises a two-hour morning tour of the historic centre of the city on Tuesdays and Thursdays (tel 21 39 29/33 12), or ask the Réunion Tourist Board for information (tel 21 00 41/21).

Some interesting sights and places:

Barachois. Once the site of a little fishing harbour where governor Mahé de Labourdonnais built an artificial landing place for boats in the 18th century, it is now a seafront park and promenade and socialising spot for strollers, idlers, and players of *pétanque* (bowls). This is an area of very French pavement cafés and restaurants, wafting out that elusive metropolitan aroma of fine food, good coffee and strong tobacco. Take away the palm trees and the profusion of exotic flowers and you could quite easily be in Paris or Marseilles. The park faces Place Sarda Garriga, where there's a fine statue of one of Réunion's most famous men, the legendary aviator **Roland Garros**, who made the first flight across the Mediterranean and won the Croix de Guerre for his exploits during the First World War. On the seafront boulevard is the **Hôtel de la Prefecture de St Denis**, an imposing old (1733) colonial building that was once the headquarters of the French East India Company. It now houses the offices of the island's Prefect, or administrator. Old cannons flank the entrance and in front of the building is a statue of the Prefect's most illustrious predecessor, governor Mahé de Labourdonnais. Off Avenue de la Victoire is the **Cathédrale de St Denis**, built between 1829 and 1832, with its fountain, tacked on in 1854. Almost opposite the cathedral is the old (1759)

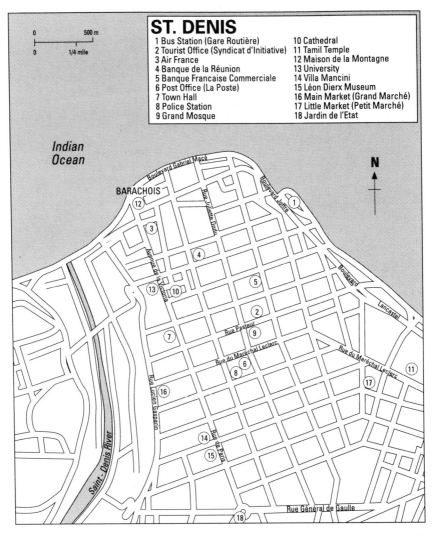

ST. DENIS

1 Bus Station (Gare Routière)
2 Tourist Office (Syndicat d'Initiative)
3 Air France
4 Banque de la Réunion
5 Banque Francaise Commerciale
6 Post Office (La Poste)
7 Town Hall
8 Police Station
9 Grand Mosque
10 Cathedral
11 Tamil Temple
12 Maison de la Montagne
13 University
14 Villa Mancini
15 Léon Dierx Museum
16 Main Market (Grand Marché)
17 Little Market (Petit Marché)
18 Jardin de l'Etat

University. It has had a varied existence. Built as a college for a religious order, it was in turn a barracks, a shipping office, and a maternity hospital. It was damaged by fire in 1993. Heading south, at the junction of rue de la Compagnie, is the **Monument aux Morts**, the towering war memorial to the dead of two world wars. On the same side of the street is the **Hôtel de Ville** at 14 rue de Paris, the town hall which was built in 1860 and used until 1977, and on the next block heading south, at **15 rue de Paris**, is an impressive villa that is a fine example of 18th century carpentry work, where Léon Dierx, the man acclaimed in Paris after the death of Mallarmé in 1898 as the 'Prince of Poets,' was born on 31 March 1838. The house was the island home of former French prime minister Raymond Barre and is now used as offices of the General Council. Another superb Creole house is the **Villa Mancini** which mounts modern arts and photographic exhibitions. It is now known as the **Artothèque** (tel 41 75 00), and is open daily except Monday. Entrance is free. The **Leon Dierx Museum** is more an art gallery than a museum and houses the most famous collection of art in the Indian Ocean. The museum, at 28 rue de Paris, has an exceptional collection of modern art, including a Picasso bronze, some sketches by Gauguin, and works by Dégas, Delacroix, Cézanne, Chagall, Bourdelle, Carrière, Guillaumin, Redon, Van Dongen, and Vlaminck. It was founded in 1911 by two Creole scholars, Marius and Ary Leblond, in a building that was formerly an episcopal palace. There is special access for the disabled. Entrance is free. It is open from 9am to noon and 1pm to 5pm (tel 20 24 82).

Jardin de l'Etat. The 12-acre (5 ha) State Gardens at the end of the rue de Paris were laid out in 1817 and hold more than 7,000 exotic plants and trees from all over the tropics. At the end of the gardens is the **Muséum d'Histoire Naturelle** in a building dating back to 1855 that once housed the Colonial Council, and is now a classified National Heritage building. The museum is worth a visit, if only to see its enormous **coelacanth**, caught in the Comoros, and an even rarer specimen of the extinct **crested Bourbon bird**. There are also other vanished island species, including giant tortoises and dugongs, as well as fauna from other south-west Indian Ocean islands, and rocks and minerals from Réunion and Madagascar. Open Monday to Saturday from 10am to 5pm. Closed on public holidays. Entrance fee for adults is FF10, children FF5 (tel 20 02 19, fax 21 33 93).

At 32 rue du Maréchal Leclerc is the **Grand Mosquée**, one of three on the island ministering to Réunion's 20,000 Muslims. The **Tamil Temple**, is also on rue de Maréchal Leclerc, and not far away, on rue St Anne, is the **Buddhist Pagoda**.

Le Grand Marché, at 2 rue Maréchal Leclerc, is the city's main market and a good place to browse among Réunion and Madagascar handicrafts, spices and other products. It's open daily from 8.30am to 6.30pm. About a mile (2 km) east of the main market is **Le Petit Marché** a bustling, colourful fruit and veg market. In the Chaudron quarter in the east of St Denis, now the site of a new university campus, is the **Parc Zoologique**, where the main attraction is a bevy of Madagascan lemurs. There are pony rides for children, shady squares to lounge in, and a swimming pool nearby. It costs FF10 to get in (tel 28 28 73).

Jardin de Cendrillon. (Cinderella's Garden). This unusual ¾-acre (3,000 sq m) garden at 48 Route des Palmiers, La Montagne, is up at nearly 1,500 ft (450 m). It has an impressive collection of traditional island plants and flowers, particularly varieties of roses that have been developed on Réunion. There is a nursery where you can buy rare plants. Prior booking is recommended for guided tours of 4-30 people. Individual visits are not allowed. Admission is FF30 per person (tel 23 63 28, fax 86 32 88).

Take a **sunset walk** at St Bernard, 1,312 ft (400 m) up above the city, for some fine views. At 2,624 ft (800 m) is Le Brûlé where you'll find **hiking trails** leading to Cascade Maniquet and La Roche Ecrite, a 7,470 ft (2,277m) rock outcrop which dominates the north of the island and drops sharply down to the cirques of Mafate and Salazie. The peak is named after a stone covered with graffiti.

THE NORTH COAST

Round and about St Denis you'll find the Ilet Quinquina to the east for picnics and swimming; the Montauban market gardens, which supply the city with its fruit and vegetables, are at La Bretagne; Morne des Patates à Durand, or Pic Adam, at Piton Bois de Nèfles, has magnificent views over the coastline. Inland are the Providence botanical paths supervised by the National Forest Authority

(ONF). For air enthusiasts, **St Marie** is where pilot Marcel Goulette landed an aircraft on the island at Gillot for the first time on 29 November 1929, on the site of the present international airport. Steam train buffs should visit Grand Chaloupe, between St Denis and La Possession, a former railway station where a Schneider 030T locomotive, Réunion's first mobile historical monument, can be seen. **La Possession** and nearby **Le Port** to the west of St Denis are unprepossessing places and their main interest is historical in the former instance and mercantile in the latter. La Possession is where in 1642 Sieur Jacques de Pronis took possession of the island for France; Le Port was established in the 19th century when a harbour was excavated to give the island its first safe haven for shipping.

ACCOMMODATION

Classified Hotels. A double room costs from FF520-750 a night at a three-star hotel and FF260-420 at one and two star hotels.

Saint-Denis: (Apavou-Best Western Group), 2 rue Doret (tel 21 80 20, fax 21 97 41). Three star hotel right in the historical heart of the city, 15 minutes from the international airport, facing the ocean and alongside the Barachois seafront gardens and promenade, 118 rooms, shopping arcade, snack-bar, bar, *L'Oasis* restaurant serves French and Creole cuisine, close to the casino, evening entertainment in the bar Monday to Saturday, breakfast costs FF75.

Mercure Creolia: (Accor Group), 14 rue du Stade, Montgaillard (tel 94 26 26, fax 94 27 27, e-mail: creolia@guetali.fr). Three star hotel with 107 air-conditioned rooms overlooking St Denis, a short stroll from the town centre and near the airport (free pick up service). Two restaurants: *Le Kalou Pile*, serves Creole and French cuisine, and *La Varangue*, gym, swimming-pool, tennis court, sauna, jacuzzi, piano bar, Tuesday and Thursday evening entertainment, breakfast FF70.

Juliette Dodu: 31 rue Juliette Dodu (tel 20 91 20, fax 20 91 21). A few minutes from the Indian Ocean and 15 minutes from the international airport, this three star hotel occupies what was once the house of national heroine Juliette Dodu. 43 rooms, private parking, jacuzzi, restaurant, room service, library, breakfast FF65.

The other three star hotel, 5 miles (8 km) from the city, is *Domaine des Jamroses:* 6 Chemin du Colorado, La Montagne (tel 23 59 00, fax 23 93 37). Set in a 5-acre (2 ha) tropical park overlooking the sea, 12 spacious rooms in a Creole residence, *Les Jamroses* restaurant, which has a terrace and panoramic view, serves French gourmet cuisine, squash, sauna, jacuzzi, swimming pool, billiards, mountain biking, breakfast included.

Central Hotel: 37 rue de la Compagnie (tel 94 18 08, fax 21 64 33, e-mail: central.hotel@wanadoo.fr). Two star hotel situated in the capital, 10 minutes from the airport, close to the main shopping area, 57 rooms, bar, car park, *Le Central* restaurant for French cuisine and snacks, breakfast included.

Jardin de Bourbon: 18 rue du Verger (tel 40 72 40, fax 30 32 28). Two-star tourist residence in the upper reaches of the city, 181 rooms in a tropical setting, bathroom with bath, spa, underground car park, breakfast FF30.

Lancastel: (Apavou Group), 6 rue Henri Vavasseur (tel 94 70 70, fax 20 12 05). Two stars, 135 rooms facing the ocean, five minutes from the airport, pub and *La Taverne* restaurant for grills and other cuisine open daily, car park, breakfast FF35.

Marianne: 5 Ruelle Boulot (tel 21 80 80, fax 21 85 00). Two stars, 24 rooms, a stone's throw from the town centre and the State Gardens, 24 rooms, three rooms with kitchenette, continental breakfast included.

Also near the State Gardens is *Les Manguiers* two-star tourist residence (9 rue des Manguiers, tel 21 25 95, fax 20 22 23).

Mascareignes Hotel: 3 rue Laférrière (tel 21 15 28, fax 21 24 19). One star, 12 rooms in the city centre, TV lounge, breakfast included.

Non-Classified Hotels range from FF120-FF410 (£12-39/US$17-60) a night.

Austral: 20 rue Charles Gounod (tel 94 45 67).

Abis Hotel: 14/16 rue Juliette Dodu (tel 20 45 45).

L'Ocean: Boulevard de l'Ocean (tel 41 43 08).

Select Hotel: 1a rue des Lataniers (tel 41 13 50).

Fleur de Mai: 1a rue du Moulin à Vent (tel 41 51 81).

Tourist Hotel: 24 Allée Bonnier (tel 21 11 72).

Les Palmiers: 34 rue Voltaire (tel 20 36 46).

Le Cap Vert: 17 Avenue de Lattre de Tassigny, St Clotilde (tel 92 05 05).

Hotel du Centre: 272 rue Maréchal Leclerc (tel 41 73 02, fax 94 17 33).

Furnished Flats

Esmiot Louis: 195 Allée des Topazes, Bellpierre (tel 21 77 56). Costs FF1,050 (£100/US$152) a week.

Kucero Yvo: 54 rue du Couvent (tel 41 16 68).

Le Home Fleury de Cendrillon: 48 Route des Palmiers, La Montagne (tel/fax 23 63 28). Two and four bedrooms, FF200 a night for two people, with a minimum stay of three nights.

For more information on these, **self-catering gîtes** and **B&B** places (see *Accommodation* in *Practical Information*).

EATING OUT

You have a choice of around 130 places to eat in St Denis. There are lots of up-market restaurants, pavement cafés, coffee shops, take-away places, and small Chinese restaurants known for their fried noodles and Cantonese rice, but in a city where even an ordinary meal can make a big hole in your wallet, we found a tiny but great place to eat – tasty, generous helpings at reasonable prices. Oddly enough this is opposite one of the most expensive hotels in the capital, the St Denis.

There's not much room in *Le P'Tit Comptoir* ('The Little Counter'), but it's worth jamming in with blue-collar workers at lunchtime to taste owner Francis Faux-Farjon's omelettes, panine, salads, and giant pitta – a heap of spicy lamb in a Tunisian kebab bread roundel specially baked for him. The pitta costs FF35 (£3/US$5), a ham salad FF18-24, a huge baguette sandwich the same, and cold beers and fruits drinks FF10. *Le P'Tit Comptoir* is at 1 rue Doret (tel 20 40 00).

At 34 rue de la Compagnie is the *Deutsche Stube/Brasserie Allemande* where you'll get a hearty helping of goulash with noodles for FF70, the plat du jour for FF55, salad for FF15, an omelette for FF19, and a stein of draught beer for FF56. It's open every day except Sunday (tel 21 14 26). For French cuisine with a Rhone Valley flavour try *Le Val Rhonnais* at 44 rue Monthyon (tel 41 41 70). The menu runs from FF85-140. One of the owners is an examiner at the local cookery college and the restaurant is sometimes closed while he supervises examinations, so phone first.

Classified Restaurants include:

Le Labourdonnais: 14 rue Amiral Lacaze (tel 21 44 26, fax 21 56 32). French cuisine, this is *tres* up-market and expensive.

Le Bancoul: Le Chaudron, Parc des Expositions (tel 29 22 76). Creole cuisine.

Chez Piat: 60 rue Pasteur (tel 21 45 76, fax 94 30 48), French cuisine.

Le Fangourin: 11 Boulevard Doret (tel 20 27 92), Madagascan and Creole cuisine.

Le Palmeraie: rue du Verger (tel 40 72 40), grills and other dishes.

Le Roland Garros: 2 Place du 20 Decembre, Barachois (tel 41 44 37, fax 41 08 21), opposite the tourist office. French and Creole cuisine.
La Saladière: 32 Boulevard Lancastel (tel 21 49 41), French cuisine.
Le Rogation: 83 rue St Marie (tel 41 52 55, fax 21 06 24), gourmet cuisine.
Le St Bernard: 146 Chemin du Père Rimbaud, La Montagne (tel 23 62 90), Creole cuisine.
La Terrasse: 39 rue Felix Guyon (tel 20 07 85), Creole and French cuisine.
Nouvelle Orleans: 12 rue de la Compagnie (tel 20 27 74), Creole and French cuisine.
For hamburgers with all the trimmings there's McDonald's, at 11 rue de la Victoire.

ENTERTAINMENT

Théatre de Champ Fleuri, Avenue André Malraux (tel 41 11 41, fax 41 55 71), is a modern theatre with a seating capacity of 910 people and an exhibition gallery. Various concerts, dance shows, plays, conferences, movies and visual arts exhibitions. For information on shows and events the ticket office is open from Monday to Friday 10am to 6.30pm, Saturday from 10am to 8.30pm. The **Centre Dramatique de l'Ocean Indien** has sound and light productions and seating for 270 people. It is at the Theatre du Grand Marché, 2 rue Maréchal Leclerc (tel 20 33 99, fax 21 01 60, e-mail: centre-dramatique.reunion@ wanadoo.fr). At **Palaxa** good vibrations are guaranteed in this converted warehouse where you can listen to folk music and new sounds from Réunion and other Indian Ocean islands, 300 seats, 23 rue Leopold Rambaud, St Clotilde (tel 21 87 58, fax 21 42 38).

St Denis has two **cinemas**, the *Plaza* at 79 rue Pasteur (tel 21 04 36); and the *Ritz* at 53 rue Juliette Dodu (tel 20 09 52).

There are many **music bars**, including:
Atmosphère: 78 rue Juliette Dodu (tel 41 32 32).
Banana's Café: a discothèque pub, open from 6.30pm, closed on Monday, corner of rue de Paris and rue de Nice (tel 20 31 32).
Le Blue Lagoon: at the St Denis Hotel is open from 11.30am to midnight, and there's also music at *La Distillerie* piano bar daily except on Saturday and Sunday, 2 rue Doret (tel 21 80 20).
Café Moda: 75 rue Pasteur (tel 41 99 41).
Le Karaoke: open Monday to Saturday from 6pm to 2am, 4 rue Maréchal Leclerc (tel 41 18 19).
Pub Alexander: open every day for lunch and dinner, closed on Sunday and public holidays, 108 rue Pasteur (tel 21 19 32).
Saxo: piano jazz club, open from Monday to Saturday from 6.30pm, at 20 rue de Nice (tel 20 11 99).

Night-Clubs

Le Byblos: Bas de la Rivière (tel 20 03 00).
Le First: open every night from 10pm except on Sunday and Monday, 8 Avenue de la Victoire (tel 41 68 25).
Le Gin Get: open Tuesday to Saturday from 10pm until dawn, rue André Malraux (tel 41 65 65).
Le Privilege: closed on Sunday and Monday, Bas de la Rivière (tel 20 03 00).
When you have danced the night away try *Thalassorun*, Résidence des Jardins de Bourbon (tel/fax 30-1515), where you have a choice of jacuzzis, steam baths, sauna, multi-jet shower, airbaths, essential oil massages, seaweed body wrap, music and relaxation therapy, FF150-300. Medical staff are on hand and include a doctor, physiotherapist, osteopath, and a dietitian.

SHOPPING

One unusual way to buy gifts for friends and family – and save yourself the trouble of lugging them home yourself – is to buy packs or hampers of local and regional specialities and have them delivered in 48-72 hours anywhere from Scandinavia to Greece. Several companies specialise in this service and you can order from lists which include fresh flowers, tropical fruits, chocolates, rum, honey, liqueurs, pâté, Creole sausage, samosas, smoked pork, vegetables, spices, cheese and Creole pastries. Prices range from FF249 (£24/US$36) to around FF499 (£48/US$72). For more details contact *Panier Malin* (tel 53 57 93); *ColiSam Express* (tel 21 33 89). At the Roland Garros airport you'll find *Point Colipays*, which has a showroom where you can first see what you are ordering. It's open Monday to Friday from 8.30am to 6.30pm (tel 28 99 99).

Distillerie J Chatel at 72 Avenue Eudoxie Nonge, St Clotilde, is not easy to find, but it's worth the effort. It's open Monday to Friday from 8am to noon and 2pm to 5pm. There's a boutique selling punch and rums of Réunion. Free tastings (tel 28 01 90).

Street Markets. There are popular street markets at Chaudron and St Clotilde on Wednesday and Sunday morning; Les Camelias, on Friday morning; and at La Source on Thursday morning. (See also *Shopping* page 239).

THE WEST COAST

The west coast is known as the *côte sous le vent*, or the leeward side of the island, protected from the trade winds. This is the most popular side of the island for anyone in search of **beaches** and **water sports**. It has nearly 19 miles (30 km) of beaches, although not all of them are white sand. Some are pebbly and others of rather uninviting black or grey sand, the result of ancient volcanic action and erosion. The resort towns conjure up the best of the south of France and lie along the island's own riviera route south. The main holiday towns on this coast are **St Gilles les Bains** 25 miles (40 km) from St Denis, and **St Leu**. In between are dotted other pleasant villages.

ST PAUL

The west coast really starts at **St Paul**, 17 miles (28 km) from the capital and is the first beach on the coast heading south, 2 miles (3 km) of black sand. The town was Réunion's first capital, although there are not all that many traces left of its early occupation. In the centre the *mairie*, or town hall, is an imposing colonial building that was the headquarters established by the French East India Company on the island in 1767 and there are some fine examples of Creole architecture in the town. The town really comes to life on Friday afternoon and Saturday morning when its two popular street markets open for business on the seafront. For the energetic, there's a well-marked paved path inland from the main RN1 road called *Sentier le Tour des Roches*, which is a pleasant 2-hour amble up the slopes past an old water mill and through pleasant palm and banana plantations to look-out points with good views over St Paul. There's also a more demanding hike along an unsurfaced path up the slopes, which follows a stream up the **Ravine du Bernica**, whose quiet beauty is said to have been an inspiration for local poet Leconte de Lisle.

At **Etang de St Paul** only a few minutes away from the town and its supermarkets, lies **Parc Amazone**, a peaceful aquatic and botanical world where you can take a boat ride through a maze of waterways in the 988-acre (400 ha) marsh, its banks a tangled mass of papyrus and bulrushes and the haunt of **green herons** and other waders. The park is a sanctuary for about 15 different nesting birds, and migratory birds from as far afield as the arctic circle have been recorded here. You can paddle or row yourself around, or join a guided tour by canopied boat. The nature reserve is open every day except Monday, from 10am to 6pm (tel 45-1532. The Marine Cemetery (*Cimetière Marin*) on the shore has a macabre interest. The locals say it is where you will find the graves of thieves and honest men buried side by side. The notorious pirate, Olivier le Vasseur, better known as *La Buse* ('The Buzzard') is buried here. He was hanged in 1730 in Réunion for plundering ships of the French East India Company. His grave, marked with the skull and crossbones, is the first you see as you enter the cemetery. Alongside the grave of *La Buse* is a cannon which was once mounted on his ship *La Victorieux*. The famous French poet Charles Leconte de Lisle (1818-1894), is also buried here. There are usually more flowers – and the odd bottle of rum – left on the pirate's grave than on the poet's. There's also another sea captain buried here, Eraste Feuillet, who died in 1830 at the age of 29, 'a victim of his generosity,' according to his epitaph. He apparently gave his pistol to the man whose own had misfired in a duel the two men were fighting. Feuillet's opponent thanked him, and then shot him dead. Opposite the seaside cemetery you can see caves at the foot of the cliff, which are said to have been the home of the first settlers. These are known as *Grotte des Premiers Francais*, the 'Cave of the first Frenchmen'.

ST PAUL TO PITON MAÏDO

This steeply winding 15½-mile (25 km) route from sea level to 7,183 ft (2,190 m) on the edge of the rugged Mafate cirque is a drive best started fairly early in the morning. Although it isn't far you should allow at least 2 hours to negotiate the narrow road and hairpin bends, as well as to stop and admire the stupendous views. An early start should get you to the summit by 9am, which means you'll miss the mist which blankets everything as the morning wears on. As the road climbs the air takes on a nip and the scent of flowers, particularly geraniums, whose leaves and stalks are distilled to make an essential oil prized by the perfumiers of Europe. As you get higher the landscape changes to forests of acacias, mimosa, and tamarind trees. The road ends at the Maïdo car park and a choice of paths leads you up to the rim of the cirque, where the **view over the Mafate cirque** will take your breath away. There's a small wooden snack bar at the car park, open from 6am to 6pm and serving coffee, tea, beers, sandwiches, snacks and a Réunion speciality gateau stuffed with fruit.

You'll undoubtedly also find Gèrard Basson at his stand outside the hut ready to take you for a tandem parapente or flight by parachute, from the heights to the coast. No experience is necessary and anyone from 6 to 80 can parapente. If he's not there, you can contact Gérard Basson at Ecole Parapente Jean-Claude Betemps (tel 54 78 67 or 66 64 98). A baptismal flight costs FF400-500, depending on altitude.

When you stand of the knife-edge of the Mafate Cirque you'll realise why there's no road in and why the only access to the cirque is by foot or helicopter. Don't forget to take a camera, or no one will ever believe your description of this fantastic sweep of mountains, the highest peaks in the island. In a panoramic view from north to south you'll see **La Roche Ecrite** (7,469 ft/2,277 m), **Le Cimendef** (7,301 ft/2,226 m), and **Le Morne du Fourche** (7,200 ft/2,195 m) which separate the Salazie and Mafate cirques. The peaks of **Le Gros Morne** (9,810 ft/2,991 m) and the **Piton des Neiges** (10,070 ft/3,070 m) rise from the range marking the centre of the three cirques. To the south the **Col du Taïbit** (6,832 ft/2,083 m) and the peak of **Grand Bénard** (9,499 ft/2,896 m) divide Mafate from the Cilaos cirque.

On the way down from Maïdo you can get a quick lunch at any one of the many village cafés and restaurants on the road, or you could enjoy the view from the restaurant at the *Parc-Hôtel du Maïdo* (tel 32 52 52), which has a menu starting at about FF80.

The area around **Petite France** is the heart of the geranium oil industry, and you'll drive through acres of scented gardens on either side of the road. Many of these plots have a wayside stall or shack where you can smell and buy the product.

ACCOMMODATION

There is one **Classified Hotel** in Petite France, near the Piton Maïdo and about 30 minutes from St Paul. A double chalet costs from FF500-800, breakfast is an additional FF40. It is the two-star *Parc-Hotel du Maïdo* (Anthurium Group), inside a 62-acre (25 ha) park an altitude of nearly 5,000 ft (1,500 m), overlooking the ocean. There are 24 Creole double chalets, with shower and living room. The club-house has a lounge with fireplace, bar and restaurant offering Creole and French traditional cuisine, snooker, volleyball, archery, mountain biking, and walking, Route du Maïdo, Petite France (tel 32 52 52, fax 32 52 00, e-mail: maido@oceane.fr).

Also in Petite France is *Auberge des Acacias*, a furnished flat which costs about FF120 a night, 406 Route du Maïdo (tel 32 36 36).

Non-Classified Hotels. These range from FF200-260 and include the *Caillou Blanc:* 20 rue des Merles, Plateau Caillou (tel 55 71 55); and *Forgerie de la Baie:* 8 Boulevard du Front de Mer (tel 45 57 17).

Furnished Flats prices vary from FF150-200:
Hoareau: 13 Chemin Prosper, Bellemene (tel 55 56 79).
La Caz des Orangers: Sans Souci (tel 44 05 25).
Villa Lazarre: 11 Chemin des Adams, La Plaine (tel 44 11 05).
Villa Mango's: 87 rue des Sereins, Plateau Cailloux (tel 55 71 01).

EATING OUT

For Creole food try:
Au Relais de Canbaie: 59 Avenue Piton Tréport (tel 45 59 38).
Au Tamarin: 93 rue Marius and Ary Leblond (tel 22 65 73).
Chez Floris: 46a rue de la Croix (tel 22 69 81).
Forgeraie de la Baie: 8 Boulevard du Front de Mer (tel 45 57 17).
L'Auberge Gourmande: 120 Chemin Cresence, Tan Rouge (tel 37 77 82 0).
Quai Gilbert: Front de Mer (tel 22 52 74).

For European cuisine:
Gargantua: 323 Chaussée Royale (tel 45 03 24).
Provençal: 43 a rue Labourdonnais (tel 22 64 33).
Rialto: serves Italian dishes (tel 45 21 31).

The following serve Asian meals:
Chez Paul: CD4 Savannah (tel 45 32 53).
Chez Theng: 1 rue de la Baie (tel 45 19 41).
Etoile des Neiges: 5 rue Leconte de Lisle (tel 22 54 48).
Tonton Paul: 6 rue Millet (tel 22 56 05).
Tropic Lunch: Route de Savannah (tel 45 12 09).

For grills:
Baie des Pirates: 17 route des Premiers Français (tel 45 23 23).
Le Loup: 192 rue Marius and Ary Leblond (tel 45 60 13).

ENTERTAINMENT

There is one cinema, the **Splendid** at 146 rue Marius and Ary Leblond (tel 45 45

29), and a nightclub **Le Zenith**, at 40 Route du Front de Mer (tel 45 29 48).

ST GILLES LES HAUTS
At St Gilles les Hauts is the **Musée de la Villèle**, a museum in a Creole-style mansion built in 1787 at the end of a century which saw the height of the island's plantation society and its attendant black slavery. This 47-acre (19 ha) estate was the home of the notorious Marie-Anne-Ombeline Desbassyns, who is an island legend for her alleged cruelty to her 300 slaves. She died in 1846 at the age of 93 and is buried next to the **Chapelle Pointue** across the road from the museum. In the old slave hospital you can watch short videos on the history of slavery. Admission to the museum is FF10. It's open every day except Tuesday from 9.30am to noon, and 2pm to 5pm (tel 55 64 10, fax 55 51 91). In the area at **L'Eperon**, is an old mill now used as a workshop by local artists and craftsmen of the *Village Artisanal* to produce work for sale to visitors. It's open every day except Sunday, from 8.30am to noon and 1.30pm to 6pm (tel 22-7301. Nearby is the **Ravine de St Gilles** with its three waterfalls, the *bassins* Malheur, Aigrettes and Cormoran, which draw crowds of picnickers at the weekend and on public holidays. The path to the ravine starts at L'Eperon Café.

On the coast between St Paul and St Gilles les Bains lies a perfect gem of a place called **Boucan Canot**. The beach here is the favourite with people from the capital and gets crowded at the weekends and on public holidays. This is the place for topless tanning, swimming, snorkelling, and simply lazing. Open-fronted seafood restaurants line the little promenade and the beach boutiques stock things you really need on holiday, as well as interesting souvenirs. There's a range of large postcards at FF2.50, for instance, that feature island fruits, drinks, flowers, food and architecture and are good enough to frame.

ACCOMMODATION
Classified Hotels. These range in price from FF280 for a two-star hotel, to FF730 for three-stars, and FF1,100 for four stars:

Le Boucan Canot (three-star) Boucan Canot (tel 24 41 20, fax 24 02 77). Anthurium Group hotel, on the fringe of the famous Boucan Canot beach, 50 rooms, and a restaurant known for its excellent cooking.

Marina (two stars) 6 Allée des Pailles en Queue (tel 33 07 07, fax 33 07 00), at Boucan Canot beach, 10 self-catering studio flats, private car park, breakfast FF30.

Non-Classified Hotels range in price from FF180-700.

La Villa du Soleil: Boucan Canot (tel 24 38 69), breakfast FF25.

ST GILLES LES BAINS
Is better known simply as St Gilles. This is Réunion's holiday capital, with its villagey laid-back atmosphere, good restaurants, trendy discos, night-clubs and a marina, every kind of watersport, lagoons protected by offshore reef, and dazzling stretches of beach. The main beach is **Roches Noires**, which is also a popular surfing spot. The town is a good place to use as a base from which to explore the west coast. The **Garden of Eden**, at l'Hermitage les Bains is a botanical collection of more than 900 spice, perfume, sacred, magical and medicinal plants of Réunion. The garden is divided into botanical zones and includes a rice paddy and a Zen garden with seats if you feel in a meditative mood. It's open every day except Monday from 10am to 6pm. Entrance is FF35 for adults, children from 4-13 FF20, teenagers and students FF25, senior citizens FF30. An explanatory English/French/German booklet is available. Allow about 1 1/2 hours for your visit (tel 33 83 16).

ACCOMMODATION

Classified Hotels. These range in price from FF280 for a two-star hotel, to FF730 for three-stars, and FF1,100 for four stars:

Alamanda Hotel: (two stars) 81 Avenue de Bourbon (tel 33 10 10, fax 24 02 42, e-mail: alamanda.hotel@alamanda.fr). Near Hermitage lagoon, 58 rooms, bar, shop, TV room, tennis, gym, evening entertainment on Tuesday and Friday, barbecue and music during lunch on Sunday, *L'Alamanda* restaurant serves Creole and French cuisine and is open every day. Breakfast FF45.

L'Archipel: (three stars) Grand Fond (tel 24 05 34, fax 24 47 24). Near St Gilles and the beaches, 66 rooms, free bus shuttle service to St Gilles centre and beaches, excursions, scuba-diving lessons in the swimming pool, tennis. *Le Garden* restaurant serves French, Creole and Chinese cuisine. Breakfast costs FF60.

Le Blue Beach: (three stars) Avenue de la Mer, Les Filaos (tel 24 50 25, fax 24 36 22). Accor Group hotel, close to Hermitage beach, 56 rooms, including 22 suites, bar, swimming pool, sports and leisure facilities nearby. *Le Blue Beach* restaurant serves French and Creole cuisine next to the swimming pool. Breakfast FF60.

Le Caro Beach Hotel: (three stars) rue du Port (tel 24 42 49, fax 24 34 46). In the heart of the town on the Roches Noires beach, a few minutes from the fishing port and market, 44 rooms, 12 flats, breakfast FF60.

Le Grand Hotel des Mascareignes: (three stars Apavou Group) Boucan Canot (tel 24 36 24, fax 24 37 24). About 2 miles (3 km) from St Gilles and a short walk from Boucan Canot beach, 153 rooms, two tennis courts, swimming pool, two jacuzzis, evening entertainment, *Le Longane* restaurant serves gourmet cuisine, and *Le Souimanga* snack bar, piano bar, disco open from 10pm on weekends, breakfast FF70.

Le Maharani: (three stars) 28 rue du Boucan (tel 33 06 06, fax 24 32 97). About 2 miles (3 km) from the town centre, 55 rooms. *Le Tandjore* restaurant serves Indian cuisine, Indian evening Fridays, swimming pool, jacuzzi, deep-sea fishing, snooker, table tennis, music on Tuesday, Wednesday, Fridays and Saturdays, theme evenings, breakfast FF60.

Le Nautile: (three stars) 60 rue Lacaussade (tel 33 88 88, fax 33 88 89). At the Hermitage lagoon, two small two-storey buildings with 43 rooms, jacuzzi, library, breakfast FF60.

Le Novotel Coralia: (three stars) L'Hermitage (tel 24 44 44, fax 24 01 67). An Accor Group hotel set in a 7-acre (3 ha) park, 173 rooms. Creole evenings with traditional folk dance show once a week. Barbecue evenings with music on Wednesday and Saturday. *Le Papayer* restaurant serves Creole and French cuisine and is open every day, *Case Tortue* serves snacks from 9am to 5pm. Breakfast FF75.

Les Aigrettes: (two stars Apavou Group) Chemin Bottard (tel 33 05 05, fax 24 30 50). Set on a hillside in a tropical garden, the hotel overlooks the seaside resort, 87 rooms, free shuttle bus to town and beaches, tennis court, evening activities from Monday to Saturday, *Le Ravenal* restaurant serves Creole and French cuisine and is open every day. Breakfast included.

Les Créoles: (three star) Avenue de Bourbon (tel 33 09 09, fax 33 09 19). Is near the yachting harbour and the lagoon at Hermitage. It has 42 spotless air-conditioned rooms with bathroom, mini-bar. *Les Creoles* restaurant serves excellent Creole and French cuisine, and the bar, next to the sparkling swimming pool, is a friendly spot for a cocktail at sundown. Breakfast is included. A friendly, helpful English-speaking staff make for a pleasant stay.

For a change of pace, sister hotel *Le Récif:* (Avenue de Bourbon, tel 24 50 51, fax 24 38 85), is across the road in a tropical park, 32 double rooms, 22 one-bedroom bungalows, and 22 two-bedroom bungalows. The bar is open from 10am to 10pm offering a variety of tropical punches and there's a popular restaurant, swimming pool, volley-ball, tennis, aerobics, entertainment every night, breakfast included.

Les Palmes: (two stars) 205 rue du Général de Gaulle (tel 24 47 12, fax 24 30 62). Five minutes from the beach and harbour, 21 bungalows with private balcony and bath, breakfast FF35.

Saint-Alexis: (four stars) 44 Route de Boucan Canot, St Gilles les Bains (tel 24 42 04, fax 24 00 13). Near the centre of St Gilles les Bains, 42 rooms, 12 with direct access to the swimming pool, jacuzzi. *Le Grand Hunier* restaurant is well-known for its gourmet food, and *La Brigantine* serves grills. Breakfast is an additional FF100.

Swalibo: (three stars Anthurium Group) 9 rue des Salines (tel 24 10 97, fax 24 64 29). In the heart of La Saline, five minutes from the beach, 30 rooms, lounge with snooker, TV and video, small library, swimming pool, jacuzzi, beach equipment free, breakfast included.

Tourist Residences from FF360-600:

Les Brisants: (three stars Anthurium Group) Avenue de Bourbon (tel 24 50 51, fax 24 38 85). Next to shopping area of Hermitage, 12 flats, restaurant, bar, breakfast FF65.

Les Filaos: (two stars) 101 Avenue de Bourbon (tel 24 50 09, fax 24 28 09).Two minutes from the sea, 44 rooms, grills served in pavilion, themed evenings, starting point for many rambles.

Non-Classified Hotels range in price from FF180-700.

Ancre Marine: rue du Général de Gaulle (tel 24 31 32).

Hotel de la Plage: 20 rue de la Poste (tel 24 06 37), breakfast FF28.

L' Abri Côtier: 129 rue du Général de Gaulle (tel 24 44 64).

Les Bougainvilliers: 27 Ruelle des Bougainvilliers, Hermitage (tel 33 82 48), breakfast FF35.

Les Emeraudes: Grand Find (tel 24 20 20).

Les Villas du Lagon: 28 rue du Lagon, L'Hermitage (tel 33 34 46), breakfast FF85.

Vacoa: 54 rue Antoine de Bertin (tel 24 12 48).

Furnished Flats. There are more than 60 and vary from FF180-500. Among them are:

Auberge des Deux Domes: 17 Chemin de la Vanille (tel 24 46 29).

Duo d'Etoiles: 38 Avenue de Bourbon (tel 24 00 46).

Bungalows du Voyageur: 7 Allée des Flamboyants, L'Eperon (tel 55 80 73).

Kitoko Locations: close to the lagoon, five bungalows, 2 rue Lacaussade, La Saline les Bains (tel 33 81 81, fax 33 81 82).

Les Badamiers: 27 rue des Badamiers (tel 33 82 79).

Les Boucaniers: near the beach at Boucan Canot, 15 studios and apartments, 29 Route de la Plage (tel 24 23 89, fax 24 46 95).

L'Ilot Vert: five apartments, 1 rue des Salines (tel 33 92 11, fax 33 92 12).

Meubles Guyot: close to town centre and beach, kitchenette, TV, English spoken, 6 Lotissement Souris Blanche, Trois Bassins (tel 65 15 38, fax 33 92 37, e-mail: neguyot@oceanes.fr).

Paul and Virginie's: in the town centre, rue du St Alexis, Residence Diane, Appartment 8 (tel 29-4856, fax 65-9140).

Residence Ikebana: 32a, rue des Chenes, Trou d'Eau (tel 33-1435).

Villa Etoile de Mer: 76 rue A Lacaussade (tel 24 69 92).

EATING OUT

For excellent fish and seafood dishes try *Brasserie du Port*, at St Gilles harbour (Rue des Brisants, tel 24 02 02). Nearby are other seafood restaurants offering the same sort of menu, but at around twice the price.

Chez Loulou: 84-86 rue de Général de Gaulle (tel 24 46 36 for the restaurant, and 24 40 41 for the boutique). Is a gift shop, boulangerie, patisserie and restaurant all rolled into one, and it's something of a local landmark in St Gilles.

Other than the ones in hotels, you can choose from another 80 or more restaurants.

For Creole:

Authentique: 181 rue Général de Gaulle (tel 33 00 70).

Mangouste: 24 Avenue de Bourbon (tel 24 57 26).

Le Paille en Queue: at the Casino de St Gilles, Hermitage (tel 24 55 38).

Varangue des Roches Noires: 21 rue de la Poste (tel 24 01 12).

Zingade: Hermitage (tel 33 84 12).

European cuisine is served at:

Au Coin de Pêche: Place Paul Julius Bénard (tel 24 01 14).

Chez Nous: 122 rue de Général de Gaulle (tel 24 08 08).

La Citerne: Village Artisanal de l'Eperon (tel 55 52 70).

Copacabana: 20 rue des Mouettes (tel 24 16 31).

Native: Place Paul Julius Bénard (tel 33 19 34).

Planch'Alizes Quai Ouest: Plage de la Saline les Bains (tel 24 62 61).

Italian food at:

Laetitia: Place Paul Julius Bénard (tel 24 49 64).

Napoli: 2 rue des Dodos (tel 33 91 33).

Piccolo: rue du Général de Gaulle (tel 24 51 51).

Oriental food:

P'Tit Grec at Centre Commercial le Forum (tel 24 50 31).

Auberge du Bonheur: tel 24 09 97.

Palais de L'Orient: Route Nationale 1 (tel 24 68 99 0).

Grills are on the menu at:

Ecumeur: 122 rue Général de Gaulle (tel 33 04 05).

Elixir: 15 rue de la Plage (tel 33 04 53).

Hacienda Cocobeach: Place de l'Hermitage (tel 33 81 43).

ENTERTAINMENT

The **Théâtre de Plein Air** (Route du Theatre, tel 24 47 71, fax 24 38 22), is an open-air theatre with seating for 1,000 people. It is open from March to December and features concerts, dance shows, plays, and films. The ticket office is open from Monday to Friday 10am to 6.30pm, Saturday 11am to 8.30pm. There is also a cinema, the **Grand Écran** at Zac de l'Hermitage (tel 24 46 66).

If you are into boogying the night away there are lots of nightclubs, including:

Dancing des Roches Noires: Rue du Général de Gaulle (tel 24 44 15).

Le Moulin du Tango: 9 Avenue des Mascareignes, L'Hermitage (tel 24 53 90).

Le Privé: Avenue du Gal de Gaulle, Route Nationale (tel 24 04 17).

Le Pussy Cat: 1 rue des Iles Eparses (tel 24 05 11).

Le Swing: Route Nationale, Grand Fond (tel 24 45 98).

You'll find pubs and cabaret at **Chez Nous** (122 rue du Gal de Gaulle, tel 24 08 08); **Mamounia** (50 Avenue du Gal de Gaulle tel 24 09 99); **Marlin** at the Hotel le Maharani in Boucan Canot, and **Piccolo** (99 rue de Général de Gaulle, tel 24 51 51).

There are two theatres: the **Theatre Komela** (125 rue du Général Lambert, tel 34 79 94); and **Le Séchoir** (28 rue Adrien Lagourgue, Piton St Leu, tel 34 31 38).

SHOPPING

At **Jacques Hutin** (2 Mail de Rodrigues, tel 24 44 91), you can buy postcards, posters, guides. It is open from 9.30am to 12.30pm and 3.30pm to 7.30pm. Closed Sunday and Monday morning. **Patisserie Loïk Olivier** (5 rue de la Plage, tel 24 33 73, fax 24 37 78), is a French pastry shop where all the pastries are made with local products. It is open Monday to Friday from 6.30am to 12.30pm and 3pm to 7pm. **La Tee-Shirterie** offers an incredible choice of 5,000 T-shirts, swimsuits and beach-wear at Le Forum in the town centre (tel 24 31 88). **Taka Maka**, at 4 rue de la Plage (tel 24 47 47), has the same sort of gear.

Mathieu Creations, sells handicrafts made from flowers. It is open on Wednesday from 2pm to 5pm, Papier Antaimoro, 10 Route Nationale 1, Saline les Bains (tel/fax 33 97 45). The **Village Artisanal de L'Eperon**, exhibits and sells pottery, ceramics, silkscreen prints, watercolours, dried flowers, handicrafts, furniture, and there's also an art gallery. It is open Monday to Saturday from 9am to noon and 2pm to 6pm, Route du Theatre, rue Leconte de Lisle, Village de l'Eperon (tel 22 73 01).

ST LEU

Is renowned for its **surfing** spots and is a regular venue for international surfing competitions. Apart from its surfing and **diving** opportunities St Leu also has some places of interest to visitors. One of these, the **turtle farm**, is not everyone's cup of tea. The church of **Notre Dame de la Salette** was built in 1760 and is one of the oldest churches on Réunion. Water in the nearby waterfall is regarded as holy. There is an annual pilgrimage on 19 September to the chapel to commemorate the fact that St Leu was spared the cholera epidemic of 1859 which devastated the populations of St Denis and St Louis. In the town is the **Church of Colimacons**, from which you can get some splendid views of the coast.

Coral Turtle Farm at Pointe des Châteaux, is a breeding centre, supplying the island with turtle meat and shell. The marine turtle breeding programme encompasses 7,000-10,000 turtles, ranging from hatchlings to six-year-olds. A curio shop sells turtle products, such as turtle belts, tortoiseshell bracelets and earrings, and tinned turtle stew. The farm complies with international regulations on the protection of marine turtles and has developed a discovery and awareness programme which recounts the origin of sea turtles, their biological features and various species. The farm is open every day, including public holidays, from 9am to 6pm. Entrance is FF30 (tel 34 81 10, fax 34 76 87).

On the Route des Colimacons is **Le Jardin Naturel** ('Natural Garden') which overlooks St Leu and has a botanical path devoted to Réunion's natural environment. There is a tree nursery and several hundred plant species, including such rare flowers as the desert rose, as well as a collection of young palms from all over the world, and a collection of succulents from America, Africa and Madagascar. There's a nursery where more than 500 species of tropical plants are for sale (tel/fax 24 71 30, e-mail: natural@guetali.fr).

Set in an agricultural estate founded at the end of the 19th century, the **Mascarin National Botanical Conservatory** is a green showcase for Réunion's flora, with gardens and arboretums housing medicinal plants, spices, palms, and bamboos set out on 17 acres (7 ha). It is open every day except Monday, from 9am to 5pm. Entrance for adults is FF25, children FF10, Domaine des Colimacons (tel 24 92 27, fax 24 85 63).

The **Stella Matutina Agricultural and Industrial Museum** between St Leu and Piton St Leu, is a former sugar factory, with exhibitions on four levels representing the economic, social and cultural history of the island from the 16th century to the present. There is a research area (multimedia, photo library), boutique, restaurant, and picnic area. It is open every day except Monday, from 9.30am to 5.30pm. Entrance is FF40 for adults, FF20 for children, Allée des Flamboyants (tel 34 16 24, fax 34 12 66). The *Stella* restaurant at the museum is open every day except Monday, from 11am to 3pm (tel 34 07 15).

Between the Stella Matutina Agricultural and Industrial Museum and the Stella village is the **Réunion Ostrich Farm** on 10 acres (4 ha) of savannah. You can walk around the pens and look at the ostriches and emus. Ostrich meat is available for lunch on Saturday and Sunday (bookings necessary). The farm is open every day from 9am to 6pm (6.30pm in summer). Admission is FF25 (tel 34 00 05, fax 35 31 66).

About 3 miles (4 km) south of St Leu are the salt marshes of **Pointe du Sel**, where salt is still produced by traditional manual methods. There's an admission charge of FF10, and you can buy salt from a shop there (tel 34 27 88, fax 34 27 87). Near Pointe du Sel is **Le Souffleur**, or blowhole, which can spout an impressive geyser if sea conditions are right. It's best seen at night when there's a full moon.

ACCOMMODATION
Classified Hotels. There are two three-star hotels charging from FF350-450 (£34-43/US$50-63) a night for a double room:

Iloha (three stars Anthurium Group) Pointe des Chateaux (tel 34 89 89, fax 34 89 90). Close to the ocean, in a 6-acre (2.5 ha) park, overlooking the bay famous for its surfing, 50 bungalows for 2-6 people with kitchenette, and 14 double rooms, two tennis courts. Restaurant serves Creole and Mediterranean cuisine, open-air bar at the swimming pool, breakfast FF60.

Paladien Apolonia (three stars) Boulevard Bonnier (tel 34 62 62, fax 34 61 61). Near the sea, 128 rooms, activities organised every day free of charge (surfing, mountain biking, aquaerobics). *Apolonia Paladien* restaurant serves Creole, Chinese, Indian and French cuisine. Evening entertainment from Tuesday to Sunday. Boutique, billiards, fitness room, breakfast included.

Further south at **Les Avirons** is *Les Fougeres* (two stars, Anthurium Group; 53 Route des Merles, tel 38 32 96, fax 38 30 26), in the western upper reaches of Le Tévelave, 15 rooms, restaurant, daily barbecue, buffet lunch on Sunday, breakfast FF30.

Non-Classified Hotels. Rate varies around FF300:
Centre de Vacances et de Loisirs: 9 Allée Bonnier (tel 34 74 19).
Les Pêcheurs: 27 Avenue des Alizés (tel 34 91 25), has six bungalows.
Trou de Jarre: 28 Chemin Vaudeville (tel 54 80 26), has two bungalows.

Furnished Flats cost between FF150-280:
Aux Battants de Lames: 10 rue du Général Lambert (tel/fax 34 80 18), four bungalows.
Bungalows Murat: 89 Chemin Dubuisson (tel 34 85 04, fax 34 75 71).
On the same road are *Au Clin d'Ceil de L'Ocean:* tel 34 44 21; and *Sci Sycomore:* tel/fax 25 82 12.
Caze'Oceane: 6b Chemin Mutel la Chaloupe (tel 54 89 40).
Le Paille en Queue: 153a Chemin Dubuisson (tel/fax 34 46 45). 3 miles (5 km) from the town centre, English spoken.
Residence des Alizes: 48b Avenue des Alizes (tel 34 89 12, fax 34 83 99).
Villa Anassane: 57a Chemin Casimir (tel/fax 34 02 06).
Villa Laurence: 10a Chemin Albert Hoareau (tel 34 06 29, fax 26 83 76).
There are also self-catering gîtes and B&Bs (see *Accommodation* in *Practical Information* page 227).

EATING OUT
Creole and European food served at:
Auberge du Relais: 127 Route Nationale (tel 34 81 85).
Cabane au Sel: Pointe au Sel (tel 34 30 71).
Case Creole: 83 rue A Bègue (tel 54 74 10).
Lagon: 2a rue du Lagon (tel 34 79 13).

There's Asian food at:
Bienvenue: 95 rue A Bégue, La Chaloupe (tel 54 89 56). *Palais d'Asie:* 5 rue de l'Etang (tel 34 80 41).
Souffleur: Route Nationale (tel 26 61 03).

SHOPPING
Art Ecaille designs, manufactures, and sells hand-made jewellery. It is open Monday to Friday from 8am to noon and 1pm to 5pm, closed on Saturday and Sunday, 14 Cité des Pêcheurs (tel 34 71 24, fax 34 84 36).

SPORT AND RECREATION

The west coast offers a wide range of sporting activities, especially in and on the water and in the air. Deep-sea fishing, scuba-diving and snorkelling, and surfing are popular, and you can go paragliding and hang-gliding.

DEEP-SEA FISHING
Hire boats, departing from **St Gilles** harbour:
Abaco: skipper Joël Leguen (tel 24 36 10).
Abalone: skipper Marc Lagadec (tel 22 72 72).
Alopia: skipper Modéran Delamarre (tel 68 44 06).
Blue Marlin: skipper Marcel You-Seen (tel 65\ 22 35).
Maevasion: skipper Jean-Paul Bellour (tel 85 23 46).
Octopus II: skipper Thierry Raynaud (tel 34 39 17).
From **Le Port** yachting harbour:
Jolly Jumper I: skipper Guy Morvan (tel 24 48 94).
Marine Océn: skipper Alix Maillot (tel 43 98 35).
From **St Pierre** harbour:
Autres Mers: tel 86 64 34.
Rapetou II: skipper Karl Gonthier (tel 86 47 64).

SCUBA-DIVING

St Gilles les Bains
Aress: Centre de Plongée Beuchat (tel/fax 24 32 79). Offers all-level training sessions, FF200 for first exploring dive.
Bleu Marine Réunion: Port de Plaisance (tel 24 22 00, fax 24 30 04, mobile 0262-858083). For first timers, exploring and training sessions at all levels, night diving, children diving and snorkelling, FF210 for first exploration dive, English-speaking instructor.
Cereps: Enceinte Portuaire (tel 24 40 12, fax 44 24 86, mobile 0262-857092). First dives and exploring.
Club Subaquatique Réunionnais (CIP): (tel 24 34 11) first and exploration dives for all levels.
Corail Plongée: Zone Portuaire (tel 24 37 25, fax 24 46 38, mobile 0262-861482).

Initiation, and underwater exploration, training courses, FF200 for first dive.
Manta Plongée: Plage de la rue Brisants (tel/fax 24 37 10). Beginners, all level exploring, diving school, FF200 for first exploring dive.
Mascareignes Plongée: Enceinte Portuaire (tel 44 27 74, mobile 0262-855755). Diving equipment for hire, training, initiation dives, FF160 for first dive.
O Sea Bleu: Enceinte Portuaire (tel/fax 33 16 15). All levels of teaching, underwater cameras for hire, FF200 for exploration dive.

St Leu

Abyss Plongée: 7 Boulevard Bonnier (tel 34 79 79, fax 34 72 06). Initiation, exploration dives, training courses, FF200 a dive.
Atlantis: Route des Colimacons, Pointe des Châteaux (tel/fax 34 77 47, mobile 0262-653038, e-mail: atlantis@guetali.fr). First time divers, training courses.
Réunion Plongee: 13 ZA Pointe des Châteaux (tel/fax 34 77 77, mobile 0262-856637). First timers, children diving, night diving.
St Leu Plongée: Pointe des Châteaux (tel/fax 34 73 65). Initiation diving, night dives on request, FF200 for first dive.

SURFING

St Gilles les Bains

École de Body Board et Surf des Roches Noires: 4a Lot. des Charmilles (tel/fax 24 63 28, mobile 0262-860059). Offers initiation, advanced and competition training courses for surfing, body-boarding, and long-boarding. Equipment is available, transfer from hotel to surfing spot, rates on request.
Trois Bassins Surfing School: (tel 66 02 45) has initiation and training sessions, open throughout the year, transfer from hotel to surfing spot, introductory sessions cost about FF200.

You can hire or buy surfing gear – Quiksilver, Billabong, Strussy – at **High Surf**, 15 rue de la Plage des Roches Noires (tel 24 24 24).

THE SOUTH COAST

The south coast is known locally as the wild coast, although it doesn't really live up to this name until you get to the Grands Bois area, between St Pierre and St Joseph and follow the coast around to Tremblet, in the shadow of the Piton de la Fournaise ('Furnace Peak') volcano. **St Pierre** is the capital of the south, and other significant towns on the coast are **Etang-Salé les Bains**, **St Louis**, **St Joseph**, and **St Philippe**. Inland from St Pierre is **Entre-Deux**, a hopping off point for mountain trails. Most of the beaches in this part of the island are black sand, where they are not pebbly, although there is the odd white stretch.

ETANG-SALÉ

Although this is a holiday town, it is in an area that is very much an agricultural community. The most popular area for visitors is the wonderful **Etang-Salé national forest** with its picnic spots and its 5-acre (2 ha) **Bird Sanctuary**, which contains exotic as well as indigenous species. **Le Gouffre** ('abyss') is an enormous jagged crack in the black lava cliffs south of the town, where waves roar and foam up like a whale spouting. The 12-acre (5 ha) **Croc Parc** (Route Forestière, between Etang-Salé and Etang-Salé les Bains; tel 91 40 41, fax 91 41 00) is in the middle of a forest planted with indigenous trees and has nearly 200 Nile crocodiles in four pools, ranged according to their age and size. You can watch them being fed, or you can admire a pool and garden full of peacocks, pheasants, swans, and ducks. There's a boutique selling croc souvenirs. The park is open daily from 9.30am to 5.30pm in winter, until 6.30pm in summer, admission for adults is FF40.

ACCOMMODATION
Classified Hotels.
Le Caro Beach Village: (three stars) 2 Avenue de l'Ocean (tel 91 79 79, fax 91 79 80). Close to the beach in a large tropical garden, 44 rooms, 12 flats, from FF420 (£40/US$60) a night for a double room, breakfast FF60.

Furnished Flats
Les Grains D'Sable: 5 rue du Roussillon (tel 27 11 46, fax 27 18 05).
Pierre Wolter: 42 Avenue de Bretagne (tel/fax 26 65 67).

Camping
At *Camping Municipal* rue Octave Bénard, Etang-Salé (tel 91 75 86), a site costs from FF80 a day; more if you want electricity, water is available on site. You'll need your own tent and there is no restriction on length of stay.

EATING OUT
Apart from restaurants in the hotels there are lots of other restaurants, serving mainly French, Creole, and Asian food.
Carangue: serves Creole and Asian, 1 rue Payet (tel 91 70 87).
Ete Indien: European and Creole dishes, Route Nationale (tel 26 67 33).
Etoile du Sud: Creole cuisine, 66 Avenue Raymond Barre (tel 26 51 49).
Fishbone: 56 Route Nationale (tel 91 70 82) European meals.
Ripaille: Avenue Raymond Barre (tel 26 36 16) Creole and Asian food.

ST LOUIS
This is not a popular tourist area as unending fields of sugarcane provide a monotonous, if lush, landscape broken only by the chimney of the region's only sugar mill. The best thing the town itself offers is the bus, or road, to the cirque of **Cilaos**.

Outside the town, however, there are some places of interest. The **House of India** ashram, or cultural and spiritual centre, houses a display of Indian musical instruments and a library of religious and philosophical books. There are fire-walking ceremonies here in February. It is situated on the road to Gol, where you'll find **Le Gol** sugar factory. You can arrange to visit the factory (tel 91 05 47 extension 308, or 26 10 12). The tiny village of **Les Makes** is 9 miles (15 km) up the road above St Louis and has an **observatory** at 3,281 ft (1,000 m). Book for night astronomy sessions at the Plaine des Makes Observatory (tel 37 86 83, fax 37 87 24, e-mail: obs.astronomique@wanadoo.fr). Admission is FF25 for adults, FF15 for children under 12. Guided tours on Saturdays and Sundays, and weekdays for groups are available.

Another 7 miles (11 km) into the heights from Les Makes will reward you with an exceptional view of Cilaos cirque from a viewpoint appropriately called *La Fênetre* ('The Window'). The village of **La Rivière** on the way back to town is noted as a *Centre Artisanal du Bois*, where local craftsmen turn out excellent furniture, specialising in reproductions of French colonial pieces (tel 39 06 12). Another little hill town, **Les Avirons**, is also known for its reproduction furniture, as well as canework. To the east of St Louis is the broad **Rivière St Etienne**, where a lagoon is a favourite local weekend leisure spot, especially for *le pique-nique*.

ENTRE-DEUX

A quiet holiday village famed for its concentration of Creole houses and exotic gardens, Entre-Deux takes its name from the fact that it lies between two rivers. The village is the start of several **hiking paths** leading to the top of **Dimitile** mountain at 6,027 ft (1,837 m). This is a hike only for the fit as even with a dawn start it takes most of the day to get up and down again. The view of Cilaos cirque alone makes it worth the effort. Don't forget to check the weather forecast before setting out. Guides are available. Contact the local tourist office in the centre of the village (tel 39 69 80).

There are also guided tours around local gardens and the Creole houses. The **Exotica Garden** (tel 35 65 45, fax 35 65 44) on Route de Entre-Deux has collections of flowers, 800 varieties of cactus and succulent plants, and 80 different palms. It's set in a 12-acre (5 ha) coconut grove and is a fragrant world of more than 8,000 plant species. There are also geological displays, as well as orchid and anthurium greenhouses. Fruit drinks are served at a refreshment stall.

ACCOMMODATION

Non-Classified Accommodation: ranging in price from FF180-300.
Case Manin: 115 rue Payet (tel 39 69 60).
Dijoux Christianne: 31 Chemin Grand Fond Intérieur (tel 39-6956).
Ilet Creole: rue Fontaine (tel 39 67 19).

Furnished Flats
Les Pluies d'Or: costs from FF160 (tel/fax 39 62 30).
In nearby Ravine des Cabris:
Lisette D'Eurveilher: which costs FF1,200 a week, is at 29 Route Départementale 27 (tel 49 44 10).
Le Mahavel: costing FF2,520 (£242/US$365) a week for six people, 19 Chemin Lucien (tel 37 28 93, e-mail: jl.defaud@wanadoo.fr).

EATING OUT

Bar le Squash: Ravine des Citrons (tel 39 68 68); *Coq:* rue de Commerce (tel 39 55 69); *Escale le Dimitile:* rue Jean Lauret (tel 39 65 27) all serve a variety of dishes.
Le Grillardin: 4 rue Hubert Delisle (tel 39 68 68) serves Creole and European cuisine.
At Ravine des Cabris are:
Case: 27 Chemin Rural (tel 49 55 31); and *Le Domaine:* 76 Chemin Recherchant (tel 49 53 67) which serves Creole food.

SHOPPING

At Entre-Deux you can buy local products from **D Grondin**, 188 Route du Bras-Long (tel 39 63 10); **Jardin Gourmand** 31 Chemin Grand Fond Intérieur (tel 39 69 56); **AR Ledoyen** 10 Impasse du Radier (tel 39 61 79); **MA Richauvet** 8 Chemin des Rêves (tel 39 69 20; and **V Tetia** 137 Chemin Jean Lauret (tel 39 56 51).

LE TAMPON

The largest town inland from St Pierre, it's on the road to the Plaine des Cafres, the main starting point for a drive to the volcano. Apart from this, it's simply a town on the road, although it is styled as the island's **geranium capital**.

ACCOMMODATION

Classified Hotels. There are two one-star hotels which cost about FF250 (£24/US$36) a night for a double room.

L'Outre Mer: 8 rue de Bourbon (tel 57 30 30, fax 57 29 29). Between the sea and the mountain, 35 rooms, breakfast FF50.

Les Orchidées: 3 rue Jules Ferry (tel 27 11 15, fax 27 77 03). In a quiet district at 2,067 ft (630 m), 10 rooms, restaurant, FF250 a night for a double room, breakfast FF25.

There is only one **non-classified hotel** in Le Tampon:

Sud Hotel: 106 rue Marius and Ary Leblond, Le Tampon (tel 27 07 90). FF150, breakfast FF25.

Furnished Flats costs from FF1,200-1,600 (£115-154/US$174-232) a week.

Chez Madame Mézino: 81 rue Alexandre Fleming (tel/fax 27 22 38).

Chez Orlando: 3 Allée St Exupéry, Trois Mares (tel 27 12 35). 10 minutes from the town, private parking.

Gîte Tamponna: 62 Chemin Epidor Hoareau, Trois Mares (tel/fax 27 38 22), 10 minutes from the town centre.

Le Ficus; 31 Chemin Léon (tel 27 76 56), about a mile (2 km) from the town.

Les Palmiers: 8 rue Andre Malraux (tel/fax 59 74 49), private parking.

EATING OUT

Most of the restaurants serve **Creole and European food**:

Mambo: 7 rue Docteur Henri Roussel (tel 57 22 00).

Au Comptoir de la Crêpe: 275 rue Hubert Delisle (tel 27 60 23).

Fiesta: has Italian meals, 186 rue Hubert Delisle (tel 57 43 59).

For **Chinese** try *Le Bongo:* 182 rue Hubert Delisle (tel 57 69 69).

For **Asian** *Tonkinoise:* 158 rue Marius and Ary Leblond (tel 27 09 14).

ST PIERRE

The town, one of Réunion's largest communes, is a mix of a pulsing seaside resort and a more ramshackle commercial and industrial centre going about its everyday business. It is, however, the portal to the wilder regions of the south, and its yacht-filled **old port**, **lagoon** and a fine stretch of **white sand beach** add to its interest. In the 22 miles (35 km) from St Pierre to St Philippe, where the geographical south ends, there's a succession of inviting coves and lagoons, and attractive villages, both on the coast and inland. St Pierre has put to good use several of its old French East India Company buildings. An old coffee warehouse built in 1736 now houses the **Hôtel de Ville**, or town hall, on rue Méziaire Guignard. The St Pierre *Médiathèque* ('Library and Media Centre') is also in former company premises built in 1765. St Pierre has a lively **market** selling food, handicrafts and souvenirs on rue Victoire le Vigoureux, not far from the seafront. It's open Monday to Saturday from 6am to 7pm and Sunday from 7am to noon. If you are interested in rum and the way it's made, you can visit **Isautier House**, open Monday to Friday, from 8am to noon and from 2pm to 4pm (tel 96 11 96).

Réunion's biggest and most famous mosque, the **Mosque Atyaboul-Massajid**, is on rue Francois de Mahy. Although a modern construction – it was built in 1972 – the mosque has an impressive entrance and an interior remarkable for its calligraphy, the work of Comorian sculptor Ali Lazindrou.

Most of Réunion's cemeteries seem to have a strange fascination and the one in St Pierre is no exception. Here you'll find the tomb of **Sitarane**, an infamous bandit and black magic sorcerer who for all the stories of his murderous activities is still remembered by the Creoles with awe, if not affection. He was executed for his crimes in 1911. The cemetery is at the western end of the beachfront Boulevard Hubert Delisle, where his grave is a magnet for the same sort of offerings that the pirate tomb of Olivier le Vasseur attracts in the marine cemetery at St Paul. The **Vieux Domaine** ('Old Estate') at Ravine des Cabris has a magnificent orchard behind a charming old Creole house. Leisure options include ox-cart and pony rides, a *ti-train* ('little train') ride, bowls, and a traditional village. Fruits and other products are on sale. Guided visits from Tuesday to Sunday from 10am to noon and 2pm to 6pm. There's also a Creole restaurant which is open on Sunday. Admission to the estate is FF25 for adults (tel 49 53 67, fax 49 86 00).

Outside the town at La Ravine Blanche is the **Tamil temple** of *Narassinga-Péroumal-Kovil*. The picturesque village of **Terre Sainte** ('Holy Land') is a little fishing port surrounded by banyan trees.

Further along the coast towards St Joseph are the **beaches** of Grande Bois, Grande Anse, and **Manapany les Bains**, a popular spot because of its protected natural rock swimming pool and its gourmet restaurant, *Le Manapany*. At Grande Anse you can see some ancient **lime kilns** which have been carefully restored. A little path leads up to a hillock clothed in casuarina trees from which you'll get a good view of the rocky coast and **Petite Ile**, the only island off Réunion's coast. This rocky islet is a haven for a colony of nesting seabirds. On the slopes above the coastal road is the village and area also known as Petite Ile. Vetiver grows in uplands here, an Indian grass whose roots are used to produce an aromatic essence. Its long leaves are also used as thatch and to make hats and bags.

ACCOMMODATION

Classified Hotels. These range from two to three stars and vary in price from FF230-750 (£22-72/US$33-109) for double rooms.

Alizé Plage: (two stars) Boulevard Hubert Delisle (tel 35 22 21, fax 25 80 63). At the beach, seven Creole-style rooms with views of sea and mountain, restaurant, pub with music, themed evenings, breakfast FF50.

Les Chrysalides: (two stars) 6 rue Caumont (tel 25 75 64, fax 25 22 19). On the outskirts of St Pierre, near the lagoon, 16 rooms, breakfast FF35.

Le Demotel: (three stars) 8 Allée des Lataniers, Grand Bois (tel 31 11 60, fax 31 17 51). Between St Pierre and Grand Bois beaches, along a cliff with superb views, 30 bungalows, jacuzzi, pool, helicopter flights, evening entertainment, *Grill Fish* restaurant serves Creole and European cuisine. Breakfast FF50.

Le Nathania: (three stars) 12 rue Francois de Mahy (tel 25 04 57, fax 35 27 05). A short walk from the beach, port, casino and night clubs, 9 rooms, restaurant open every day, breakfast FF50.

Le Sterne-Protea: (three stars Protea Group), Boulevard Hubert Delisle (tel 25 70 00, fax 35 01 41, e-mail: sterne@guetali.fr). On the seafront, near the harbour, 50 rooms, the *Vanille et Lambrequin* restaurant serves Creole and French cuisine, and the *Piscine* brásserie at the swimming pool has delicious hot and cold buffets, pub, casino next door, French billiards, evening entertainment three days a week, breakfast FF60.

Le Suffren: (three stars) 14 rue Suffren (tel 35 19 10, fax 25 99 43). In the city centre, near the beachfront boulevard, 18 rooms, hiking, deep-sea fishing, private car park, bar, restaurant serves Creole and Asian food. Breakfast FF55

Non-Classified Hotels range in price from FF150-200, extra charge for breakfast FF15-35.

Le Tamarin: 64 rue Père Favron, Ravine Blanche (tel 25 30 60).

Star Hotel: 88 rue Conde, Ravine des Cabris (tel 27 20 69).

Tropic Hotel: 2 rue Auguste Babet (tel 25 90 70).

Furnished Flats. There are more than 10 and vary in price from FF100-250 a night, among them:

Au 'Ti Bru: 13 rue Francois Isautier (tel 96 01 41).

Chez Papa Daya: 27 rue du Four à Chaux (tel 25 64 87).

Les Adelaides: 144 Route Nationale, Terre Sainte (tel 25 86 75).

Les Meubles St Pierrois: 4a rue St Rose (tel 25 08 27, fax 35 36 28).

Residence Vacances Isabelle: 27 Boulevard Hubert Delisle (tel 38 58 88).

Tropic Loc: 3 rue Amiral Lacaze (tel 25 78 32).

EATING OUT

There are more than 60 places to eat in and around town from ice-cream parlours and hamburger joints to gourmet restaurants.

For **Creole and European dishes** try:

Alize Plage: Boulevard Hubert Delisle (tel 35 22 21).

Le Bistroquet: 8 Boulevard Hubert Delisle (tel 25 04 67).

Le Retro: 34 Boulevard Hubert Delisle (tel 25 33 06).

Caris et Rougails: 64 rue Caumont (tel 25 87 22).

Le Flamboyant: corner of Désiré Barquisseau and Four à Chaux (tel 35 02 15).

Le Pierrefonds: Route de l'Entre-Deux (tel 49 84 05).

Italian food at *Cabanon:* Boulevard Hubert Delisle (tel 25 71 46).

Caprice d'Italie: 7 rue Archambaud (tel 96 36 60).

Dolce Vita: rue Marius and Ary Leblond (tel 25 46 37).

Osteria on the corner of Archambaud and Marius and Ary Leblond (tel 25 14 15).

Asian food is served at:

Bons Enfants: 124 rue des Bons Enfants (tel 25 08 27).

Coq de Chine: 7 rue Auguste Babet (tel 25 05 54).

Restaurant Pekin: 49 rue Luc Lorion (tel 25 36 09).

Restaurant Thai: 54 rue Caumont (tel 35 30 95).

Restaurant Agadir: at 5 rue August Babet (tel 35 32 45).

Grilled meals can be found at:

Case Bretonne: 7 rue Archambaud (tel 35 33 61).

Goutali: 2 rue Marius and Ary Leblond (tel 25 04 78).

SHOPPING

The South Region Tourist Office in St Pierre has a wide range of local crafts, books, maps, and postcards. It is open Monday to Friday from 9am to 5.45pm and Saturday 9am to 3.45pm in summer, and Monday to Friday from 8.30am to 5.15pm, Saturday 9am to 3.45pm in winter. It's in a red tin-roofed building called the **Café de la Gare**. Walk through and there's a toilet and the Laurent Perrier snack bar and restaurant (17 Boulevard Hubert Delisle, tel 25 02 36, fax 25 71 19).

ST JOSEPH

This little village of 26,000 people is pretty in a dilapidated sort of way, with colourful lilliputian houses clustered at the mouth of the magnificent valley of the Rivière des Remparts in an area known for bags and basketwork made from the fronds of the *vacoa* (pandanus). The best view of the Rivière des Remparts is from the head of the valley at **Nez de Boeuf**, 19 miles (30 km) to the north on the road to the Piton de la Fournaise volcano. At **Langevin** an impressive road winds its way up a valley, alongside a number of pretty waterfalls. The road ends at **Grand Galet**, where a hiking trail runs up to the volcano.

The **Plaine des Gregues** is the heart of the island's saffron industry. The fine golden power produced is not really saffron but *curcuma*, or turmeric. **La Maison du Curcuma** ('Turmeric House') 14 Chemin du Rond (tel 37 54 66, fax 37 61 16), is dedicated to this spice produced from the surrounding fields of yellow crocus. You can also taste candied *tangor*, a type of local orange, and sweet-and-sour ginger, depending on the season. A range of products and recipes are on sale. It's open seven days a week from 9am to noon and from 1.30pm to 5.00pm.

ACCOMMODATION
Non-Classified Hotel
Manapany Bay Bungalow: 170 Boulevard de l'Ocean (tel 64 94 91), three bungalows at FF1,800 (£173/US$261) a week each.

Furnished Flats from FF1,500-2,200 a week.
Le Bengali: 17 rue Raphaël Babet (tel 56 54 01).
L'Eau Forte: 137a Boulevard de l'Ocean, Manapany les Bains (tel 56 32 84, e-mail: eau-forte@wanadoo.fr).
La Villa du Barrage Chez Franco: 21 Route de Grand Galet, Rivière Langevin (tel/fax 37 22 45).

EATING OUT
Crêperie de Grand Coude: 9 rue Théophile Gauthier (tel 56 25 90).
Le Benjoin: 114 Route de la Passerelle (tel 56 23 90) Creole cuisine.
La Case: 31 rue Leconte Delisle (tel 56 41 66) European and Creole cuisine.
Les Hirondelles: rue Raphaël Babet (tel 56 17 88) Creole and Asian meals.
Le Tajine: 23 Chemin de la Marine (tel 37 32 51) Oriental food.
Pizzeria Bella Attina: 109 rue Marcel Pagnol (tel 37 35 67) Italian.

SHOPPING
The **Association Vetiver** (Maison de Quartier Bézave, 180 CD3; tel 37 62 58) is open on Wednesday to Friday from 9am to 4pm; and the **Co-op Miel** sells honey. It is open on Monday to Friday from 9am to noon and 2pm to 5pm, and can be found at Zone Artisanale des Grègues (tel 56 00 29). You can also buy local products at **les Fleurettes** Route Nationale 2, Langevin (tel 56 59 86); and at **Pisciculture de Langevin** Grand Galet (tel 56 00 65).

ST PHILIPPE
A small village at the southernmost tip of Réunion, St Philippe is where the road turns the corner to head up the east coast back to St Denis, 57 miles (92 km) away. On the way is a volcanic promontory, called *Cap Méchant* ('Vicious Cape') which offers a view of why it's called the wild coast. The extensive lush green vegetation thins out in places until you are past the lava-scorched area below the volcano. On either side of St Philippe are **Les Puits**, four mysterious wells excavated in the lava. Nobody knows why they were dug or who made them. Also in this area of blackened lava is **Notre Dame de la Paix**, a cave next to the road which contains an altar and rows of pews. Several trails lead into the **Mare Longue Forest**, and on the botanical path you'll see some of the last *bois de couleurs* ('coloured woods') of Réunion. The **Mare Longue botanical reserve** contains 173 acres (70 ha) of tropical forest, with giant trees with such names as *bois de pomme* ('potato tree'), *bois de fer batard* ('pig-iron tree') and *joli coeur* ('pretty heart'). St Philippe also maintains a botanical reserve at **Pointe de la Table** in the volcanic Brûlé area.

The south is the production centre for many of the island's spices and essential oils and one place that will give you a better understanding of some of the plants and aromatics used in this industry is the **Spice and Fragrance Garden**, a 7-acre (3 ha) enterprise that has been cultivating them for the past 200 years. Here you'll see some of Réunion's most important tropical plants, such as vanilla, cloves, pepper, cinnamon and cardamom, which grow here in lush, humid surroundings. A guide is on hand to take you around. In season – October to January – you can taste a variety of exotic fruits and watch a manual pollination demonstration of the vanilla orchid. The garden is on the Chemin Forestière de Mare Longue. There are two guided tours a day at 10.30am and 2.30pm. Bookings for these must be made 24 hours in advance, during office hours (9am to 5pm) at the St Philippe Tourist Office (tel 37 10 43/10 97). As you leave St Philippe to start up the east coast you enter the region known as *pays brûlé* ('burnt country'). For several miles there are jagged piles of scoria and petrified rivers of lava along the road which are a reminder that the volcano is still violently active.

ACCOMMODATION
Classified hotel
Le Baril: (two stars Anthurium Group) Route Nationale 2 (tel 37 01 04, fax 37 07 62). Overlooking the ocean, 14 rooms, restaurant serves Creole and Chinese cuisine, swimming pool, FF380 (£36/US$55) a night for a double room.

There are also self-catering gîtes, stop-over and holiday gîtes and B&Bs on the south coast.

EATING OUT
On the way from St Joseph, at Cap Méchant, Basse Vallée:
Le Cap Méchant: (tel 37 08 80) which serves Creole and Asian dishes.
L'Etoile de Mer: (tel 37 04 60) which serves Creole and Chinese cuisine.
Otherwise try:
Carpe-Diem: 71 Route Nationale 2, Le Baril (tel 37 08 76) Creole food.
Chez Laurent: 26 Route Nationale 2, Le Baril (tel 37 03 07) Creole and Asian food.
La Canot: 15b rue Leconte Delisle (tel 37 00 36) European and Creole food.
Le Chamaron: 34 Route Nationale 2 (tel 37 07 07) Creole and Asian meals.
La Marmite du Pêcheur: Route Nationale 2, Ravine Ango (tel 37 01 01) European and Creole cuisine.

SHOPPING
In St Philippe **Escale Bleue** (7 Route Nationale 2, Le Tremblet, tel 37 03 99) is a vanilla processing shop; and on the way to St Philippe at Basse Vallée is the **Association Cass'le Coin**, which sells wickerwork, local baskets (*bertelles*), bags, handbags, hats, and lampshades. It is open Monday to Saturday from 9am to 4pm and Sunday from 1pm to 4pm (rue Labourdonnais, tel 37 09 61, fax 37 04 89). You can also visit **Vacoa Sud Maison de L'Artisanat'** which sells handicrafts made from *vacoa* (palm fibre). It is open daily from 9am to noon and 1pm to 5pm, and has demonstrations on Tuesday and Friday (8 Route Nationale 2, Le Baril, tel 37 10 25).

ENTERTAINMENT
The theatre in **St Pierre** is the **Bato Fou** at rue de la Republique (tel 25 65 01). **Théâtre Luc Donat** is in **Le Tampon** and seats 600 people. On Tuesday, Friday and Saturday there are variety shows, jazz and folk concerts, dance shows, plays, conferences, and exhibitions. There is also an annual humour festival in June. Bookings at the theatre on Monday to Friday 9am to noon and 2pm to 5.45pm, Saturday at 9am to noon. A seat costs between FF40 and FF150, depending on the show, 20 rue Victor Le Vigoureux (tel 27 24 36, fax 57 17 57).

Cinemas
In **St Pierre** there is the **Rex**, rue Auguste Babet (tel 25 01 01); **Roxy**, 53 rue Désiré Barquisseau (tel 35 34 90; and **Salle Moulin a Café**, rue Pasteur, Ravine des Cabris

(tel 49 82 58). At **Entre-Deux** the **OMCT de L'Entre-Deux** is at 115 rue Payet (tel 39 69 60); at **Le Tampon** the **Eden**, 72 Route Hubert Delisle (tel 57 14 89); and at **St Joseph** there's the **Royal** (tel 56 55 59).

Night-Clubs

In **St Pierre** there is **Appolo Night** at 15 Route du Père Maître (tel 49 58 91); **Chapiteau**, (Montvert les Bas, tel 31 00 81) open Saturday and on the eve of public holidays; **Prestige** (15 Route de Bois d'Olives, tel 49 50 18); **Refuge** (Ravine des Cabris, tel 49-5632); and **Star Club** (240 rue Presbytère, tel 35 33 62) open Friday, Saturday and on the eve of public holidays, free admission for women on Fridays.
In **St Joseph**, you'll find the **Le Moulin Rouge** at 52 rue Maréchal Leclerc which is open on Saturday and Sunday (tel 56 27 40).

Pubs and Cabarets

There are lots of pubs in **St Pierre**, some with cabaret, such as **Le Bato Fou**, open every Friday (rue de la Republique, tel 25 65 61); **Cabaret St Jeff** with theme evenings every night (Boulevard Hubert Delisle, tel 25 76 92); **Pub Malone's** (Boulevard Hubert Delisle (tel 25 81 41), a South African pub with bands and music videos, as well as 20 different kinds of beer and an equally formidable range of whisky brands; **L'Endroit** (42 Boulevard Hubert Delisle, tel 96 39 61) a piano bar at Casino du Sud, open from Monday to Saturday from 6pm to 2am; and **Ananas Café** at rue Auguste Babet (tel 96 01 08).

You might also enjoy an evening of **astronomy** at the Observatoire Astronomique des Makes, Les Makes de St Louis (tel 37 86 83).

EAST COAST

ST PHILIPPE TO ST BENOIT

This is *la côte au vent*, the windy side of the island, which has kept it pleasantly undeveloped and agricultural, with a charm all its own. The trade winds mean the coast gets lots of rain. Tropical spices, coffee and, since the first half of the 19th century, sugarcane, have made this fertile, well-watered region a prosperous one. Vanilla is also cultivated extensively, either between the sugarcane stands, or twining around wooden stakes made of candle-wood. A century ago, the harvesting of these huge plantations, especially in the north-east, was extremely labour intensive. After slavery was abolished in 1848 thousands of contract Tamil Indian labourers were brought into Réunion and since 1860 have had a strong influence on the area, which is evident from the many brightly coloured Tamil temples around the countryside. The southern end of the coast is dominated by the **Piton de la Fournaise** ('Furnace Peak') volcano, which from time to time still blows its top to send rivers of molten lava pouring down its flanks to the sea. On one memorable occasion it added an estimated 62-74 acres (25-30 ha) to the size of the island. This explains why you'll find no houses for a considerable distance along the coast in the volcano's preferred path to the sea, and which is why the area is known as 'the burnt country.' Main towns on the east coast between St Philippe and the capital are **St Rose, St Benoit, Bras Panon, St André** and **St Suzanne**.

Several **trails** meander through the Grand Brûlé forest at **Takamaka** and **Tremblet**. Outside Grand Brûlé is a turn-off signposted **Symbiose pour Volcan et Oiseau**, ('Symbiosis for volcano and bird'), which is a weird group of statues mounted on a disused drilling rig near the 1976 lava flow and left by the sculptor to be shaped further by erosion, wind, time, and maybe further eruptions. Between here and the Piton St Rose area you can see some **impressive lava flows**. In one place the 1992 eruption poured lava down the slopes to stop only a few yards from the road. Even more spectacular is the evidence of the April 1977 volcanic eruption which burnt hundreds of acres of forest and destroyed about 30 houses around **Piton St Rose**. In the village itself stands a little pastel-coloured roadside church which religious islanders still regard as the site of a miracle. As the lava bubbled down from the volcano and through the village the flow split into two separate streams around the church, leaving it untouched (the police barracks were also spared). The church, now known as **Notre Dame de la Lave**, still stands surrounded by hardened black lava. Near the village is a beautiful little spot called **Anse des Cascades** ('Waterfall Cove') where colourful fishing boats lie on the hard, surrounded by soothingly quiet groves of vacoa and tall coconut palms. From the water's edge you can see the cascades tumbling down the cliff to the sea. There's a small bar and restaurant, the *Restaurant Anse des Cascades* (tel 47 20 42), where you can relax if you don't want to picnic al fresco. Another pleasant spot at **St Rose** is the village's harbour at La Marine, where Chez Louiso's snack bar stands incongruously next to three old cannons pointing out to sea. On a nearby grassy knoll is a towering black lava stele, a monument to a British naval officer killed in battle when St Rose was attacked by a British fleet in 1809. Between Piton Bellevue and the sea at St Rose is **Bananaland**, which promises to introduce you to the magical universe of the banana, its history, botany, and uses, during a one-hour circuit of the plantation. It's open every day from 10am to 4.30pm and admission is FF25 for adults and FF10 for children (tel 87 21 47). The road to St Anne crosses la Rivière de l'Est by way of a concrete span that runs parallel with the much more attractive old (1894) **Pont d'Anglais** suspension bridge on the seaward side of the road. It's worth a halt to admire this astonishing piece of Victorian era engineering, which was said to have been the longest suspension bridge in the world when it was completed. There are some pleasant grassy picnic spots at either end of the bridge, if you ignore the American-style spray-can graffiti on the new bridge's concrete buttresses.

The village of **St Anne** is noted for what is probably to most unusual church in Réunion, the **Eglise de St Anne**, with a façade that is a rococo confection of cement that calls to mind Disneyland and the Spanish architecture of Gaudí. The lavishly ornamented floral twirls and curlicues were added to the 1857 church by priest Father Dodemberger after he arrived from Alsace in 1922. The church is a proclaimed historical monument and its cherubims, rosettes and crenellations were used to good affect by Francois Truffaut in his film *La Sirène du Mississippi*.

ACCOMMODATION

St Anne has a non-classified hotel *Jorest'Lacase:* 159 Chemin Morange (tel 50 52 75) which costs about FF80 a night. There are also a couple in **St Rose** which cost about FF160 a night: *Le Poisson Rouge:* 503 Route Nationale (tel 47 32 51) breakfast FF20, and *Rose des Laves:* 84 Chemin du Petit Brûle (tel 47 38 77) one bungalow.

In the middle of **St André** next to a shopping centre is the *Ile de France:* 50 rue du Stade (tel 58 18 50, fax 58 18 55) 30 rooms, at FF230 a night, breakfast FF50.

There are also self-catering gîtes and B&Bs on the east coast (see *Accommodation* in *Practical Information*).

EATING OUT
St André

There are a couple of dozen restaurants to choose from. In Champ Borne, Joël Manglou runs a restaurant at his *Ferme Auberge* (1440 Chemin Bel Ombre) where he mixes Creole food with Creole music. Manglou has won local and international prizes for both his cooking and for songs he has written (tel 46-0918).

Creole and European cooking is also available at:

Beau Rivage: Vieille Eglise, Champ Borne (tel 46 08 66).

Champ Borne: 370 Route Champ Borne (tel 46 16 67).

La Coupole: commercial centre (tel 46 94 77).

Printanier: 558 Avenue de Bourbon (tel 46 56 00).

Restaurant du Mât: 1050 Route de Salazie (tel 46 05 59).

Saint-André: 804 rue de la Gare (tel 46 74 31).

Asian food is served at:

Hacienda: 1221 Avenue Ile de France (tel 46 30 05).

Jouvancourt: 433 Chemin Jouvancourt (tel 46 57 15).

Lilas: 587 Avenue Ile de France (tel 46 75 52).

Restaurant du Centre: 52 Chemin Deschanets (tel 46 03 51).

Restaurant Law-Shun: 866 Avenue de Bourbon (tel 46 04 08).

There are also two country inns serving food, the *Auberge le Desert:* Bras des Chevrettes (tel 46 64 43); and *Savriama:* 1085 Chemin 80, Rivière du Mât les Bas (tel 46 69 84).

ST BENOIT

St Benoit is an agricultural and fishing centre, and the biggest commune on the east coast. The town lost a lot of its old charm in the 1950s when it was swept by fire. Many of its houses were rebuilt in concrete. The area surrounding it offers some scenic spots, such as the **Rivière des Marsouins**, ('Porpoise River'), a river flowing down from the hills behind the town, narrow and wild in its upper reaches and broad and calm at its mouth where you might be lucky enough to see *bichiques* being netted. These are fish small fry used to make a popular local curry.

Two roads leading out from the west of St Benoit take you into the upper reaches above the village. One road, the D53, climbs up the Marsouins river valley, a 9-mile (15 km) drive to the Takamaka hydro-electric plant at 2,605 ft (794 m) and stunning view of the **Cascade de l'Arc en Ciel** succession of falls. On the way is the hamlet of **Bethlehem**, which is known for its fruit, especially litchis. There are picnic and river swimming areas here. The other road, the N3, runs right across the island to St Pierre through the Plaine des Palmistes and the Plain des Cafres. This will take you, via a turn-off 6 miles (10 km) out of town, to **Grand Etang**, a large forbidding stretch of water that is a major mountain lake enclosed by steep heights clad in the luxuriant vegetation typical of this area. There's a path around the lake. On the way, about 4 miles (6 km) from St Benoit, you can visit **La Domaine de la Confiance** ('Confidence Estate'), which is an old sugar plantation with the inevitable ruined sugar mill and sumptuous 18th century **Creole mansion**, set in an imposing garden. Entrance is free and it's open every day. You can eat in the private residence if you book (tel 50 90 50, fax 50 97 27). Not far away is the **Forêt de Ravenales** ('Traveller's Tree Forest'), where there's a pleasant short walk with views over St Benoit and its environs. In the industrial zone of town at Beaufonds you can take a guided tour of the **Distillerie Rivière du Mât** where you can see sugar transformed from molasses to alcohol and finally rum. Tours last about 30 minutes on Wednesdays during the sugar processing season, July to December, and cost FF20 (tel 50 27 32).

Réunion is still the world's largest producer of natural vanilla and **Bras Panon** is the island's vanilla capital, with its largest co-operative. The **Co-operative de Vanille** deals with about 75% of Réunion's vanilla production, and on a guided tour and through videos you can see the different stages of vanilla processing from the harvest to the drying of the wonderfully scented pods. On the premises is a well-stocked shop selling the co-operative's products, as well as other local specialities and handicrafts. Its restaurant *Le Vani-la* serves vanilla-based dishes. The co-op is open Monday to Friday, including public holidays, from 8am to noon and 1.30pm to 5pm, Saturday 9am to noon and 1.30pm to 5pm. Admission is FF25 (tel 51 70 12, fax 51 61 74). Bras Panon derives its name from a tributary, a *bras*, or arm, of the Rivière des Roches which crosses the old Panon estate. Near the mouth of this 'Rock River' is a freshwater lagoon between the coast and an offshore bar which is a popular place for **canoeing and windsurfing**. Follow the river along the small Beauvallon road up to a lovely waterfall called **Bassin de la Paix** ('Peace Pool'). Further up is **Bassin de la Mer** ('Sea Pool'), but this is only accessible by 4x4 vehicle or a 30-minute hike.

The large vanilla and sugar plantations of the region are a legacy of the island's colonial past, but they are still an important part of Réunion's agricultural economy. **St André** has one of the largest Indian communities in Réunion, descendants of the early indentured plantation workers, and places of interest include the **Kali Kovil**, on the Avenue de l'Ile de France, with its monumental gateway, known as the *Gopuram*, and the **Le Colosse** temple in Champ Borne. The Kali temple is open to visitors, once they have removed their shoes. December-January is the time you can watch impressive Tamil fire-walking ceremonies. In Champ Borne there's also the ruined shell of **St Nicolas Church**, which was, as the locals say, subjected to the outrage of a tidal wave thrown up in 1962 by Cyclone Jenny. Every October the ruins are dressed in flowers and palm fronds as part of *la semaine bleu*, the town's 'Blue Week' festival. Visitors are welcomed. In front of the church is an outlet of the organisation for Réunion Craft Development (ADAR), which has hundreds of hand-made products for sale, such as bamboo vases, rugs, paintings, animals carved out of pine cones and local straw back-packs known as *bertels*. It's open every day (tel 46 77 92/14 69).

Another attraction is the **Maison de la Vanille** ('Vanilla House') at 466 rue de la Gare (tel 46 00 14), which is in the gardens of a Creole working estate. There's an informative tour lasting 30 minutes, which includes a documentary film and a synoptic panels exhibition, after which you can buy dried vanilla, vanilla craftwork, and other mementoes of your visit at the estate shop, but nothing is cheap. You can also drink tea on the terrace, vanilla tea, of course. Open every day except Monday, from 9am to 11.30am, and 2pm to 5.20pm. Admission FF20.

For the sheer pleasure of sharing her passion for **orchids** with you, local resident Mrs Audifax will let you see her incredible greenhouse collection at her home on Chemin Rio. There's no charge, just phone first (tel 46 13 37). Another private home in St André worth a visit is the house of disabled Alexis Mahavande on ruelle Ponama. He has a genius for recycling throwaway rubbish, turning it into replicas of ships, Creole houses, and bonsai trees. Until his disabling accident, Alexis Mahavande was the caretaker of **Valliamée House**, so he can give you some useful insights before you visit this magnificently restored colonial mansion in St André.

If you happen to be in St André at the right lunar time in February you could enjoy the street **dragon dance** with which the local Chinese community welcomes in the Chinese New Year. At **Bois Rouge**, on the way to St Suzanne, you can take a guided tour of the sugar-refinery there during the harvest season, July to mid-December (tel 41 36 94 refinery; or 46 91 63 tourist office).

ACCOMMODATION
Classified Hotels. There are two in St Benoit (one a tourist hotel) and cost FF330-400 (£32-38/US$48-58), with breakfast an additional FF50.

Hostellerie de la Confiance: (tel 52 32 81) Anthurium Group, tourist hotel. 7 rooms in a beautiful old garden, with swimming pool, gourmet restaurant.

L'Armony: Route Nationale, La Marine (tel 50-8650, fax 50-8660). Apavou Group hotel, on a hill overlooking the Indian Ocean, 50 rooms, restaurant, starting point for many rambles, *L'Arum* restaurant serves gourmet cuisine.

Non-Classified Hotels. Range in price from FF200-250 and include:
Le Grand Etang: breakfast included, 300 Route des Plaines (tel 50-9430).
Le Bouvet: breakfast FF20 (tel 50-1496).
You can also try *Jean-Francois Sautron:* 37 Chemin Cratère, Bras Canot (tel 23 73 41), a furnished flat in the centre of the town which costs about FF1,700 a week.

EATING OUT
Creole and European cuisine is available at:
Bouvet: 75 rue Amiral Bouvet (tel 50 14 96).
Camus: rue Georges Pompidou (tel 50 28 78).
Grand Etang: 300 Chemin des Plaines (tel 50 94 30).
Hostellerie de la Confiance: tel 50 90 50.
Italian food is served at:
Dauphin Gourmand: 2a rue Amiral Bouvet (tel 50 42 82).
Asian food can be found at:
Café de Chine: Place du Marché (tel 50 12 47).
Chez Georget: 47 rue Amiral Bouvet (tel 50 22 74).
Le Beauvallon: Rivière des Roches (tel 50 42 92).

ST SUZANNE
12 miles (20 km) from St Denis and the last town of any consequence on the east coast, St Suzanne is very much another sugar town. It's best known for its hand-made bamboo bird cages, its lighthouse, a waterfall, and an old sugar estate. The **Phare de Bel-Air**, or Bel-Air lighthouse, stands on the rocks to the west of the town; the **Cascade Niagara** might have a grandiose name but this 100 ft (30 m) waterfall on the St Suzanne River, a short walk through the canefields above the town, is a pretty spectacle and a popular picnic spot at weekends. Further up, not far from the village of Bagatelle, is another waterfall called **Bassin Boeuf**. The pride of St Suzanne is the **Domaine du Grand Hazier** ('Grand Hazier Estate'), which is regarded as a noble representative of all the 18th century estates on the east coast. The 300-year-old estate is a French historical monument. After a guided tour of the Creole mansion you can stroll through the 5-acre (2 ha) garden, a vegetable garden and an orchard where tropical fruit trees and native species grow. However, you can visit only if you have made an advance booking (tel 52 32 81), admission is FF35, children under 12 free. Near the bus station in the centre of town you'll find the 19th century **Church of St Suzanne**. In front of the church is a memorial to the dead of two world wars, bearing a statue of a *poilu*, the French private soldier of World War I.

ENTERTAINMENT
There are two cinemas in **St Benoit**, the **Cristal**, at rue Montfleury (tel 50 44 09); and the **Office Culturel Benedictin** (12 Chemin Morange, tel 51 15 73), as well as one theatre **Compagnie Acte 3**, at Bras-Fusil (tel 50 53 33). The cinema in **St Rose** is the **OMSL** on Route Nationale (tel 47 27 48); and the theatre is the **Roz d'Zil**, Ravine Glissante (tel 47 36 06). In **St André** you will find the **Salle Multimedia Guy Alphonsine** cinema at 270 rue de la Gare (tel 46 63 15); and the **Mi Amuse Theatre** at rue de la Gare (tel 46 04 38).

SHOPPING

The **St Benoit Tourist Office** (Centre d'Affaires Agora, Route des Plaines, tel 50 21 29, fax 50 88 49) has local products and handicrafts for sale. It is open Monday to Saturday 9am to noon and 2pm to 5pm.

In **St Anne** you can also try the **Maison de L'Artisanat** (Place de l'Eglise, tel 51 02 57) which is open Monday to Friday 9am to 5pm, Saturday 9am to noon.

At the **St Andre Tourist Office** (66 Centre Commercial, tel 46 91 63, fax 46 52 16) you will find wickerwork, T-shirts, postcards, jewellery, and confectionery. It is open on Tuesday to Friday from 8.30am to noon and 1.30pm to 5.30pm, Saturday 8.30am to noon and 1.30pm to 4.20pm. An interesting stop is at the **Co-operative de Vanille de Bras-Panon** (Vanilla Co-operative) 21 Route Nationale (tel 51 70 12), which is open Monday to Friday from 8am to noon and 1.30pm to 5pm, Saturday 9am to noon and 1.30pm to 5pm. The **Vanilla House** in **St Andre** is open Tuesday to Sunday from 9am to 11.30am and 2pm to 5.30pm. You will find it at 466 rue de la Gare (tel 46 00 14).

THE HIGH PLAINS AND VOLCANO

The N3 road slices the island into two unequal parts, running the 39 miles (62 km) between St Pierre and St Benoit through **Les Hauts Plaines** ('The High Plains') which lie between the stupendous mountain cirques to the north-west and the active volcano Piton de la Fournaise to the south-east. From St Pierre the road traverses the **Plaine des Cafres**, named after the runaway black slaves who once hid out in the region, and the **Plaine des Palmistes** named after a variety of edible palm now protected and to be found mainly in the foothills of the Cilaos and Salazie cirques. The main towns and villages along the N3 are **Le Tampon**, **La Plaine des Cafres**, at 4,265 ft (1,300 m) one of the highest inhabited places on the island, **Bourg Murat**, and **La Plaine des Palmistes**, the last village before St Benoit – 12 miles (20 km) away – or the first if you are coming the other way. Apart from providing a **wonderful scenic drive** on the elevated tableland between the leeward and windward coasts the main attraction of these settlements is that most of them are jumping off points for mountain and forest roads and trails and en route to the dramatic lunar landscape of the **Plaine des Sables** ('Plain of Sands') on the approach to the volcano towering into the mists at 8,632 ft (2,631 m). The **Piton de la Fournaise** is aptly named 'Furnace Peak.' Reliable records show that between 1910 and 1999 the volcano erupted 79 times, an average of almost one eruption a year. There have been fairly long periods of dormancy, of course; there were no eruptions at all from 1992 until 1998, when it made up for lost time with two cataclysmic eruptions that belched out an estimated 2-million cubic metres of magma. The last eruptions occurred between March and September 1999. All this makes the Piton de la Fournaise one of the most interesting places in the world to vulcanologists and geologists, who can gaze into a crater 5 miles (8 km) in diameter and unravel the whole history of volcanic action in a relatively young (500,000 years) caldera. There are two main craters: the central Dolomieu, which is the active, larger, one and the smaller Bory crater, which has not muttered since 1791.

If your interest is not so specialised you can get a good insight into what makes the volcano tick before you peer into the real thing by visiting the **Maison du Volcan** ('Volcano House') in the centre of Bourg Murat village, the departure point on the N3 road for the volcanic heights. This modernistic building houses several expositions covering everything volcanic from history and documentation to an art gallery and a boutique. It's open every day except Monday from 9.30am to 5.30pm, admission FF40 for adults and varying prices for others including FF15 for the physically handicapped. Guided tours can be booked (tel 59 00 26, fax 59 16 71). From Bourg Murat the road winds up past **Nez de Boeuf** ('Ox's Nose') at 2,240 ft (683 m), from where on a clear day there's a fine view of the Rivière des Remparts threading the gorge way down below. Further along, the Commerson Crater gives you a foretaste of what's to come at the end of the road, which traverses the vast red and black scoria expanse of the Plaine des Sables to the Pas de Bellecombe view site. There's a rather dilapidated unmanned small information building at the car park here, from where a rocky path leads a few hundred yards along the crater rim to the start of a steep path, well marked with splashes of white paint, down to the interior of the crater. At the edge of the crater is an interesting ceramic table which tells you that distances from Piton de la Fournaise to the following are:

Bombay	3,063 miles	(4,930 km)
Brazil	7,059 miles	(11,360 km)
Mauritius	112 miles	(180 km)
Moscow	6,183 miles	(9,950 km)
New York	10,756 miles	(17,310 km)
Paris	5,903 miles	(9,500 km)
Peking	6,040 miles	(9,720 km)
Seychelles	820 miles	(1,320 km)
Sydney	6,015 miles	(9,680 km)
Antananarivo	541 miles	(870 km)
Tokyo	6,710 miles	(10,800 km)

The fumarole-pocked crater really is an awesome sight and at the eastern edge of the rim the ramparts have been shattered to open up an immense natural chute, ready when necessary to funnel more volcanic porridge down to the sea below. The highlight of the trek into and across what is known as the Enclosure is to walk around the precarious lip of the Dolomieu crater and get a whiff of its sulphurous entrails.

Caution take water with you if you are going to hike down into the crater, make sure you are wearing strong footwear, and take a copy of the IGN Piton de la Fournaise 4406 RT map (see *Maps and Guides*) if you plan to scale the heights on the opposite side and tackle one of the many hiking trails in the area. Mist comes and goes all the time and can make path-finding difficult. Lightweight windproofs and waterproofs are also a good idea. Hiking routes and times are best discussed beforehand with local guides. The Gîte du Pas de Bellecombe (tel 21 28 96), can be of help in this regard. If you are driving, allow a good half-day for the trip to the volcano from either St Pierre or St Benoit. The best way to view the volcano in its entirety, of course, is from a helicopter. There's a **volcano observatory** at La Plaine des Cafres where vulcanologists keep a finger on the Furnace Peak's pulse, ready to warn coastal villages of any impending danger (tel 27 52 92). You can't fault the Réunionese on business acumen. Within an hour or the observatory giving advance warning of the July 1999 eruption local shops were selling T-shirts emblazoned with *volcano la pété!* (something along the lines of 'thar she blows').

On the other side of the valley from the N3 are walks to a number of **beauty spots**. The road through Bois Court from La Plaine des Cafres takes you to a viewsite above the gloomy valley at **Grand Bassin** and its cascade. If you want to visit this isolated community it is a 1½ hour hike down, and at least double that to get back up. There is also an excellent view of the mountain ramparts of the south-eastern edge of Cilaos cirque. From La Plaine des Palmistes you can take a 2 mile (3 km) stroll to sparkling **Cascade Biberon** ('Feeding Bottle') in the wooded Ravine Sèche. There's an icy pool below the 787 ft (240 m) cascade where you can cool off. The village and its surrounds are a draw in summer for other islanders who come to enjoy the cooler altitude – and the annual *Miel Vert* ('Green Honey') festival at the end of January – and in winter when they descend on the settlement for the annual Goyaviers festival. The *goyavier* is a much sought-after acidic red berry – not a guava – which grows in the forests around here. This is also cheese country and the berry goes well with *Tommette des Plaines*, a local cheese which is pepped up with chillies and spices. The Bèbour Forest lies along the road from La Plaine des Palmistes towards the Cirque of Salazie. Nearly 11 miles (18 km) of paths criss-cross this picturesque forest area, with its tamarind trees, orchids, white arum lilies, giant tree ferns, and goyavier trees laden with the prized red berries between May and July.

ACCOMMODATION

Plaine des Cafres
Classified Hotels. These range from the tourist hotels, with no stars that cost from FF160 (£15/US$23) for a double, to two star hotels from FF360 (£35/US$52).

Adret: (two stars) 137 Route Forestière du Volcan (tel 59 00 85, fax 59 09 34). On the road to the volcano at 5,397 ft (1,645 m), a non-smoking hotel, 12 rooms, hiking trails, horse trekking, mountain bike, volcano weather forecast, family restaurant serving Creole meals. Breakfast of local farm products FF35.

L'Ecrin: (two stars) (tel 59 02 02, fax 59 36 10), is 100 yards (100 m) from the Volcano House at Bourg Murat and another good starting point from which to explore the high plains, 9 bungalow rooms, *Panoramic* restaurant serves Creole and European cuisine. Breakfast FF30.

Les Géraniums: (two stars) on the RN3 road at the 24 km mark (tel 59 11 06, fax 59 21 83). Close to Maison du Volcan (Volcano House) and starting point to numerous hikes, 16 rooms, panoramic view of Piton des Neiges, Bois Court, Dimitile mountain, restaurant, breakfast FF50.

Also near Volcano House are *Le Volcan:* (two stars tel 27 50 91, fax 59 17 21), breakfast FF50; and *L'Auberge de Volcan:* (tourist hotel tel 27 50 91, fax 59 17 21) 8 bungalow rooms, breakfast FF25.

La Diligence: (tourist hotel) Route Nationale 3, Bourg Murat (tel 59 10 10, fax 59 11 81), is a good setting-off point for horseback rides and hikes, 26 rooms, bar, tennis court, French bowls, sauna, mountain bike, restaurant, breakfast FF32.

There are a couple of **non-classified** places to stay at Plaine des Cafres, which range between FF160-220. They are *L'Auberge la Fermete* (Chemin du Bois Court; tel 27 50 08) breakfast FF20 and *L'Auberge du 24eme* (36 rue du Père Favron; tel 59 08 60), breakfast FF20.

Furnished Flats vary in price from FF75-400:
Les Pelargoniums: 40a Petite Ferme, Route de Notre Dame de la Paix, Plaine des Cafres (tel/fax 59 02 51).
L'Accueil: 24 rue Marie Poitevin, Plaine des Cafres (tel 59 15 88).

Plaine des Palmistes
Classified Hotels. Like those in Plaine des Cafres these range from the tourist hotels, with no stars that cost from FF160 for a double, to two star hotels from FF360.

Hotel des Plaines: (three stars Logis de France) 2ème Village (tel 51 31 97, fax 51 45 70), is up at 3,609 ft (1,100 m) on a grassy plateau in the heart of Plaine des Palmistes, 14 rooms, restaurant (with fireplace) serving French and Creole cuisine, table tennis, billiards.

Les Azalées: (one star), 80 rue de la Republique (tel 51 34 24, fax 28 17 97). At 3,609 ft (1,100 m), 36 bungalow rooms, breakfast FF35.

Furnished Flats vary in price from FF75-400:
   Les Orchidées: 59 rue Richard Adolphe, Petite Plaine, Plaine des Palmistes (tel 51 33 43, fax 51 46 37, e-mail: rene.gentet@wanadoo.fr).
   Poïny Toplan: 5 rue Delmas Hoareau, Petite Plaine, Plaine des Palmistes (tel 46 07 99).

EATING OUT
Nearly all the restaurants at **Plaine des Palmistes** serve **Creole and European** food:
Auberge du Pommeau: rue Depeindray d'Ambelles (tel 51 40 70).
Café Gregue: 175 rue de la République (tel 51 42 01).
Clos des Mimosas: 7 Allée des Goyaviers (tel 51 31 59).
Cryptomérias: Chemin de la Petite Plaine (tel 51 38 15).
La Marmite: rue de la République (tel 51 44 49).
Petite Case: 289a rue de la République (tel 51 48 08).
Platanes: 167 rue de la République (tel 51 31 69).
Relais de la Cascade: 2 rue Raphaël Babet (tel 51 31 48).
Relais du Village: rue de la République (tel 51 42 71).
For a change the *Combava* at 28 rue de la République serves **Indian** food.
Creole and European food are also generally served at restaurants at **Plaine des Cafres**
L'Auberge du Bois Court: 2b rue Raphael Douyère, Bois Court (tel 59 29 29).
Auberge du Volcan: Bourg Murat (tel 27 50 91).
Chez Cocotier: 39 Piton Ravine Blanche (tel 59 08 30).
Fermette: 48 Route de Bois Court (tel 27 50 08).
Lyssandra: 35 Route Nationale 3 (tel 59 20 65).
Relais: Route de Bois Court (tel 59 28 28).
Lovers of **Italian** food should try *Kios'Q Pizza* at Chemin du Repos (tel 59 25 31).

ENTERTAINMENT
There are two nightclubs, the **Malibu Club** in Plaine des Palmistes (tel 51 38 21); and theTwist Pavillon in Plaine des Cafres (tel 59 21 80).

SHOPPING
Fonderie de Bourbon (Domaine des Tourelles; tel/fax 51 42 94) in Plaine des Palmistes, is a foundry manufacturing workshop, where you can watch moulding and art foundry. Free admission, closed on Tuesdays. **Kiosque Piment Martin** (1 rue de la Republique, Ravine Plate; tel 51 32 83) sells specialities made from hot peppers and local goyavier berries. Open daily from 9am to 6pm.
   At Plaine des Cafres is the **Boutique de Volcan** (Route Nationale 3; tel 59 29 12) which sells a wide range of local products related to the volcano. Open Tuesday to Sunday from 10am to 12.45pm and 1.45pm to 6pm. **Canelle et Vetiver** (9 rue Alfred Picard, Bourg Murat; tel 59 06 53) is a Creole house where you can buy handicrafts made from cinnamon and vetiver, and miniature souvenirs made from other fragrant woods. It is open daily from 8am to 7pm. **Chant d'Etelle** (Route du Volcan; tel 59 11 00) has hand-made perfumed candles for sale. Open Tuesday to Sunday from 10am to 6pm. **Comptoir Austral** (207 Route Nationale 3, Bourg Murat; tel 59 09 31) has Indian Ocean-style artwork. Open Tuesday and Bank holidays from 9.30am to 6pm. **Palais du Fromage** (Route du Volcan, rue Alfred Picard; tel 59 27 15) is a 'cheese palace' specialising in local farm cheeses. Open 9am to 7pm, closed on Monday.

THE CIRQUES

Volcanic activity in the centre of Réunion ceased about half a million years ago, leaving the island's highest point, **Piton des Neiges**, the hub of an area of collapsed volcanoes which time and weather have sculpted into three vast amphitheatres called cirques because of their almost perfect circular shape. The three cirques are Cilaos, Salazie, and Mafate. Each is about 6 miles (10 km) in diameter, each is enclosed by high mountain ramparts, but each has a distinct character of its own. The only features they have in common are the gigantic canyons carved out of their girdling mountains over the millennia by tumultuous rivers in search of exits from the craters. In the early days of island settlement the cirques provided ideal places of refuge for the escaped slaves known as *marrons* and the only time anyone else ventured into their fastness was with a gun to shoot wild goats or runaways. Records of the time suggest that the latter was the preferred sport of the French planters and garrison soldiers. Throughout the early 19th century poor white farmers left the coastal regions to settle the fertile cirques and descendants of these two groups now make up most of the scattered Creole communes. These cirques are literally at the heart of the island's attractions and are unique in the Indian Ocean. Cilaos and Salazie are accessible by road; to explore Mafate you have to go on foot or by helicopter.

CILAOS
Cilaos is the most southerly and driest of the three cirques. Although its slopes have fewer waterfalls than its neighbours it was water which first put Cilaos on the map. Three **thermal mineral springs** were discovered here in 1819 at 3,342 ft (1,019 m) above sea level, pouring out 3,000 gallons (13,638 litres) of water an hour at 97°F (36°C). By the end of the 19th century they had established Cilaos as a health spa and resort town. In 1826, a freed slave named Figaro was granted permission to live in what is now Ilet à Cordes and that is the date from which the Cilaos cirque was officially settled. Cilaos lies 4,003 ft (1,220 m) above sea level and is 70 miles (113 km) from St Denis. Although it is only 23 miles (37 km) from the coastal town of St Louis, it takes about two hours to negotiate a remarkable road that has been described as being the result of every trick in the engineer's book. It is an exciting and at times terrifying drive, with hairpin bends, tunnels, unrailed precipitous drops, and a dizzying spot where the road loops back on itself in a turn appropriately known as the *boucle*, or the buckle. It's tough on drivers (and passengers) but a mountain biker's idea of heaven. There are viewsites along the road and, as you get higher, the odd local selling craftwork and bottles of the sweet wines produced in the cirque. Cilaos is a pretty little village sitting in the shadow of the Piton des Neiges. It is well served by hotels and restaurants, some of the most scenically located grouped around the tranquil lake on its outskirts. The hot springs that first brought the infirm and ailing to Cilaos saw a decline after the area was devastated by a cyclone in 1948. The natural source was tapped again in 1987 when the Irénée Accot Thermal Establishment opened on the Route de Bras Sec to once again soothe aches and pains with the mineral-impregnated waters. Cilaos offers more than hot water and cold, crisp air. The women of Cilaos are famed for their needlework, which you can admire in the **Maison de la Broderie**, an embroidery workshop which had its beginnings at the turn of the last century when Dr Jean-Marie MacAuliffe started a needlework school for his daughter, Angèle. This eventually developed into the 'Embroidery House,' a workshop producing embroidered children's clothing, bridal gowns, baptismal dresses, table napkins, and other items. You can buy these items here, or from one of the street vendors. The centre is open Monday to Saturday, from 9am to noon and 2pm to 5pm,

Sunday and public holidays from 9am to noon. Admission, which includes a guided tour, costs FF5. The workshop is at 4 rue des Ecoles (tel 31 77 48, fax 31 80 54). Up the road from the workshop is Philippe Turpin's **studio** (tel 31 73 64), where there is a permanent exhibition of the copper engravings this artist produces. You can buy etchings of traditional island scenes, as well as others with themes inspired by magic and fantasy.

Cilaos is well known for its **hiking and trekking trails**, and several pleasant country walks radiate from here. **Bassin Bleu** is a pretty stretch of water, where you can take a refreshing swim. The Sources footpath, a walk of about 4 miles (6 km), takes you through a forest for a view of the *Bonnet du Prêtre* ('Priest's Hat'), a summit which looks like a bishop's mitre; the road leading to Bras Sec village passes through a lovely forest of Japanese cedars; and there's a two-hour walk which starts near the Hotel des Thermes along a **botanical path** to Roche Merveilleuse. The **Maison de la Montagne** will give you more information about these walks and about more serious trails, such as the ones leading to the summit of Piton de la Neiges and others into the cirques of Salazie and Mafate. They will also book accommodation at mountain gîtes for you, provide weather forecasts, and tell you where you can hire a local guide. The Maison de la Montagne is in the same building as the **Cilaos Tourism Office** at 2 rue MacAuliffe and is open Monday to Saturday from 8.30am to 12.30pm and 1.30pm to 5.30pm. On Sundays and public holidays they are open from 9am to 1pm (tel 31 71 71, fax 31 80 54). The tourism office keeps the same hours. If you have the calf muscles, an equally popular way to explore the surroundings area is by mountain bike (see *Getting Around* page 220).

Cilaos is well known for its wines, although they are not rated all that high by island wine lovers. Sweet white and red wines are produced and sell at about FF40 a bottle, although you'll pay less if you buy from a roadside vendor. Decide on the quality for yourself at the **Wine House** (tel 31 79 69) which is open Monday to Friday, from 9am to noon, and 1.30pm to 4pm. Guided tours and a tasting cost FF15. The other specialities on which Cilaos prides itself are its lentils – which accompany most Creole dishes in the local hotels and restaurants – and the local corn-fed duck.

ACCOMMODATION

Classified Hotels. These range from one to three stars, and vary in price from FF260 (£28/US$38) to FF630 (£60/US$91) for a double room:

Hotel des Thermes (two stars) 8 rue des Sources (tel 31 89 00, fax 31 74 73). Close to the village centre, 28 rooms, one suite, tennis court, thermal baths, *La Lentillière* restaurant serves French and Creole cuisine and is open every day. Breakfast is included in the rate.

Hotel du Cirque (one star) 27 rue du Père Boiteau (tel 31 70 68, fax 31 80 46). Family-run hotel, 35 rooms, fitness room, *Le Chêne* restaurant serves Creole, French and Chinese cuisine. Breakfast included.

Le Vieux Cep (two stars Anthurium Group) 2 rue des Trois Mares (tel 31 71 89, fax 31 77 68). In the centre of the village close to the shops, 44 rooms, bar, badminton, table tennis, restaurant serves French and Creole food. Breakfast included.

Les Chenets (three stars) Chemin des Trois Mares (tel 31 85 85, fax 31 87 17). Creole hotel in the town, 17 rooms with mountain views, restaurant serving Creole cuisine, two saunas, one steam bath, library, free transport from helipad to hotel. Sporting activities include mountain biking, tennis, canyoning, rock climbing and hiking trails. Extra charge for breakfast.

There are 10 **Non-Classified Hotels** in Cilaos ranging from FF80-FF320 a night, among them:

Auberge du Haneau: 5 Chemin du Seminaire (tel 31 70 94), breakfast included.
Auberge du Lac: 5 Chemin du Seminaire (tel 31 70 94) breakfast FF30.
Auberge le Grand Benaré: 5 Chemin du Seminaire (tel 31 70 94), breakfast FF25.
Case Bleue: 15 rue Alsace Corre (tel 31 77 88), breakfast FF20.
Clair de Lune: rue Winceslas Rivière (tel 31 88 03), breakfast included.
Hotel les Aloes: 14 rue St Louis (tel 31 81 00), breakfast included.
Jade du Cirque: 4 rue des Glycines (tel 31 87 58), breakfast included.

Furnished Flats range in price from FF150-250 a night:
Auberge du Mont Fleuri: 19 Chemin Saül Bras Sec (tel 25 77 61), breakfast FF20.
Gilette Gonthier: 9 rue des Fleurs Jaunes (tel 31 71 35), five minutes from the centre.
Idmont: 5 Chemin des Trois Mares (tel 31 85 80).
Residence des Montagnes: 22 Route du Cap, Palmiste Rouge (tel 31 91 26).
There are also self-catering gîtes, gîtes d'etape, and B&Bs (see *Accommodation* in *Practical Information* page 227).

EATING OUT

The most popular and certainly one of the largest restaurants in **Cilaos** is in the hotel *Le Vieux Cep* (the Old Vinestock). If you don't mind crowds of tourists, rather than locals, you'll enjoy the food and the size of the helpings. Make sure you get a taste of the lentils for which Cilaos is famous. Most of the classified restaurants are in the local hotels, although there are other restaurants, some of them on the picturesque lake near Cilaos, the *Mare à Joncs*.
There is mainly **Creole** food on offer:
Auberge du Grand Benaré: 5 rue Winceslas Rivière (tel 31 78 29).
Auberge du Lac: 13 rue Mare à Joncs (tel 31 86 22).
Café Lunch: rue Mare à Joncs (tel 31 87 54).
Chez Noe: 40 rue du Père Boiteau (tel 31 79 53).
Gin-Pub: 12 rue du Père Boiteau (tel 31 71 97).
Jade du Cirque: 4 rue des Glycines (tel 31 87 58).
Moulin a Café: 68 rue du Père Boiteau (tel 31 80 80).
Restaurant le Stade: 31 rue de St Louis (tel 31 75 09).

ENTERTAINMENT

There is a cinema in **Cilaos**, the **OMJA Cilaos**, at 2 rue des Ecoles (tel 31 73 25). You can also relax at the **Etablissement Thermal 'Irénée Accot,'** (Route de Bras Sec; tel 31 72 27, fax 31 76 57) relaxation and fitness centre in spectacular surroundings, personal attendance, four whirlpools, seaweed baths, sauna, shiatsu bed (for acupressure massage), work-out room, jacuzzi, beauty salon for face and body treatments, a fitness trail, a rest and a relaxation area with colour and music therapy, spa cures and fitness programmes.

SALAZIE

This is the largest, wettest and the most lush of the three cirques, watered by at least a hundred perennial falls and cascades, in reality rivers descending vertically down the cliffs, and drenched by rains brought by the tradewinds to the windward side of Réunion. It is also the most accessible cirque from St Denis, 25 miles (41 km) away. The main village **Hell-Bourg** can be reached by car in well under two hours from the capital and in less than an hour from St André 10 miles (16 km) away. Its impressive gorges and peaks mean it is also the most flown over by helicopter-borne tourists. Salazie sits at the foot of Piton des Neiges, watered by Rivière du Mât and its tributaries. The cirque's first inhabitants were fugitive slaves who fled there in the 18th century and found sanctuary among the wild peaks and canyons. A prominent peak, Piton de 'Anchaing, is named after one of them. Anchaing and his wife Heva lived high in the cirque for 10 years before smoke from their fire attracted attention and a slave-hunting party recaptured them. The couple had raised a family during their years in the cirque and it's reported that their erstwhile owner was pleased to receive interest on his long-frozen capital in the shape of seven more little slaves for his fields. The first free settler was Theodore Cazeau, who arrived with his family around 1830. At one stage the Cazeaus were isolated by heavy floods and lived for 43 days solely on pumpkins. Around the same time, the Salazie crater was explored and a 90°F (32°C) medicinal spring was found bubbling up from its floor, the last trace of the old volcano. This spring at 2,616 ft (797 m) above sea level gushed a natural concoction tasting like warm soda-water with a bouquet of its principal ingredients – soda, magnesium, lime, iron and sodium. The ruined blue-tiled **Old Spa Baths** below the village are all that's left today of the place which remained popular until the spring dried up during the cyclone of 1948. Between 1838 and 1841, Governor de Hell promoted settlement and agriculture in the cirque, and the village of Hell-Bourg came into being, named in his honour. The exploitation of the thermal spring, and the malaria then prevalent at the coast, transformed Hell-Bourg into a healthy hill station, a status it enjoyed until malaria was eradicated and people turned to more modern medicaments for their stiff joints. Like the road up to Cilaos, the approach to this cirque is spectacular. The little hamlet of Salazie is at the entrance to the cirque. Just beyond the village the road forks, the right fork leading to the hamlet of **Grand Ilet**, 21 miles (34 km) away in the shadow of La Roche Ecrit, and the left to Hell-Bourg, which is 6 miles (9 km) further up the winding road.

In Salazie there's a cultural museum, the **Ecomusée** (tel 47 86 86); and **Santons de Salazie** Artists' Residence at Mare à Poule d'Eau (Moorhen Pond), between Salazie and Hell-Bourg, which is an exhibition centre showcasing the cirque and island culture. Between Salazie and Hell-Bourg are the lacy **Voile de la Mariée** ('Bride's Veil Falls'), which drop into a ravine in a succession of cascades from heights often lost in the clouds. The village of Hell-Bourg is a living museum of traditional Creole architecture. Neat, freshly painted little houses, each with wooden shutters for protection against the tropical storms which spill in from the Indian Ocean, line quaint streets surrounded by prolific gardens. Vegetables thrive here. The most popular vegetable is chou-chou, variously known in other countries as choko, chayote, mirliton, christophine, and vegetable pear. It grows on a vine whose leaves are also an ingredient in local brèdes, or stews. Chou-chou appear in many Creole recipes and it is generally acknowledged that the best of all grow in Salazie.

There are plenty of **hiking trails** to choose from around Hell-Bourg, with full day hikes to Les Sources Pétrifiantes, and Piton d'Anchaing, a popular trail to the summit at 4,436 ft (1,352 m) where you get stunning views over the entire cirque. There's also a two-day hike to the Piton des Neiges. This is another highly popular trek, which can be started either in Cilaos or Hell-Bourg. From Réunion's highest point you can see the entire island. One of the many footpaths leading from Hell-Bourg heads towards Belouve lodge, through one of the most magnificent forests on Réunion. In Hell-Bourg, opposite the church, you'll find **Folio House** (5 rue Amiral-Lacaze; tel 47 80 98) through whose ivy-covered entrance gate is a *guétali* (pavilion), a citrus orchard, and a terraced vegetable garden. Walk through the house and you'll get a rare insight into bygone Creole life. The exuberant garden harbours a variety of plants, including orchids, anthuriums, and an alley of century-old camellias. It's open 7 days a week from 9am to 11.30 am and 2pm to 5.30pm. Admission is FF20, children under 10 free. Near the Relais des Cimes there's a well-marked route to the **Parc Piscicole d'Hell-Bourg**, which is a trout breeding farm where you can hook your own lunch and have it cooked to order at the nearby restaurant. The farm is open every day from 9am to 6pm and costs FF7 if you don't fish. If you do, entry is free, but you pay by weight for your catch. The **Hell-Bourg library** is a refurbished Creole house (tel 47 83 47), and it's worth strolling down the main street just to look at the shop fronts, the Creole houses, and an unlikely police station at the end of a lovely garden with statues.

ACCOMMODATION

Classified Hotels. There is only one, the *Le Relais des Cimes* (two stars Anthurium Group, rue de Général de Gaulle, Hell-Bourg; tel 47 81 58, fax 47 82 11), at FF284 (£27/US$41) a night, in Hell-Bourg village centre, close to the shops, starting point for numerous hiking trails, 17 rooms, mountain biking, canyoning, restaurant serving Creole and Madagascan food, breakfast FF36.

Furnished Flats (all in Hell-Bourg) range in price from FF300 a night (minimum stay of two nights) to FF420:

La Caféière: Chemin Bellevue (tel/fax 34 84 43), two apartments.
Chez Bègue: 28 rue du Général de Gaulle (tel 47 84 43).
Chez Festin: Rob Pont (tel 46 54 61).
L'Orchidée Rose: 5 rue de l'Hotel (tel 47 87 22).
Ti Case: Sentier Bélouve (tel 47 87 80).

The youth hostel in Hell-Bourg is in the Maison Morange, on the Chemin de la Cayenne. If it's full you can camp in the grounds. There are also self-catering gîtes in Cilaos and Salazie, gîte d'étape, and B&Bs (see *Accommodation* in *Practical Information* page 227).

EATING OUT

First a word of warning to anyone impressed by the fame of one of Réunion's so-called top restaurants, the *Relaise des Cîmes:* in Hell-Bourg. This served up the worst food we ate in Réunion. Maybe they are resting on their laurels, and maybe it's time for the Guild of French Provinces, to which the restaurant belongs, to send an inspector around to reassess the cuisine.

Other less pretentious ones to try are:
Chez Alice: Hell-Bourg (tel 47 86 24).
Lotus et Chouchoux: Pont de l'Escalier (tel 47 62 87).
L'Orchidée Rose: 5 rue de l'Hotel, Hell-Bourg (tel 47 87 22).
Le Voile de la Mariée: Chemin Xavier Fontaine (tel 47 53 54), French and Creole cuisine.
P'Tit Bambou: rue Georges Pompidou (tel 47 51 51, fax 47 65 78), Creole, Chinese and French cuisine, closed on Wednesday.
For **Italian** there is *La Cafrine* at rue Georges Pompidou (tel 47 66 06) and you can get **fast-food** at *Ti Case Snack:* Chemin Bélouve (tel 47 87 80).

MAFATE

The fact that there is no natural access road into the cirque of Mafate means that it has remained one of the wildest and most pristine of the island's mountain areas and if you like trekking Mafate is the most exciting cirque of the three. If you don't drop in by helicopter (see *Getting Around*) you have a choice of four main trails to take you into this incredibly rugged cirque, where houses and hamlets perch on the odd level volcanic shelf, or cling to cliffs over vertiginous gorges. You can get an idea of the terrain just be peering over the edge of the cirque from Piton Maïdo (see

West Coast) for a bird's-eye view of a valley hemmed in by soaring peaks piercing billowing clouds. You can also get a good view of it from the viewsite at **Cap Noir** at 4,265 ft (1,300 m) above La Possession, with the bonus of a good view of the Rivière des Galets on its way down to Le Port; and from Bord Martin at 5,217 ft (1,590 m). The most spectacular treks in are the Cilaos-Marla and Col de Fourche-La Nouvelle trails. The former is also known as the Route de Ilet à Cordes and runs past the Col du Taïbit (6,834 ft/2,083 m) by way of Ilet des Salazes, before dropping down again to Marla. This is a challenging walk but worth the slog for the wonderful views it offers of the island. From Col de Fourche-La Nouvelle, the trail makes a short descent through a tamarind forest to drop down to the little hamlet of La Nouvelle, which is the main settlement in Mafate.

La Nouvelle sits at a hiking trail junction and is your best hope of finding anything you might have forgotten to pack. Other, smaller, hamlets in the cirque are Marla, Aurère, Ilet à Bourse, Roche Plate, and Grand Place near the spot where the Rivière des Galets ('River of Shingle') exits from the cirque. There are a number of gîtes offering basic accommodation for hikers. Most of the trails in Mafate call for trail savvy and a high degree of physical fitness as all your exertions will be at between 4,921 ft (1,500 m) and 9,843 ft (3,000 m). It is extremely unwise to venture into this cirque without first getting information and advice from experts, such as those at Maison de la Montagne, 10 Place du Barachois, St Denis (tel 90 78 78, fax 90 78 70, e-mail: nature@oceanes.fr).

ACCOMMODATION
There are two guest-houses in Mafate cirque (Both at La Nouvelle), *Alain Begue* (tel 43 43 10) and *Joseph Cuvelier* (tel 43 49 63).

SHOPPING
The tourist office in **Cilaos**, at 2 rue MacAuliffe (tel 31 78 03, fax 31 70 30), has a permanent handicrafts exhibition, open Monday to Saturday from 8.30am to 12.30pm and 1.30pm to 5.30pm, Sunday and public holidays from 9am to 1pm. The embroidery of Cilaos is renowned on the island. You can view examples and buy them at the **Maison de la Broderie** (Embroidery House) (4 rue des Ecoles; tel 31 77 48, fax 31 80 38), which also has other local crafts for sale. It's open Monday to Saturday from 9am to noon and 2pm to 5pm, Sunday and public holidays 9am to noon. There's an admission of FF5 per person, which includes a guided tour and demonstration.

Chai de Cilaos (34 rue des Glycines; tel 31 79 69, fax 31 79 70), has wine tastings and Cilaos wines for sale. They're not great, but they make an unusual memento or gift. It's open Monday to Friday 9am to noon and 2pm to 5pm.

In Salazie, **Cazanou** (rue Charles de Gaulle, Hell-Bourg; tel 47 88 23) has *vacoa* (pandanus) and straw products, wood, bamboo, local food, and garments for sale. It is open Tuesday to Sunday from 9am to 6pm. **Le Bambou** (tel 47 84 90) sells furniture and other articles made from, guess what, bamboo. It's open daily from 8.30am to 5.30pm. **Epicevasion**, is a spice shop at 25 rue du Général de Gaulle, Hell-Bourg (tel 47 89 27). It is open daily, except Monday, from 9am to noon and 1pm to 6pm.

INDEX